Mastering Windows Presentation Foundation

Master the art of building modern desktop applications on Windows

Sheridan Yuen

BIRMINGHAM - MUMBAI

Mastering Windows Presentation Foundation

Copyright © 2017 Packt Publishing

First published: February 2017

Production reference: 1130217

Published by Packt Publishing Ltd.
Livery Place
35 Livery Street
Birmingham
B3 2PB, UK.
ISBN 978-1-78588-300-2

www.packtpub.com

Credits

Author

Sheridan Yuen

Reviewer

Alex Golesh

Commissioning Editor

Edward Gordon

Acquisition Editor

Chaitanya Nair

Content Development Editor

Zeeyan Pinheiro

Technical Editor

Kunal Chaudhari

Copy Editor

Pranjali Chury

Project Coordinator

Vaidehi Sawant

Proofreader

Safis Editing

Indexer

Rekha Nair

Graphics

Kirk D'Penha

Production Coordinator

Shantanu N. Zagade

About the Author

Sheridan Yuen is a Microsoft .NET MCTS and Oracle Java SCJP certified software developer, living in London, England. His passion for coding made him stand out from the crowd right from the start. From his second year onward at university, he was employed to be a teaching assistant for the first year student coding workshops and has since returned as a guest lecturer.

Among other prestigious positions, he was the primary software developer for the Ministry of Sound group for four years, working on their main music business application, responsible for creating their multi award winning albums. This application managed to increase its users' productivity by up to 80% in some cases.

In addition to this, he architected a unique ticket scanning application for their award winning nightclub, making it the first club in the world to introduce scanned ticket entry across all streams for their clients. Coming from a musical background and being a qualified audio engineer, with experience of record production and digital audio, this post was a perfect union.

He soon became a popular figure in the C# and WPF sections of the Stack Overflow, "question and answer" website, being awarded enough reputation by the community members to raise him to well within the top half percent of all users. While authoring this book and other projects have kept him away for some time, he is keen to return to continue to help new users to get to grips with WPF.

I would like to thank my long suffering girlfriend Jemma, who has regularly had to make do without my company for the best part of a year, for her patience while I was composing and writing this book and the many examples in it. I'd also like to thank Chaitanya from Packt Publishing for convincing me to write this book in the first place and without who, this book would not have been written.

Finally, I would like to thank Mary Thomson, Professor Sarah Barman and Professor James Orwell in particular, from Kingston University, London, who inspired me to change the direction of my previous career and planted the seed of curiosity that has taken me so far. I would also like to thank James for encouraging me to move from the Bachelor's Degree course to the integrated Master's Degree that I ended up gaining and for all of the benefits that this brought with it.

About the Reviewer

Alex Golesh is an international expert in XAML-based technologies such as Universal Windows Platform (Windows, Windows Phone, HoloLens, Xbox One), Xamarin.Forms, WPF, and Silverlight. Also, Alex specializes in cloud-based solutions such as Microsoft Azure. Alex developed training solutions for Microsoft Learning on Windows Phone and Windows 8 and delivers workshops for developers and enterprises. Alex leads the architecture and development process in multiple projects for his clients.

www.PacktPub.com

For support files and downloads related to your book, please visit www.PacktPub.com.

Did you know that Packt offers eBook versions of every book published, with PDF and ePub files available? You can upgrade to the eBook version at www.PacktPub.com and as a print book customer, you are entitled to a discount on the eBook copy. Get in touch with us at service@packtpub.com for more details.

At www.PacktPub.com, you can also read a collection of free technical articles, sign up for a range of free newsletters and receive exclusive discounts and offers on Packt books and eBooks.

https://www.packtpub.com/mapt

Get the most in-demand software skills with Mapt. Mapt gives you full access to all Packt books and video courses, as well as industry-leading tools to help you plan your personal development and advance your career.

Why subscribe?

- Fully searchable across every book published by Packt
- Copy and paste, print, and bookmark content
- On demand and accessible via a web browser

Customer Feedback

Thanks for purchasing this Packt book. At Packt, quality is at the heart of our editorial process. To help us improve, please leave us an honest review on this book's Amazon page at `https://goo.gl/yuUApD`.

If you'd like to join our team of regular reviewers, you can email us at `customerreviews@packtpub.com`. We award our regular reviewers with free eBooks and videos in exchange for their valuable feedback. Help us be relentless in improving our products!

Table of Contents

Preface

While it can be easy to construct a basic form using WPF, it takes a lot more to fully understand what WPF can do for us and how best to use it. It has a steep learning curve and it can be difficult to comprehend this very different way of working. This book aims to help you to get over that initial hill and continue to fully enable you to implement any given requirement.

This book will start by providing you the foundation knowledge on how to improve your workflow and what to do when you have problems. It will build upon this foundation by introducing the base layer of the application that will serve all that comes after it. We will then take a detour to cover data binding in detail.

The book will then turn to the User Interface (UI) and how to get the most out of the built-in and custom WPF controls. It will make clear which customization methods are best to utilize in a wide range of scenarios, avoiding the need to rewrite existing functionality. Other tips and tricks will also be provided to enable you to create your own visually stunning UIs.

The final section of the book will introduce the concluding ways for you to polish your applications, from adding practical animations and data validation, to improving application performance. The book will end by explaining how to deploy the applications that you have been working so hard on and discuss other things that you can now achieve with your new found knowledge.

What this book covers

Chapter 1, *A Smarter Way of Working with WPF*, introduces the Model, View, View Model (MVVM) software architectural pattern and the benefits of using it with WPF.

Chapter 2, *Debugging WPF Applications*, provides essential tips on various methods of debugging WPF applications, ensuring the ability to iron out any problems that may occur.

Chapter 3, *Writing Custom Application Frameworks*, introduces the indispensable concept of application frameworks, with early examples that will be built upon as the book progresses. By the end of the book, you will have a fully functioning Framework with which to build your applications upon.

Chapter 4, *Becoming Proficient with Data Binding,* demystifies data binding and clearly demonstrates how to use it in a practical application. A plethora of examples will help you to understand which binding syntax to use in any given situation and to be confident that their bindings will work as expected.

Chapter 5, *Using The Right Controls for The Job,* explains which controls to use in particular situations and describes the various ways to modify them when required. It clearly outlines how to customize existing controls and how to create custom controls when required.

Chapter 6, *Mastering Practical Animations,* explains the ins and outs of WPF Animations, detailing lesser known functionality. It concludes with a number of ideas for practical animations and continues to build upon the custom application framework.

Chapter 7, *Creating Visually Stunning User Interfaces,* offers advice for getting the most out of the WPF visuals, while remaining practical, and provides handy tips on making applications stand out from the crowd.

Chapter 8, *Implementing Responsive Data Validation,* presents a number of methods of data validation to suit every situation and continues to build upon the custom application framework. It covers full, partial, instant, and delayed validation and a variety of different ways to display validation errors.

Chapter 9, *Completing That Great User Experience,* provides tips for creating applications with a great user experience. Concepts introduced here, such as asynchronous data access and keeping the end users well informed, will substantially improve the existing custom application framework.

Chapter 10, *Improving Application Performance,* lists a number of ways to increase the performance of WPF applications from freezing resources to implementing virtualization. Readers that follow these tips and tricks can rest assured that their WPF applications will perform as optimally as they can.

Chapter 11, *Deploying Your Masterpiece Application,* covers the final requirement for all professional applications—deployment. It includes the older method of using the Windows Installer software, along with the more common and up-to-date method of using ClickOnce functionality.

Chapter 12, *What Next?,* summarizes what you have learned from this book and suggests what you can do with many of your various new skills. It provides you with further ideas on extending the application framework.

What you need for this book

As with all WPF development, you'll need to have the .NET Framework and a version of Microsoft's Visual Studio integrated development environment software installed on your computer.

You'll be able to use versions as old as 2010, but in order to use the code in the book that takes advantage of the latest .NET Framework improvements, you'll need to use one of the newer versions. Note that any edition of Visual Studio can be used, from the top of the line Enterprise edition to the free Community (2015) edition.

Who this book is for

This book is for working developers with a basic to moderate level of knowledge about Windows Presentation Foundation and for those interested in improving their practical day to day WPF skills. It will also be of special interest to individuals wanting to know more about application architecture and those wanting to improve the look of their user interfaces.

Conventions

In this book, you will find a number of text styles that distinguish between different kinds of information. Here are some examples of these styles and an explanation of their meaning.

Code words in text, database table names, folder names, filenames, file extensions, pathnames, dummy URLs, user input, and Twitter handles are shown as follows: "There are two other useful properties declared by the `Grid` class."

A block of code is set as follows:

```
public string Name
{
  get { return name; }
  set
  {
    if (name != value)
    {
      name = value;
      NotifyPropertyChanged("Name");
    }
  }
}
```

Any command-line input or output is written as follows:

```
System.Windows.Data Error: 17 : Cannot get 'Item[]' value (type
'ValidationError') from '(Validation.Errors)' (type
'ReadOnlyObservableCollection`1').
BindingExpression:Path=(Validation.Errors)[0].ErrorContent;
DataItem='TextBox' (Name=''); target element is 'TextBox' (Name='');
target property is 'ToolTip' (type 'Object')
ArgumentOutOfRangeException:'System.ArgumentOutOfRangeException:
Specified argument was out of the range of valid values.
```

New terms and **important words** are shown in bold. Words that you see on the screen, for example, in menus or dialog boxes, appear in the text like this: "The **Cancel** button has been declared in the second row and column."

Warnings or important notes appear in a box like this.

Tips and tricks appear like this.

Reader feedback

Feedback from our readers is always welcome. Let us know what you think about this book-what you liked or disliked. Reader feedback is important for us as it helps us develop titles that you will really get the most out of. To send us general feedback, simply e-mail feedback@packtpub.com, and mention the book's title in the subject of your message. If there is a topic that you have expertise in and you are interested in either writing or contributing to a book, see our author guide at www.packtpub.com/authors.

Customer support

Now that you are the proud owner of a Packt book, we have a number of things to help you to get the most from your purchase.

Downloading the example code

You can download the example code files for this book from your account at `http://www.p acktpub.com`. If you purchased this book elsewhere, you can visit `http://www.packtpub.c om/support` and register to have the files e-mailed directly to you.

You can download the code files by following these steps:

1. Log in or register to our website using your e-mail address and password.
2. Hover the mouse pointer on the **SUPPORT** tab at the top.
3. Click on **Code Downloads & Errata**.
4. Enter the name of the book in the **Search** box.
5. Select the book for which you're looking to download the code files.
6. Choose from the drop-down menu where you purchased this book from.
7. Click on **Code Download**.

Once the file is downloaded, please make sure that you unzip or extract the folder using the latest version of:

- WinRAR / 7-Zip for Windows
- Zipeg / iZip / UnRarX for Mac
- 7-Zip / PeaZip for Linux

The code bundle for the book is also hosted on GitHub at `https://github.com/PacktPubl ishing/Mastering-Windows-Presentation-Foundation`. We also have other code bundles from our rich catalog of books and videos available at `https://github.com/PacktPublish ing/`. Check them out!

Downloading the color images of this book

We also provide you with a PDF file that has color images of the screenshots/diagrams used in this book. The color images will help you better understand the changes in the output. You can download this file from `https://www.packtpub.com/sites/default/files/down loads/MasteringWindowsPresentationFoundation_ColorImages.pdf`.

Errata

Although we have taken every care to ensure the accuracy of our content, mistakes do happen. If you find a mistake in one of our books-maybe a mistake in the text or the code-we would be grateful if you could report this to us. By doing so, you can save other readers from frustration and help us improve subsequent versions of this book. If you find any errata, please report them by visiting http://www.packtpub.com/submit-errata, selecting your book, clicking on the **Errata Submission Form** link, and entering the details of your errata. Once your errata are verified, your submission will be accepted and the errata will be uploaded to our website or added to any list of existing errata under the Errata section of that title.

To view the previously submitted errata, go to https://www.packtpub.com/books/conten t/supportand enter the name of the book in the search field. The required information will appear under the **Errata** section.

Piracy

Piracy of copyrighted material on the Internet is an ongoing problem across all media. At Packt, we take the protection of our copyright and licenses very seriously. If you come across any illegal copies of our works in any form on the Internet, please provide us with the location address or website name immediately so that we can pursue a remedy.

Please contact us at copyright@packtpub.com with a link to the suspected pirated material.

We appreciate your help in protecting our authors and our ability to bring you valuable content.

Questions

If you have a problem with any aspect of this book, you can contact us at questions@packtpub.com, and we will do our best to address the problem.

1
A Smarter Way of Working with WPF

When **Windows Presentation Foundation** (**WPF**) was first released as part of the .NET Framework version 3.0 in 2006, it was billed as the future of desktop application **Graphical User Interface** (**GUI**) languages and supporters claimed that it would put an end to the previous GUI technology, Windows Forms. However, as time passed, it has fallen far short of this claim.

There are three main reasons that WPF has not taken off as widely as previously expected. The first reason has nothing to do with WPF and stems from the recent push to host everything in the cloud and having web interfaces rather than desktop applications. The second reason relates to the very steep learning curve and the very different way of working that is required to master WPF.

The last reason is that it is not a very efficient language and if a WPF application has lots of 'bells and whistles' in, then either the client computers will need to have additional RAM and/or graphics cards installed, or they could face a slow and stuttering user experience.

This explains why many companies that make use of WPF today are in the finance industry, where they can afford to upgrade all users' computers to be able to run their applications optimally. This book will aim to make WPF more accessible to the rest of us by providing practical tips and tricks to help build our real-world applications more easily and more efficiently.

One of the simplest changes with the biggest workflow improvements that we can make to improve the way we work with WPF is to follow the MVVM software architectural pattern. It describes how we can organize our classes to make our applications more maintainable, testable, and generally simpler to understand. In this chapter, we will take a closer look at this pattern and discover how it can help us to improve our applications.

After discovering what MVVM is and what its benefits are, we'll learn several new ways to communicate between the various components in this new environment. We'll then focus on the physical structure of the code base in a typical MVVM application and investigate a variety of alternative arrangements.

What is MVVM and how does it help?

Model-View-View Model (**MVVM**) is a software architectural pattern that was famously introduced by John Gossman on his blog back in 2005 and is now commonly used when developing WPF applications. Its main purpose is to provide a *Separation of Concerns* between the business model, the **User Interface** (**UI**), and the business logic. It does this by dividing them into three distinct types of core components: Models, Views, and View Models. Let's take a look at how they are arranged and what each of these components represent.

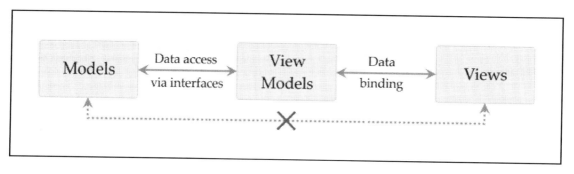

As we can see here, the **View Models** component sits between the **Models** and the **Views** and provides two-way access to each of them. It should be noted at this point that there should be no direct relationship between the **Views** and **Models** components and only loose connections between the other components. Let's now take a closer look at what each of these components represent.

Models

Unlike the other MVVM components, the Model constituent comprises of a number of elements. It encompasses the business data model along with its related validation logic and also the **Data Access Layer** (**DAL**), or data repositories, that provide the application with data access and persistence.

The data model represents the classes that hold the data in the application. They typically mirror the columns in the database more or less, although it is common that they are hierarchical in form, and so may require joins to be performed in the data source in order to fully populate them. One alternative would be to design the data model classes to fit the requirements in the UI, but either way, the business logic or validation rules will typically reside in the same project as the data model.

The code that is used to interface with whatever data persistence technology is used in our application is also included within the Models component of the pattern. Care should be taken when it comes to organizing this component in the code base, as there are a number of issues to take into consideration. We'll investigate this further in a while, but for now, let's continue to find out more about the components in this pattern.

View Models

The View Models can be explained easily; each View Model provides its associated View with all of the data and functionality that it requires. In some ways, they can be considered to be similar to the old Windows Forms code behind files, except that they have no direct relationship with the View that they are serving. A better analogy, if you're familiar with MVC, would be that they are similar to the Controllers in the **Model-View-Controller** (**MVC**) software architectural pattern. In fact, in his blog, John describes the MVVM pattern as being a variation of the MVC pattern.

They have two-way connections with the Model component in order to access and update the data that the Views require, and often, they transform that data in some way to make it easier to display and interact with in the UI. They also have two-way connections with the Views through data binding and property change notification. In short, View Models form the bridge between the Model and the View, which otherwise have no connection to each other.

However, it should be noted that the View Models are only loosely connected to the Views and Model components through their data binding and interfaces. The beauty of this pattern enables each element to be able to function independently from each other.

To maintain the separation between the View Models and the View, we avoid declaring any properties of UI-related types in the View Model. We don't want any references to UI-related DLLs in our View Models project, and so we make use of custom `IValueConverter` implementations to convert them to primitive types. For example, we might convert `Visibility` objects from the UI to plain `bool` values or convert the selection of some colored `Brush` objects to an `Enum` instance that is safe to use in the View Model.

Views

The Views define the appearance and layout of the UI. They typically connect with a View Model through the use of their `DataContext` property and display the data that it supplies. They expose the functionality provided by the View Model by connecting its commands to the UI controls that the users interact with.

In general, the basic rule of thumb is that each View has one associated View Model. This does not mean that a View cannot data bind to more than one data source or that we cannot reuse View Models. It simply means that, in general, if we have a class called `SecurityView`, it is more than likely that we'll also have an instance of a class named `SecurityViewModel` that will be set as the value of that View's `DataContext` property.

Data binding

One often overlooked aspect of the MVVM pattern is its requirement for data binding. We could not have the full Separation of Concerns without it, as there would be no easy way of communicating between the Views and View Models. The XAML markup, data binding classes, and `ICommand` and `INotifyPropertyChanged` interfaces are the main tools in WPF that provide this functionality.

The `ICommand` interface is how commanding is implemented in the .NET Framework. It provides behavior that implements and even extends the ever useful Command pattern, in which an object encapsulates everything needed to perform an action. Most of the UI controls in WPF have `Command` properties that we can use to connect them to the functionality that the commands provide.

The `INotifyPropertyChanged` interface is used to notify binding clients that property values have been changed. For example, if we had a `User` object and it had a `Name` property, then our `User` class would be responsible for raising the `PropertyChanged` event of the `INotifyPropertyChanged` interface, specifying the name of the property each time its value was changed. We'll look much deeper into all of this later, but now let's see how the arrangement of these components help us.

So how does MVVM help?

One major benefit of adopting MVVM is that it provides the crucial Separation of Concerns between the business model, the UI, and the business logic. This enables us to do several things. It frees the View Models from the Models, both the business model and the data persistence technology. This in turn enables us to reuse the business model in other applications and swap out the DAL and replace it with a mock data layer so that we can effectively test the functionality in our view models without requiring any kind of real data connection.

It also disconnects the Views from the View logic that they require, as this is provided by the View Models. This allows us to run each component independently, which has the advantage of enabling one team to work on designing the Views, while another team works on the View Models. Having parallel work streams enables companies to benefit from vastly reduced production times.

Furthermore, this separation also makes it easier for us to swap the Views for a different technology without needing to change our Model code. We may well need to change some aspects of the View Models, for example, the new technology used for the Views may not support the `ICommand` interface, but in principal, the amount of code that we would need to change would be fairly minimal.

The simplicity of the MVVM pattern also makes WPF easier to comprehend. Knowing that each View has a View Model that provides it with all the data and functionality that it requires means that we always know where to look when we want to find where our data bound properties have been declared.

Is there a downside?

There are, however, a few drawbacks to using MVVM, and it will not help us in every situation. The main downside to implementing MVVM is that it adds a certain level of complexity to our applications. First, there's the data binding, which can take some time to master. Also, depending on your version of Visual Studio, data binding errors may only appear at runtime and can be very tricky to track down.

Then, there are the different ways to communicate between the Views and View Models that we need to understand. Commanding and handling events in an unusual way takes a while to get used to. Having to discover the optimal arrangement of all the required components in the code base also takes time. So, there is a steep learning curve to climb before we can become competent at implementing MVVM for sure. This book will cover all of these areas in detail and attempt to lessen the gradient of that learning curve.

However, even when we are well practiced at the pattern, there are still occasional situations when it wouldn't make sense to implement MVVM. One example would be if our application was going to be very small, it would be unlikely that we would want to have unit tests for it or swap out any of its components. It would, therefore, be impractical to go through the added complexity of implementing the pattern when the benefits of the Separation of Concerns that it provides were not required.

Debunking the myth about code behind

One of the great misconceptions about MVVM is that we should avoid putting any code into the code behind files of our Views. While there is some truth to this, it is certainly not true in all situations. If we think logically for a moment, we already know that the main reason to use MVVM is to take advantage of the Separation of Concerns that its architecture provides. Part of this separates the business functionality in the View Model from the user interface-related code in the Views. Therefore, the rule should really be we should avoid putting any business logic into the code behind files of our Views.

Keeping this in mind, let's look at what code we might want to put into the code behind file of a View. The most likely suspects would be some UI-related code, maybe handling a particular event, or launching a child window of some kind. In these cases, using the code behind file would be absolutely fine. We have no business-related code here, and so we have no need to separate it from the other UI-related code.

On the other hand, if we had written some business-related code in a View's code behind file, then how could we test it? In this case, we would have no way to separate this from the View, no longer have our Separation of Concerns and, therefore, would have broken our implementation of MVVM. So in cases like this, the myth is no longer a myth... it is good advice.

However, even in cases like this where we want to call some business-related code from a View, it *is* possible to achieve without breaking any rules. As long as our business code resides in a View Model, it can be tested through that View Model, so it's not so important where it is called from during runtime. Understanding that we can always access the View Model that is data bound to a View's `DataContext` property, let's look at this simple example:

```
private void Button_Click(object sender, RoutedEventArgs e)
{
  UserViewModel viewModel = (UserViewModel)DataContext;
  viewModel.PerformSomeAction();
}
```

Now, there are some who would balk at this code example, as they correctly believe that Views should not know anything about their related View Models. This code effectively ties this View Model to this View. If we wanted to change the UI layer in our application at some point or have designers work on the View, then this code would cause us a problem. However, we need to be realistic... what is the likelihood that we will really need do that?

If it is likely, then we really shouldn't put this code into the code behind file and instead handle the event by wrapping it in an Attached Property, and we'll see an example of this in the next section. However, if it is not at all likely, then there is really no problem with putting it there. Let's follow rules when they make sense for us to follow them rather than blindly sticking to them because somebody in a different scenario said they were a good idea.

One other situation when we can ignore this 'No code behind' rule is when writing self-contained controls based on the `UserControl` class. In these cases, the code behind files are often used for defining Dependency Properties and/or handling UI events and for implementing general UI functionality. Remember though, if these controls are implementing some business-related functionality, we should write that into a View Model and call it from the control so that it can still be tested.

There is definitely perfect sense in the general idea of avoiding writing business-related code in the code behind files of our Views and we should always try to do so. However, we now hopefully understand the reasoning behind this idea and can use our logic to determine whether it is ok to do it or not in each particular case that may arise.

Learning how to communicate again

As we tend not to handle UI events directly, when using MVVM, we need alternative ways to implement the same functionality that they provide. Different methods are required to reproduce the functionality of different events. For example, the functionality of the `SelectionChanged` event of a collection control is typically reproduced by data binding a View Model property to the `SelectedItem` property of the collection control.

```
<ListBox ItemsSource="{Binding Items}"
    SelectedItem="{Binding CurrentItem}" />
```

In this example, the setter of the `CurrentItem` property will get called by the WPF Framework each time a new item is selected from the `ListBox`. Therefore, instead of handling the `SelectionChanged` event in the code behind, we can call any method directly from the property setter in the View Model:

```
public TypeOfObject CurrentItem
{
  get { return currentItem; }
  set
  {
    currentItem = value;
    DoSomethingWithTheNewlySelectedItem(currentItem);
  }
}
```

Note that we need to keep any methods that we call from data bound property setters from doing too much, as the time that it takes to execute them could negatively affect the performance when entering data. However, in this example, we would typically use this method to start an asynchronous data access function using a value from the current item or alter the value of another property in the View Model.

Many other UI events can be replaced with some form of `Trigger` in the XAML markup directly. For example, imagine that we had an `Image` element that was set as the `Content` property value of a `Button` control and that we wanted the `Image` element to be semi-transparent when the `Button` was disabled. Instead of handling the `UIElement.IsEnabledChanged` event in the code behind file, we could write a `DataTrigger` in a `Style` that we could apply to the `Image` element:

```
<Style x:Key="ImageInButtonStyle" TargetType="{x:Type Image}">
  <Setter Property="Opacity" Value="1.0" />
  <Style.Triggers>
    <DataTrigger Binding="{Binding IsEnabled,
      RelativeSource={RelativeSource FindAncestor,
      AncestorType={x:Type Button}}, FallbackValue=False}"
```

```
      Value="False">
      <Setter Property="Opacity" Value="0.5" />
    </DataTrigger>
  </Style.Triggers>
</Style>
```

Binding syntax will be covered in detail in Chapter 4, *Becoming Proficient With Data Binding*, but in short, the binding in this DataTrigger is specifying the target as the IsEnabled property of the ancestor (or parent) of the Image element with a type of Button. When this binding target has a value of False, the Opacity property of the Image will be set to 0.5 and set back to its original value when the target property value is True. Therefore, the Image element in our Button will become semi-transparent when the Button is disabled.

Introducing the ICommand interface

When it comes to button clicks in WPF and MVVM, instead of handling the well-known Click event, we typically use some form of command that implements the ICommand interface. Let's take a look at an example of a basic standard command:

```
using System;
using System.Windows.Forms;
using System.Windows.Input;

public class TestCommand : ICommand
{
  public event EventHandler CanExecuteChanged;

  public void Execute(object parameter)
  {
    MessageBox.Show("You executed a command");
  }

  public bool CanExecute(object parameter)
  {
    return true;
  }
}
```

Please note that in this book, we will display code with two-space tabs, instead of the more commonly used four-space tabs, in order to enable more characters of each code snippet to fit onto each line.

We can see that it has an `Execute` method, where the functionality that the command provides is performed. The `CanExecute` method is called by the `CommandManager` at various points over time, when it believes that the output value may have changed. We'll cover this in more detail later, but basically, raising the `CanExecuteChanged` event is one of the ways to trigger the `CommandManager` to do this. The output of the `CanExecute` method specifies whether the `Execute` method can be called or not.

You can imagine how cumbersome it would be if we had to create one of these classes for every action that we needed to implement. Furthermore, there is no context of where the command was called from other than the single command parameter. This means that if we wanted the command to add an item into a collection, we would have to put both the collection and the item to add into another object so that they could both be passed through the single input parameter.

When using MVVM, rather than implementing the commands in the standard way, we tend to use a single, reusable implementation that allows us to handle actions with standard methods directly in the View Model. This enables us to use commands without having to create a separate class for each one. There are a number of variations of this command, but its simplest form is shown here:

```
using System;
using System.Windows.Input;

public class ActionCommand : ICommand
{
  private readonly Action<object> action;
  private readonly Predicate<object> canExecute;

  public ActionCommand(Action<object> action) : this(action, null) { }

  public ActionCommand(Action<object> action,
    Predicate<object> canExecute)
  {
    this.action = action;
    this.canExecute = canExecute;
  }

  public event EventHandler CanExecuteChanged
  {
    add { CommandManager.RequerySuggested += value; }
    remove { CommandManager.RequerySuggested -= value; }
  }

  public bool CanExecute(object parameter)
  {
```

```
      return canExecute == null ? true : canExecute(parameter);
  }

  public void Execute(object parameter)
  {
    action(parameter);
  }
}
```

This is typically used in the View Model classes, as shown in the following example, where the command functionality comes from the `Save` method and the `bool` return value of the `CanSave` method determines whether the command can execute or not:

```
public ICommand SaveCommand
{
  get { return new ActionCommand(action => Save(),
    canExecute => CanSave()); }
}
```

A safer way to ensure that the command is never called *by code* when the `CanExecute` condition is not satisfied would be to make this alteration; however, please note that the `CommandManager` will always perform this check before calling any commands anyway:

```
public void Execute(object parameter)
{
  if (CanExecute(parameter)) action(parameter);
}
```

Full credit for this custom command should go to Josh Smith, as his `RelayCommand` class was the first implementation like this that I came across, although there are several variations to be found online. The beauty of this particular implementation should not be underestimated. Not only is it simple, elegant, and saves us from writing large amounts of code, but it also makes testing our functionality much easier, as our command code can now be defined right in our View Models.

The `action` parameter of type `Action<object>` will hold the reference to the method that will be called when the command is executed and the `object` generic parameter relates to the optionally used command parameter. The `canExecute` parameter of type `Predicate<object>` will hold the reference to the method that will be called to verify whether the command can be executed or not and its `object` generic parameter relates to the optionally used command parameter again.

The `CanExecuteChanged` event should be raised whenever the `canExecute` parameter value changes. It is typically handled by command sources, such as the `Button` control, to set their `IsEnabled` property value appropriately. When a command source receives a notification that this event has been raised, it will call the `ICommand.CanExecute` method to check the new value. Therefore, when a command can execute, its data bound control will be enabled and when it can't, its data bound control will be disabled.

The `CommandManager.RequerySuggested` event will be raised when the `CommandManager` detects a change in the UI that could reflect on whether a command could execute or not. For example, this could be due to a user interaction, such as the selection of an item in a collection or some other change in focus. Therefore, connecting one to the other seems to be a logical thing to do. In fact, an example of this is actually found in the source code of the .NET `RoutedCommand` class. We'll look at this `ActionCommand` again and in more detail in Chapter 3, *Writing Custom Application Frameworks*, but for now, let's move on to the next method of communication.

Handling events in Attached Properties

There is one way to handle events in WPF without having to resort to writing code in the code behind file of a View. Using Attached Properties, we can encapsulate the handling of events and effectively expose their behavior using properties that we can data bind to in our Views. Let's take a look at a simple example using the `PreviewKeyDown` event:

```
public static DependencyProperty OnEnterKeyDownProperty =
  DependencyProperty.RegisterAttached("OnEnterKeyDown",
  typeof(ICommand), typeof(TextBoxProperties),
  new PropertyMetadata(OnOnEnterKeyDownChanged));

public static ICommand GetOnEnterKeyDown(DependencyObject dependencyObject)
{
  return (ICommand)dependencyObject.GetValue(OnEnterKeyDownProperty);
}

public static void SetOnEnterKeyDown(DependencyObject dependencyObject,
  ICommand value)
{
  dependencyObject.SetValue(OnEnterKeyDownProperty, value);
}

public static void OnOnEnterKeyDownChanged(
  DependencyObject dependencyObject,
  DependencyPropertyChangedEventArgs e)
{
```

```
    TextBox textBox = (TextBox)dependencyObject;
    if (e.OldValue == null && e.NewValue != null)
       textBox.PreviewKeyDown += TextBox_OnEnterKeyDown;
    else if (e.OldValue != null && e.NewValue == null)
       textBox.PreviewKeyDown -= TextBox_OnEnterKeyDown;
  }

  private static void TextBox_OnEnterKeyDown(object sender, KeyEventArgs e)
  {
    if (e.Key == Key.Enter || e.Key == Key.Return)
    {
      TextBox textBox = sender as TextBox;
      ICommand command = GetOnEnterKeyDown(textBox);
      if (command != null && command.CanExecute(textBox))
        command.Execute(textBox);
    }
  }
```

As can be seen in this example, the event is handled by attaching an event handler in the normal way, except that all relating code is encapsulated within the class that declares the Attached Property. Let's take a closer look. First, we declare an Attached Property named OnEnterKeyDown of type ICommand in a class named TextBoxProperties, and we pass a reference of our handling method to the PropertyChangedCallback delegate parameter of the PropertyMetadata constructor.

The GetOnEnterKeyDown and SetOnEnterKeyDown methods represent the normal way to get and set Attached Property values. In the unfortunately named OnOnEnterKeyDownChanged method, which will be called when the property value changes, we look at the NewValue and OldValue values of the DependencyPropertyChangedEventArgs input parameter in order to decide whether we need to attach or detach the event handler to the 'PreviewKeyDown event of the relevant TextBox.

If the OldValue value is null and the NewValue value is not null, it means that there was no previous value, and so the property is being set for the first time. In this case, we want to attach the event handler. Conversely, when the OldValue value is not null and the NewValue value is null, it means that there previously was a value, which has been removed, so we should detach the event handler.

Finally, the `TextBox_OnEnterKeyDown` event handling method first detects whether either the *Enter* key or the *Return* key were pressed. If one was pressed, the data bound `ICommand` instance is checked for `null` and if the command can execute, it is then executed. Therefore, we have effectively wrapped a `PreviewKeyDown` event in an Attached Property and can now execute any command that has been data bound to it when the user presses *Enter* on their keyboard.

In order to use this Attached Property, we must first add an XML namespace prefix for our `Attached` folder in the XAML file of the View that this functionality is required in. Note that the `TextBoxProperties` class will be declared in the `Attached` folder of the Views project and so, its namespace will be as follows:

```
xmlns:Attached="clr-namespace:CompanyName.ApplicationName.Views.Attached;
    assembly=CompanyName.ApplicationName.Views"
```

Microsoft's convention for naming these prefixes is for the first character to be a lowercase letter, but it has always made more sense to me to simply use the last segment of the declared namespace, which will start with a capital letter. Once you have defined the prefix, you can use the Attached Property, as shown in the following example:

```
<TextBox Attached:TextBoxProperties.OnEnterKeyDown="{Binding Command}" />
```

Any UI events that we might need to handle in our applications can be encapsulated in Attached Properties in this same way. At first, this might seem to be a complicated way to handle events, compared with having a simple handler in a code behind file, but once we have a collection of these properties declared, we will find ourselves having to create fewer and fewer new ones. Think of them as simply being a reusable way of converting events into properties.

Making use of delegates

Delegates are very similar to events and, in fact, events can be thought of as a particular kind of delegate. They are a very simple tool to use to pass a signal or message from one place to another in the program. Unlike when creating custom events, we are not forced to use particular input parameters, for example, some form of the `EventArgs` class. We are totally unconstrained when creating custom delegates and are able to define our own method signatures, including both input and output parameter types.

As most of you will already be familiar with events and event handling, you'll already inadvertently know how to use delegates too. Let's look at a simple example. Imagine that we have a parent View Model that spawns child View Models and that one of these child View Models is paired with a View that enables administrative users to select security permissions. Now, let's imagine that the parent View that relates to the parent View Model has a menu that needs to be updated depending on the user's selection in the child View. How do we notify the parent View Model upon selection?

This is where delegates save the day. Keeping this example simple initially, let's say that we just need to notify the parent View Model that a particular change has been made so that it can refresh the current user's security permissions from a database. In this case, we only need to pass a signal, so we can create a delegate with no input or output parameters. We can declare it in the View Model that will be sending the signal, in this case, the child View Model.

```
public delegate void Signal();
```

Note that we define it in the same way that we define an abstract method, except that the `abstract` keyword is replaced with the `delegate` keyword after the access modifier. In short, a delegate defines a type that references a method with a particular signature. Now that we have defined our signaling delegate, we need to create a way for elements outside the View Model to use it. For this, we can simply create a property of the type of our new delegate *in the same View Model*:

```
public Signal OnSecurityPermissionChanged { get; set; }
```

As we don't need any property change notifications for this property, we can save ourselves some typing and take advantage of the .NET Auto-Implemented Property syntax. Bear in mind that delegates work in a multicast way like events, meaning that we can attach more than one handler to each one. In order to do this, we need to use the += operator to add handlers for the delegate, and in this example, we would want to do that in the parent View Model when the child View is instantiated:

```
ChildViewModel viewModel = new ChildViewModel();
viewModel.OnSecurityPermissionChanged += RefreshSecurityPermissions;
```

Here, we have assigned the `RefreshSecurityPermissions` method in the parent View Model to be the handler for this delegate. Note that we omit the parenthesis and the input parameters if there were any when attaching the handler. Now, you may be wondering, "What does the method signature of this handler look like?", but you already have the answer to this. If you remember, we declared the delegate with the signature of the method that we want to handle it. Therefore, any method that shares this signature can be a handler for this type of delegate:

```
private void RefreshSecurityPermissions()
{
   // Refresh user's security permissions when alerted by the signal
}
```

Note that the name used is irrelevant and all that matters when matching the delegate signature are the input and output parameters. So, we now have our delegate declared and hooked up to a handler in the parent View Model, but it's still not going to do anything because we haven't actually called it yet. In our example, it's the child View Model that is going to call the delegate because that's the object that needs to send out the information, or signal in this case.

When calling delegates, we must always remember to check for `null` before trying to use them because there may be no handlers attached. In our example, we'd call our `Signal` delegate via the `OnSecurityPermissionChanged` property at the point that we need to send the signal from the child View Model, let's say in reaction to a user changing their own security permissions:

```
if (OnSecurityPermissionChanged != null) OnSecurityPermissionChanged();
```

Alternatively, we could do so using the more concise null conditional operator in C# version 6.0, which calls the delegate's `Invoke` method if it is not null:

```
OnSecurityPermissionChanged?.Invoke();
```

Note that we do need to include the parenthesis when calling the delegate in the first example even though `OnSecurityPermissionChanged` is a property. This is because the delegate type of the property relates to a method and it is that method that we are calling. Please bear in mind that the first of these methods is not thread safe, so if thread safety is important for your application, then you will need to use the latter way.

We now have the complete picture, but while it is common to have a signal-sending delegate such as this, it is not overly useful because it only passes a signal with no other information. In many real-world scenarios, we would typically want to have some sort of input parameter so that we could pass some information, rather than just a signal.

For example, if we wanted to be notified with details each time a user selected a different item from a collection control in the UI, we could add a `CurrentItem` property into a generic `BaseCollection` class in our application and data bind it to the data bound collection control's `SelectedItem` property. This `CurrentItem` property would then be called by the WPF Framework each time a user makes a new selection, and so we can call our new delegate from its property setter:

```
protected T currentItem;

public virtual CurrentItemChange CurrentItemChanged { get; set; }

public virtual T CurrentItem
{
  get { return currentItem; }
  set
  {
    T oldCurrentItem = currentItem;
    currentItem = value;
    CurrentItemChanged?.Invoke(oldCurrentItem, currentItem);
    NotifyPropertyChanged();
  }
}
```

Delegates can be used to communicate between any related classes as long as they have access to the class that exposes the delegate so that they can attach a handler. They are commonly used to send information between child Views or View Models and their parents, or even between Views and View Models, but they can also be used to pass data between any two connected parts of the application.

Structuring the application code base

Now that we have a better understanding of the MVVM pattern, let's look at how we might implement it in a WPF application. What should the folder structure of our application be like? Clearly, we'll need somewhere to put our Models, Views, and View Models; however, how we arrange them will somewhat depend on the overall size of our application.

As we have heard, very small projects do not really suit MVVM because implementing it can involve a lot of preparation and often, the benefits do not apply. For small WPF applications, we would typically have just one project in our WPF application. In these cases, our classes would be separated into different folders within the single project.

With larger scale applications, we arrange our classes in the same basic structure, but as there are more classes and more chance that we want to reuse some of this code, it makes sense to use separate projects instead of folders. Either way, our classes should end up with the same CLR namespaces, as they tend to follow the structure of the application, regardless of whether those classes were separated using folders or projects.

While the CLR namespace in our startup project might be something along the lines of `CompanyName.ApplicationName`, the namespace of the classes in the Models component would be, or start with, `CompanyName.ApplicationName.Models`. For the purpose of the remainder of this book, we will assume that we are dealing with a large-scale WPF application and using projects for the separation of our classes.

There is nothing in the MVVM pattern that dictates what structure our code base should have, although there are clues. We will clearly need `Views` and `ViewModels` projects, but the `Models` project is less clearly defined. There are several elements within the Models component of MVVM, but we don't necessarily want to group them all into a single project in our code base. There are other projects that will be required too.

Let's visualize some possible structures so that we can get started with building our application.

```
CompanyName.ApplicationName (Solution)
    CompanyName.ApplicationName (Startup Project)
        Images
        Resources
    CompanyName.ApplicationName.Converters
    CompanyName.ApplicationName.DataProviders
        Interfaces
    CompanyName.ApplicationName.Extensions
    CompanyName.ApplicationName.Managers
        Interfaces
    CompanyName.ApplicationName.Models
        Business
    CompanyName.ApplicationName.ViewModels
        Commands
        Business
            Collections
            Delegates
            Enums
            Interfaces
    CompanyName.ApplicationName.Views
        Attached
        Business
        Controls
    Test.CompanyName.ApplicationName.Managers
    Test.CompanyName.ApplicationName.Mocks
    Test.CompanyName.ApplicationName.ViewModels
```

CompanyName.ApplicationName (Solution)
    CompanyName.ApplicationName (Startup Project)
        Images
        Resources
    CompanyName.ApplicationName.Converters
    CompanyName.ApplicationName.DataModels
        Collections
        Delegates
        Enums
        Interfaces
    CompanyName.ApplicationName.Extensions
    CompanyName.ApplicationName.Managers
    CompanyName.ApplicationName.Models
        DataControllers
        DataProviders
        Interfaces
    CompanyName.ApplicationName.ViewModels
        Commands
    CompanyName.ApplicationName.Views
        Attached
        Controls
    Test.CompanyName.ApplicationName.Managers
    Test.CompanyName.ApplicationName.Mocks
    Test.CompanyName.ApplicationName.ViewModels

These examples offer an insight into what the project structure of an MVVM-based WPF application might look like. However, nothing is set in stone and we are free to rename and to reorganize our application projects as we see fit. The important thing is how the components are connected together rather than the arrangement of the application files.

After we have developed a number of WPF applications, we get a feel for which project names and which structure we prefer, so I'd suggest trying a few variations and seeing which you feel more comfortable working with. Of course, some of us may not have the luxury of being able to create or alter the structure of the application that we work on. Let's first focus on the projects common to both example structures.

We see that the `Images` and `Resources` folders reside in the startup project. While this is customary, they *can* technically reside in any project or even in their own project. However, I prefer to keep them in this project because it provides a marginal performance benefit. Typically, when using MVVM, the only other files in the startup project will be the `MainWindow.xaml`, `App.xaml` (and their constituent code behind files), and `app.config` files.

The `Images` folder contains the images and icons that are displayed in the UI controls, whereas the `Resources` folder normally contains any resource files, such as XML schemas or text or data files that are used by the application.

The next project is named `Converters` and is fairly self-explanatory. It only contains classes that have implemented the `IValueConverter` interface and are used for converting data bound values in the Views. These classes are all reusable and the DLL from this project should be kept up to date and shared amongst our other applications.

Both examples show an `Extensions` project, but this is entirely optional and not a requirement of the MVVM pattern. I just happen to find Extension methods to be an essential part of .NET development, having built up a large collection of invaluable helper methods. After getting used to being able to call `Add` on an `IEnumerable` instance or `ToObservableCollection` on a query result for example, I now reuse them in every application. We'll see some examples of these in Chapter 3, *Writing Custom Application Frameworks,* Chapter 8, *Implementing Responsive Data Validation,* and Chapter 9, *Completing That Great User Experience.*

The next common project that we can see is a project called `Managers`. Others may prefer to call this `Engines`, `Services`, or something similar, but that is just a personal preference, and either way, the content will be the same. In this project, we typically find a number of classes that together provide a wide variety of functionality to the View Models. For example, in this project, we might find classes named `ExportManager`, `FeedbackManager`, `HardDriveManager`, `WindowManager`, and so on.

It is important to have a project like this, where we have one common place to provide all of the required specialized functionality for our application, rather than having to repeat the code in each View Model that requires that certain functionality. These classes are totally reusable between applications and this arrangement also promotes behavioral consistency throughout the application.

For example, without consolidating all of our functionality in this project, we might be tempted to copy and paste certain bits of code from one View Model to another. If the code then requires a change in the future, we may not remember that it has been copied and only update it in one View Model, thereby breaking the consistency of the application.

Another benefit to utilizing a project like this is that it reduces the number of references that the other projects need. The `Managers` project will typically require many references to be added, whereas the View Model and other classes that make use of its functionality will only need to add a single reference to this project.

Some or all of the functionality from these classes can be exposed through a `BaseViewModel` class and can therefore be made available to every View Model. We'll see more about this in `Chapter 3`, *Writing Custom Application Frameworks*, but for now, let's start to look at the differences between the two structures.

In the first structure example, the `Business` folder within the `Models` project simply represents the business data models of the application. There's no real need to have these classes in a separate `Business` folder other than the fact that it highlights that they are connected with the `ViewModels.Business` View Models and the `Views.Business` Views.

Technically, the data model classes in our application should represent our business objects and not contain any properties that bear no relevance to the business model, such as properties named `CurrentItem` or `IsSelected`. If this were the case and they were defined in their own project, as shown in the first example, then we could reuse their DLL in our other business applications. Alternatively, perhaps we already have a DLL representing the business model from another application that we will be reusing in the next application.

In either of these cases, we would need to add other folders into the `ViewModels` project in which we would implement an additional View Model class for each business model class to be displayed. This arrangement is shown in the `ViewModels.Business` folder of the first example and demonstrates the separation of the data model from the Views.

In these classes, we would encapsulate each public business model property in a new property that raised change notification and add any further properties required by the UI. It would look similar to the following example, where the BaseBusinessViewModel class simply implements the INotifyPropertyChanged interface:

```
using System;

namespace CompanyName.ApplicationName.Models.Business
{
  public class User
  {
    public User(Guid id, string name, int age)
    {
      Id = id;
      Name = name;
      Age = age;
    }

    public Guid Id { get; set; }

    public string Name { get; set; }

    public int Age { get; set; }
  }
}

using System;
using CompanyName.ApplicationName.Models.Business;

namespace CompanyName.ApplicationName.ViewModels.Business
{
  public class UserViewModel : BaseBusinessViewModel
  {
    private User model;
    private bool isSelected = false;

    public UserViewModel(User model)
    {
      Model = model;
    }

    public User Model
    {
      get { return model; }
      set { model = value; NotifyPropertyChanged(); }
    }
```

```
      public Guid Id
      {
        get { return Model.Id; }
        set { Model.Id = value; NotifyPropertyChanged(); }
      }

      public string Name
      {
        get { return Model.Name; }
        set { Model.Name = value; NotifyPropertyChanged(); }
      }

      public int Age
      {
        get { return Model.Age; }
        set { Model.Age = value; NotifyPropertyChanged(); }
      }

      public bool IsSelected
      {
        get { return isSelected; }
        set { isSelected = value; NotifyPropertyChanged(); }
      }
    }
  }
```

When implementing this pattern, after each data object was loaded from the data source, it would need to be wrapped in one of these View Model classes before being displayed in the UI:

```
User user = new User(Guid.NewGuid(), "John Smith", 25);
UserViewModel userViewModel = new UserViewModel(user);
```

Following the pattern in the first example structure through to the `Views` project, we see that it also contains a `Business` folder. Typically, we could find a small, individual object-sized View there for each of these business model-related View Models. However, in the vast majority of applications, this additional level of separation between the business model and the UI is simply unrequired. Also, following this pattern adds a small overhead to all implementation and data access times.

For some, a viable alternative would be to simply add the properties and property change notification required by the UI straight into the data model classes. If we don't need this separation, then there is little point in writing all of the extra code. I am a great fan of Agile practices and one of the twelve principles from the *Manifesto for Agile Software Development* summarizes this point perfectly:

> *"Simplicity–the art of maximizing the amount of work not done–is essential"*

This simpler, alternative implementation is shown in the `DataModels` project of the second example, where the business model classes are combined with the UI-related properties along with the business rules or validation logic.

In other types of applications, you may find a separate validation layer that sits between the DAL and the code behind the UI layer. As we'll see in `Chapter 8`, *Implementing Responsive Data Validation*, with WPF, we can build validation right into the business classes, along with the properties that they are validating.

This `DataModels` project contains a number of sub-folders, grouping similar types of classes together. The `Collections` folder typically contains an extension of the `ObservableCollection<T>` class for each data model class in the application. The `Enums` folder is also often well used in most WPF applications, as enumerations are great to use when data bound to either radio buttons or checkboxes.

The interfaces found in the `Interfaces` folder are essential to enable the functionality of the base classes, as we'll see in `Chapter 3`, *Writing Custom Application Frameworks*. If we're likely to use a large number of delegates in our application, then it also makes sense to organize them into a separate `Delegates` folder as well. Otherwise, if a delegate is strongly tied to a particular class, they can just be declared locally in the classes that will be raising them.

One other alternative would be to have a single class in the `Models` project that encapsulates all of the application delegates, although this would require prefixing the name of this class to the delegate names when using them, for example, `Delegates.CloseRequest`. Declaring each delegate in the class that uses them enables us to reference them directly, for example, `CloseRequest`.

The data model classes in this project could be thought of as View Models too, although View Models that only serve the display of individual objects, as opposed to those that serve the main application Views. They would have a base class that implements the `INotifyPropertyChanged` interface like the main View Models, but then it would also typically implement a validation error interface too.

They also differ from the main application View Models because they generally provide no functionality other than validation to their associated Views. We can think of these classes as mere data containers with a few extra properties to enable effective communication with the UI.

When following this structure, we can render these individual object-sized View Models in the UI using data templates, so we generally don't need to declare a separate View for each of them. Furthermore, we may want to display the same objects differently in different parts of the application, or even switch their display in response to some user action and that is also easier to accomplish with data templates.

This explains why these objects do not reside in the View Models project along with the main application View Models. If you remember, each View Model should only have one associated View. For the purpose of this book, this simpler, alternative implementation is the pattern that we will be following. Now, let's continue by investigating the DAL of the application.

The `DataProviders` project from the first example is responsible for providing access to the persisted data source of the application. Another commonly used name is `Repositories`, but again, you can call it what you like. The important thing is that it has an essential `Interfaces` folder that contains one or more interfaces that form the connection between the data source(s) and the rest of the application.

The `DataProviders` and `Interfaces` folders in the second example appear within the `Models` project, but they have the same responsibilities. Either way, it is through the use of these interfaces that we are able to disconnect the data source and replace it with a mock source of some kind when testing. We will look at an example of this in Chapter 3, *Writing Custom Application Frameworks*, but for now, let's continue.

The `ViewModels` project is fairly easy to understand, as it just contains View Models. You may be wondering why there is a `Commands` folder inside it. If we were using commands in the old fashioned way, writing a separate class for each command, then we could end up with a great many classes and that would probably warrant putting them into their own project.

However, if you remember, we will be using only one single command, the `ActionCommand`. As this will be used by the View Model classes alone, it makes sense to include it in their project. We've already covered the differences in the View Models and Views projects between the two example structures, so let's finish off looking at the remaining common parts.

We often find an `Attached` folder in the `Views` project that contains the Attached Properties that are used in the application. As these classes contain View-related code and are only used by the Views, it is logical that they should reside here. Alongside that, we see the `Controls` folder where we find reusable user controls and/or custom controls, such as a custom textbox that spawns a child window to help with editing when clicked or a custom clock face that can be used to enter a time.

At the bottom of both example structures, we see the test projects that contain the code that tests our application. If your application needs testing, this is a good pattern to follow. By prefixing the name of the projects that we will be testing with a `Test` domain, they will all appear in the Visual Studio Solution Explorer in one group, either above or below the other projects, and in the same order as the projects being tested.

The `Mocks` project typically hosts the application objects to be used while testing the application. This would normally include any mock data generation or provider classes and mock `Manager` classes. We may need to create these mock `Manager` classes if we don't want to use expensive resources while testing, or in case they access any UI elements that we also want to avoid when testing. Let's take a look at an example of one possible method of a `UiThreadManager` class:

```
public Task RunAsynchronously(Action method)
{
   return Task.Run(method);
}
```

This method is fairly straightforward and enables us to pass a reference to any method that we want to run asynchronously. It simply passes the method reference to the `Task.Run` method and lets it do its thing. It can be called like this:

```
UiThreadManager.RunAsynchronously(() => GenerateReports());
```

However, running code asynchronously in unit tests can have unpredictable results that may make them fail. Therefore, when testing, we need to use a `MockUiThreadManager` class and implement its `RunAsynchronously` method, as follows:

```
public Task RunAsynchronously(Action method)
{
   Task task = new Task(method);
   task.RunSynchronously();
   return task;
}
```

In this method, we can see that we use the `RunSynchronously` method of the `Task` class to run the referenced method synchronously, or in other words, immediately and on the same thread. In effect, this simply bypasses the functionality of the original method. Using these mock objects enable us to run different code while testing than we do at runtime. We'll see more examples of these mock objects in Chapter 3, *Writing Custom Application Frameworks*, but let's first take a look back at what we have covered so far.

Summary

In this chapter, we have discovered what the MVVM architectural pattern is and the benefits of using it when developing WPF applications. We're now in a better position to decide which applications to use it with and which not to. We started looking into the various new ways of communicating between the various components of this pattern and also investigated the most common ways of organizing our source code. We are now ready to start setting out our own application structures.

In the next chapter, before we properly get started building our application, we'll look at several methods of the sometimes tricky task of debugging our data bound values. We'll discover other useful tips and tricks that we can use to help us to iron out any problems that may occur in our applications so that once we start building, we'll be able to avoid wasting time with problems that may arise.

2
Debugging WPF Applications

When our WPF programs don't work as expected, we need to debug them, as we would with any other language. However, at first it can seem to be a daunting task, as WPF is very different from other languages. For example, when declaring a Dependency Property, we normally add a CLR property wrapper for convenience. However, the WPF Framework won't call it when the property value is changing, so we'd wait a long time for a break point in that setter to be hit.

When we're testing our newly developed code, we need to be able to check the values of our data bound properties, and there are a number of ways to do that, although some are far from obvious. In this chapter, we'll investigate a number of important sources of information to help us to locate the mistakes in our code.

We'll discover a variety of tactics to help us when debugging the data bound values and find out how to track down the actual cause of a problem when faced with the dreaded `XamlParseException`. We'll cover all of these topics in detail shortly, but for now, let's first start with the absolute basics.

Utilizing the Output window

When we've made changes to our XAML, but don't see what we are expecting to see in the UI, the first place to look for errors is in the **Output** window of Visual Studio. If this window is not already visible, then you can display it by selecting the **Output** option from the **View** menu or by pressing *Ctrl + W* and then *O*.

However, if you have a binding error, but don't see any reference to it in the **Output** window, it could be because your Visual Studio is not currently set up to output debug information to it. You can turn this functionality on in the Visual Studio **Options** dialog window.

Navigate to **Tools** | **Options** | **Debugging** | **Output Window** | **General Output Settings**.

The **General Output Settings** section has several options that you can turn on and off. The most important ones are **All debug output** and **Exception Messages**, but it is generally good practice to leave them all set to **On**. When set, binding errors will be displayed in the **Output** window in the following format:

```
System.Windows.Data Error: 40 : BindingExpression path error:
'ViewName' property not found on 'object' ''MainViewModel'
(HashCode=3910657)'. BindingExpression:Path=ViewName;
DataItem='MainViewModel' (HashCode=3910657); target element is 'TextBox'
(Name='NameTextBox'); target property is 'Text' (type 'String')
```

Let's take a closer look at this error. The plain English translation for this would be as follows:

- There is no public property named `ViewName` in the object of type `MainViewModel` with a `HashCode` value of `3910657`
- The error was raised from a `Binding.Path` value that was specified as `ViewName`, which was set on the `Text` property of a `TextBox` named `NameTextBox`

This could be rewritten with descriptive names rather than specific details, like this:

```
System.Windows.Data Error: 40 : BindingExpression path error:
'PropertyOfBindingSource' property not found on 'object'
''TypeOfBindingSource' (HashCode=HashCodeOfBindingSource)'.
BindingExpression:Path=UsedBindingPath; DataItem='TypeOfBindingSource'
(HashCode=HashCodeOfBindingSource); target element is
'TypeOfBindingTarget' (Name='NameOfBindingTarget'); target property is
'PropertyOfBindingTarget' (type 'TypeOfBindingTargetProperty')
```

Now that we have our 'key' to explain what these values represent, we can see that they are really very descriptive. Not only are we provided with the name of the data bound UI control, if it is set, and the used binding path, but also the type of the data source, along with the hash code of the actual instance of that type that is being used.

These errors highlight the mistakes that have been made in the XAML files. The type of errors displayed in this window will include incorrectly labeled binding paths, such as using non-existent property names, or otherwise invalid binding source paths. While it won't catch every problem, there is a way to make it output additional information that could help us to track down our more elusive problems. In order to do this, first display the following **Options** dialog window:

 Navigate to **Tools** | **Options** | **Debugging** | **Output Window** | **WPF Trace Settings**.

Here, you can find a number of options, each with a variable level of output; **Animation, Data Binding, Dependency Properties, Documents, Freezable, HWND Hosting, Markup, Name Scope, Resource Dictionaries** and **Routed Events**. The various levels of output and their meanings are as follows:

- **Critical**: Enables tracing of **Critical** events only
- **Error**: Enables tracing of **Critical** and **Error** events
- **Warning**: Enables tracing of **Critical**, **Error**, and **Warning** events
- **Information**: Enables tracing of **Critical**, **Error**, **Warning**, and **Information** events
- **Verbose**: Enables tracing of **Critical**, **Error**, **Warning**, **Information**, and **Verbose** events
- **ActivityTracing**: Enables tracing of **Stop**, **Start**, **Suspend**, **Transfer**, and **Resume** events

It is fairly common to permanently have the **Data Binding** option set to **Warning** or **Error**, with the other options set to **Off**. The general rule of thumb when using these options is to use the minimum level required, except when trying to find problems, because they will slow down the running of the application. It should be noted however, that this extra debug trace output will not affect Release builds at all.

If you set the **Data Binding** entry to an output of **Verbose** or **All** and look in the **Output** window when running your application, you will understand why it will negatively affect performance. Even when not displaying this debug information in the **Output** window, the WPF Framework will still be performing a great number of checks when there are binding errors. It is, therefore, very important to clear up all errors and warnings that are displayed, to minimize the amount of work that the Framework does when trying to resolve them.

Putting Presentation Trace Sources to work

As useful as it is, there are certain occasions when using the **Output** window will not suffice. Perhaps we have far too much output to look through now and would like to view it on the way home from work, or maybe we need to see this kind of debug trace information after our application has been deployed. In these cases and others, it's time to enable the WPF Presentation Trace Sources.

There are a number of different trace sources that we can employ to output detailed tracing data for us. The choice is the same as that found in the **WPF Trace Settings** options and in fact, after setting the values there, the **Output** window has already been showing us the debug trace output. By default, WPF uses a `DefaultTraceListener` object to send the information to the **Output** window, but we can override that and/or configure the output to be sent to a text and/or XML file instead or as well.

In order to do this, we need to alter our `app.config` file, which is found in the root folder of our startup project. We'll need to add a `system.diagnostics` section and within it, add `sources`, `switches`, and `sharedlisteners` elements. The `switches` element holds the switch that determines the output level, as specified in the previous section.

The `sharedlisteners` element specifies which kind of output we want to utilize. The three types are:

- `System.Diagnostics.ConsoleTraceListener`: Sends the traces to the **Output** window
- `System.Diagnostics.TextWriterTraceListener`: Outputs to a text file
- `System.Diagnostics.XmlWriterTraceListener`: Outputs to an XML file

Finally, we need to add a `source` element for each trace source that we want to listen to, and specify which switch and listener we want to use with it. Therefore, we are able to output different trace sources to different media and with different levels of output. These trace sources are the same as those found in the **WPF Trace Settings** options, although in the configuration file, we need to specify their full names.

The choices are as follows:

- `System.Windows.Media.Animation`
- `System.Windows.Data`
- `System.Windows.DependencyProperty`
- `System.Windows.Documents`
- `System.Windows.Freezable`

- System.Windows.Interop.HwndHost
- System.Windows.Markup
- System.Windows.NameScope
- System.Windows.ResourceDictionary
- System.Windows.RoutedEvent
- System.Windows.Shell

Let's see an example configuration file:

```xml
<?xml version="1.0" encoding="utf-8"?>
<configuration>
  <startup>
    <supportedRuntime version="v4.0" sku=".NETFramework,Version=v4.6.1" />
  </startup>
  <system.diagnostics>
    <sources>
      <source name="System.Windows.Data" switchName="Switch">
        <listeners>
          <add name="TextListener" />
        </listeners>
      </source>
    </sources>
    <switches>
      <add name="Switch" value="All" />
    </switches>
    <sharedListeners>
      <add name="TextListener"
        type="System.Diagnostics.TextWriterTraceListener"
        initializeData="Trace.txt" />
    </sharedListeners>
    <trace indentsize="4" autoflush="true"></trace>
  </system.diagnostics>
</configuration>
```

Focusing on the system.diagnostics section from the example, we see that there is one source element that is specifying the System.Windows.Data source (for data binding information), the switch named Switch and the TextListener listener. Looking first in the switches section, we find the switch named Switch, and note that it is set with an output level of All.

Below this, in the `sharedlisteners` element, we see the listener named `TextListener`. This listener is of type `System.Diagnostics.TextWriterTraceListener` and this outputs to a text file which is specified by the value of the `initializeData` attribute. We end with a `trace` element that sets the tab size of the text document to four spaces and ensures that data is flushed out of the buffer after each write to prevent trace data being lost due to a crash.

To set a less verbose output, we can simply alter the switch to use one of the other levels of output, as follows:

```
<add name="Switch" value="Error" />
```

As mentioned earlier, WPF can use a `DefaultTraceListener` object to send trace information to the **Output** window when particular options are set in Visual Studio. The name of this listener is `Default`. In order to stop the default behavior of this `DefaultTraceListener`, we can remove it using our `source` element, as follows:

```
<source name="System.Windows.Data" switchName="Switch">
  <listeners>
    <add name="TextListener" />
    <remove name="Default" />
  </listeners>
</source>
```

It's good to be aware of this fact, because if we also configured our own `ConsoleTraceListener` object, we could end up with our **Output** window duplicating trace events. However, it is also possible to add multiple listeners into each `source` element if required.

```
<source name="System.Windows.Data" switchName="Switch">
  <listeners>
    <add name="TextListener" />
    <add name="OutputListener" />
  </listeners>
</source>
```

We can also add different listeners for different sources.

```
<source name="System.Windows.Data" switchName="Switch">
  <listeners>
    <add name="TextListener" />
  </listeners>
</source>
<source name="System.Windows.DependencyProperty" switchName="Switch">
  <listeners>
    <add name="OutputListener" />
```

```
    </listeners>
  </source>
  ...
  <sharedListeners>
    <add name="TextListener"
      type="System.Diagnostics.TextWriterTraceListener"
      initializeData="Trace.txt" />
    <add name="OutputListener"
      type="System.Diagnostics.ConsoleTraceListener" />
  </sharedListeners>
```

Different output levels for different sources can be added as follows:

```
<source name="System.Windows.Data" switchName="ErrorSwitch">
  <listeners>
    <add name="TextListener" />
  </listeners>
</source>
<source name="System.Windows.DependencyProperty" switchName="AllSwitch">
  <listeners>
    <add name="OutputListener" />
  </listeners>
</source>
...
<switches>
  <add name="AllSwitch" value="All" />
  <add name="ErrorSwitch" value="Error" />
</switches>
```

One neat feature that the WPF Presentation Trace Sources provide is the ability to create our own custom trace sources.

```
<source name="CompanyName.ApplicationName" switchName="Switch">
  <listeners>
    <add name="TextListener" />
  </listeners>
</source>
```

Note that the DefaultTraceListener was already configured to send information to the **Output** window in the **WPF Trace Settings** options mentioned in the previous section, so the traces from this source will also be sent to the **Output** window automatically. If you have not set those options, but want to view the trace output there, then you will need to manually add a reference to the ConsoleTraceListener to this source as shown in the preceding code snippets.

In code, we are now able to output custom trace information to this source.

```
TraceSource traceSource = new  TraceSource("CompanyName.ApplicationName");
traceSource.TraceEvent(TraceEventType.Information, eventId, "Data loaded");
// Alternative way to output information with an event id of 0
traceSource.TraceInformation("Data loaded");
```

To specify different levels of importance, we use the `TraceEventType` enumeration.

```
traceSource.TraceEvent(TraceEventType.Error, eventId, "Data not loaded");
```

After outputting the debug information, we can optionally flush the existing listeners to ensure that they receive the events in the buffers before continuing.

```
traceSource.Flush();
```

Finally, we need to ensure that we close the `TraceSource` object to free resources when we have outputted the necessary information.

```
traceSource.Close();
```

The best part of this tracing functionality is the fact that we can turn it on and off using the configuration file, either at design time, runtime, or even on production versions of the application. As the configuration file is basically a text file, we can manually edit it and then restart the application so that it reads the new configuration.

Imagine that we had two switches in our file and that our default configuration used the switch named `OffSwitch`, so that there was no tracing output.

```
<source name="CompanyName.ApplicationName" switchName="OffSwitch">
  <listeners>
    <add name="TextListener" />
  </listeners>
</source>
...
<switches>
  <add name="AllSwitch" value="All" />
  <add name="OffSwitch" value="Off" />
</switches>
```

Now imagine that we have deployed our application and it is installed on a user's computer. It's worth noting at this point that the actual deployed configuration file that is created from the `app.config` file will have the same name as the executable file. In our case, it would be named `CompanyName.ApplicationName.exe.config` and would reside in the same folder as the executable file.

If this installed application was not behaving correctly, we could locate this configuration file, and simply change the switch to the one named `AllSwitch`.

```
<source name="CompanyName.ApplicationName" switchName="AllSwitch">
  <listeners>
    <add name="TextListener" />
  </listeners>
</source>
```

After restarting the application, the new configuration would be read and our custom traces would be written to the specified text file. One alternative to restarting the application would be to call the `Refresh` method of the `Trace` class, which has the same effect of initiating a new read of the configuration file.

```
Trace.Refresh();
```

This method call can even be connected to a menu item or other UI control to enable tracing to be turned on and off without having to restart the application. Using either of these methods of refreshing the configuration file, we can attain important debug information from our software, even when it is in production. However, great care should be taken to ensure that text or XML file tracing is not permanently enabled on released software, as it will negatively affect performance.

While the WPF Presentation Trace Sources are typically available by default these days, in a few cases, we may need to manually enable this tracing functionality by adding the following registry key.

```
HKEY_CURRENT_USER\Software\Microsoft\Tracing\WPF
```

Once the `WPF` registry key has been added, we need to add a new `DWORD` value to it, name it `ManagedTracing` and set its value to 1. We should then have access to the WPF Presentation Trace Sources. We've now seen a number of ways of finding the information that we need at runtime, but what about if the application won't even run?

Discovering inner exceptions

When we are building the content of our Views, we often make the odd typographical mistake here and there. Perhaps, we mistype the name of one of our properties in a binding path, or copy and paste some code that references other code that we have not copied.

At first, it may appear to be quite difficult to find the source of these types of errors, because when we run our application, the actual error that is raised by Visual Studio is usually of type XamlParseException and bares no direct relation to the actual error. The additional information provided is also of little help. Here is a typical example.

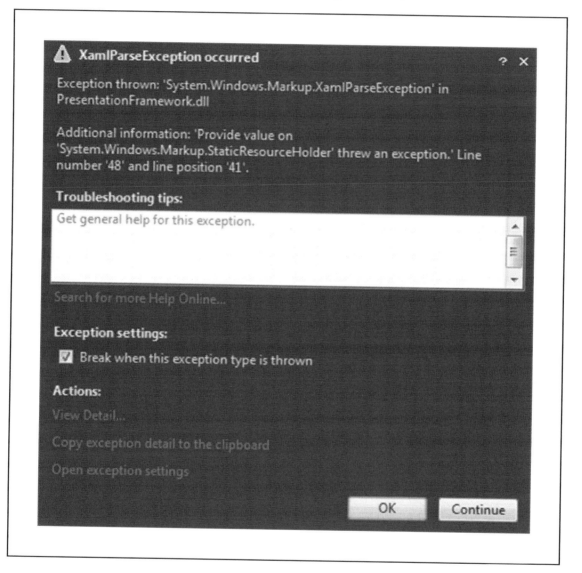

Let's investigate this further. We can see that the additional information supplied here says-`'Provide value on 'System.Windows.Markup.StaticResourceHolder' threw an exception.' Line number '48' and line position '41'`.

Now let's try to break this down to some meaningful information. Firstly, it is clear that the exception was thrown by the `System.Windows.Markup.StaticResourceHolder` class. By itself, this information is not very useful, but at least we know that the problem has something to do with a `StaticResource` that could not be resolved.

The next bit of information that we can gather from this message is that the problem occurred on line 48 and position 41. However, without informing us of which file this relates to, this information is also not very useful. The **Exception** dialog window shown in the preceding screenshot will often have a line pointing to the line and position in the current file, which can also be another red herring. In this particular case, it was indeed false information as there was no error there, but at least that tells us that the problem has not arisen from the current file.

The trick to finding out what caused the real problem that occurred is for us to click the **View Detail...** link in the window. This will open the **View Detail** window, where we can see all of the property values of the `XamlParseException`. Looking at the `StackTrace` and `TargetSite` property values won't help in the way that they usually do with normal exceptions. However, if we open up and inspect the `InnerException` property value, we can finally find out what actually happened. Let's do that with our example.

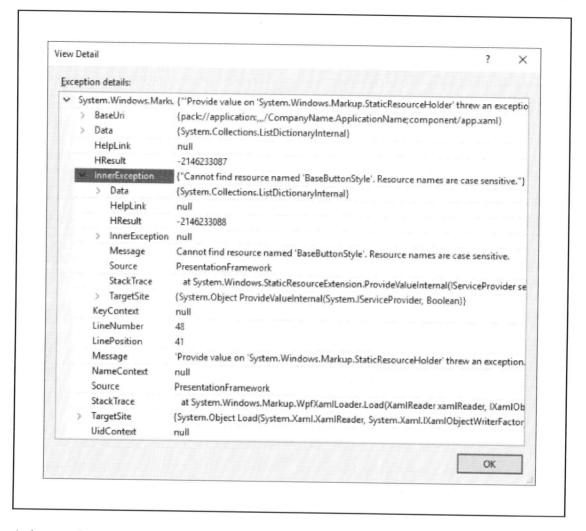

At last, we have something that we can work with. The `InnerException.Message` property value states: `"Cannot find resource named 'BaseButtonStyle'. Resource names are case sensitive"`.

Therefore, our offending object references the `BaseButtonStyle` style. A quick search for `'BaseButtonStyle'` through the solution files in Visual Studio will locate the source of the problem. In this case, our problem lay in the `Application.Resources` section of the `App.xaml` file. Let's take a closer look:

```
<Style x:Key="SmallButtonStyle" TargetType="{x:Type Button}"
    BasedOn="{StaticResourceBaseButtonStyle}">
```

```
    <Setter Property="Height" Value="24" />
    <Setter Property="Width" Value="24" />
</Style>
```

Here we can see a style that is based on another style, but the base style is apparently missing. It is this missing base style that is the `StaticResource` named `BaseButtonStyle` that caused this error. We can fix this problem easily by either creating the referenced base style in the `App.xml` file, or by removing the `BasedOn` property from the `SmallButtonStyle` style.

We should always bear in mind that errors like these will most likely reside in the code that we have just been editing, so that also helps us to narrow down the search. It is therefore beneficial to run the application often when implementing XAML that may contain errors, as the more code we write between checking our progress, the more code we need to look through to find the problem.

Debugging data bound values

So far, we have seen that we can utilize a number of sources of information to help with tracking down the causes of our problems. However, what about actual debugging? In other GUI languages, we can add breakpoints at various locations in our code and watch our values changing as we step through our code. While we can also do this with WPF applications, it is not always so obvious where to put our breakpoints to ensure that program execution will hit them.

If you remember from the previous chapter, the `CommandManager.RequerySuggested` event is raised when the `CommandManager` detects a change in the UI that could reflect on whether a command could execute or not. Well, it turns out that two of the conditions that the `CommandManager` looks out for is when the application window is either activated or deactivated and we can take advantage of this to help us when debugging. Note that the application window is deactivated when the user moves focus from it and is reactivated when the user returns focus to it.

Therefore, while running the application side by side with Visual Studio, we can put a breakpoint in any method that is being used as a `canExecute` handler for our `ActionCommand` class, thereby removing focus from the application. Now, when we click back on the WPF application, the focus will be returned to it.

This will cause the `CommandManager.RequerySuggested` event to be raised and as a result, the `canExecute` handler will be called and our breakpoint will be hit. This basically means that we are able to get the program execution into our View Models to debug parameter values any and every time that we need to. Let's see what else we can do to help fix our data binding errors.

Outputting values to UI controls

One of the simplest ways of working out what values our data bound properties have is to just data bind them to other UI controls that have a textual output. For example, if we have a collection of items and we want to do something with the selected item, but whatever that is isn't working, we need to verify that our binding to that selected item is correct.

To visualize the result of the binding, we can simply copy and paste the binding path to the `Text` property of a `TextBox` and run the application. If our binding path is correct, we'll see something output in the `TextBox` and if not, we'll know that the problem that we're having is in fact, down to the binding path. We can therefore use this method to verify that objects that don't normally have a textual output are at least correctly data bound or not.

This simple technique can help in any situation where the faulty data binding is not already rendered in a text-based UI control. For example, we might need to debug a data bound value because a particular visual effect that is created with a `DataTrigger` is not working and we need to determine whether the problem is related to the UI control or the data binding path.

Catching changing Dependency Property values

As we saw at the beginning of this chapter, the WPF Framework won't call the CLR property wrappers of our Dependency Properties when the property values are changing. However, there is a way to accomplish this using callback handlers. In fact, we've already seen an example of this when we were looking at the creation of the `OnEnterKeyDown` Attached Property. Let's remind ourselves what that looked like:

```
public static DependencyProperty OnEnterKeyDownProperty =
  DependencyProperty.RegisterAttached("OnEnterKeyDown",
  typeof(ICommand), typeof(TextBoxProperties),
  new PropertyMetadata(OnOnEnterKeyDownChanged));

...

public static void OnOnEnterKeyDownChanged(
```

```
    DependencyObject dependencyObject, DependencyPropertyChangedEventArgs e)
{
    TextBox textBox = (TextBox)dependencyObject;
    if (e.OldValue == null && e.NewValue != null)
        textBox.PreviewKeyDown += TextBox_OnEnterKeyDown;
    else if (e.OldValue != null && e.NewValue == null)
        textBox.PreviewKeyDown -= TextBox_OnEnterKeyDown;
}
```

For this Attached Property, we used a particular overload of the
`DependencyProperty.RegisterAttached` method that accepts a `PropertyMetadata`
object, which enabled us to assign a `PropertyChangedCallback` handler to the property.
Note that there is an identical overload for the `DependencyProperty.Register` method
for declaring Dependency Properties.

Program execution will enter these `PropertyChangedCallback` handlers each time their
related Dependency Property changes and so that makes them perfect for debugging their
values. While we don't often need to attach these handlers, it only takes a moment to add
one when we need to and they enable us to find out what's going on with the Dependency
Property values at runtime.

Exploiting converters

If we're having a problem with a data binding that uses an `IValueConverter` to convert
the data bound value from one type to another, then we can place a breakpoint into the
`Convert` method of the converter. As long as we have correctly set up the converter, we can
be sure that the breakpoint will be hit when the binding is evaluated at runtime. If it doesn't
get hit, that will mean that we have not set it up correctly.

However, even when we are not already using a converter on a binding that is not
displaying the value that we are expecting, we can still add one just for this purpose. We
can either add an existing converter to the binding, if we have one of the relevant type, or
we can create a simple converter specifically for the purpose of debugging and use that
instead. Let's take a look at how we might do this.

```
[ValueConversion(typeof(object), typeof(object))]
public class DataBindingDebugConverter : IValueConverter
{
    public object Convert(object value, Type targetType, object parameter,
        CultureInfo culture)
    {
        if (Debugger.IsAttached) Debugger.Break();
        return value;
```

```
  }

  public object ConvertBack(object value, Type targetType,
    object parameter, CultureInfo culture)
  {
    if (Debugger.IsAttached) Debugger.Break();
    return value;
  }
}
```

As you can see from the preceding code snippet, it's a very simple implementation of the `IValueConverter` interface. We start by specifying that we are converting from `object` to `object` in the `ValueConversion` attribute, thereby outlining that we are not actually converting any data bound values in this converter. The rest of the class represents a typical converter class, but without any conversion code.

The only real point of interest here are the two calls to the `Debugger.Break` method from the `System.Diagnostics` assembly. When the program execution reaches either of these method calls, it will automatically break, just as if there were breakpoints set on these lines.

Therefore, when using this converter, we don't even need to set a breakpoint; we can just plug it into the binding, run the program and investigate the value of the `value` input parameter. Note the use of the `Debugger.IsAttached` property in the `if` statements, which are used to ensure that execution will not break in a production environment if this converter is accidentally left connected. It can be attached like any other converter.

```
xmlns:Converters="clr-namespace:CompanyName.ApplicationName.Converters;
  assembly=CompanyName.ApplicationName.Converters"
...
<UserControl.Resources>
  <Converters:DataBindingDebugConverter x:Key="Debug" />
</UserControl.Resources>
...
<ListBox ItemsSource="{Binding Items, Converter={StaticResource Debug}}" />
```

Summary

In this chapter, we've investigated the best ways to track down our coding problems. We've looked at the various debug tracing outputs that we have access to and even discovered how to output our own custom trace information. We discovered that the exceptions that are thrown in WPF often hide their useful information in their `InnerException` properties. Finally, we found out a number of tips and tricks to use when trying to find errors with our data bound values.

The next chapter delves deeply into the subject of application frameworks and we get started on constructing our own. We find out about the benefit of base classes and discover alternative ways to implement our framework functionality. The chapter will finish off by investigating a variety of techniques to ensure that our applications maintain the essential Separation of Concerns that MVVM provides.

3
Writing Custom Application Frameworks

In this chapter, we will investigate application frameworks and the benefits that they can bring us. We find out the differences between providing this functionality via base classes and interfaces and also discover other ways to build the functionality into our frameworks. The chapter will finish off by investigating a variety of techniques to ensure that our applications maintain the essential Separation of Concerns that MVVM provides.

What is an application framework?

In the simplest terms, an application framework is comprised of a library of classes that together, provide the most common functionality required by an application. By using an application framework, we can vastly reduce the amount of work and time that is required to create the various parts of the application. In short, they support the future development of the application.

In typical three-tier applications, the framework often extends through all layers of the application; the Presentation Layer, the Business Layer, and the Data Access Layer. In a WPF application using the MVVM pattern, we can therefore see aspects of the application framework in all three components of the pattern; the Models, the View Models, and the Views.

Apart from the obvious benefits of the reduced production times and effort involved in creating our application components, application frameworks also provide many additional benefits. Typical application frameworks promote reusability, which is one of the core aims of **Object-Oriented Programming (OOP)**. They do this by providing generic interfaces and/or base classes that can be used to define the various application components.

By reusing these application framework interfaces and base classes, we also instill a sense of uniformity and consistency throughout the application. Furthermore, as these frameworks generally provide additional functionality, or services, the developers working on the application can save further time when requiring this particular functionality.

Concepts like modularity, maintainability, testability, and extensibility can also be realized by using an application framework. These frameworks often come with the ability to run individual components independently of each other and this fits WPF and the MVVM pattern extremely well. Additionally, application frameworks can also supply patterns of implementation to further simplify the process of constructing new application components.

Different frameworks are created for different technologies and WPF already have a few publicly available. Some are relatively lightweight, like the **MVVM Light Toolkit** and the **WPF Application Framework** (**WAF**), while others are more heavyweight, such as **Caliburn.Micro** and the now, open source **Prism**. While it is likely that you may have used one or more of these frameworks at work, instead of investigating these in this chapter, we'll look at how to create our own lightweight custom framework, that will implement just the features that we need.

Encapsulating common functionality

Probably the most commonly used interface in any WPF application would be the `INotifyPropertyChanged` interface, as it is required to correctly implement data binding. By providing an implementation of this interface in our base class, we can avoid having to repeatedly implement it in every single View Model class. It is therefore, a great candidate for inclusion in our base class. There are a number of different ways to implement it depending on our requirements, so let's take a look at the most basic first:

```
public virtual event PropertyChangedEventHandler PropertyChanged;

protected virtual void NotifyPropertyChanged(string propertyName)
{
  if (PropertyChanged != null)
    PropertyChanged(this, new PropertyChangedEventArgs(propertyName));
}
```

In all forms of this implementation, we first need to declare the `PropertyChanged` event. This is the event that will be used to notify the various binding sources and targets of changes to the data bound values in our application. Note that this is the only requirement of the `INotifyPropertyChanged` interface. There is no `NotifyPropertyChanged` method that we have to implement, so you may well come across differently named methods that perform the same functionality.

Of course, without the method, just implementing the event would do nothing. The basic idea of this method is that as usual, we first check for `null`, and then raise the event, passing the raising class instance as the `sender` parameter and the name of the property that changed in the `PropertyChangedEventArgs`. We have already seen that the null conditional operator in C# 6.0 provides us with a shorthand notation for this.

```
PropertyChanged?.Invoke(this, new PropertyChangedEventArgs(propertyName));
```

Note that the declared access modifier on this method is `protected`, to ensure that all View Models that derive from this base class will have access to it, while non-deriving classes will not. Furthermore, the method is also marked as `virtual`, so that the derived classes can override this functionality if required. In the View Models, this method would be called from a property like this:

```
private string name = string.Empty;

public string Name
{
  get { return name; }
  set
  {
    if (name != value)
    {
      name = value;
      NotifyPropertyChanged("Name");
    }
  }
}
```

However, a new attribute was added in .NET 4.5, that gives us a shortcut to use with this implementation. The `CallerMemberNameAttribute` class enables us to automatically obtain the name of the method caller, or more specifically in our case, the name of the property that called the method. We can use it with an optional input parameter with a default value, like this:

```
protected virtual void NotifyPropertyChanged(
  [CallerMemberName]string propertyName = "")
{
  PropertyChanged?.Invoke(this,
    new PropertyChangedEventArgs(propertyName));
}
```

The calling property can then be simplified to this:

```
public string Name
{
  get { return name; }
  set { if (name != value) { name = value; NotifyPropertyChanged(); } }
}
```

It's worth noting at this point that in .NET 4.5.3, another improvement to calling the most basic implementation of this method was introduced. The `nameof` operator also enables us to avoid using strings to pass the property name, as passing strings can always be error prone. This new operator basically converts the name of a property to a string at compile-time, so the end result is exactly the same as passing the string, but less error prone. Using the preceding property, let's see how this is used:

```
NotifyPropertyChanged(nameof(Name));
```

There are also other tricks that we can employ too. For example, we often need to notify the Framework that more than one property value has changed at once. Visualize a scenario where we have two properties named `Price` and `Quantity` and a third property named `Total`. As you can imagine, the value of the `Total` property will come from the calculation of the `Price` value multiplied by the `Quantity` value.

```
public decimal Total
{
  get { return Price * Quantity; }
}
```

However, this property has no setter, so where should we call the NotifyPropertyChanged method from? The answer is simple. We need to call it from both of the constituent property setters, as they can both affect the resulting value of this property.

Traditionally, we would have to call the NotifyPropertyChanged method once for each constituent property and once for the Total property. However, it is possible to rewrite our implementation of this method to enable us to pass multiple property names to it in a single call. For this, we can make use of the params keyword to enable any number of input parameters.

```
protected void NotifyPropertyChanged(params string[] propertyNames)
{
  if (PropertyChanged != null)
  {
    foreach (string propertyName in propertyNames)
    {
      PropertyChanged(this, new PropertyChangedEventArgs(propertyName));
    }
  }
}
```

When using the params keyword, we need to declare an array type input parameter. However, this array merely holds the input parameters and we do not need to supply an array when calling this method. Instead, we provide any number of input parameters of the same type and they will be implicitly added to the array. Going back to our example, this enables us to call the method like this:

```
private decimal price = 0M;

public decimal Price
{
  get { return price; }
  set
  {
    if (price != value)
    {
      price = value;
      NotifyPropertyChanged(nameof(Price), nameof(Total));
    }
  }
}
```

We therefore have a variety of different ways to implement this method, depending on what suits our requirements. We can even add a number of overloads of the method to provide the users of our framework with more choices. We'll see a further enhancement to this method later, but for now, let's see what our `BaseViewModel` class might look like so far:

```
using System.ComponentModel;

namespace CompanyName.ApplicationName.ViewModels
{
  public class BaseViewModel : INotifyPropertyChanged
  {
    #region INotifyPropertyChanged Members

    public event PropertyChangedEventHandler PropertyChanged;

    protected void NotifyPropertyChanged(params string[] propertyNames)
    {
      if (PropertyChanged != null)
      {
        foreach (string propertyName in propertyNames)
        {
          PropertyChanged(this,
            new PropertyChangedEventArgs(propertyName));
        }
      }
    }

    protected virtual void NotifyPropertyChanged(
      [CallerMemberName]string propertyName = "")
    {
      PropertyChanged?.Invoke(this,
        new PropertyChangedEventArgs(propertyName));
    }

    #endregion
  }
}
```

To summarize, we started with an interface that declared a single event. The interface itself provides no functionality and in fact, we as the implementers have to provide the functionality, in the form of the `NotifyPropertyChanged` method and the calling of that method each time a property value changes. But the reward for doing this is that the UI controls are listening and responding to those events and so by implementing this interface, we have gained this additional data binding capability.

However, we can provide functionality in our application framework in a number of different ways. The two main ways are through the use of base classes and interfaces. The main difference between these two approaches relate to the amount of development that the users of our framework will have to accomplish in order to create the various application components.

When we use interfaces, we are basically supplying a contract that the developers will have to honor, by providing the implementation themselves. However, when we use base classes, we are able to provide that implementation for them. So generally, base classes provide ready written functionality, whereas interfaces rely on the developers to provide some or all of that functionality for themselves.

We've just seen an example of implementing an interface in our View Model base class. Let's now take a look at what else we can encapsulate in our other framework base classes and compare the differences between providing features or functionality in base classes and interfaces. Let's turn our attention to our Data Model classes now.

In base classes

We have seen that in a WPF application, it is essential for us to have an implementation of the `INotifyPropertyChanged` interface in our View Model base class. Likewise, we will also need a similar implementation in our Data Model base class. Remember that when Data Models are mentioned here, we are discussing the business model classes that are combined with the View Model properties and functionality from the second application structure example in `Chapter 1`, *A Smarter Way Of Working With WPF*.

All of these `DataModel` classes will need to extend their base class, because they will all need to have access to its `INotifyPropertyChanged` implementation. As we progress through the chapters in this book, we will see more and more reasons why we need separate base classes for our Data Models and View Models. For example, let's imagine that we want to provide these Data Models with some simple auditing properties and investigate what our base class might look like:

```
using System;

namespace CompanyName.ApplicationName.DataModels
{
  public class BaseDataModel : INotifyPropertyChanged
  {
    private DateTime createdOn;
    private DateTime? updatedOn;
    private User createdBy, updatedBy;
```

```
public DateTime CreatedOn
{
  get { return createdOn; }
  set { createdOn = value; NotifyPropertyChanged(); }
}

public User CreatedBy
{
  get { return createdBy; }
  set { createdBy = value; NotifyPropertyChanged(); }
}

public DateTime? UpdatedOn
{
  get { return updatedOn; }
  set { updatedOn = value; NotifyPropertyChanged(); }
}

public User UpdatedBy
{
  get { return updatedBy; }
  set { updatedBy = value; NotifyPropertyChanged(); }
}

#region INotifyPropertyChanged Members

...

#endregion
  }
}
```

Here we see our auditing properties, along with the hidden INotifyPropertyChanged implementation that we saw earlier. For now, let's keep the implementation the same as that of the BaseViewModel class. Note that using this particular base class would result in all derived classes getting access to these properties, whether they needed them or not.

We might then decide to declare another base class, so that we can have one that provides access to our implementation of the INotifyPropertyChanged interface and one that extends that base class and adds the new auditable properties shown earlier. In this way, all derived classes can make use of the INotifyPropertyChanged interface implementation and the classes that require the auditable properties as well can derive from the second base class.

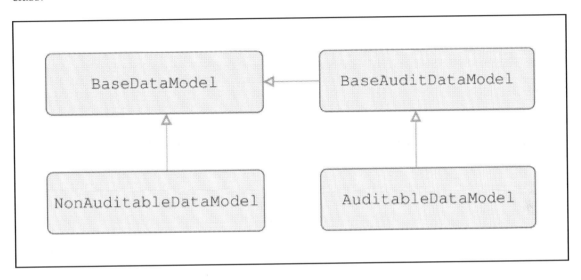

For this basic example, we seem to have solved our problem. If these auditable properties were the only properties that we wanted to provide to our derived classes, then this would not be such a bad situation. However, an average a framework will typically provide far more than this.

Let's now imagine that we wanted to provide some basic undo capability. We'll see an example of this later in this chapter, but for now we'll keep this simple. Without actually specifying the required members of this new base class, let's just think about this first.

Now we have a situation where we already have two different base classes and we want to provide some further functionality. Where should we declare our new properties? We could derive from either one, or indirectly, from both of the existing base classes, as shown in the following diagram, in order to create this new "synchronizable" base class.

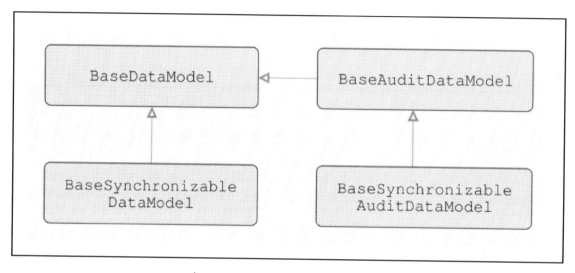

So now, we could have four different base classes that the developers, that use our framework, could extend. There could be some confusion as to exactly which base class they need to extend, but overall, this situation is still just about manageable. However, imagine if we want to provide some additional properties or functionality in one or more levels of base class.

In order to enable every combination of functionality from these base classes, we could end up with as many as eight separate base classes. Each additional level of functionality that we provide will either double the total number of base classes that we have, or mean that the developers sometimes have to derive from a base class with functionality or properties that they do not require. Now that we have uncovered a potential problem of utilizing base classes, let's see if declaring interfaces can help with this situation.

Through interfaces

Going back to our auditing example, we could have declared these properties in an interface instead. Let's see what that might look like:

```
using System;

namespace CompanyName.ApplicationName.DataModels.Interfaces
{
  public interface IAuditable
  {
    DateTime CreatedOn { get; set; }

    User CreatedBy { get; set; }

    DateTime? UpdatedOn { get; set; }

    User UpdatedBy { get; set; }
  }
}
```

Now, if a developer requires these properties, they can implement this interface as well as extending the Data Model base class.

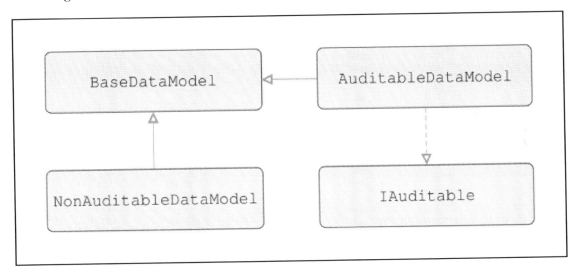

```
using System;
using CompanyName.ApplicationName.DataModels.Interfaces;

namespace CompanyName.ApplicationName.DataModels
{
```

```
public class Invoice : BaseDataModel, IAuditable
{
  private DateTime createdOn;
  private DateTime? updatedOn;
  private User createdBy, updatedBy;

  public DateTime CreatedOn
  {
    get { return createdOn; }
    set { createdOn = value; NotifyPropertyChanged(); }
  }

  public User CreatedBy
  {
    get { return createdBy; }
    set { createdBy = value; NotifyPropertyChanged(); }
  }

  public DateTime? UpdatedOn
  {
    get { return updatedOn; }
    set { updatedOn = value; NotifyPropertyChanged(); }
  }

  public User UpdatedBy
  {
    get { return updatedBy; }
    set { updatedBy = value; NotifyPropertyChanged(); }
  }
}
```

Initially then, it seems as though this could be a better way to go, but let's continue to investigate the same scenario that we looked at with the base classes. Let's now imagine that we want to provide the same basic undo capability using interfaces. We didn't actually investigate which members would be required for this, but it will require both properties and methods.

This is where the interface approach starts to break down somewhat. We can ensure that implementers of our ISynchronization interface have particular properties and methods, but we have no control over their implementation of those methods. In order to provide the ability to undo changes, we need to provide the actual implementation of these methods, rather than just the required scaffolding.

If this was left up to the developers to implement each time they used the interface, they might not implement it correctly, or perhaps they might implement it differently in different classes and break the consistency of the application. Therefore, to implement some functionality, it seems as though we really do need to use some kind of base class.

However, we also have a third option that involves a mix of the two approaches. We could implement some functionality in a base class, but instead of deriving our Data Model classes from it, we could add a property of that type, so that we can still access its public members.

We could then declare an interface that simply has a single property of the type of this new base class. In this way, we would be free to add the different functionality from different base classes to just the classes that require them. Let's look at an example of this:

```
public interface IAuditable
{
   Auditable Auditable { get; set; }
}
```

This `Auditable` class would have the same properties as those in the previous `IAuditable` interface shown in the preceding code. The new `IAuditable` interface would be implemented by the Data Model classes by simply declaring a property of type `Auditable`.

```
public class User : IAuditable
{
   private Auditable auditable;

   public Auditable Auditable
   {
      get { return auditable; }
      set { auditable = value; }
   }

   ...
}
```

It could be used by the framework, for example, to output the names of each user and when they were created into a report. In the following example, we use the **Interpolated Strings** syntax that was introduced in C# 6.0 for constructing our string. It's like the `string.Format` method, but with the method call replaced with a $ sign and the numerical format items replaced with their related values.

```
foreach (IAuditable user in Users)
{
    Report.AddLine($"{user.Name} created on {user.Auditable.CreatedOn}");
}
```

Most interestingly, as this interface could be implemented by many different types of object, the preceding code could also be used with objects of different types. Note this slight difference:

```
List<IAuditable> auditableObjects = GetAuditableObjects();
foreach (IAuditable user in auditableObjects)
{
    Report.AddLine($"{user.Name} created on {user.Auditable.CreatedOn}");
}
```

It's worth pointing out this useful ability to work with objects of different types is not limited to interfaces. This can also be achieved just as easily with base classes. Imagine a View that enabled the end user to edit a number of different types of object. We could use this very similar code to display a confirmation of the changes from each object back to the user:

```
List<BaseSynchronizableDataModel> baseDataModels = GetBaseDataModels();
foreach (BaseSynchronizableDataModel baseDataModel in baseDataModels)
{
    if (baseDataModel.HasChanges)
        FeedbackManager.Add(baseDataModel.PropertyChanges);
}
```

We have a number of choices when it comes to encapsulating pieces of pre-packaged functionality into our Data Model classes. Each of these methods that we have investigated so far have strengths and weaknesses. If we're sure that we want some pre-written functionality in every one of our Data Model classes, like that of the `INotifyPropertyChanged` interface, then we can simply encapsulate it in a base class and derive all of our model classes from that.

If we just want our models to have certain properties or methods that can be called from other parts of the framework, but are not concerned with the implementation, then we can use interfaces. If we want some combination of the two ideas, then we can implement a solution using the two methods together. It is up to us to choose the solution that best fits the requirements in hand.

With Extension methods

There is a further method of providing additional functionality to the developers of our application that was mentioned when investigating the application structures in the Chapter 2, *Debugging WPF Applications*. It is through the use of Extension methods. If you are not familiar with this amazing .NET feature, Extension methods enable us to write methods that can be used on objects that we did not create.

At this stage, it's worth pointing out that we don't generally write Extension methods for classes that we have declared. There are two main reasons for this. The first is that we created these classes and so we have access to their source code and can therefore simply declare new methods in these classes directly.

The second reason is that there will be a reference to our Extensions project added to most other projects, including our DataModels project, so that they can all take advantage of the extra capabilities. Therefore, we can't add references to any of our other projects into the Extensions project, because it would create circular dependencies.

You are probably aware of Extension methods already, although perhaps inadvertently, as most of the LINQ methods are Extension methods. Once declared, they can be used just like the ordinary methods that were declared within the various classes that we are extending, although they are differentiated by having different icons in the Visual Studio IntelliSense display.

The basic principle when declaring them is to have a static class, where each method has an extra input parameter prefixed with the `this` keyword, that represents the object being extended. Note that this extra input parameter must be declared first in the parameter list and that it will not be visible in IntelliSense when calling the method on an instance of an object.

Extension methods are declared as static methods, but are typically called using instance method syntax. A simple example should help to clarify this situation. Let's imagine that we want to be able to call a method on each item in a collection. In fact, we'll see an example of this being used in our `BaseSynchronizableCollection` class later in this chapter, but now, let's see how we can do this:

```
using System;
using System.Collections.Generic;

namespace CompanyName.ApplicationName.Extensions
{
  public static class IEnumerableExtensions
  {
    public static void ForEach<T>(this IEnumerable<T> collection,
      Action<T> action)
    {
      foreach (T item in collection) action(item);
    }
  }
}
```

Here we see the `this` input parameter that specifies the instance of the target type that this Extension method is called on. Remember that this won't appear in the parameter list in IntelliSense in Visual Studio, unless it is called through the static class itself, as shown in the following code.

```
IEnumerableExtensions.ForEach(collection, i => i.RevertState());
```

Inside this method, we simply iterate through the collection items, calling the `Action` specified by the `action` input parameter and passing in each item as the parameter. After adding a `using` directive to the `CompanyName.ApplicationName.Extensions` namespace, let's see how this this method is more usually called:

```
collection.ForEach(i => i.PerformAction());
```

So you can now see the power of Extension methods and the benefits that they can bring us. If some functionality that we want is not already provided by a certain class in the .NET Framework, then we can simply add it in. Take this next example.

Here is an Extension method that has been sorely missed from the existing LINQ Extension methods. As with the other LINQ methods, this one also works on the `IEnumerable<T>` interface and therefore, also any collection that extends it:

```
public static IEnumerable<TSource> DistinctBy<TSource, TKey>(
  this IEnumerable<TSource> source, Func<TSource, TKey> keySelector)
{
  HashSet<TKey> keys = new HashSet<TKey>();
  foreach (TSource element in source)
  {
    if (keys.Add(keySelector(element))) yield return element;
  }
}
```

Let's first look at the declaration of this method. We can see that our source collection will be of type `TSource`. Note that this is exactly the same as if the generic type parameter were named `T` like our other examples, except that this provides a little more detail as to the use of this type parameter. This naming has come from the `Enumerable.OrderBy<TSource, TKey>` method, where the `TSource` type parameter represents our source collection.

Next, we notice that the method name is suffixed by two generic type parameters; first the `TSource` parameter and then the `TKey` parameter. This is because we require two generic type parameters for the input parameter of type `Func<TSource, TKey>`. If you're not familiar with the `Func<T, TResult>` delegate, as Microsoft call it, it simply encapsulates any method that has a single input parameter of type `T` and returns a value of type `TResult`, or in our case, `TKey`.

"Why are we using this `Func<T, TResult>` delegate?", I hear you asking. Well it's simple really. Using this class, we can provide the developers with an object of the same type as those in the source collection and the ability to select a member of that class, in particular, the property that they want to perform the distinct query on. Before looking at the rest of this method, let's see it in use:

```
IEnumerable<User> distinctUsers = Users.DistinctBy(u => u.Department);
```

Let's envisage that we had a `Department` property in our `User` class and a collection of these users. Now let's imagine that we wanted to find out which departments our users belonged to. This method would return a single member from each distinct department.

So in this case, we are actually interested in the departments that the users belong to and not the users themselves. If we wanted to find out the distinct ages of the users, we could simply use this method again, but specify the `Age` property instead of the `Department` property.

Referring back to the source code for this method, the `User` class represents the `TSource` parameter and this is shown in the Lambda expression in the example as the `u` input parameter. The `TKey` parameter is determined by the type of the class member that is selected by the developer. In this case, by the string `Department` value. This example could be written slightly differently to make it clearer:

```
distinctUsers = Users.DistinctBy((User user) => user.Department);
```

So our `Func<TSource, TKey>` can be seen here, with a `User` input parameter and a string return value. Now let's focus on the magic of our method. We see a `HashSet` of type string in our case, being initialized. This type of collection is essential to this method as it allows only unique values to be added.

Next, we iterate through our source collection, of type `User` in this case, and attempt to add the relevant property value of each item in the collection into the `HashSet`. In our case, we're adding the names of the departments into this `HashSet`.

If the department value is unique and the `HashSet<T>.Add` method returns `true`, we yield, or return that item from our source collection. The second and each subsequent time that a used department value is read, it is rejected. This means that only the first items with unique department values are returned from this method.

We've now managed to create our very own LINQ-style Extension method. However, not all of our Extension methods need to be so ground breaking. Often, they can be used to simply encapsulate some commonly used functionality. In a way, we can use them as simple convenience methods. Take a look at the following example that is used in the *With Converters* section later in this chapter.

```
namespace CompanyName.ApplicationName.Extensions
{
  public static class EnumExtensions
  {
    public static string GetDescription(this Enum value)
    {
      FieldInfo fieldInfo = value.GetType().GetField(value.ToString());
      if (fieldInfo == null) Enum.GetName(value.GetType(), value);
      DescriptionAttribute[] attributes = (DescriptionAttribute[])
        fieldInfo.GetCustomAttributes(typeof(DescriptionAttribute), false);
      if (attributes != null && attributes.Length > 0)
        return attributes[0].Description;
      return Enum.GetName(value.GetType(), value);
    }
  }
}
```

In this method, we attempt to get the `FieldInfo` object that relates to the instance of the relevant enumeration provided by the `value` input parameter. If the attempt fails, we simply return the name of the particular instance. If we succeed however, we then use the `GetCustomAttributes` method of that object, passing the type of the `DescriptionAttribute` class, to retrieve an array of attributes.

If we have declared a value in the `DescriptionAttribute` of this particular enumeration instance, then it will always be the first item in the attribute array. If we have not set a value, then the array will be empty and we return the name of the instance instead. Note that as we used the base `Enum` class in this method, we are able to call this method on any enumeration type.

When creating these methods, it should be noted that there is no requirement to put them into separate classes that are split by type, as we have done here. There are no specified naming conventions either and in fact, it is also totally viable to put all of your Extension methods into a single class. However, if we have a large number of Extension methods of a particular type, then it can help with maintenance to have this separation.

Before moving on, let's take a look at one final example of these Extension methods. One of the most useful traits of an Extension method is the ability to add new or missing functionality to existing classes from the .NET Framework. For example, let's see how we can define a simple `Count` method for the `IEnumerable` class:

```
public static int Count(this IEnumerable collection)
{
  int count = 0;
  foreach (object item in collection) count++;
  return count;
}
```

As we can see, this method requires little explanation. It literally just counts the number of items in the `IEnumerable` collection and returns that value. As simple as it is, it proves to be useful, as we'll see in a later example. Now that we have investigated Extension methods, let's turn our attention to another way of building further abilities into our framework, this time focusing on the Views component.

In UI controls

One other common way to include functionality in an application framework is to encapsulate it into custom controls. In doing so, we can expose the required functionality using Dependency Properties, while hiding the implementation details. This is also another great way to promote reusability and consistency throughout the application. Let's take a look at a simple example of a `UserControl` that wraps the functionality of the `System.Windows.Forms.FolderBrowserDialog` control:

```
<UserControl
  x:Class="CompanyName.ApplicationName.Views.Controls.FolderPathEditField"
  xmlns="http://schemas.microsoft.com/winfx/2006/xaml/presentation"
  xmlns:x="http://schemas.microsoft.com/winfx/2006/xaml"
  xmlns:mc="http://schemas.openxmlformats.org/markup-compatibility/2006"
  xmlns:d="http://schemas.microsoft.com/expression/blend/2008"
  xmlns:Controls="clr-namespace:CompanyName.ApplicationName.Views.Controls"
  mc:Ignorable="d" d:DesignHeight="28" d:DesignWidth="300">
  <TextBox Name="FolderPathTextBox"
    Text="{Binding FolderPath, RelativeSource={RelativeSource
    AncestorType={x:Type Controls:FolderPathEditField}}, FallbackValue='',
    UpdateSourceTrigger=PropertyChanged}" Cursor="Arrow"
    PreviewMouseLeftButtonUp="TextBox_PreviewMouseLeftButtonUp" />
</UserControl>
```

This simple `UserControl` just contains a textbox with its `Text` property data bound to the `FolderPath` Dependency Property that is declared in our control's code behind. Remember that it is perfectly acceptable to use the code behind of a `UserControl` for this purpose when using MVVM. Note that we have used a `RelativeSource` binding here, because nothing has been set to this control's `DataContext` property. We'll find out much more about data binding in the next chapter, but for now, let's continue.

You may notice that we have attached a handler for the `PreviewMouseLeftButtonUp` event in the code behind and as no business-related code is being used there, this is also perfectly acceptable when using MVVM. The only other notable code here is that we set the `Cursor` property to show an arrow when users mouse over our control. Let's now take a look at the code behind of the `UserControl` and see how the functionality is encapsulated:

```
using System;
using System.Windows;
using System.Windows.Controls;
using System.Windows.Input;
using FolderBrowserDialog = System.Windows.Forms.FolderBrowserDialog;

namespace CompanyName.ApplicationName.Views.Controls
{
```

```
public partial class FolderPathEditField : UserControl
{
  public FolderPathEditField()
  {
    InitializeComponent();
  }

  public static readonly DependencyProperty FolderPathProperty =
    DependencyProperty.Register(nameof(FolderPath),
    typeof(string), typeof(FolderPathEditField),
    new FrameworkPropertyMetadata(string.Empty,
    FrameworkPropertyMetadataOptions.BindsTwoWayByDefault));

  public string FolderPath
  {
    get { return (string)GetValue(FolderPathProperty); }
    set { SetValue(FolderPathProperty, value); }
  }

  public static readonly DependencyProperty OpenFolderTitleProperty =
    DependencyProperty.Register(nameof(OpenFolderTitle),
    typeof(string), typeof(FolderPathEditField),
    new FrameworkPropertyMetadata(string.Empty,
    FrameworkPropertyMetadataOptions.BindsTwoWayByDefault));

  public string OpenFolderTitle
  {
    get { return (string)GetValue(OpenFolderTitleProperty); }
    set { SetValue(OpenFolderTitleProperty, value); }
  }

  private void TextBox_PreviewMouseLeftButtonUp(object sender,
    MouseButtonEventArgs e)
  {
    if (((TextBox)sender).SelectedText.Length == 0 &&
      e.GetPosition(this).X <= ((TextBox)sender).ActualWidth -
      SystemParameters.VerticalScrollBarWidth)
      ShowFolderPathEditWindow();
  }

  private void ShowFolderPathEditWindow()
  {
    string defaultFolderPath = string.IsNullOrEmpty(FolderPath) ?
      Environment.GetFolderPath(Environment.SpecialFolder.MyDocuments)
      : FolderPath;
    string folderPath = ShowFolderBrowserDialog(defaultFolderPath);
    if (folderPath == string.Empty) return;
    FolderPath = folderPath;
```

```
        }

        private string ShowFolderBrowserDialog(string defaultFolderPath)
        {
            FolderBrowserDialog folderBrowserDialog = new FolderBrowserDialog();
            folderBrowserDialog.Description = OpenFolderTitle;
            folderBrowserDialog.ShowNewFolderButton = true;
            folderBrowserDialog.SelectedPath = defaultFolderPath;
            folderBrowserDialog.ShowDialog();
            return folderBrowserDialog.SelectedPath;
        }
    }
}
```

We start with our `using` directives and see an example of a using alias directive. In this case, we don't want to add a normal `using` directive for the `System.Windows.Forms` assembly because it contains many UI-related classes that have names that clash with those in the required `System.Windows` assembly.

To avoid these conflicts, we can create an alias for the single type that we are interested in using from that assembly. To clarify, Microsoft decided not to reinvent the wheel, or in this case, the `FolderBrowserDialog` control, in the `System.Windows` assembly and so we need to use the one from the `System.Windows.Forms` assembly.

Looking at this class, we see that much of this code is taken up with the declarations of the Dependency Properties of the control. We have the `FolderPath` property that will hold the file path of the folder that is selected from the `Windows.Forms` control and the `OpenFolderTitle` property that will populate the title bar of the `FolderBrowserDialog` window when displayed.

Next, we see the `TextBox_PreviewMouseLeftButtonUp` event handler that handles the `PreviewMouseLeftButtonUp` event of the single textbox in our control. In this method, we first verify that the user is not selecting text from, or scrolling the textbox and then if true, we call the `ShowFolderPathEditWindow` method.

In order to verify that the user is not selecting text, we simply check the length of the `SelectedText` property of the `TextBox`. In order to confirm that the user is not scrolling the textbox, we compare the relative horizontal position of the user's click with the length of the `TextBox` minus the width of the vertical scroll bar to ensure that their mouse is not over the scroll bar.

The `ShowFolderPathEditWindow` method first prepares to display the `Windows.Forms` control. It sets the `defaultFolderPath` variable to either the current value of the `FolderPath` property, if one is set, or the current user's `Documents` folder, using the `Environment.GetFolderPath` method and the `Environment.SpecialFolder.MyDocuments` enumeration.

It then calls the `ShowFolderBrowserDialog` method to launch the actual `FolderBrowserDialog` control and retrieve the selected folder path. If a valid folder path is selected, we set its value to the data bound `FolderPath` property directly, but note that we could have set it in other ways.

It would be very easy to add an `ICommand` property to our control in order to return the selected folder path instead of using this direct assignment. This could be useful in cases where we don't want the data bound value to be set instantly, for example, if the control was used in a child window that needed a confirmation button to be clicked before the data bound value could be updated.

The `ShowFolderBrowserDialog` method utilizes the `defaultFolderPath` variable and the `OpenFolderTitle` property when setting up the actual `FolderBrowserDialog` control. Note that this `OpenFolderTitle` property is simply here to demonstrate how we can expose the required properties from the `FolderBrowserDialog` element in our control. In this way, we can encapsulate the use of the `Windows.Forms` control and assembly within our control.

Note that we could have added extra Dependency Properties to enable the users of our framework to have further control over the settings in the `FolderBrowserDialog` control. In this basic example, we simply hardcoded a positive value for the `FolderBrowserDialog.ShowNewFolderButton` property, but we could have exposed that as another property.

We could have also added a browse button and maybe even a clear button to clear the selected folder value. We could have then added additional `bool` Dependency Properties to control whether those buttons should be displayed or not. There are many other ways that we could improve this control, but it still demonstrates how we can encapsulate functionality into our Views components. We'll see another View-related way to capture little snippets of functionality in the following section.

With converters

Converters are yet another way that we can package up useful functionality in our framework. We've already seen a useful example of the `IValueConverter` interface in Chapter 2, *Debugging WPF Applications*, but while that was a very simple example, converters can actually be very versatile.

Long before Microsoft introduced their `BooleanToVisibilityConverter` class, developers had to create their own versions. We often need to convert the `UIElement.Visibility` enumeration to or from a variety of different types and so it is a good idea to start with a `BaseVisibilityConverter` class that can serve multiple converter classes. Let's see what that entails.

```
using System.Windows;
using System.Windows.Data;

namespace CompanyName.ApplicationName.Converters
{
  public abstract class BaseVisibilityConverter
  {
    public enum FalseVisibility { Hidden, Collapsed }

    protected Visibility FalseVisibilityValue { get; set; } =
      Visibility.Collapsed;

    public FalseVisibility FalseVisibilityState
    {
      get { return falseVisibilityState == Visibility.Collapsed ?
        FalseVisibility.Collapsed : FalseVisibility.Hidden; }
      set { falseVisibilityState = value == FalseVisibility.Collapsed ?
        Visibility.Collapsed : Visibility.Hidden; }
    }

    public bool IsInverted { get; set; }
  }
}
```

This converter requires one value to represent the visible value and as there is only one corresponding value in the `UIElement.Visibility` enumeration, that will clearly be the `Visibility.Visible` instance. It also requires a single value to represent the invisible value.

As such, we declare the `FalseVisibility` enumeration with the two corresponding values from the `UIElement.Visibility` enumeration and the `FalseVisibilityValue` property to enable users to specify which value should represent the false state. Note that the most commonly used `Visibility.Collapsed` value is set as the default value.

The users can set the `FalseVisibilityState` property when using the control and this sets the protected `FalseVisibilityValue` property internally. Finally, we see the indispensable `IsInverted` property that is optionally used to invert the result. Let's see what our `BoolToVisibilityConverter` class looks like now:

```
using System;
using System.Globalization;
using System.Windows;
using System.Windows.Data;

namespace CompanyName.ApplicationName.Converters
{
  [ValueConversion(typeof(bool), typeof(Visibility))]
  public class BoolToVisibilityConverter : BaseVisibilityConverter,
    IValueConverter
  {
    public object Convert(object value, Type targetType,
      object parameter, CultureInfo culture)
    {
      if (value == null || value.GetType() != typeof(bool))
        return DependencyProperty.UnsetValue;
      bool boolValue = IsInverted ? !(bool)value :(bool)value;
      return boolValue ? Visibility.Visible : FalseVisibilityValue;
    }

    public object ConvertBack(object value, Type targetType,
      object parameter, CultureInfo culture)
    {
      if (value == null || value.GetType() != typeof(Visibility))
        return DependencyProperty.UnsetValue;
      if (IsInverted) return (Visibility)value != Visibility.Visible;
      return (Visibility)value == Visibility.Visible;
    }
  }
}
```

We start by specifying the data types involved in the implementation of the converter in the `ValueConversion` attribute. This helps tools to know what types are being used in the converter, but also makes it clear to the users of our framework. Next, we extend our `BaseVisibilityConverter` base class and extend the required `IValueConverter` interface.

In the `Convert` method, we first check the validity of our `value` input parameter, then if valid, we convert it to a `bool` variable, taking the `IsInverted` property setting into consideration. We return the `DependencyProperty.UnsetValue` value for invalid input values. Finally, we resolve the output value from this `bool` variable to either the `Visibility.Visible` instance, or the value of the `FalseVisibilityValue` property.

In the `ConvertBack` method, we also check the validity of our `value` input parameter first. We return the `DependencyProperty.UnsetValue` value for invalid input values again, otherwise we output a `bool` value that specifies whether the input parameter of type `Visibility` is equal to the `Visibility.Visible` instance, while again taking the value of the `IsInverted` property into consideration.

Note that use of the `IsInverted` property enables users to specify that elements should become visible when the data bound `bool` value is `false`. This can be incredibly useful when we want to have one object visible upon a certain condition and another object hidden dependent upon the same condition. We can declare two converters from this class like this:

```
xmlns:Converters="clr-namespace:CompanyName.ApplicationName.Converters;
  assembly=CompanyName.ApplicationName.Converters"
...
<Converters:BoolToVisibilityConverter x:Key="BoolToVisibilityConverter" />
<Converters:BoolToVisibilityConverter
  x:Key="InvertedBoolToVisibilityConverter" IsInverted="True" />
```

As stated, we often need to convert to and from the `UIElement.Visibility` enumeration from a variety of different types. Let's see an example of a conversion to and from the `Enum` type now. The principle is the same as the last example, where a single data bound value represents the `Visibility.Visible` instance and all other values represent the hidden or collapsed state:

```
using System;
using System.Globalization;
using System.Windows;
using System.Windows.Data;

namespace CompanyName.ApplicationName.Converters
{
  [ValueConversion(typeof(Enum), typeof(Visibility))]
  public class EnumToVisibilityConverter : BaseVisibilityConverter,
    IValueConverter
  {
    public object Convert(object value, Type targetType,
      object parameter, CultureInfo culture)
    {
```

```
    if (value == null || (value.GetType() != typeof(Enum) &&
      value.GetType().BaseType != typeof(Enum)) ||
      parameter == null) return DependencyProperty.UnsetValue;
    string enumValue = value.ToString();
    string targetValue = parameter.ToString();
    bool boolValue = enumValue.Equals(targetValue,
      StringComparison.InvariantCultureIgnoreCase);
    boolValue = IsInverted ? !boolValue : boolValue;
    return boolValue ? Visibility.Visible : FalseVisibilityValue;
  }

  public object ConvertBack(object value, Type targetType,
    object parameter, CultureInfo culture)
  {
    if (value == null || value.GetType() != typeof(Visibility) ||
      parameter == null) return DependencyProperty.UnsetValue;
    Visibility usedValue = (Visibility)value;
    string targetValue = parameter.ToString();
    if (IsInverted && usedValue != Visibility.Visible)
      return Enum.Parse(targetType, targetValue);
    else if (!IsInverted && usedValue == Visibility.Visible)
      return Enum.Parse(targetType, targetValue);
    return DependencyProperty.UnsetValue;
  }
 }
}
```

Again, we start by specifying the data types involved in the implementation of the converter in the ValueConversion attribute. In the Convert method, we first check the validity of our value input parameter, then if valid, we convert it to the string representation of the value. This particular class uses the parameter input parameter to pass the specified enumeration instance that will represent the visible value and so it is set to the targetValue variable as a string.

We then create a bool value by comparing the current enumeration instance with the target instance. Once we have our bool value, the last two lines replicate those in the BoolToVisibilityConverter class.

The ConvertBack method implementation is somewhat different. Logically speaking, we are unable to return the correct enumeration instance for a hidden visibility, as it could be any value except the visible value passed through the parameter input parameter.

As such, we are only able to return that specified value if the element is visible and the IsInverted property is `false`, or if it is not visible and the IsInverted property is `true`. For all other input values, we simply return the `DependencyProperty.UnsetValue` property to state that there is no value.

Another incredibly useful thing that converters can do is to convert individual enumeration instances to particular images. Let's look at an example that relates to our FeedbackManager, or more accurately, the Feedback objects that get displayed. Each Feedback object can have a particular type that is specified by the FeedbackType enumeration, so let's first see that.

```
namespace CompanyName.ApplicationName.DataModels.Enums
{
  public enum FeedbackType
  {
    None = -1,
    Error,
    Information,
    Question,
    Success,
    Validation,
    Warning
  }
}
```

To make this work, we obviously need a suitable image for each enumeration instance, except for the None instance. Our images will reside in the root folder of the startup project.

```
using System;
using System.Globalization;
using System.Windows;
using System.Windows.Data;
using System.Windows.Media;
using CompanyName.ApplicationName.DataModels.Enums;

namespace CompanyName.ApplicationName.Converters
{
  [ValueConversion(typeof(Enum), typeof(ImageSource))]
  public class FeedbackTypeToImageSourceConverter : IValueConverter
  {
    public object Convert(object value, Type targetType,
      object parameter, CultureInfo culture)
    {
      if (value == null || value.GetType() != typeof(FeedbackType) ||
        targetType != typeof(ImageSource))
        return DependencyProperty.UnsetValue;
      string imageName = string.Empty;
```

```
    switch ((FeedbackType)value)
    {
      case FeedbackType.None: return null;
      case FeedbackType.Error: imageName = "Error_16"; break;
      case FeedbackType.Success: imageName = "Success_16"; break;
      case FeedbackType.Validation:
      case FeedbackType.Warning: imageName = "Warning_16"; break;
      case FeedbackType.Information: imageName = "Information_16"; break;
      case FeedbackType.Question: imageName = "Question_16"; break;
      default: return DependencyProperty.UnsetValue;
    }
    return $"pack://application:,,,/CompanyName.ApplicationName;
      component/Images/{imageName}.png";
  }

  public object ConvertBack(object value, Type targetType,
    object parameter, CultureInfo culture)
  {
    return DependencyProperty.UnsetValue;
  }
  }
}
```

Once again, we start by specifying the data types involved in the converter in the `ValueConversion` attribute. In the `Convert` method, we check the validity of our `value` input parameter before casting it to a `FeedbackType` instance if valid. We then use a `switch` statement to generate the relevant image name for each enumeration instance.

If an unknown instance is used, we return the `DependencyProperty.UnsetValue` value. In all other cases, we use String Interpolation to build up the full file path of the relevant image and then return it from the converter as the converted value. As the `ConvertBack` method in this converter has no valid use, it is not implemented and simply returns the `DependencyProperty.UnsetValue` value.

You may have noticed that we specified the `ImageSource` type in the `ValueConversion` attribute, but we returned a string. This is possible because XAML uses the relevant type converter to convert the string into an `ImageSource` object automatically for us. Exactly the same thing occurs when we set an `Image.Source` property with a string in XAML.

As with other parts of our framework, we can make our converters even more useful, when we combine functionality from other areas. In this particular example, we utilize one of the Extension methods that was shown earlier in this chapter. To remind you, the `GetDescription` method will return the value of the `DescriptionAttribute` that is set on each enumeration instance.

The `DescriptionAttribute` enables us to associate any string value with each of our enumeration instances, so this is a great way to output a user friendly description for each instance. An example of this would be as follows:

```
public enum BitRate
{
  [Description("16 bits")]
  Sixteen = 16,
  [Description("24 bits")]
  TwentyFour = 24,
  [Description("32 bits")]
  ThirtyTwo = 32,
}
```

In this way, instead of displaying the names of the instances in a `RadioButton` control for example, we could display the more humanized descriptions from these attributes. Let's have a look at this converter class now.

```
using System;
using System.Globalization;
using System.Windows;
using System.Windows.Data;
using CompanyName.ApplicationName.Extensions;

namespace CompanyName.ApplicationName.Converters
{
  [ValueConversion(typeof(Enum), typeof(string))]
  public class EnumToDescriptionStringConverter : IValueConverter
  {
    public object Convert(object value, Type targetType,
      object parameter, CultureInfo culture)
    {
      if (value == null || (value.GetType() != typeof(Enum) &&
        value.GetType().BaseType != typeof(Enum)))
        return DependencyProperty.UnsetValue;
      Enum enumInstance = (Enum)value;
      return enumInstance.GetDescription();
    }

    public object ConvertBack(object value, Type targetType,
      object parameter, CultureInfo culture)
    {
      return DependencyProperty.UnsetValue;
    }
  }
}
```

As we're now accustomed to doing, we start by specifying the data types used in the converter in the `ValueConversion` attribute. In the `Convert` method, we again check the validity of our `value` input parameter and return the `DependencyProperty.UnsetValue` value if it is invalid.

If it is valid, we cast it to a `Enum` instance and then use the power of our Extension method to return the value from each instance's `DescriptionAttribute`. In doing so, we are able to expose this functionality to our Views and to enable the users of our framework to utilize it directly from the XAML. Now that we have a general understanding of the various ways that we can encapsulate functionality into our framework, let's focus on starting construction of our base classes.

Constructing a custom application framework

There will be different requirements for different components, but typically, the properties and functionality that we build into our Data Model base classes will be utilized and made more useful by our other base classes, so let's start by looking at the various Data Model base classes first.

One thing that we need to decide is whether we want any of our Data Model base classes to be generic or not. The difference can be subtle, but important. Imagine that we want to add some basic undo functionality into a base class. One way that we can achieve this would be to add an object into the base class that represents the unedited version of the Data Model. In an ordinary base class, it would look like this:

```
private object originalState;

public object OriginalState
{
  get { return originalState; }
  private set { originalState = value; }
}
```

In a generic base class, it would look like this:

```
public abstract class BaseSynchronizableDataModel<T> : BaseDataModel
{
  private T originalState;

  public T OriginalState
  {
```

```
      get { return originalState; }
      private set { originalState = value; }
   }
}
```

To make this property more useful, we'll need to add some further methods. First, we'll see the non-generic versions.

```
public abstract void CopyValuesFrom(object dataModel);

public virtual object Clone()
{
  object clone = new object();
  clone.CopyValuesFrom(this);
  return clone;
}

public abstract bool PropertiesEqual(object dataModel);
```

Now let's look at the generic versions:

```
public abstract void CopyValuesFrom(T dataModel);

public virtual T Clone()
{
  T clone = new T();
  clone.CopyValuesFrom(this as T);
  return clone;
}

public abstract bool PropertiesEqual(T dataModel);
```

The last few members of this base class would be the same for both versions.

```
public bool HasChanges
{
  get { return originalState != null && !PropertiesEqual(originalState); }
}

public void Synchronize()
{
  originalState = this.Clone();
  NotifyPropertyChanged(nameof(HasChanges));
}

public void RevertState()
{
  Debug.Assert(originalState != null, "Object not yet synchronized.");
```

```
    CopyValuesFrom(originalState);
    Synchronize();
    NotifyPropertyChanged(nameof(HasChanges));
  }
```

We started with the OriginalState property which holds the unedited version of the Data Model. After that, we see the abstract CopyValuesFrom method that the developers will need to implement and we'll see an example of that implementation shortly. The Clone method simply calls the CopyValuesFrom method in order to perform a deep clone of the Data Model.

Next, we have the abstract PropertiesEqual method that the developers will need to implement in order to compare each property in their classes with those from the dataModel input parameter. Again, we'll see this implementation shortly, but you may be wondering why we don't just override the Equals method, or implement the IEquatable.Equals method for this purpose.

The reason why we don't want to use either of those methods is because they, along with the GetHashCode method, are used by the WPF Framework in various places and they expect the returned values to be immutable. As our object's properties are very much mutable, they cannot be used to return the values for those methods. Therefore, we have implemented our own version. Let's return to the description of the remainder of this code.

The HasChanges property is the property that we would want to data bind to a UI control to indicate whether a particular object had been edited or not. The Synchronize method sets a deep clone of the current Data Model to the originalState field and importantly, notifies the WPF Framework of a change to the HasChanges property. This is done because the HasChanges property has no setter of its own and this operation will affect its value.

It is very important that we set a cloned version to the originalState field, rather than simply assigning the actual object reference to it. This is because we need to have a completely separate version of this object to represent the unedited version of the Data Model. If we simply assigned the actual object reference to the originalState field, then its property values would change along with the Data Model object and render it useless for this feature.

The RevertState method first checks that the Data Model has been synchronized and then copies the values back from the originalState field to the model. Finally, it calls the Synchronize method to specify that this is the new, unedited version of the object and notifies the WPF Framework of a change to the HasChanges property.

So, as you can see, there are not many differences between these two versions of the base class. In fact, the differences can be seen more clearly in the implementation of the derived classes. Let's now focus on their implementations of the example abstract methods, starting with the non-generic versions.

```
public override bool PropertiesEqual(object genreObject)
{
  if (genreObject.GetType() != typeof(Genre)) return false;
  Genre genre = (Genre)genreObject;
  return Name == genre.Name && Description == genre.Description;
}

public override void CopyValuesFrom(object genreObject)
{
  Debug.Assert(genreObject.GetType() == typeof(Genre), "You are using
    the wrong type with this method.");
  Genre genre = (Genre)genreObject;
  Name = genre.Name;
  Description = genre.Description;
}
```

Before discussing this code, let's first see the generic implementations.

```
public override bool PropertiesEqual(Genre genre)
{
  return Name == genre.Name && Description == genre.Description;
}

public override void CopyValuesFrom(Genre genre)
{
  Name = genre.Name;
  Description = genre.Description;
}
```

At last, we can see the difference between using generic and non-generic base classes. Without using generics, we have to use object input parameters, which will need to be cast to the appropriate type in each of the derived classes before we can access their properties. Attempting to cast inappropriate types causes Exceptions, so we generally try to avoid these situations.

On the other hand, when using a generic base class, there is no need to cast, as the input parameters are already of the correct type. In short, generics enable us to create type-safe data models and avoid duplicating type specific code. Now that we have seen the benefit of using generic classes, let's take a pause from generics for a moment and look at this base class a bit closer.

Some of you may have noticed that the only places where the WPF Framework is notified of changes to our `HasChanges` property is in the `Synchronize` and `RevertState` methods. However, in order for this functionality to work properly, we need to notify the Framework every time the values of any properties are changed.

We could rely on the developers to call the `NotifyPropertyChanged` method, passing the `HasChanges` property name each time they call it for each property that changes, but if they forgot to do this, it could lead to errors that could be difficult for them to track down. Instead, a better solution would be for us to override the default implementation of the `INotifyPropertyChanged` interface from the base class and notify changes to the `HasChanges` property for them each time it is called.

```
#region INotifyPropertyChanged Members

protected override void NotifyPropertyChanged(
  params string[] propertyNames)
{
  if (PropertyChanged != null)
  {
    foreach (string propertyName in propertyNames)
    {
      if (propertyName != nameof(HasChanges)) PropertyChanged(this,
        new PropertyChangedEventArgs(propertyName));
    }
    PropertyChanged(this,
      new PropertyChangedEventArgs(nameof(HasChanges)));
  }
}

protected override void NotifyPropertyChanged(
  [CallerMemberName]string propertyName = "")
{
  if (PropertyChanged != null)
  {
    if (propertyName != nameof(HasChanges)) PropertyChanged(this,
      new PropertyChangedEventArgs(propertyName));
    PropertyChanged(this,
      new PropertyChangedEventArgs(nameof(HasChanges)));
  }
}
```

```
#endregion
```

The first method will raise the `PropertyChanged` event, passing the name of the `HasChanges` property just once, regardless of how many property names were passed to the method. The second method also performs a check to ensure that it will refrain from raising the event with the `HasChanges` property name more than once, so these implementations remain efficient.

Now our base class will work as expected and the `HasChanges` property will correctly update when other properties in the Data Model classes are changed. This technique can also be utilized in other scenarios, for example, when validating our property values, as we'll see later in `Chapter 8`, *Implementing Responsive Data Validation*. For now though, let's return to see what else we can achieve with generics.

Another area where generics are often used relates to collections. I'm sure that you're all aware that we tend to use the `ObservableCollection<T>` class in WPF applications, because of its `INotifyCollectionChanged` and `INotifyPropertyChanged` implementations. It is customary, but not essential, to extend this class for each type of Data Model class that we have.

```
public class Users : ObservableCollection<User>
```

However, instead of doing this, we can declare a `BaseCollection<T>` class that extends the `ObservableCollection<T>` class and adds further functionality into our framework for us. The users of our framework can then extend this class instead.

```
public class Users : BaseCollection<User>
```

One really useful thing that we can do is to add a generic property of type `T` into our base class, that will represent the currently selected item in a data bound collection control in the UI. We could also declare some delegates to notify developers of changes to either selection or property values. There are so many short cuts and helper methods that we can provide here, dependent on requirements, so it's worth spending some time investigating this. Let's take a look a few possibilities.

```
using System.Collections.Generic;
using System.Collections.ObjectModel;
using System.ComponentModel;
using System.Linq;
using System.Runtime.CompilerServices;
using CompanyName.ApplicationName.Extensions;

namespace CompanyName.ApplicationName.DataModels.Collections
{
  public class BaseCollection<T> :
```

```csharp
    ObservableCollection<T>, INotifyPropertyChanged
    where T : class, INotifyPropertyChanged, new()
{
  protected T currentItem;

  public BaseCollection(IEnumerable<T> collection) : this()
  {
    foreach (T item in collection) Add(item);
  }

  public BaseCollection(params T[] collection) :
    this(collection as IEnumerable<T>) { }

  public BaseCollection() : base()
  {
    currentItem = new T();
  }

  public virtual T CurrentItem
  {
    get { return currentItem; }
    set
    {
      T oldCurrentItem = currentItem;
      currentItem = value;
      CurrentItemChanged?.Invoke(oldCurrentItem, currentItem);
      NotifyPropertyChanged();
    }
  }

  public bool IsEmpty
  {
    get { return !this.Any(); }
  }

  public delegate void ItemPropertyChanged(T item,
    string propertyName);

  public virtual ItemPropertyChanged CurrentItemPropertyChanged
    { get; set; }

  public delegate void CurrentItemChange(T oldItem, T newItem);

  public virtual CurrentItemChange CurrentItemChanged { get; set; }

  public T GetNewItem()
  {
    return new T();
```

```
}

public virtual void AddEmptyItem()
{
  Add(new T());
}

public virtual void Add(IEnumerable<T> collection)
{
  collection.ForEach(i => base.Add(i));
}

public virtual void Add(params T[] items)
{
  if (items.Length == 1) base.Add(items[0]);
  else Add(items as IEnumerable<T>);
}

protected override void InsertItem(int index, T item)
{
  if (item != null)
  {
    item.PropertyChanged += Item_PropertyChanged;
    base.InsertItem(index, item);
    if (Count == 1) CurrentItem = item;
  }
}

protected override void SetItem(int index, T item)
{
  if (item != null)
  {
    item.PropertyChanged += Item_PropertyChanged;
    base.SetItem(index, item);
    if (Count == 1) CurrentItem = item;
  }
}

protected override void ClearItems()
{
  foreach (T item in this)
    item.PropertyChanged -= Item_PropertyChanged;
  base.ClearItems();
}

protected override void RemoveItem(int index)
{
  T item = this[index];
```

```
    if (item != null) item.PropertyChanged -= Item_PropertyChanged;
    base.RemoveItem(index);
}

public void ResetCurrentItemPosition()
{
    if (this.Any()) CurrentItem = this.First();
}

private void Item_PropertyChanged(object sender,
    PropertyChangedEventArgs e)
{
    if ((sender as T) == CurrentItem) CurrentItemPropertyChanged?.
        Invoke(currentItem, e.PropertyName);
    NotifyPropertyChanged(e.PropertyName);
}

#region INotifyPropertyChanged Members

    ...

#endregion
    }
}
```

There's quite a lot to digest here, so let's go carefully over each part. We start with our private member of type `T` that will back our `CurrentItem` property. We then find a few overloads of the constructor that enable us to initialize our collection from either a collection, or any number of input parameters of the relevant type.

Next, we see the `CurrentItem` property from the `Chapter 1`, *A Smarter Way Of Working With WPF*, again, but now with some further context. If a class has subscribed to the `CurrentItemChanged` property, we will call the delegate from here, passing both the new and old values of the current item. The `IsEmpty` property is just an efficient convenience property for our developers to call when they need to know whether the collection has any content or not.

After this, we see the collection delegates and the relevant property wrappers that enable the developers that will use our framework to make use of them. Next, we see the convenient `GetNewItem` and `AddEmptyItem` methods, which both generate a new item of the `T` generic type parameter, before returning or adding them to the collection respectively. This is the reason that we needed to add the `new()` generic type constraint to the class definition; this type constraint specifies that the generic type used must have a parameterless constructor.

And now we reach the various `Add` methods of the collection; note that every way to add an item to the collection must be handled, so that we can attach our `Item_PropertyChanged` handler to the `PropertyChanged` event of each added item to ensure consistent behavior.

We therefore call our `Add` methods from all other overloads and helper methods and call the base `Collection.Add` method from there. Note that we actually attach our handler inside the `InsertItem` method, as this overridden method is called from the `Add` methods in the `Collection` class.

Likewise, the protected `SetItem` method will be called by the `Collection` class when items are set using the index notation, so we must handle that too. Similarly, when items are removed from the collection, it is equally, if not more, important to remove the reference to our event handler from each object. Failing to do so can result in memory leaks, as the reference to the event handler can keep the Data Model objects from being disposed by the garbage collector.

As such, we also need to handle every method of removing objects from our collection. To do this, we override a few more protected methods from the `Collection` base class. The `ClearItems` method will be called internally when users call the `Clear` method on our collection. Equally, the `RemoveItem` method will be called when users call any of the public removal methods, so it is the optimal place to remove our handler.

Skipping the `ResetCurrentItemPosition` method for now, at the bottom of the class, we reach the `Item_PropertyChanged` event handling method. If the item that has had the property changed is the current item in the collection, then we raise the `ItemPropertyChanged` delegate that is connected with the `CurrentItemPropertyChanged` property.

For every property change notification, regardless of whether the item is the current item or not, we then raise the `INotifyPropertyChanged.PropertyChanged` event. This enables the developers that use our framework to be able to attach a handler to the `PropertyChanged` event directly on our collections and be able to discover when any property has been changed on any of the items in the collection.

You may also have noticed a few places in the collection class code where we set the value of the `CurrentItem` property. The option chosen here is to always select the first item in the collection automatically, but it would be a simple change to have the last item selected instead, for example. As always, these kinds of details will depend on your specific requirements.

Another benefit of declaring these base collection classes is that we can utilize the properties and extend the functionality that is built into our base Data Model classes. Thinking back to the simple example of our `BaseSynchronizableDataModel` class, let's see what we could add into a new base collection class to improve this functionality.

Before we can do this however, we need to be able to specify that the objects in our new collection have implemented the properties and methods from the `BaseSynchronizableDataModel` class. One option would be to declare our new collection class like this:

```
public class BaseSynchronizableCollection<T> : BaseCollection<T>
    where T : BaseSynchronizableDataModel<T>
```

However, in C#, we can only extend a single base class, while we are free to implement as many interfaces as we like. A more preferable solution would therefore be for us to extract the relevant synchronization properties from our base class into an interface, add that to our base class definition.

```
public abstract class BaseSynchronizableDataModel<T> :
    BaseDataModel, ISynchronizableDataModel<T>
    where T : BaseDataModel, ISynchronizableDataModel<T>, new()
```

We could then specify this new generic constraint on our new collection class like this:

```
public class BaseSynchronizableCollection<T> : BaseCollection<T>
    where T : class, ISynchronizableDataModel<T>, new()
```

Note that any other generic constraints that are placed on the `BaseSynchronizableDataModel` class will also need to be added to the `where T` part of this declaration. If for example, we needed to implement another interface in the base class and we did not add the same constraint for the `T` generic type parameter in the base collection class, then we would get a compilation error when attempting to use instances of our base class as the `T` parameter. Let's now look at this new base class:

```
using System.Collections.Generic;
using System.ComponentModel;
using System.Linq;
using CompanyName.ApplicationName.DataModels.Interfaces;
using CompanyName.ApplicationName.Extensions;

namespace CompanyName.ApplicationName.DataModels.Collections
{
  public class BaseSynchronizableCollection<T> : BaseCollection<T>
    where T : class, ISynchronizableDataModel<T>,
    INotifyPropertyChanged, new()
  {
```

```
public BaseSynchronizableCollection(IEnumerable<T> collection) :
  base(collection) { }

public BaseSynchronizableCollection(params T[] collection) :
  base(collection as IEnumerable<T>) { }

public BaseSynchronizableCollection() : base() { }

public virtual bool HasChanges
{
  get { return this.Any(i => i.HasChanges); }
}

public virtual bool AreSynchronized
{
  get { return this.All(i => i.IsSynchronized); }
}

public virtual IEnumerable<T> ChangedCollection
{
  get { return this.Where(i => i.HasChanges); }
}

public virtual void Synchronize()
{
  this.ForEach(i => i.Synchronize());
}

public virtual void RevertState()
{
  this.ForEach(i => i.RevertState());
}
  }
}
```

While remaining simple, this base collection class provides some powerful functionality. We start off with the class declaration, with its generic type constraints that are inherited from both our target T type classes and our `BaseCollection<T>` class. We've then implemented the constructor overloads and passed initialization duties straight to the base class.

Note that had we wanted to attach an additional level of event handlers to our collection items, we would follow the pattern from the base class, rather than calling the base class constructors in this way.

The `HasChanges` property can be used as a flag to detect whether any item in the collection has any changes or not. This would typically be tied to the `canExecute` parameter of a save command, so that the save button would become enabled when any item in the collection had been edited and disabled if the changes were undone.

The `AreSynchronized` property simply specifies whether the items in the collection have all been synchronized or not, but the real beauty of this class is in the `ChangedCollection` property. Using a simple LINQ filter, we return only the items from the collection that have changes. Imagine a scenario where we enable the user to edit multiple items at once. With this property, our developers could extract just the items that they need to save from the collection with zero effort.

Finally, this class provides one method to enable the synchronization of all of the items in the collection at once and another to undo the changes of all of the edited items in the collection likewise. Note the use of the custom `ForEach` Extension method in these last two methods; if you remember from the earlier *With Extension methods* section, it enables us to perform an action on each item in the collection.

Through the use of the properties and methods of our Data Model base classes by other parts of our framework, we are able to extend their functionality further. While building composite functionality from different components in this way is generally optional, it can also be necessary, as we'll see later in the book.

The more common functionality that we can build into our application framework base classes, the less work the developers that use our framework will have to do when developing the application. However, we must plan carefully and not force the developers to have unwanted properties and methods in order to extend a particular base class that has some other functionality that they do want.

Typically, there will be different requirements for different components. The Data Model classes will generally have more base classes than the View Models because they play a bigger role than the View Models. The View Models simply provide the Views with the data and functionality that they require. However, the Data Model contain that data, along with validation, synchronization and possibly animation methods and properties. With this in mind, let's look again at the View Model base class.

We have already seen that we will need an implementation of the `INotifyPropertyChanged` interface in our base class, but what else should we implement? If every View will be providing some specific functionality, such as saving and deleting items for example, then we can also add commands straight into our base class and abstract methods that each derived View Model class will have to implement.

```
public virtual ICommand Refresh
```

```
  {
    get
    {
      return new ActionCommand(action => RefreshData(),
        canExecute => CanRefreshData());
    }
  }

  protected abstract void RefreshData();

  protected abstract bool CanRefreshData();
```

Again, it is important to declare this command as being virtual, in case the developers need to provide their own, different implementation of it. An alternative to this arrangement would be to just add abstract properties for each command, so that the individual implementations would be completely up to the developers.

```
  public abstract ICommand Save { get; }
```

While on the subject of commands, you may remember our basic implementation of the `ActionCommand` from Chapter 1, *A Smarter Way Of Working With WPF*. At this point, it is worth taking a short detour to investigate this further. Note that while the basic implementation shown works well for most of the time, it can catch us out occasionally and we may notice that a button hasn't become enabled when it should have.

Let's look at an example of this. Imagine that we have a button in our UI that opens a folder for the user and is enabled when a certain condition is met in the `ICommand.CanExecute` method. Let's say that this condition is that the folder should have some content. After all, there's no point in opening an empty folder for the user.

Now let's imagine that this folder will be filled when the user performs some other operation in the UI. The user clicks the button that starts this folder-filling function and the application begins to fill it. At the point that the filling function is complete and the folder now holds some content, the open folder button should become enabled, as its associated command's `CanExecute` condition is now `true`.

Nevertheless, the `CanExecute` method won't be called at that point and why should it? The button and indeed, the `CommandManager` class has no idea that this background process was occurring and that the condition of the `CanExecute` method has now been met. Luckily, we have a couple of options to address this situation.

One option is to raise the `CanExecuteChanged` event manually to make the data bound command sources recheck the output of the `CanExecute` method and update their enabled state accordingly. To do this, we could add another method into our `ActionCommand` class, but we would have to rearrange a few things first.

The current implementation doesn't store any references to the event handlers that get attached to the `CanExecuteChanged` event. They're actually being stored in the `CommandManager` class, as they're just passed straight through for the `RequerySuggested` event to handle. In order to be able to raise the event manually, we'll need to store our own references to the handlers and to do that, we'll need an `EventHandler` object.

```
private EventHandler eventHandler;
```

Next, we'll need to add the references to the handlers that get attached and remove those that get detached, while still passing references of them through to the `RequerySuggested` event of the `CommandManager`.

```
public event EventHandler CanExecuteChanged
{
  add
  {
    eventHandler += value;
    CommandManager.RequerySuggested += value;
  }
  remove
  {
    eventHandler -= value;
    CommandManager.RequerySuggested -= value;
  }
}
```

The final change to our `ActionCommand` class is to add the method that we can call to raise the `CanExecuteChanged` event when we want the command sources of the UI controls to retrieve the new `CanExecute` value and update their enabled states.

```
public void RaiseCanExecuteChanged()
{
  eventHandler?.Invoke(this, new EventArgs());
}
```

We are now able to raise the `CanExecuteChanged` event whenever we need to, although we'll also need to change our use of the `ActionCommand` class to do so. Whereas previously, we were simply returning a new instance each time its getter was called, we'll now need to keep a reference to each command that we want to have this ability.

```
private ActionCommand saveCommand = null;

...

public ICommand SaveCommand
{
  get { return saveCommand ?? (saveCommand =
    new ActionCommand(action => Save(), canExecute => CanSave())); }
}
```

If you are unfamiliar with the `??` operator shown in the preceding code, it is known as the null-coalescing operator and it simply returns the left-hand operand if it is not `null`, or the right-hand operand if it is. In this case, the right-hand operand will initialize the command and set it to the `saveCommand` variable. Then, to raise the event, we call the new `RaiseCanExecuteChanged` method on our `ActionCommand` instance when we have completed our operation.

```
private void ExecuteSomeCommand()
{
  // Perform some operation that fulfils the canExecute condition
  // then raise the CanExecuteChanged event of the ActionCommand
  saveCommand.RaiseCanExecuteChanged();
}
```

While our method is built into the `ActionCommand` class, at times we may not have access to the particular instance that we need to raise the event on. It should therefore be noted at this point that there is another, more direct way that we can get the `CommandManager` class to raise its `RequerySuggested` event.

In these cases, we can simply call the `CommandManager.InvalidateRequerySuggested` method. We should also be aware that these methods of raising the `RequerySuggested` event will only work on the UI thread, so care should be taken when using them with asynchronous code. Now that our short command-related detour is complete, let's return to take a look at what other common functionality we might want to put into our View Model base class.

If we have chosen to use generic base classes for our Data Models then we can take advantage of that in our `BaseViewModel` class. We can provide generic methods that utilize members from these generic base classes. Let's take a look at some simple examples.

```
public T AddNewDataTypeToCollection<S, T>(S collection)
  where S : BaseSynchronizableCollection<T>
  where T : BaseSynchronizableDataModel<T>, new()
{
  T item = collection.GetNewItem();
  if (item is IAuditable)
    ((IAuditable)item).Auditable.CreatedOn = DateTime.Now;
  item.Synchronize();
  collection.Add(item);
  collection.CurrentItem = item;
  return item;
}

public T InsertNewDataTypeToCollection<S, T>(int index, S collection)
  where S : BaseSynchronizableCollection<T>
  where T : BaseSynchronizableDataModel<T>, new()
{
  T item = collection.GetNewItem();
  if (item is IAuditable)
    ((IAuditable)item).Auditable.CreatedOn = DateTime.Now;
  item.Synchronize();
  collection.Insert(index, item);
  collection.CurrentItem = item;
  return item;
}

public void RemoveDataTypeFromCollection<S, T>(S collection, T item)
  where S : BaseSynchronizableCollection<T>
  where T : BaseSynchronizableDataModel<T>, new()
{
  int index = collection.IndexOf(item);
  collection.RemoveAt(index);
  if (index > collection.Count) index = collection.Count;
  else if (index < 0) index++;
  if (index > 0 && index < collection.Count &&
    collection.CurrentItem != collection[index])
    collection.CurrentItem = collection[index];
}
```

Here, we see three simple methods that encapsulate more common functionality. Note that we must specify the same generic type constraints that are declared on our bass classes. Failure to do so would either result in compilation errors or us not being able to use our Data Model classes with these methods.

The `AddNewDataTypeToCollection` and `InsertNewDataTypeToCollection` methods are almost identical and start by creating a new item of the relevant type using the `GetNewItem` method of our generic `BaseSynchronizableCollection` class. Next, we see another use for our `IAuditable` interface. In this case, we set the `CreatedOn` date of the new item if it implements this interface.

Because we declared the generic type constraint on the `T` type parameter that specifies that it must be, or extend, the `BaseSynchronizableDataModel` class, we are able to call the `Synchronize` method to synchronize the new item. We then add the item to the collection and set it as the value of the `CurrentItem` property. Finally, both methods return the new item.

The last method performs the opposite action; it removes an item from the collection. Before doing so, it checks the item's position in the collection and sets the `CurrentItem` property to the next item if possible, or the next nearest item if the removed item was the last item in the collection.

Once again, we see how we can encapsulate commonly used functionality into our base class and save the users of our framework both time and effort re-implementing this functionality in each View Model class themselves. We can package up any common functionality that we require in this manner. Having now seen several examples of providing functionality in our base classes, let's now turn our attention to providing separation between the components of our framework.

Separating the Data Access Layer

Now that we've had a look at providing a variety of functionality through our base classes and interfaces, let's investigate how we can provide the Separation of Concerns that is crucial when using the MVVM pattern. Once again, we turn to the humble interface to help us to achieve this. Let's view a simplified example:

```
using System;
using CompanyName.ApplicationName.DataModels;

namespace CompanyName.ApplicationName.Models.Interfaces
{
    public interface IDataProvider
```

```
    {
        User GetUser(Guid id);

        bool SaveUser(User user);
    }
}
```

We start off with a very simple interface. Of course, real applications will have a great many more methods than this, but the principal is the same, regardless of the complexity of the interface. So here, we just have a GetUser and a SaveUser method that our DataProvider classes need to implement. Now let's look at the ApplicationDataProvider class:

```
using System;
using System.Data.Linq;
using System.Linq;
using CompanyName.ApplicationName.DataModels;
using CompanyName.ApplicationName.Models.Interfaces;

namespace CompanyName.ApplicationName.Models.DataProviders
{
    public class ApplicationDataProvider : IDataProvider
    {
        public ApplicationDataContext DataContext
        {
            get { return new ApplicationDataContext(); }
        }

        public User GetUser(Guid id)
        {
            DbUser dbUser = DataContext.DbUsers.SingleOrDefault(u => u.Id == id);
            if (dbUser == null) return null;
            return new User(dbUser.Id, dbUser.Name, dbUser.Age);
        }

        public bool SaveUser(User user)
        {
            using (ApplicationDataContext dataContext = DataContext)
            {
                DbUser dbUser =
                    dataContext.DbUsers.SingleOrDefault(u => u.Id == user.Id);
                if (dbUser == null) return false;
                dbUser.Name = user.Name;
                dbUser.Age = user.Age;
                dataContext.SubmitChanges(ConflictMode.FailOnFirstConflict);
                return true;
            }
        }
    }
}
```

```
    }
```

This `ApplicationDataProvider` class uses some simple LINQ to SQL to query and update a database for the `User` specified by the provided `id` value. That means that this particular implementation of the interface requires a connection to a database. We want to avoid having this dependency when testing our application, so we'll need another implementation of the interface to use for testing purposes. Let's take a look at our mock implementation now.

```
using System;
using CompanyName.ApplicationName.DataModels;
using CompanyName.ApplicationName.Models.Interfaces;

namespace Test.CompanyName.ApplicationName.Models.DataProviders
{
    public class MockDataProvider : IDataProvider
    {
        public User GetUser(Guid id)
        {
            return new User(id, "John Smith", 25);
        }

        public bool SaveUser(User user)
        {
            return true;
        }
    }
}
```

In this `MockDataProvider` implementation of the `IDataProvider` interface, we can see that the data is just manually mocked. In fact, it just returns the one single `User` from the `GetUser` method and always returns `true` from the `SaveUser` method, so it's fairly useless.

In a real-world application, we would either utilize a mocking framework, or manually mock up some more substantial testing data. Still, this will suffice for the point that we are focusing on here. Now that we've seen the classes involved, let's look at how they might be used.

The idea is that we have some sort of `DataController` class or classes that sit between the `IDataProvider` interface and the View Model classes. The View Model classes request data from the `DataController` class and in turn, it requests data through the interface. It therefore mirrors the methods of the interface and typically introduces some extra functionality, such as feedback handling for example. Let's see what our simplified `DataController` class looks like:

```
using System;
using CompanyName.ApplicationName.DataModels;
using CompanyName.ApplicationName.Models.Interfaces;

namespace CompanyName.ApplicationName.Models.DataControllers
{
  public class DataController
  {
    private IDataProvider dataProvider;

    public DataController(IDataProvider dataProvider)
    {
      DataProvider = dataProvider;
    }

    protected IDataProvider DataProvider
    {
      get { return dataProvider; }
      private set { dataProvider = value; }
    }

    public User GetUser(Guid id)
    {
      return DataProvider.GetUser(id);
    }

    public bool SaveUser(User user)
    {
      return DataProvider.SaveUser(user);
    }
  }
}
```

As we can see, the `DataController` class has a private member variable of type `IDataProvider`, which is populated in its constructor. It is this variable that is used to access the application data source. When the application is running, an instance of our `ApplicationDataProvider` class is used to instantiate the `DataController` class and so our actual data source is used.

```
DataController dataController =
    new DataController(new ApplicationDataProvider());
```

However, when we are testing our application, we can use an instance of our `MockDataProvider` class to instantiate the `DataController` class instead, thereby eliminating our dependency to the actual data source.

```
DataController dataController = new DataController(new MockDataProvider());
```

In this way, we can swap out the code that provides the data for the View Models, while keeping the rest of the code unchanged. This enables us to test the code in the View Models without having to be connected to our actual data storage device. In the next section, we'll see better ways to initialize these classes, but for now, let's see what else our `DataController` class could do for us.

Interfaces become more useful when they are used by parts of the application framework, other than the implementing classes. Apart from than defining some auditing properties and having the possibility of outputting their values, our earlier `IAuditable` interface example is not overly useful. We could however, extend its functionality further in our `DataController` class, by automatically updating its values. We'll need to add some more members to achieve this:

```
using CompanyName.ApplicationName.DataModels.Interfaces;

...

public User CurrentUser { get; set; }

...

private void SetAuditUpdateFields<T>(T dataModel) where T : IAuditable
{
    dataModel.Auditable.UpdatedOn = DateTime.Now;
    dataModel.Auditable.UpdatedBy = CurrentUser;
    return dataModel;
}
```

We first need to add a property of type `User` that we will use to set the value of the current user of the application. This can be set as new users login to the application. Next, we need a method to update the "updated" values of our `IAuditable` interface. Again, we add a generic type constraint to ensure that only objects that implement our interface can be passed into this method. The result of this is that the developers that use our application framework can easily update these values.

```
public bool SaveUser(User user)
{
    return DataProvider.SaveUser(SetAuditUpdateFields(user));
}
```

We could add a similar method to set the "created" audit properties when adding new objects.

```
public bool AddUser(User user)
{
    return DataProvider.AddUser(SetAuditCreateFields(user));
}

...

private void SetAuditCreateFields<T>(T dataModel) where T : IAuditable
{
    dataModel.Auditable.CreatedOn = DateTime.Now;
    dataModel.Auditable.CreatedBy = CurrentUser;
    return dataModel;
}
```

Continuing this example, we could extend the constructor of our `DataController` class to accept a `User` input parameter that we can use to set our `CurrentUser` property with:

```
public DataController(IDataProvider dataProvider, User currentUser)
{
    DataProvider = dataProvider;
    CurrentUser = currentUser;
}
```

We could then expose our data source to our View Models through their base class using a CurrentUser property in the StateManager class and the DependencyManager class that we'll see in the following sections.

```
protected DataController Model
{
  get { return new DataController(
    DependencyManager.Instance.Resolve<IDataProvider>(),
    StateManager.CurrentUser); }
}
```

Essentially, anything that we need to do to the data coming from our application data source can be achieved in a single DataController class. However, if we require several different modifications, then we could alternatively create several controller classes and chain them together, with each performing their separate tasks in turn. As they could all implement the same methods, they could all potentially implement the same interface.

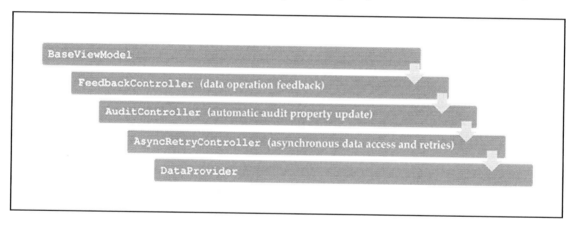

We'll see an example of this in Chapter 9, *Completing That Great User Experience*, but now that we have a good idea on how best to setup our application data source connections to provide the separation required by the MVVM pattern, we can focus on the next way of building functionality into our framework. Let's move on to discover how we can plug more complex and/or specialized functionality into our framework.

Providing services

The job of the base classes and interfaces in our application framework are to encapsulate functionality that is commonly used by our View Models and Data Models. When the required functionality is more complex, or when it involves particular resources, or external connections, we implement it in separate service, or manager classes. For the remainder of this book, we will refer to these as manager classes. In larger applications, these are typically provided in a separate project.

Encapsulating them in a separate project enables us to reuse the functionality from these classes in our other applications. Which classes we use in this project will depend on the requirements of the application that we're building, but it will often include classes that provide the ability to send e-mails, to access the end user's hard drive, to export data in various formats, or to manage global application state for example.

We will investigate a number of these classes in this book, so that we have a good idea of how to implement our own custom manager classes. The most commonly used of these classes can normally be accessed directly from the base View Model class via properties. There are a few different ways that we can expose these classes to the View Models, so let's examine them.

When a manger class is used often and for short durations each time, we can expose a new instance of them each time, like this:

```
public FeedbackManager FeedbackManager
{
  get { return new FeedbackManager(); }
}
```

However, if a manager class is required for the life of the application, because it must remember some state or configuration for example, then we typically use the `static` keyword in one way or another. The simplest option would be to declare a normal class, but expose it via a static property.

```
private static StateManager stateManager = new StateManager();

...

public static StateManager StateManager
{
  get { return stateManager; }
}
```

An alternative method of having one and only one instance of a class being instantiated and having it stay alive for as long as the application is running is for us to use the Singleton pattern. While it was all the rage twenty or so years ago, it has unfortunately recently fallen foul of more modern programming principles, such as the likes of SOLID, that states that each class should have a single responsibility.

The Singleton pattern breaks this principle as it serves whatever purpose we design it for, but it is also responsible for instantiating itself and maintaining a single access point. Before discussing the merits and pitfalls of this pattern further, let's take a look at how we might implement it in our manager class:

```
namespace CompanyName.ApplicationName.Managers
{
  public class StateManager
  {
    private static StateManager instance;

    private StateManager() { }

    public static StateManager Instance
    {
      get { return instance ?? (instance = new StateManager()); }
    }

    ...
  }
}
```

Note that it can be implemented in a variety of ways, but this particular way uses lazy initialization, where the instance is not instantiated until it is first referenced via the `Instance` property. Using the `??` operator again, the `Instance` property getter can be read as "return the one and only instantiated instance if it is not null, or if it is, instantiate the one and only instance and then return it". The significant part of this pattern is that as there is no public constructor and therefore the class cannot be externally instantiated, this property is the single way to access the internal object.

However, this is the very part that causes trouble for some developers, as this makes inheritance impossible with these classes. In our case though, we won't need to extend our `StateManager` class, so that it not a concern for us. Others may point to the problem that exposing this Singleton class as shown in the following code, will tightly couple it to the base View Model class that it is declared in.

```
public StateManager StateManager
{
   get { return StateManager.Instance; }
}
```

While this is true, what harm is that with this class? Its purpose is to maintain the state of user settings, common or default values, and values for UI display and operation statuses. It contains no resources and no real reason to avoid using it when running unit tests, so in this case, the tight coupling is inconsequential. In this regard, the Singleton pattern continues to be a useful tool in the right situations, but we should certainly be aware of its pitfalls all the same.

However, if a particular manger class does utilize resources or creates some form of connection with the outside world, for example, like an `EmailManager` would, then we will need to create an interface for it to maintain our Separation of Concerns. Remember that interfaces enable us to disconnect the actual application components and replace them with mock components while testing. In these cases, we have to expose the functionality in the base classes slightly differently.

```
private IEmailManager emailManager;

...

public BaseViewModel(IEmailManager emailManager)
{
   this.emailManager = emailManager; }
}

...

public IEmailManager EmailManager
{
   get { return emailManager; }
}
```

The general idea here is for us to have no direct contact with the manager class in hand, instead accessing its functionality through the interface methods and properties. By doing this, we are able to decouple the manager class from the View Models that use it and therefore enable them to be used independently of each other. Note that this is a very simple example of Dependency Injection.

Implementing Dependency Injection

Dependency Injection is a well-known design pattern that aids in decoupling various components of an application. If one class uses another class to perform some functionality internally, then the class that is internally used becomes a dependency of the class that uses it. It cannot achieve its objectives without it. In some cases, this is not a problem, but in others, it can represent a huge problem.

For example, let's imagine that we have a `FeedbackManager` class that is responsible for providing operational feedback to the end users. In that class, we have a `FeedbackCollection` class that holds the `Feedback` objects that are current being displayed to the current user. Here, the `Feedback` objects are a dependency of the `FeedbackCollection` object and that in turn, is a dependency of the `FeedbackManager` class.

These objects are all tightly coupled, which is usually a bad thing in software development. However, they are also tightly related by necessity. A `FeedbackCollection` object would be useless without the `Feedback` objects, as would the `FeedbackManager` object.

In this particular case, these objects require this coupling to make them useful together. This is called composition, where the individual parts form a whole, but do little on their own, so it really is no problem for them to be connected in this way.

On the other hand, let's now contemplate the connection between our View Models and our DAL. Our View Models will definitely need access to some data, so it would at first seem to make sense to encapsulate a class in our View Models that provides the data that it requires.

While that would certainly work, it would unfortunately result in the DAL class becoming a dependent of the View Model class. Moreover, it would permanently couple our View Model component to the DAL and break the Separation of Concerns that MVVM provides. The kind of connection that we require in this situation is more like aggregation, where the individual parts are useful on their own.

In these cases, we want to be able to use the individual components separately and to avoid any tight coupling between them. Dependency Injection is a tool that we can use to provide this separation for us. In the absolute simplest terms, Dependency Injection is implemented through the use of interfaces. We've already seen some basic examples of this in the `DataController` class from the *Separating the Data Access Layer* section and the `EmailManager` example from the previous section.

However, they were very basic examples and there are a variety of ways of improving them. Many application frameworks will provide the ability for the developers to use Dependency Injection to inject the dependencies into their classes and we can do the same with ours. In its simplest form, our `DependencyManager` class will simply need to register the dependencies and provide a way to resolve them when required. Let's take a look:

```
using System;
using System.Collections.Generic;

namespace CompanyName.ApplicationName.Managers
{
  public class DependencyManager
  {
    private static DependencyManager instance;
    private static Dictionary<Type, Type> registeredDependencies =
      new Dictionary<Type, Type>();

    private DependencyManager() { }

    public static DependencyManager Instance
    {
      get { return instance ?? (instance = new DependencyManager()); }
    }

    public int Count
    {
      get { return registeredDependencies.Count; }
    }

    public void ClearRegistrations()
    {
      registeredDependencies.Clear();
    }

    public void Register<S, T>() where S : class where T : class
    {
      if (!typeof(S).IsInterface) throw new ArgumentException("The S
        generic type parameter of the Register method must be an
        interface.", "S");
```

```
    if (!typeof(S).IsAssignableFrom(typeof(T))) throw
      new ArgumentException("The T generic type parameter must be a
      class that implements the interface specified by the S generic
      type parameter.", "T");
    if (!registeredDependencies.ContainsKey(typeof(S)))
      registeredDependencies.Add(typeof(S), typeof(T));
  }

  public T Resolve<T>() where T : class
  {
    Type type = registeredDependencies[typeof(T)];
    return Activator.CreateInstance(type) as T;
  }

  public T Resolve<T>(params object[] args) where T : class
  {
    Type type = registeredDependencies[typeof(T)];
    if (args == null || args.Length == 0)
      return Activator.CreateInstance(type) as T;
    else return Activator.CreateInstance(type, args) as T;
  }
 }
}
```

You may have noticed that we are using the Singleton pattern again for this class. In this case, it fits our requirements exactly again. We want one and only one instance of this class to be instantiated and we want it to stay alive for as long as the application is running. When testing, it is used to inject our mock dependencies into the View Models, so it is part of the framework that enables our Separation of Concerns.

The Count property and the ClearRegistrations method are more useful for testing than when running the application and the real action goes on in the Register and Resolve methods. The Register method registers the interface type represented by the S generic type parameter with the concrete implementation of that interface represented by the generic type parameter.

As the S generic type parameter must be an interface, an ArgumentException is thrown at runtime if the supplied type parameter class is not one. A further check is performed to ensure that the type specified by the T generic type parameter actually implements the interface specified by the S generic type parameter.

The method then verifies that the provided type parameter is not already in the `Dictionary` and adds it if it is unique in the collection. Therefore, in this particular implementation, we can only specify a single concrete implementation for each supplied interface. We could change this to either update the stored reference if an existing type was passed again, or even to store multiple concrete types for each interface. It all depends on the application requirements.

Note the generic type constraint declared on this method that ensures the type parameters will at least be classes. Unfortunately, there is no such constraint that would allow us to specify that a particular generic type parameter should be an interface. However, this type of parameter validation should be used where possible, as it helps the users of our framework to avoid using these methods with inappropriate values.

The `Resolve` methods use some simple reflection to return the concrete implementations of the interface types represented the generic type parameters used. Again, note the generic type constraints declared by these two methods, that specify that the type used for the `T` type parameter must be a class. This is to prevent the `Activator.CreateInstance` methods from throwing an `Exception` at runtime, if a type that could not be instantiated were used.

The first overload can be used for classes without any constructor parameters and the second has an additional `params` input parameter to pass the parameters to use when instantiating classes that require constructor parameters.

The `DependencyManager` class can be setup during application startup, using the `App.xaml.cs` file. To do this, we first need to find the following `StartupUri` property setting in the `Application` declaration at the top of the `App.xaml` file:

```
StartupUri="MainWindow.xaml"
```

We then need to replace this `StartupUri` property setting with the following `Startup` property setting:

```
Startup="App_Startup"
```

In this example, `App_Startup` is the name of the initialization method that we want to be called at startup. Note that as the WPF Framework is no longer starting the `MainWindow` class, it is now our responsibility to do so.

```
using System.Windows;
using CompanyName.ApplicationName.Managers;
using CompanyName.ApplicationName.ViewModels;
using CompanyName.ApplicationName.ViewModels.Interfaces;
```

```
namespace CompanyName.ApplicationName
{
  public partial class App : Application
  {
    public void App_Startup(object sender, StartupEventArgs e)
    {
      RegisterDependencies();
      new MainWindow().Show();
    }

    private void RegisterDependencies()
    {
      DependencyManager.Instance.ClearRegistrations();
      DependencyManager.Instance.Register<IDataProvider,
        ApplicationDataProvider>();
      DependencyManager.Instance.Register<IEmailManager, EmailManager>();
      DependencyManager.Instance.Register<IExcelManager, ExcelManager>();
      DependencyManager.Instance.Register<IWindowManager, WindowManager>();
    }
  }
}
```

When we want to inject these dependencies into a View Model in the application at runtime, we could use the `DependencyManager` class like this:

```
UsersViewModel viewModel =
  new UsersViewModel(DependencyManager.Instance.Resolve<IEmailManager>(),
  DependencyManager.Instance.Resolve<IExcelManager>(),
  DependencyManager.Instance.Resolve<IWindowManager>());
```

The real beauty of this system is that when testing our View Models, we can register our mock manager classes instead. The same preceding code will then resolve the interfaces to their mock concrete implementations, thereby freeing our View Models from their actual dependencies.

```
private void RegisterMockDependencies()
{
  DependencyManager.Instance.ClearRegistrations();
  DependencyManager.Instance.Register<IDataProvider, MockDataProvider>();
  DependencyManager.Instance.Register<IEmailManager, MockEmailManager>();
  DependencyManager.Instance.Register<IExcelManager, MockExcelManager>();
  DependencyManager.Instance.Register<IWindowManager, MockWindowManager>();
}
```

We've now seen the code that enables us to swap out our dependent classes with mock implementations when we are testing our application. However, we've also seen that not all of our manager classes will require this. So what exactly represents a dependency? Let's take a look at a simple example involving a UI popup message box:

```
using CompanyName.ApplicationName.DataModels.Enums;

namespace CompanyName.ApplicationName.Managers.Interfaces
{
  public interface IWindowManager
  {
    MessageBoxButtonSelection ShowMessageBox(string message,
      string title, MessageBoxButton buttons, MessageBoxIcon icon);
  }
}
```

Here we have an interface that declares a single method. This is the method that the developers will call from the View Model classes when they need to display a message box in the UI. It will use a real `MessageBox` object during runtime, but this uses a number of enumerations from the `System.Windows` namespace.

We want to avoid interacting with these enumeration instances in our View Models, as that will require adding a reference to the `PresentationFramework` assembly and tie our View Models to part of our Views component.

We therefore need to abstract them from our interface method definition. In this case, we have simply replaced the enumerations from the `PresentationFramework` assembly with custom enumerations from our domain that merely replicate the original values. As such, there is little point in showing the code for these custom enumerations here.

While it's never a good idea to duplicate code, it's an even worse idea to add a UI assembly like the `PresentationFramework` assembly to our `ViewModels` project. By encapsulating this assembly within the `Managers` project and converting its enumerations, we can expose the functionality that we need from it without tying it to our View Models.

```
using System.Windows;
using CompanyName.ApplicationName.Managers.Interfaces;
using MessageBoxButton =
  CompanyName.ApplicationName.DataModels.Enums.MessageBoxButton;
using MessageBoxButtonSelection =
  CompanyName.ApplicationName.DataModels.Enums.MessageBoxButtonSelection;
using MessageBoxIcon =
  CompanyName.ApplicationName.DataModels.Enums.MessageBoxIcon;

namespace CompanyName.ApplicationName.Managers
{
```

```
public class WindowManager : IWindowManager
{
  public MessageBoxButtonSelection ShowMessageBox(string message,
    string title, MessageBoxButton buttons, MessageBoxIcon icon)
  {
    System.Windows.MessageBoxButton messageBoxButtons;
    switch (buttons)
    {
      case MessageBoxButton.Ok: messageBoxButtons =
        System.Windows.MessageBoxButton.OK; break;
      case MessageBoxButton.OkCancel: messageBoxButtons =
        System.Windows. MessageBoxButton.OkCancel; break;
      case MessageBoxButton.YesNo: messageBoxButtons =
        System.Windows.MessageBoxButton.YesNo; break;
      case MessageBoxButton.YesNoCancel: messageBoxButtons =
        System.Windows.MessageBoxButton.YesNoCancel; break;
      default: messageBoxButtons =
        System.Windows.MessageBoxButton.OKCancel; break;
    }
    MessageBoxImage messageBoxImage;
    switch (icon)
    {
      case MessageBoxIcon.Asterisk:
        messageBoxImage = MessageBoxImage.Asterisk; break;
      case MessageBoxIcon.Error:
        messageBoxImage = MessageBoxImage.Error; break;
      case MessageBoxIcon.Exclamation:
        messageBoxImage = MessageBoxImage.Exclamation; break;
      case MessageBoxIcon.Hand:
        messageBoxImage = MessageBoxImage.Hand; break;
      case MessageBoxIcon.Information:
        messageBoxImage = MessageBoxImage.Information; break;
      case MessageBoxIcon.None:
        messageBoxImage = MessageBoxImage.None; break;
      case MessageBoxIcon.Question:
        messageBoxImage = MessageBoxImage.Question; break;
      case MessageBoxIcon.Stop:
        messageBoxImage = MessageBoxImage.Stop; break;
      case MessageBoxIcon.Warning:
        messageBoxImage = MessageBoxImage.Warning; break;
      default: messageBoxImage = MessageBoxImage.Stop; break;
    }
    MessageBoxButtonSelection messageBoxButtonSelection =
      MessageBoxButtonSelection.None;
    switch (MessageBox.Show(message, title, messageBoxButtons,
      messageBoxImage))
    {
      case MessageBoxResult.Cancel: messageBoxButtonSelection =
```

```
            MessageBoxButtonSelection.Cancel; break;
        case MessageBoxResult.No: messageBoxButtonSelection =
            MessageBoxButtonSelection.No; break;
        case MessageBoxResult.OK: messageBoxButtonSelection =
            MessageBoxButtonSelection.Ok; break;
        case MessageBoxResult.Yes: messageBoxButtonSelection =
            MessageBoxButtonSelection.Yes; break;
        }
        return messageBoxButtonSelection;
    }
  }
}
```

We start with our `using` directives and see further examples of using alias directives. In this case, we created some enumeration classes with the same names as those from the `System.Windows` namespace. To avoid the conflicts that we would have caused by adding a standard `using` directive for our `CompanyName.ApplicationName.DataModels.Enums` namespace, we add aliases to enable us to work with just the types from our namespace that we require.

After this, our `WindowManager` class simply converts the UI-related enumeration values to and from our custom enumerations, so that we can use the functionality of the message box, but not be tied to its implementation. Imagine a situation where we need to use this to output an error message.

```
WindowManager.ShowMessageBox(errorMessage, "Error", MessageBoxButton.Ok,
    MessageBoxIcon.Error);
```

When execution reaches this point, a message box will pop up, displaying an error message with an error icon and heading. The application will freeze at this point while waiting for user feedback and if the user does not click a button on the popup, it will remain frozen indefinitely. If execution reaches this point during a unit test and there is no user to click the button, then our test will freeze indefinitely and the test will never complete.

In this example, the `WindowManager` class is dependent upon having a user present to interact with it. Therefore, if the View Models used this class directly, they would also have the same dependency. Other classes might have a dependency on an e-mail server, database, or other type of resource, for example. These are the types of classes that the View Models should only interact with via interfaces.

In doing so, we provide the ability to use our components independently from each other. Using our IWindowManager interface, we are able to use our ShowMessageBox method independently of the end users. In this way, we are able to break the user dependency and run our unit tests without them. Our mock implementation of the interface can simply return a positive response each time and the program execution can continue unheeded.

```
using CompanyName.ApplicationName.DataModels.Enums;
using CompanyName.ApplicationName.Managers.Interfaces;

namespace Test.CompanyName.ApplicationName.Mocks.Managers
{
  public class MockWindowManager : IWindowManager
  {
    public MessageBoxButtonSelection ShowMessageBox(string message,
      string title, MessageBoxButton buttons, MessageBoxIcon icon)
    {
      switch (buttons)
      {
        case MessageBoxButton.Ok:
        case MessageBoxButton.OkCancel:
          return MessageBoxButtonSelection.Ok;
        case MessageBoxButton.YesNo:
        case MessageBoxButton.YesNoCancel:
          return MessageBoxButtonSelection.Yes;
        default: return MessageBoxButtonSelection.Ok;
      }
    }
  }
}
```

This simple example shows another method of exposing functionality from a source to our View Models, but without it becoming a dependency. In this way, we can provide a whole host and variety of capabilities to our View Models, while still enabling them to function independently.

We now have the knowledge and tools to build functionality into our application framework in many different ways, yet our probe into application frameworks is still not quite complete. One other essential matter is that of connecting our Views with our View Models. We'll need to decide how the users of our framework should do this, so let's look at some choices.

Connecting Views with View Models

In WPF, there are several ways to connect our Views to their data sources. We've all seen examples of the simplest method of a View setting its `DataContext` property to itself in its code behind.

```
public partial class MainWindow : Window
{
  public MainWindow()
  {
    InitializeComponent();
    DataContext = this;
  }
}
```

However, this should only ever be used for quick demonstrations and never in our real-world applications. If we need to data bind to properties declared in a View's code behind, let's say for a particular custom `UserControl`, then we should use `RelativeSource` bindings instead. We'll find out more about this in the next chapter, but for now, let's continue looking at the alternative ways to connect the Views with their data sources.

The next simplest method utilizes the data templating model that is built into the WPF Framework. This topic will also be covered in much more detail in the next chapter, but in short, a `DataTemplate` is used to inform the WPF Framework how we want it to render data objects of a particular type. The simple example below shows how we could define the visual output of our `User` objects:

```
<DataTemplate DataType="{x:Type DataModels:User}">
  <TextBlock Text="{Binding Name}" />
</DataTemplate>
```

In this example, the `DataType` property specifies which type of object this relates to and therefore, which properties the containing XAML bindings have access to. Keeping it simple for now, we just output the name of each `User` in this `DataTemplate`. When we data bind one or more `User` objects to a UI control that is in scope of this `DataTemplate`, they will each be rendered by the WPF Framework as a `TextBlock` that specifies their name.

When the rendering engine of the WPF Framework comes across a custom data object, it looks for a `DataTemplate` that has been declared for its type and if it finds one, it renders the object according to the XAML contained within the relevant template. This means that we can create a `DataTemplate` for our View Model classes that simply specifies their related View classes as the rendering output.

```xml
<DataTemplate DataType="{x:Type ViewModels:UsersViewModel}">
  <Views:UsersView />
</DataTemplate>
```

In this example, we have specified that when the WPF Framework sees an instance of our `UserViewModel` class, it should render it as one of our `UserView` classes. At this point, it will set our View Model instance to the `DataContext` property of the related View implicitly. The only downside to this method is minimal and is that we have to add a new `DataTemplate` to our `App.xaml` file for each of our View-View Model pairs.

This method of connection works View Model first, where we supply the View Model instance and the WPF Framework takes care of the rest. In these cases, we typically use a `ContentControl` that has its `Content` property data bound to a `ViewModel` property, which the application View Models are set to. The WPF Framework notes the type of the View Model that is set and renders it according to its specified `DataTemplate`.

```csharp
private BaseViewModel viewModel;

public BaseViewModel ViewModel
{
  get { return viewModel; }
  set { viewModel = value; NotifyPropertyChanged(); }
}

...

ViewModel = new UserViewModel();

...

<ContentControl Content="{Binding ViewModel}" />
```

This is the preferred version of View to View Model connections for many, as the WPF Framework is left to take care of most of the details. However, there is another way to construct these connections that adds a layer of abstraction to the process.

For this method, we need to create interfaces for each of our View Models. It's called View Model Location and it's fairly similar to the Dependency Injection example that we have already seen. In fact, we could even use our existing `DependencyManager` to achieve a similar result. Let's take a quick look at that first.

```
DependencyManager.Instance.Register<IUserViewModel, UserViewModel>();

...

public partial class UserView : UserControl
{
  public UserView()
  {
    InitializeComponent();
    DataContext = DependencyManager.Instance.Resolve<IUserViewModel>();
  }
}

...

<Views:UsersView />
```

In this example, we associate the `IUserViewModel` interface with the `UserViewModel` concrete implementation of that interface in some initialization code and later, resolve the dependency, before setting it as the View's `DataContext` value. After declaring our Views in the XAML, they automatically hook themselves up to their related View Models at runtime.

This method of connecting Views to View Models works View first, where we declare the View and it instantiates its own View Model and sets its own `DataContext`. The downside with this method is that we have to create an interface for all of our View Models and register and resolve each of them using the `DependencyManager`.

The main difference between this implementation and that of a View Model Locator is that a locator provides a level of abstraction from our Singleton class, which enables us to indirectly instantiate our View Models from the XAML, without using the code behind. They also have a little extra specific functionality that enables dummy data to be used at design time. Let's take a look at the simplest possible example.

```csharp
using CompanyName.ApplicationName.Managers;
using CompanyName.ApplicationName.ViewModels;
using CompanyName.ApplicationName.ViewModels.Interfaces;

namespace CompanyName.ApplicationName.Views.ViewModelLocators
{
  public class ViewModelLocator
  {
    public IUserViewModel UserViewModel
    {
      get { return DependencyManager.Instance.Resolve<IUserViewModel>(); }
    }
  }
}
```

Here we have a very basic View Model Locator, that simply locates a single View Model. It is important that this View Model class has an empty constructor, so that it can be instantiated from the XAML. Let's see how we can do this:

```xml
<UserControl x:Class="CompanyName.ApplicationName.Views.UserView"
  xmlns="http://schemas.microsoft.com/winfx/2006/xaml/presentation"
  xmlns:x="http://schemas.microsoft.com/winfx/2006/xaml"
  xmlns:d="http://schemas.microsoft.com/expression/blend/2008"
  xmlns:mc="http://schemas.openxmlformats.org/markup-compatibility/2006"
  xmlns:ViewModelLocators="clr-namespace:
    CompanyName.ApplicationName.Views.ViewModelLocators"
  mc:Ignorable="d" Height="30" Width="300">
  <UserControl.Resources>
    <ViewModelLocators:ViewModelLocator x:Key="ViewModelLocator" />
  </UserControl.Resources>
  <UserControl.DataContext>
    <Binding Path="UserViewModel"
      Source="{StaticResource ViewModelLocator}" />
  </UserControl.DataContext>
  <TextBlock Text="{Binding User.Name}" />
</UserControl>
```

As a side note, you may have noticed that our `ViewModelLocator` class has been declared in the `Views` project. The location of this class is not very important, but it must have references to both the `ViewModels` and the `Views` projects and this severely limits the number of projects in which it can reside. Typically, the only projects that will have access to the classes from both of these projects will be the `Views` project and the startup project.

Getting back to our example, an instance of the `ViewModelLocator` class is declared in the View's `Resources` section and this will only work if we have a parameterless constructor (including the default parameterless constructor that is declared for us if we do not explicitly declare a constructor). Without a parameterless constructor, we will receive an error in the Visual Studio designer.

Our View sets its own `DataContext` property in XAML this time, using a `BindingPath` to the `UserViewModel` property from our `ViewModelLocator` resource. The property then utilizes our `DependencyManager` to resolve the concrete implementation of the `IUserViewModel` interface and return it for us.

There are other benefits to using this pattern as well though. One problem often faced by WPF developers is that the Visual Studio WPF Designer cannot resolve the interfaces that are used back to their concrete implementations, nor can it access the application data sources during design time. The result of this is that the designer does not typically display data items that cannot be resolved.

One thing that we can do with our `ViewModelLocator` is to provide mock View Models that have dummy data returned from their properties that we can use to help visualize our Views as we construct them. To achieve this, we can make use of the `IsInDesignMode` Attached Property from the `DesignerProperties` .NET class.

```
public bool IsDesignTime
{
  get { return
    DesignerProperties.GetIsInDesignMode(new DependencyObject()); }
}
```

The `DependencyObject` object here is required by the Attached Property and in fact, is the object that is being checked. As all objects supplied here would return the same value, we are free to use a new one each time. If we are concerned that this property will be called more frequently than the garbage collector, we could opt to use a single member instead, just for this purpose.

```
private DependencyObject dependencyObject = new DependencyObject();

public bool IsDesignTime
{
```

```
    get { return DesignerProperties.GetIsInDesignMode(dependencyObject); }
  }
```

However, if we need a `DependencyObject` object just for this purpose, then we could simplify things further by extending our `ViewModelLocator` class from the `DependencyObject` class and use itself as the required parameter. Of course, this would mean that our class would inherit unwanted properties, so some might prefer to avoid doing this. Let's see how we could use this property to provide the WPF Designer with mock data at design time:

```
using System.ComponentModel;
using System.Windows;
using CompanyName.ApplicationName.Managers;
using CompanyName.ApplicationName.ViewModels;
using CompanyName.ApplicationName.ViewModels.Interfaces;

namespace CompanyName.ApplicationName.Views.ViewModelLocators
{
  public class ViewModelLocator : DependencyObject
  {
    public bool IsDesignTime
    {
      get { return DesignerProperties.GetIsInDesignMode(this); }
    }

    public IUserViewModel UserViewModel
    {
      get
      {
        return IsDesignTime ? new MockUserViewModel() :
          DependencyManager.Instance.Resolve<IUserViewModel>();
      }
    }
  }
}
```

If you look at our `UserViewModel` property, you'll see the value that we return is now dependent upon the value of the `IsDesignTime` property. If we are in design time, for example when the View file is open in the WPF Designer, then the `MockUserViewModel` class will be returned. At runtime however, the concrete implementation of our `IUserViewModel` interface that we registered with the `DependencyManager` will be returned instead.

The `MockUserViewModel` class will typically hardcode some mock data and return it from its properties when requested. In this manner, the WPF Designer will be able to visualize the data for the developers or designers, while they build the Views.

However, each View will require a new property in our locator class and we'll need to copy this conditional operator statement from the preceding code for each. As always in OOP, there is a further abstraction that we could make to hide that implementation away from the developers that will use our framework. We could create a generic base class for our View Model Locator.

```
using System.ComponentModel;
using System.Windows;
using CompanyName.ApplicationName.Managers;

namespace CompanyName.ApplicationName.Views.ViewModelLocators
{
  public abstract class BaseViewModelLocator<T> : DependencyObject
    where T : class
  {
    private T runtimeViewModel, designTimeViewModel;

    protected bool IsDesignTime
    {
      get { return DesignerProperties.GetIsInDesignMode(this); }
    }

    public T ViewModel
    {
      get { return IsDesignTime ?
        DesignTimeViewModel : RuntimeViewModel; }
    }

    protected T RuntimeViewModel
    {
      get { return runtimeViewModel ??
        (runtimeViewModel = DependencyManager.Instance.Resolve<T>()); }
    }

    protected T DesignTimeViewModel
    {
      set { designTimeViewModel = value; }
      get { return designTimeViewModel; }
    }
  }
}
```

We start by declaring an abstract class that takes a generic type parameter, which represents the interface type of the View Model that we are trying to locate. Once again, note the generic type constraint declared on the generic type parameter that specifies that the type used must be a class. This is now required because this class calls the `Resolve` method of the `DependencyManager` class and that has the same constraint declared upon it.

We have two internal members of the relevant type of View Model interface, which back the properties with the same names. There's one for our runtime View Model and one for our design time View Model. The third View Model property of the same type is the one that we will data bind to from the Views and it uses our `IsDesignTime` property to determine which View Model to return.

A nice touch in this class is that it does a lot of the connection work for the developers. They don't need to concern themselves with the implementation of the `IsDesignTime` property and this base class will even attempt to automatically resolve the concrete View Model dependency for the runtime View Model property. Therefore, the developer need only declare the following code for each View model to take advantage of this functionality:

```
using CompanyName.ApplicationName.ViewModels;
using CompanyName.ApplicationName.ViewModels.Interfaces;

namespace CompanyName.ApplicationName.Views.ViewModelLocators
{
  public class UserViewModelLocator : BaseViewModelLocator<IUserViewModel>
  {
    public UserViewModelLocator()
    {
      DesignTimeViewModel = new MockUserViewModel();
    }
  }
}
```

It could be setup in the UI with very little difference to our original locator version.

```
<UserControl x:Class="CompanyName.ApplicationName.Views.UserView"
  . . .
  <UserControl.Resources>
    <Locators:UserViewModelLocator x:Key="ViewModelLocator" />
  </UserControl.Resources>
  <UserControl.DataContext>
    <Binding Path="ViewModel" Source="{StaticResource ViewModelLocator}" />
  </UserControl.DataContext>
  . . .
</UserControl>
```

Note that although this should work automatically in newer versions of Visual Studio, you may need to provide a helping hand to the WPF Designer in older versions. The d XML namespace is used by the Designer and so we can specify a `DataContext` location to it directly at design time.

```
mc:Ignorable="d" Height="30" Width="300"
   d:DataContext="{Binding ViewModel,
   Source={StaticResource ViewModelLocator}}"
```

While there is a clear benefit to this arrangement, as always, we have to weigh up whether the cost of any such abstractions will be worth the benefits. For some, the cost of extracting an interface, declaring a mock version of it to use at design time and creating a View Model Locator for each View Model will definitely be worth the benefit of designing Views that visualize their data.

For others, it simply won't be worth it. Each time we add a level of abstraction, we have more work to achieve to arrive at the same end goal. We need to decide whether each abstraction is viable in our own situations and build our application frameworks accordingly.

Summary

We've now investigated the benefit of having an application framework and started constructing our own. We've discovered a variety of different ways to encapsulate our required functionality into our framework and know which situations to use each in. After exploring a number of manager classes, we have also begun to expose functionality from external sources, but without being tied to them.

We've managed to maintain and improve the Separation of Concerns that our application requires and should now be able to detach the various application components and run them independently of each other. We are also able to provide our View designers with mock data at design-time, while maintaining loose coupling at runtime.

In the next chapter, we will thoroughly examine the essential topic of data binding, one of the very few requirements of the MVVM pattern. We'll comprehensively cover the wide variety of binding syntax, both long and short hand notation, discover why bindings fail to work at certain times and get a better understanding of how to display our data exactly the way we want.

4

Becoming Proficient with Data Binding

In this chapter, we'll investigate the data binding syntax that is used to connect our data sources to our UI controls. We'll examine how to declare Dependency Properties, along with all of the various options that we have when doing that. We'll find out about the scope of declared bindings and unravel the finer details of data templates. Let's start at the beginning.

It is the data binding in the WPF that enables it to work so well with the MVVM pattern. It provides the connection for two-way communication between the View and the View Models components. Yet this abstraction can often lead to confusion and make tracking down problems more difficult than when using traditional methods of UI to business logic communication.

As data binding is such an important part of the MVVM pattern, we'll cover this topic thoroughly, from the basics to advanced concepts. We'll ensure that we are able to fulfil any binding requirements that we may receive.

Data binding basics

In WPF, we use the `Binding` class to create our bindings. In general, it is fair to say that every binding will contain four constituent parts. The first is the binding source; typically, this will be one of our View Models. The second is the path to the property from the source object that we would like to data bind to.

The third is the binding target; this will typically be a UI control. The fourth is the path to the property of the binding target that we want to bind to. Therefore, if one of our bindings do not work, it is most likely that one of these four things has not been set correctly.

It is important to stress that the target property will typically be from a UI control, because there is a data binding rule that states that the binding target must be a Dependency Property. The properties of most UI controls are Dependency Properties and so, this rule simply enforces that data normally travels in the direction from our View Model data sources to the binding target UI controls.

We'll examine the direction of data bound data traversal later in the chapter, but let's first focus on the syntax that is used to specify the value of the `Binding.Path` property.

Binding path syntax

Bindings can be declared either in longhand, defining an actual `Binding` element in the XAML, or in shorthand, using the markup language that is translated to a `Binding` element for us by the XAML. We'll primarily focus on the shorthand notation, as that is what we will predominantly use throughout the book.

The `Binding.Path` property is of type `PropertyPath`. This type supports a unique syntax that can be expressed in XAML using an XAML markup extension. While it can be confusing at times, there are specific rules that we can learn to make it easier. Let's investigate.

To start with, let's understand that the binding path is relative to the binding source and that the binding source is typically set by the `DataContext` property, or by the path itself. In order to bind to the whole binding source, we can specify our binding like this:

```
{Binding Path=.}
```

It can also be specified like this:

```
{Binding .}
```

Most simply, we can specify our binding like this:

```
{Binding}
```

Note that explicitly declaring the `Path` property name in this syntax is optional, when the path value is declared first. The three preceding examples are all equal. We will omit the `Path` property declaration in the bindings in this book for brevity. Let's now see the remaining property path syntax mini-language.

To data bind to most property paths, we use the same notation as we use in code. For example, when binding directly to the property of a data bound object, we just use the property name.

```
{Binding PropertyName}
```

To data bind to the property of an object that is directly referenced by a property of our binding source, we again use the same syntax that we do in code. This is known as **indirect property targeting**.

```
{Binding PropertyName.AnotherPropertyName}
```

Similarly, when data binding to an item in a collection, or a property of a collection item, we use the indexing notation from code. For example, this is how we access a property from the first item in our data bound binding source.

```
{Binding [0].PropertyName}
```

Of course, if we want to access the second item, we use a key of 1 and use a key value of 2 if we want the third item and so on. Likewise, to indirectly target a property of a collection item, where the collection is a property of our binding source, we use the following syntax.:

```
{Binding CollectionPropertyName[0].PropertyName}
```

As you can see, we are freely able to combine these various syntactical options to generate more complex binding paths. Multi-dimensional collections are also accessed in the same way as we refer to them in code.

```
{Binding CollectionPropertyName[0, 0].PropertyName}
{Binding CollectionPropertyName[0, 0, 0].PropertyName}
. . .
```

While discussing data binding to collections, note that there is a special forward slash (/) syntax that we can use to access the selected item at any time.

```
{Binding CollectionPropertyName/PropertyName}
```

This particular example would bind to the `PropertyName` property of the current item of the collection specified by the `CollectionPropertyName` property. Let's take a quick look at a more practical example:

```
<StackPanel>
  <ListBox ItemsSource="{Binding Users}"
    IsSynchronizedWithCurrentItem="True" />
  <TextBlock Text="Selected User's Name:" />
  <TextBlock Text="{Binding Users/Name}" />
</StackPanel>
```

In this basic example using our `UsersViewModel`, we data bind the `Users` collection to a listbox. Underneath, we output the value of the `Name` property from the currently selected item. Note the setting of the `IsSynchronizedWithCurrentItem` property, as without it, this forward slash binding would not work correctly.

Try removing the `IsSynchronizedWithCurrentItem` property from the example and running the application again and you will see that the current user's name will be output initially, but not updated after changes to the selected item.

Setting this property to `True` will ensure that the `ItemCollection.CurrentItem` property from the `ListBox.Items` collection is updated each time the selection changes. Note that we could also achieve this same output using the `ListBox.SelectedItem` property instead of this forward slash notation.

```
<StackPanel>
  <ListBox Name="ListBox" ItemsSource="{Binding Users}"
    IsSynchronizedWithCurrentItem="True" />
  <TextBlock Text="Selected User's Name:" />
  <TextBlock Text="{Binding SelectedItem.Name, ElementName=ListBox}" />
</StackPanel>
```

The `IsSynchronizedWithCurrentItem` property is now not needed to update the selected user's name in the `TextBlock`, because the `SelectedItem` property will take care of that. However, setting it to `True` in this case will ensure that the first item in the `ListBox` is selected and that the `TextBlock` will initially output the name of that item's user. Let's continue looking at the forward slash notation.

If you are trying to data bind to a property of an item in a collection where, the collection is itself an item of a parent collection, we can use the forward slash notation multiple times in a single binding path.

```
{Binding CollectionPropertyName/InnerCollectionPropertyName/PropertyName}
```

To clarify, this path would bind to the `PropertyName` property of the selected item of the collection specified by the `InnerCollectionPropertyName` property, which itself is the selected item of the collection specified by the `CollectionPropertyName` property.

Let's move on from collections now, to Attached Properties. In order to data bind to an Attached Property, we need to use a slightly different syntax from that used in code; we need to enclose the property name in parenthesis, along with the class name.

```
{Binding (ClassName.PropertyName)}
```

Note that when the Attached Property is a custom-declared property, we must include the XML namespace prefix inside the parenthesis with its separating colon.

```
{Binding (XmlNamespacePrefix:ClassName.PropertyName)}
```

Typically, when binding to Attached Properties, we also need to specify the binding target as well as the target property. The binding target will generally either be the object that the binding is set on, or another UI element, so we tend to see the `RelativeSource` or `ElementName` properties being used in these situations.

```
{Binding Path=(Attached:TextBoxProperties.Label),
    RelativeSource={RelativeSource AncestorType={x:Type TextBox}}}
```

We'll see an extended version of this example later in the book, but in short, it binds to the `TextBoxProperties.Label` Attached Property of the parent control of type `TextBox`. It is called from within a `ControlTemplate` and so, the parent textbox is the templated parent of the control that is being data bound.

Escaping invalid characters

When using the `PropertyPath` syntax mini-language, there may be the odd occasion when we need to escape certain characters that are used in the syntax. In general, the backslash (\) is used as the escape character and the only characters that we need to escape are as follows.

The most common character that we may need to escape in our bind paths is the closing curly bracket (}), which signals the end of a markup section. Also, if you need to use an actual backslash in your binding path, then you must escape it by preceding it with another backslash.

The only two other characters that we need to escape are the equals sign (=) and the comma character (,), which are both used to define binding paths. All other characters that we are likely to use in a binding path are deemed to be valid.

Note that there is a special character to use if we need to escape a character when inside an indexer binding expression. In these cases, instead of using the backslash character, we need to use the caret character (^) as the escape character.

Also note that when explicitly declaring bindings in XAML, we need to escape the ampersand (&) and the greater than sign (>) by replacing them with their XML Entity forms. If you need to use these characters, then replace the ampersand with & and replace the greater than sign with >.

Exploring the Binding class

The `Binding` class has more properties than we have space to discuss here, but we'll cover the most important ones in detail shortly, and briefly look at other notable properties momentarily. The `Binding` class is the top-level class in each binding, but internally it uses a lower-level class that maintains the connection between the binding source and binding target.

The `BindingExpression` class is that underlying object. When using MVVM, developers do not typically access this inner class, as we tend to keep our functionality in our View Models. However, if we are writing custom controls, then it can be useful to be aware of it.

It can be used to programmatically update the associated binding source in certain circumstances and we'll find out about that later in the chapter. For now, let's focus on what the `Binding` class can do for us.

In .NET 4.5, a great new property was added to the `Binding` class. The `Delay` property enables us to specify an amount of time in milliseconds with which to delay the update of the binding source after a change has been made to the binding target property value.

This is really useful if we are performing some heavy computational validation or other processing dependent upon the user's input in a textbox for example. To clarify this functionality further, this delay is actually restarted each time the data bound property value changes, or each key press in our example. It is typically used to update the binding source in chunks, each time the user pauses, or completes typing, somewhat like buffering.

```
<TextBox Text="{Binding Description,
    UpdateSourceTrigger=PropertyChanged, Delay=400}" />
```

The `FallbackValue` property is another useful property when it comes to performance. In order to return a value from each binding, the WPF Framework does up to four things. The first is to simply validate the target property type with the data bound value. If successful, it will then try to resolve the binding path.

Most of the time, this will work, but if not, it will then attempt to find a converter to return the value. If it can't find one, or it returns the `DependencyProperty.UnsetValue` value, it will then look to see if the `FallbackValue` property has a value to provide it with. If there is no fallback value, then a lookup is required to find the default value of the target Dependency Property.

By setting the `FallbackValue` property, we can do two things to improve performance, albeit in a slight way. The first is that, it will stop the WPF Framework from performing the lookup of the default value of the target Dependency Property. The second is that it will prevent trace statements from being fed to the **Output** window in Visual Studio and to any other trace outputs that have been setup.

The `TargetNullValue` property is similar to the `FallbackValue` property in that it enables us to provide some output when there is no data bound value from the binding source. The difference is that the `FallbackValue` property value is output when a data bound value cannot be resolved, while the `TargetNullValue` property value is used when the successfully resolved data bound value is null.

We can use this functionality to display a more humanized value than 'null', or even to provide a default message in our textbox controls for example. To do this, we could set our data bound string properties to null and set a suitable value to the `TargetNullValue` property.

```
<TextBox Text="{Binding Name, TargetNullValue='Please enter your name'}" />
```

Of course, this 'message' will actually appear in the textbox, so it's not an ideal way of providing this functionality. We'll see a better example of this later in the book, but now let's continue our exploration of the `Binding` class.

If you have any properties in your View Model that access their data asynchronously, or if they are calculated by a heavy computational process, then we need to set the `IsAsync` method to `True` on the binding.

```
<Image Source="{Binding InternetSource, IsAsync=True,
    FallbackValue='pack://application:,,,/CompanyName.ApplicationName;
    component/Images/Default.png'}" />
```

This stops the UI from being blocked while waiting for the data bound property to be calculated, or otherwise resolved. Until the binding source is resolved, the fallback value is used if set, or the default value will be used if not. In this example, we are providing a default image to be displayed until the actual image is downloaded from the internet and the binding source is resolved.

Another useful property of the `Binding` class is the `StringFormat` property. As the name hints, this uses the `string.Format` method internally to format our data bound text output. There are however, a few caveats to using this functionality. The first is that we can obviously only use a single format item, that represents the single data bound value in a normal binding. We'll find out how to use multiple values later in the chapter.

Secondly, we need to declare our format carefully, as curly brackets are used by the markup extensions and we cannot use the double quote characters ("), as the binding is already declared within double quotes. One solution is to use single quotes.

```
<TextBlock Text="{Binding Price, StringFormat='{0:C2}'}" />
```

Another option is to escape the format by using a pair of curly brackets before it.

```
<TextBlock Text="{Binding Price, StringFormat={}{0:C2}}" />
```

Most of the useful binding properties have now been discussed here, but it should be noted that there are a number of properties in the `Binding` class that are not typically used when building a WPF application with MVVM. This is because they involve event handlers and we do not normally implement event handlers when using MVVM.

For example, the three `NotifyOnSourceUpdated`, `NotifyOnTargetUpdated`, and `NotifyOnValidationError` properties relate to the raising of the `Binding.SourceUpdated`, `Binding.TargetUpdated` and `Validation.Error` Attached Events.

Likewise, the three `ValidatesOnDataErrors`, `ValidatesOnExceptions`, `ValidatesOnNotifyDataErrors` and `ValidationRules` properties all relate to the use of the `ValidationRule` class. This is a very UI-related way of validating, but this puts our business logic right into our Views component.

When using MVVM, we want to avoid this blending of components. We therefore tend to work with data elements rather than UI elements and so, we perform these kind of duties in our Data Model and/or View Model classes instead. We'll see this in Chapter 8, *Implementing Responsive Data Validation* later in the book, but now let's take a deeper look at the most important properties of the `Binding` class.

Directing data bound traffic

The direction of data traversal in each binding is specified by the `Binding.Mode` property. There are four distinct directional instances declared in the `BindingMode` enumeration, plus an additional value. Let's first take a look at the directional values and what they represent.

The first and most common value reflects the most common situation, where data flows from the binding source, say one of our View Models, to the binding target represented by a UI control. This binding mode is called **One-Way** and is specified by the `OneWay` enumeration instance. This mode is used primarily for display only, or read-only purposes and situations where the data bound values cannot be altered in the UI.

The next most common direction of travel is represented by the `TwoWay` enumeration instance and signifies that data is free to travel both from our View Models to the UI controls and also in the opposite direction. This is the most commonly used mode when data binding to form controls, when we want the users' changes to be reflected in our View Models.

The third directional enumeration instance is the `OneWayToSource` instance and is the opposite to the `OneWay` instance. That is, it specifies that data can only travel from the binding target, represented by a UI control, to the binding source, for example, one of our View Models. This mode is also useful for capturing user inputted date, when we don't need to alter the data bound values.

The final directional instance is similar to the `OneWay` instance, except that it only works once, and is represented by the `OneTime` instance. While this mode will indeed only work one time upon instantiation of its containing control, it will actually update its value each time the `DataContext` property of the relevant binding is set.

The final instance is named `Default` and as the name hints, is the default value of the `Binding.Mode` enumeration. It directs the binding to use the binding mode that was declared from the specified target property. When each Dependency Property is declared, we can specify whether a One or **Two-Way** binding mode should be used by default. If this is not specifically declared, then the property will be assigned a One-Way mode. We'll see this explained in more detail later in this chapter.

Binding to different sources

We generally set the binding source using the `FrameworkElement.DataContext` property. All UI controls extend the `FrameworkElement` class, so we can set our binding sources on any of them. This must be set for a binding to work, although it can be specified in the `Path` property, or inherited from ancestor controls, so it does not have to be explicitly set. Take a look at this simple example that assumes that a suitable binding source has been correctly set on the parent control:

```
<StackPanel>
  <TextBlock DataContext="{Binding User}" Text="{Binding Name}" />
  <TextBlock DataContext="{Binding User}" Text="{Binding Age}" />
</StackPanel>
```

Here, we set the binding source of the first `TextBlock` to a `User` object and the path to the `Name` property from that source. The second is set likewise, but with the binding source path pointing to the `Age` property instead. Note that we have set the `DataContext` property to a `User` object on each `TextBox` control individually.

While this is perfectly valid XAML, you can imagine how tiresome it would be to do this on every control that we want to data bind to in a large form. As such, we tend to take advantage of the fact that the `DataContext` property can inherit its value from any of its ancestor controls. In this way, we can simplify this code by setting the `DataContext` on the parent control instead.

```
<StackPanel DataContext="{Binding User}">
  <TextBlock Text="{Binding Name}" />
  <TextBlock Text="{Binding Age}" />
</StackPanel>
```

In fact, when developing each `Window` or `UserControl`, it is customary to set the `DataContext` on these top-level controls, so that every contained control will have access to the same binding source. This is why we create a View Model for each `Window` or `UserControl` and specify that each View Model is responsible for providing all of the data and functionality that its related View requires.

There are a few alternative ways of specifying a binding source, other than setting the `DataContext` property. One way is to use the `Source` property of the binding and this enables us to explicitly override the binding source that is inherited from the parent `DataContext`, if one was set. Using the `Source` property, we are also able to data bind to resources, as we saw in our View Model Locator example, or static values, as shown in the following snippet:

```
<TextBlock Text="{Binding Source={x:Static System:DateTime.Today},
    Mode=OneTime, StringFormat='{}© {0:yyyy} CompanyName'}" />
```

Another way involves the use of the `RelativeSource` property of the binding. Using this incredibly useful property of type `RelativeSource`, we can specify that we want to use the target control, or a parent of that control as the binding source.

It also enables us to override the binding source from the `DataContext` and is often essential when trying to data bind to View Model properties from `DataTemplate` elements. Let's adjust the earlier `DataTemplate` for our `User` Data Model to output a property from its normal `DataContext` that is set by the `DataTemplate`, and one from the View Model that is set as the `DataContext` of the parent control, using the `AncestorType` property of the `RelativeSource` class.

```
<DataTemplate DataType="{x:Type DataModels:User}">
  <StackPanel>
    <TextBlock Text="{Binding Name}" />
    <TextBlock Text="{Binding DataContext.UserCount,
      RelativeSource={RelativeSource Mode=FindAncestor,
      AncestorType={x:Type Views:UserView}}}" />
  </StackPanel>
</DataTemplate>
```

Note that setting the `Mode` property, that specifies the relative position of the binding source compared to the binding target, is optional here. Using the `AncestorType` property implicitly sets the `Mode` property to the `FindAncestor` instance, so we can declare the same binding without it, like this:

```
<TextBlock Text="{Binding DataContext.UserCount,
  RelativeSource={RelativeSource
  AncestorType={x:Type Views:UserView}}}" />
```

The `Mode` property is of the `RelativeSourceMode` enumeration type, which has four members. We've already seen an example of one instance, the `FindAncestor` member, although this can be extended using the related `RelativeSource.AncestorLevel` property, which specifies which level of ancestor in which to look for the binding source. This property is only really useful if a control has multiple ancestors of the same type, as in this following simplified example:

```
<StackPanel Tag="Outer">
  ...
  <StackPanel Orientation="Horizontal" Tag="Inner">
    <TextBlock Text="{Binding Tag, RelativeSource={RelativeSource
      Mode=FindAncestor, AncestorType={x:Type StackPanel},
      AncestorLevel=2}}" />
    ...
  </StackPanel>
</StackPanel>
```

The `TextBox` in this example will output the word `"Outer"` at runtime, because we have declared that the binding source should be the second ancestor of type `StackPanel`. If the `AncestorLevel` property had been set to one, or omitted from the binding, then the `TextBox` would output the word `"Inner"` at runtime.

The next `RelativeSourceMode` enumeration instance is `Self`, which specifies that the binding source is the same object as the binding target. Note that when using the `RelativeSource.Self` property, the `Mode` property is implicitly set to the `Self` instance. We could use this property to data bind one property of a UI control to another, as in this following example that sets the control's width value to its `Height` property to ensure that it remains a square regardless of the width.

```
<Rectangle Height="{Binding ActualWidth,
  RelativeSource={RelativeSource Self}}" Fill="Red" />
```

The `RelativeSource.TemplatedParent` property is only used to access the properties of controls from inside a `ControlTemplate`. The templated parent refers to the object that has the `ControlTemplate` applied to it. When using the `TemplatedParent` property, the `Mode` property is implicitly set to the `TemplatedParent` instance of the `RelativeSourceMode` enumeration. Let's see an example.

```
<ControlTemplate x:Key="ProgressBar" TargetType="{x:Type ProgressBar}">
  ...
  <TextBlock Text="{Binding Value,
    RelativeSource={RelativeSource TemplatedParent}}" />
  ...
</ControlTemplate>
```

In this example, the templated parent is the instance of the `ProgressBar` that will have this template applied to it and so, using the `TemplatedParent` property, we are able to access the various properties of the `ProgressBar` class from within the `ControlTemplate`. Furthermore, any binding source that is data bound to the `Value` property of the templated parent will also be data bound to the `Text` property of this internal `TextBox` element.

Moving on to the final `RelativeSource` property, `PreviousData` is only really useful when defining a `DataTemplate` for items in a collection. It is used to set the previous item in the collection as the binding source. While not often used, there can be situations where we need to compare values between neighboring items in a collection and we'll see a full example of this later in this chapter.

Although a far simpler option, the `ElementName` property of the `Binding` class also enables us to override the binding source set by the `DataContext`. It is used to data bind the property of one UI control to either the property of another control, or another property on the same control. The only requirement to use this property is that we need to name the element that we want to data bind to in our current control. Let's see an example.

```
<StackPanel Orientation="Horizontal" TextElement.FontSize="24" Margin="20">
  <CheckBox Name="Checkbox" Content="Service" Margin="0,0,10,0" />
  <TextBox Text="{Binding Service}"
    Visibility="{Binding IsChecked, ElementName=Checkbox,
    Converter={StaticResource BoolToVisibilityConverter}}" />
</StackPanel>
```

In this example, we have a service `CheckBox` and a `TextBlock`. The `Visibility` property of the `TextBlock` is data bound to the `IsChecked` property of the `CheckBox` and we make use of the `BoolToVisibilityConverter` class that we saw earlier to convert the `bool` value to a `Visibility` instance. Therefore, when the user checks the checkbox, the textbox will become visible and vice versa.

The `ElementName` property can also be used as a shortcut to accessing the parent control's `DataContext`. If we name our View `This` for example, then we can use the `ElementName` property from within a data template to data bind to a property from the parent View Model.

```
<DataTemplate DataType="{x:Type DataModels:User}">
  <StackPanel>
    <TextBlock Text="{Binding Name}" />
    <TextBlock Text="{Binding DataContext.UserCount, ElementName=This}" />
  </StackPanel>
</DataTemplate>
```

When specifying these alternative binding sources, it is important to know that we can only use one of these three different methods at once. If we were to set more than one of the binding `Source`, `RelativeSource`, or `ElementName` properties, then an exception would be thrown from the binding.

Binding with priority

On the odd occasion, we may need to specify a number of source binding paths and want to map them to a single binding target property. One way that we can do this is to use the `MultiBinding` class and we'll see an example of this in the last section of this chapter. However, there is an alternative class that we can use that provides us with some additional functionality.

The `PriorityBinding` class enables us to specify multiple bindings and gives each a priority, with the bindings that are declared first having the highest priority. The special functionality of this class is that it will display the value from the first binding that returns a valid value and if that is not the binding with the highest priority, it will then update the display with the value from the highest priority binding when it is successfully resolved.

To clarify further, this enables us to specify a binding to a normal property that will resolve immediately, while the actual value that we want to data bind to is being downloaded, calculated, or otherwise being resolved over time. This enables us to supply a default image source while the actual required image is being downloaded, or to output a message until a calculated value is ready for display. Let's look at a simple XAML example.

```
<TextBlock>
  <TextBlock.Text>
    <PriorityBinding>
      <Binding Path="SlowString" IsAsync="True" />
      <Binding Path="FastString" Mode="OneWay" />
    </PriorityBinding>
  </TextBlock.Text>
</TextBlock>
```

In the preceding example, we set the `PriorityBinding` on the `TextBlock.Text` property and inside, specify two bindings. The first has the higher priority and has the actual property value that we want to display. Note that we set the `IsAsync` property to `True`, to specify that this binding will take some time to resolve and that it should not block the UI thread.

The second binding is data bound to a normal property using a One-Way binding that simply outputs a message.

```
public string FastString
{
  get { return "The value is being calculated..."; }
}
```

By using the `PriorityBinding` element, this message will be output instantly and then updated with the actual value from the `SlowString` property when it is ready. Let's now move on and investigate one further type of `Binding` class.

Binding from within control templates

A `TemplateBinding` is a particular type of binding that is used within `ControlTemplate` elements in order to data bind to the properties of the type that is being templated. It is very similar to the `RelativeSource.TemplatedParent` property that we discussed earlier. It's a way to connect the properties of elements inside a `ControlTemplate` to the properties of elements outside the template.

```
<ControlTemplate x:Key="ProgressBar" TargetType="{x:Type ProgressBar}">
   ...
   <TextBlock Text="{TemplateBinding Value}" />
   ...
</ControlTemplate>
```

In this example from earlier that we edited slightly, we see that declaring a `TemplateBinding` is far more straightforward and less verbose than performing the same binding using the `RelativeSource.TemplatedParent` property. Let's remind ourselves what that looked like.

```
<TextBlock Text="{Binding Value,
    RelativeSource={RelativeSource TemplatedParent}}" />
```

It is generally preferable to use a `TemplateBinding` instead of the `RelativeSource.TemplatedParent` property and although they perform the same connection in the binding, there are a few differences between them. For example, a `TemplateBinding` is evaluated at compile time, whereas `TemplateBinding` is not evaluated until runtime. It can therefore also make it easier to work with.

Furthermore, it is a simpler form of binding and is missing a number of the `Binding` class properties, such as `StringFormat` and `Delay`. In addition, it places the extra constraints on the user, that it is permanently set to have a binding mode of `OneWay` and both binding target *and* binding source must be Dependency Properties. It was designed to be used in a single place with a single purpose and in that situation, it does its job well and more efficiently than its counterpart.

Binding source changes

At times, we may need to make changes to our binding sources and have those changes propagate to the binding target controls. We may want to set default values on a new form, clear old form values, or even set form labels from our View Models. In order to do this, our View Models *must* implement the `INotifyPropertyChanged` interface and this is why we build this implementation into our base View Model class.

When we data bind a binding source to a control in the UI, an event handler is attached to the `PropertyChanged` event of the source object. When a notification of a change to the property that is specified by the binding source property path is received, the control is updated with the new value.

It should be noted that the `PropertyChanged` event of the binding source will be null if no handler has specifically been attached and none of its properties have been data bound to UI controls. It is for this reason that we must always check for null, before raising this event.

All of the binding modes work in the direction of binding source to binding target, except for the `OneWayToSource` instance. However, only this and the `TwoWay` instance of the `Binding.Mode` enumeration propagate changes in the direction of the binding target to the binding source.

When the binding is working in either of these modes, it attaches a handler to the target control to listen for changes to the target property. When it receives notification of a change to the target property, its behavior is determined by the value of the binding's `UpdateSourceTrigger` property.

This property is of the enumeration type `UpdateSourceTrigger`, which has four members. The most common is the `PropertyChanged` instance and this specifies that the source property should be updated as soon as the target property has changed. This is the default value for most controls.

The `LostFocus` member is the next most common value and this specifies that the binding should update the binding source when the user moves focus from the data bound control. This option can be useful when we want to trigger validation once the user has completed entry in each textbox, rather than as they type.

The `Explicit` instance will not update the binding source without explicit instruction to do so. As we need to programmatically call the `UpdateSource` method of the internal `BindingExpression` object in order to propagate the changes to the binding source, this option is not generally used in our normal Views.

Instead, if used at all, we would find it in our `CustomControl` classes. Note that calling the `UpdateSource` method will do nothing if the binding mode is not set to one of the `OneWayToSource` or `TwoWay` instances.

If we had an instance of a textbox and we wanted to explicitly update the binding source that was data bound to its `Text` property, we can access the lower-level `BindingExpression` object from the `BindingOperations.GetBindingExpression` method and call its `UpdateSource` method.

```
BindingExpression bindingExpression =
    BindingOperations.GetBindingExpression(textBox, TextBox.TextProperty);
bindingExpression.UpdateSource();
```

Alternatively, if our binding target control class extends the `FrameworkElement` class and most do, then we can simply call the `GetBindingExpression` method on it directly and pass in the Dependency Property key that we want to update the binding from.

```
textBox.GetBindingExpression(TextBox.TextProperty);
```

The last member of the `UpdateSourceTrigger` enumeration is the `Default` instance. This is similar to the `Default` instance of the `Binding.Mode` enumeration in that it uses the value specified by each target Dependency Property and is the default value of the `UpdateSourceTrigger` property. Again, we'll find out how to set the metadata for Dependency Properties later in this chapter.

Converting data bound values

There are many times when developing a WPF application, when we need to convert a data bound property value to a different type. For example, we might want to control the visibility of some UI elements with a `bool` property in our View Model, so that we can avoid having the UI-related `Visibility` enumeration instance in it.

We might want to convert different enumeration members to different `Brush` objects, or collections to string representations of the contained collection items. We've already seen a number of examples of the `IValueConverter` interface, but let's now take a bit more of a thorough look.

```
public interface IValueConverter
{
   object Convert(object value, Type targetType, object parameter,
      CultureInfo culture);
   object ConvertBack(object value, Type targetType, object parameter,
      CultureInfo culture);
}
```

As we've already seen, the `value` input parameter of type `object` is the data bound value of the binding. The `object` return type relates to the converted value that we want to return. The `targetType` input parameter specifies the type of the binding target property and is typically used to validate the input value to ensure that the converter is being used with the expected type of data.

The `parameter` input parameter is optionally used to pass an additional value through to the converter. If used, its value can be set using the `Binding.ConverterParameter` property. Finally, the `culture` input parameter provides us with a `CultureInfo` object to correctly format textual output, when working in a culturally-sensitive application. We'll return to this in a moment, but let's first look at an example of a converter that uses the `parameter` input parameter.

```
using System;
using System.Globalization;
using System.Windows;
using System.Windows.Data;

namespace CompanyName.ApplicationName.Converters
{
   [ValueConversion(typeof(Enum), typeof(bool))]
   public class EnumToBoolConverter : IValueConverter
   {
      public bool IsInverted { get; set; }

      public object Convert(object value, Type targetType, object parameter,
         CultureInfo culture)
      {
         if (value == null || parameter == null || (value.GetType() !=
            typeof(Enum) && value.GetType().BaseType != typeof(Enum)))
            return DependencyProperty.UnsetValue;
         string enumValue = value.ToString();
         string targetValue = parameter.ToString();
```

```
      bool boolValue = enumValue.Equals(targetValue,
        StringComparison.InvariantCultureIgnoreCase);
      return IsInverted ? !boolValue : boolValue;
    }

    public object ConvertBack(object value, Type targetType,
      object parameter, CultureInfo culture)
    {
      if (value == null || parameter == null)
        return DependencyProperty.UnsetValue;
      bool boolValue = (bool)value;
      string targetValue = parameter.ToString();
      if ((boolValue && !IsInverted) || (!boolValue && IsInverted))
        return Enum.Parse(targetType, targetValue);
      return DependencyProperty.UnsetValue;
    }
  }
}
```

The idea of this converter is that we can data bind an enumeration property to a `RadioButton` or `CheckBox` control that specifies the name of a particular member. If the value of the data bound property matches the specified member, then the converter will return true and check the control. For all other enumeration members, the control will be unchecked. We could then specify a different member in each of a group of `RadioButton` controls, so that each member could be set.

In the class, we start by specifying the data types that are involved in the implementation of the converter in the `ValueConversion` attribute. Next, we see the `IsInverted` property that we saw in the `BaseVisibilityConverter` class that enables us to invert the output of the converter.

In the `Convert` method, we first check the validity of our `value` and `parameter` input parameters, and return the `DependencyProperty.UnsetValue` value if either are invalid. For valid values, we convert both parameters to their string representations. We then create a `bool` value by comparing the two string values. Once we have our `bool` value, we use it in conjunction with the `IsInverted` property to return the output value.

As with our other enumeration converter example, the `ConvertBack` method implementation is a little different again, as we are unable to return the correct enumeration instance for a false value; it could be any value except the value specified by the `parameter` input parameter.

As such, we are only able to return the specified enumeration instance if the data bound value is true and the `IsInverted` property is false, or if it is false and the `IsInverted` property is true. For all other input values, we simply return the `DependencyProperty.UnsetValue` property, which is preferred by the property system rather than the null value.

Let's see an example of this in use, with the `BitRate` enumeration that we saw in the previous chapter. Let's first look at the simple View Model.

```
using System.Collections.ObjectModel;
using CompanyName.ApplicationName.DataModels.Enums;
using CompanyName.ApplicationName.Extensions;

namespace CompanyName.ApplicationName.ViewModels
{
  public class BitRateViewModel : BaseViewModel
  {
    private ObservableCollection<BitRate> bitRates =
      new ObservableCollection<BitRate>();
    private BitRate bitRate = BitRate.Sixteen;

    public BitRateViewModel()
    {
      bitRates.FillWithMembers();
    }

    public ObservableCollection<BitRate> BitRates
    {
      get { return bitRates; }
      set { if (bitRates != value) { bitRates = value;
        NotifyPropertyChanged(); } }
    }

    public BitRate BitRate
    {
      get { return bitRate; }
      set { if (bitRate != value) { bitRate = value;
        NotifyPropertyChanged(); } }
    }
  }
}
```

This class just contains a collection of type `BitRate`, which will hold all possible members and a selection property of type `BitRate`, which we will data bind to the various `RadioButton` elements using our new converter. Note the use of the `FillWithMembers` Extension method in the constructor. Let's first see that:

```
public static void FillWithMembers<T>(this ICollection<T> collection)
{
  if (typeof(T).BaseType != typeof(Enum))
    throw new ArgumentException("The FillWithMembers<T> method can only be
    called with an enum as the generic type.");
  collection.Clear();
  foreach (string name in Enum.GetNames(typeof(T)))
    collection.Add((T)Enum.Parse(typeof(T), name));
}
```

In the `FillWithMembers` Extension method, we first check that the collection that the method is called on is of an enumeration type and throw an `ArgumentException` if it's not. We then clear the collection, in case it has any pre-existing items in it. Finally, we iterate through the result of the `Enum.GetNames` method, parsing each string name to the relevant enumeration member and casting it to the correct type, before adding it to the collection.

Let's now see the XAML for the View:

```
<UserControl x:Class="CompanyName.ApplicationName.Views.BitRateView"
  xmlns="http://schemas.microsoft.com/winfx/2006/xaml/presentation"
  xmlns:x="http://schemas.microsoft.com/winfx/2006/xaml"
  xmlns:mc="http://schemas.openxmlformats.org/markup-compatibility/2006"
  xmlns:d="http://schemas.microsoft.com/expression/blend/2008"
  xmlns:Converters="clr-namespace:CompanyName.ApplicationName.Converters;
    assembly=CompanyName.ApplicationName.Converters"
  mc:Ignorable="d" d:DesignHeight="60" d:DesignWidth="300">
  <UserControl.Resources>
    <Converters:EnumToBoolConverter x:Key="EnumToBoolConverter" />
  </UserControl.Resources>
  <GroupBox Header="Audio Quality" HorizontalAlignment="Left"
    VerticalAlignment="Top" Padding="5">
    <StackPanel>
      <RadioButton Content="16 bits" IsChecked="{Binding BitRate,
        Converter={StaticResource EnumToBoolConverter},
        ConverterParameter=Sixteen}" VerticalContentAlignment="Center" />
      <RadioButton Content="24 bits" IsChecked="{Binding BitRate,
        Converter={StaticResource EnumToBoolConverter}, ConverterParameter=
        TwentyFour}" VerticalContentAlignment="Center" />
      <RadioButton Content="32 bits" IsChecked="{Binding BitRate,
        Converter={StaticResource EnumToBoolConverter},
        ConverterParameter=ThirtyTwo}" VerticalContentAlignment="Center" />
    </StackPanel>
  </GroupBox>
</UserControl>
```

In this View, we setup the `Converters` XML namespace prefix and then declare an instance of the `EnumToBoolConverter` class in the `Resources` section. We then declare a `StackPanel` containing three `RadioButton` elements inside a `GroupBox`. Each `RadioButton` element is data bound to the same `BitRate` property from our View Model, using the converter from the resources.

Each button specifies a different enumeration member in its binding's `ConverterParameter` property and this is passed through to the converter in the `parameter` input parameter. If a `RadioButton` is checked, its true value is passed to the converter and converted to the value specified by its `ConverterParameter` value and the `BitRate` property is updated with that value. The output of this code looks like the following figure:

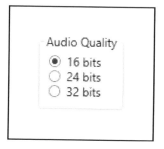

Note that if we had a large number of enumeration members, or the members were changed regularly, declaring each one manually in the UI like this example might not be such a good idea. In these cases, we could generate the same UI with less work, utilizing a `DataTemplate` object. We'll see an example of this later in this chapter, but for now, let's return to the input parameters of our converter.

The final input parameter in the `Convert` and `ConvertBack` methods is the `culture` parameter of type `CultureInfo`. In non-international applications, we can simply ignore this parameter, however if globalization plays a part in your application, then using this parameter is essential.

It enables us to correctly format any textual output that we may have in our converter using the `object.ToString` method and keep it in line with the rest of the text in the application. We can also use it in the various `Convert` class methods to ensure that numerals are also correctly output in the right format. Globalization is beyond the scope of this book and so we'll move on now.

Binding multiple sources to a single target property

In WPF, there is another, more common way to data bind to multiple binding sources at once and to perform some sort of conversion from the various values to a single output value. In order to achieve this, we need to use a `MultiBinding` object in conjunction with a class that implements the `IMultiValueConverter` interface.

The `MultiBinding` class enables us to declare multiple binding sources and a single binding target. If the `Mode` or `UpdateSourceTrigger` properties of the `MultiBinding` class are set, then their values are inherited by the contained `binding` elements, unless they have different values set explicitly.

The values from the multiple binding sources can be combined in one of two ways; their string representations can be output using the `StringFormat` property, or we can use a class that implements the `IMultiValueConverter` interface to generate the output value. This interface is very similar to the `IValueConverter` interface, but works with multiple data bound values instead.

When implementing the `IMultiValueConverter` interface, we do not set the `ValueConversion` attribute that we are accustomed to setting in the `IValueConverter` implementations that we have created.

In the `Convert` method that we need to implement, the `value` input parameter of type `object` from the `IValueConverter` interface is replaced by an object array named `values`, which contains our input values.

In the `ConvertBack` method, we have an array of type `Type` for the types of the binding targets and one of type `object` for the return types. Apart from these slight differences, these two interfaces are the same. Let's look at an example to help clarify the situation.

Imagine a scenario where a healthcare application needs to display a patient's weight measurements over time. It would be helpful if we could output an indicator of whether each consecutive measurement was higher or lower than the previous one, to highlight any unhealthy trends.

This can be implemented using the `RelativeSource.PreviousData` property mentioned earlier, a `MultiBinding` object and an `IMultiValueConverter` class. Let's first take a look at how we implement the `IMultiValueConverter` interface.

```
using System;
using System.Globalization;
using System.Windows;
using System.Windows.Data;

namespace CompanyName.ApplicationName.Converters
{
  public class HigherLowerConverter : IMultiValueConverter
  {
    public object Convert(object[] values, Type targetType,
      object parameter, CultureInfo culture)
    {
      if (values == null || values.Length != 2 || values[0] == null ||
        values[1] == null || values[0].GetType() != typeof(int) ||
        values[1].GetType() != typeof(int))
        return DependencyProperty.UnsetValue;
      int intValue = (int)values[0];
      int previousValue = (int)values[1];
      return intValue > previousValue ? "->" : "<-";
    }

    public object[] ConvertBack(object value, Type[] targetTypes,
      object parameter, CultureInfo culture)
    {
      return new object[2] { DependencyProperty.UnsetValue,
        DependencyProperty.UnsetValue };
    }
  }
}
```

We start our implementation with the customary validation of the input values. In this specific converter, we are expecting two values of type `int` and so verify that we have that before continuing. If valid, we cast our two values to `int` and compare them, returning the appropriate string based direction arrow, dependent on the result of the comparison.

As the `ConvertBack` method is not required for our example, we simply return an object array that contains two `DependencyProperty.UnsetValue` values. Let's take a quick look at our View Model next.

```
using System.Collections.Generic;

namespace CompanyName.ApplicationName.ViewModels
{
  public class WeightMeasurementsViewModel : BaseViewModel
  {
    private List<int> weights =
      new List<int>() { 90, 89, 92, 91, 94, 95, 98, 99, 101 };

    public List<int> Weights
    {
      get { return weights; }
      set { weights = value; NotifyPropertyChanged(); }
    }
  }
}
```

Here, we have a very simple View Model, with just one field and property pair. We've just hard coded a few test values to demonstrate with. Let's now take a look at our View.

```
<UserControl
  x:Class="CompanyName.ApplicationName.Views.WeightMeasurementsView"
  xmlns="http://schemas.microsoft.com/winfx/2006/xaml/presentation"
  xmlns:x="http://schemas.microsoft.com/winfx/2006/xaml"
  xmlns:mc="http://schemas.openxmlformats.org/markup-compatibility/2006"
  xmlns:d="http://schemas.microsoft.com/expression/blend/2008"
  xmlns:Converters="clr-namespace:CompanyName.ApplicationName.Converters;
    assembly=CompanyName.ApplicationName.Converters"
  xmlns:System="clr-namespace:System;assembly=mscorlib"
  mc:Ignorable="d" d:DesignHeight="90" d:DesignWidth="300">
  <UserControl.Resources>
    <Converters:HigherLowerConverter x:Key="HigherLowerConverter" />
  </UserControl.Resources>
  <Border BorderBrush="Black" BorderThickness="1" CornerRadius="5"
    HorizontalAlignment="Left" VerticalAlignment="Top">
    <ItemsControl ItemsSource="{Binding Weights}" Margin="20,20,0,20">
      <ItemsControl.ItemsPanel>
        <ItemsPanelTemplate>
          <StackPanel Orientation="Horizontal" />
        </ItemsPanelTemplate>
      </ItemsControl.ItemsPanel>
      <ItemsControl.ItemTemplate>
        <DataTemplate DataType="{x:Type System:Int32}">
          <StackPanel Margin="0,0,20,0">
```

```
            <TextBlock Text="{Binding}" />
            <TextBlock HorizontalAlignment="Center">
              <TextBlock.Text>
                <MultiBinding
                  Converter="{StaticResource HigherLowerConverter}">
                  <Binding />
                  <Binding
                    RelativeSource="{RelativeSource PreviousData}" />
                </MultiBinding>
              </TextBlock.Text>
            </TextBlock>
          </StackPanel>
        </DataTemplate>
      </ItemsControl.ItemTemplate>
    </ItemsControl>
  </Border>
</UserControl>
```

After the `Converters` XML namespace prefix and the declared `HigherLowerConverter` element in the `Resources` section, we have a bordered `ItemsControl` that is data bound to the `Weights` property of the View Model that is set as the `DataContext` of this View. Next, we see a horizontal `StackPanel` element being used as the `ItemsPanelTemplate` in the `ItemsControl.ItemsPanel` property. This simply makes the collection control display items horizontally instead of vertically.

Note that in the following `DataTemplate` object, we need to specify the data type and so need to import the `System` namespace from the `mscorlib` assembly to reference the `Int32` type. The binding to the `Text` property in the first `TextBlock` specifies that it is binding to the whole data source object, which is simply an integer in this case.

The binding to the `Text` property in the second `TextBlock` is where we are using our `MultiBinding` and `IMultiValueConverter` elements. We set our `HigherLowerConverter` class to the `Converter` property of the `MultiBinding` object and inside this, we specify two binding objects. The first is again binding to the integer value and the second uses the `RelativeSource.PreviousData` property to data bind to the previous integer value. Let's now see the output of this example:

```
90   89   92   91   94   95   98   99   101
     <-   ->   <-   ->   ->   ->   ->   ->
```

Each value after the first have an arrow displayed underneath, that specifies whether it is higher or lower than the previous value. While the visual output of this example could be improved, it does still highlight the worrying trend of the weight measurements continually increasing towards the end of the sample data. This useful technique can be used in any situation when we need to compare current data values with previous values, such as when displaying share prices, or stock levels.

Dependency Properties

We've already seen some examples of Dependency Properties in previous chapters, but now let's take a more thorough look. We have a large number of options that we can use when declaring these properties, some more commonly used than others. Let's investigate the standard declaration first, by defining an `Hours` property of type `int` in a class named `DurationPicker`.

```
public static readonly DependencyProperty HoursProperty =
    DependencyProperty.Register(nameof(Hours), typeof(int),
    typeof(DurationPicker));

public int Hours
{
  get { return (int)GetValue(HoursProperty); }
  set { SetValue(HoursProperty, value); }
}
```

As with all Dependency Properties, we start by declaring the property as `static` and `readonly`, because we only want a single, immutable instance of it. This also enables us to access it without an instance of our class.

Note that this `readonly` declaration does *not* mean that we cannot set the value of our property. Unlike normal CLR properties, we do not store the values of our Dependency Properties in a field that backs the property.

Instead, they are stored in a separate dictionary and our declared `DependencyProperty` here is merely the identifier that is used to access the values from that dictionary. This is the reason that we need to dynamically get and set the actual values using the `GetValue` and `SetValue` methods, passing the property.

The result of this arrangement is that it saves a huge amount of memory, because only Dependency Property values that have been explicitly set will be stored in the dictionary, while default values are read from the declared Dependency Properties instead.

To declare each property and create our key to the dictionary, we use the `Register` method of the `DependencyProperty` class. This method has a number of overloads, but all of them require the following information; the name and type of the property and the type of the declaring class, or *owner type* as Microsoft prefer to call it.

The overloaded methods both have an additional input parameter of type `PropertyMetadata`. We'll return to this shortly, but for now let's focus on the last overload that also enables us to attach a `ValidateValueCallback` handler to our property.

As the name suggests, this is solely used for validation purposes and we cannot alter the data bound value in this method. Instead, we are simply required to return true or false to specify the validity of the current value. Let's see how we can attach this handler to our property and what its method signature is.

```
public static readonly DependencyProperty HoursProperty =
  DependencyProperty.Register(nameof(Hours), typeof(int),
    typeof(DurationPicker), new PropertyMetadata(12, ValidateHours));

private static bool ValidateHours(object value)
{
  int intValue = (int)value;
  return intValue > 0 && intValue < 25;
}
```

Note that the `ValidateValueCallback` delegate does not provide us with any reference to our class and so, we cannot access its other properties from this static context. In order to compare the current value with other property values, or to ensure that certain conditions are met, we can use another overload of the `PropertyMetadata` input parameter of the `DependencyProperty.Register` method. Let's now return to focus on the `PropertyMetadata` input parameter.

Setting metadata

Using the overloads of the `PropertyMetadata` constructor, we can optionally set a default value for the property and attach handlers to be called when the value changes, or when it is being re-evaluated. Let's update our example to attach a `PropertyChangedCallback` handler now.

```
public static readonly DependencyProperty HoursProperty =
   DependencyProperty.Register(nameof(Hours), typeof(int),
   typeof(DurationPicker), new PropertyMetadata(OnHoursChanged));

private static void OnHoursChanged(DependencyObject dependencyObject,
   DependencyPropertyChangedEventArgs e)
{
   // This is the signature of PropertyChangedCallback handlers
}
```

Note that our `PropertyChangedCallback` handler must also be declared as static in order to be used from the static context of the declared `DependencyProperty` as shown in the preceding code. However, we may have a situation where we need to call an instance method rather than a static method and in these cases, we can declare an anonymous method that calls our instance method like this.

```
public static readonly DependencyProperty HoursProperty =
   DependencyProperty.Register(nameof(Hours),
   typeof(int), typeof(DurationPicker),
   new PropertyMetadata((d, e) => ((DurationPicker)d).OnHoursChanged(d,e)));

private void OnHoursChanged(DependencyObject dependencyObject,
   DependencyPropertyChangedEventArgs e)
{
   // This is the signature of non-static PropertyChangedCallback handlers
}
```

Anonymous methods comprised of Lambda expressions can appear confusing, so let's first extract the relevant code.

```
(d, e) => ((DurationPicker)d).OnHoursChanged(d, e))
```

This could be re-written to make the example somewhat clearer.

```
(DependencyObject dependencyObject, DependencyPropertyChangedEventArgs e)
   =>
   ((DurationPicker)dependencyObject).OnHoursChanged(dependencyObject, e))
```

Now we can clearly see the input parameters of the `PropertyChangedCallback` handler, followed by the anonymous method body. Inside this method, we simply cast the `dependencyObject` input parameter to the type of the declaring class and then call the non-static method from the cast instance of the class, passing the input parameters through, if required.

As we saw in the Chapter 2, *Debugging WPF Applications*, the CLR properties that provide convenient access to our Dependency Properties will not be called by the WPF Framework when their values change. Using this `PropertyChangedCallback` handler is how we are able to perform actions upon value changes, or to debug the changing values.

The last overload of the `PropertyMetadata` constructor additionally enables us to provide a `CoerceValueCallback` handler, which provides the platform for us to perform any custom data validation that we may require for our properties. Unlike the `PropertyChangedCallback` delegate, it requires us to return the output value of the property, so this enables us to tweak the value before returning it. Here is a simple example that shows how we can adjust our property values.

```
public static readonly DependencyProperty HoursProperty =
  DependencyProperty.Register(nameof(Hours),
  typeof(int), typeof(DurationPicker),
  new PropertyMetadata(0, OnHoursChanged, CoerceHoursValue));

...

private static object CoerceHoursValue(DependencyObject dependencyObject,
  object value)
{
  // Access the instance of our class from the dependencyObject parameter
  DurationPicker durationPicker = (DurationPicker)dependencyObject;
  int minimumValue = 1, maximumValue = durationPicker.MaximumValue;
  int actualValue = (int)value;
  return Math.Min(maximumValue, Math.Max(minimumValue, actualValue));
}
```

In this simple example, we first cast the `dependencyObject` input parameter, so that we can access its `MaximumValue` property. Let's assume that our `DurationPicker` control can work with either twelve or twenty-four hour time formats and so we need to determine the current upper hour limit. We can therefore constrain our `Hours` property value to be between one and this upper limit.

When using the `CoerceValueCallback` handler, there is a special case that enables us to effectively cancel a change in value. If your code detects what your requirements specify to be a wholly invalid value, then you can simply return the `DependencyProperty.UnsetValue` value from the handler.

This value signals to the property system that it should discard the current change and return the previous value instead. You could even use this technique to selectively block changes to a property until a certain condition is met elsewhere in the class, for example.

That sums up the useful, but fairly limited options that we have with our `PropertyMetadata` object, although it should be noted that there are a number of classes that derive from this class that we can use in its place and each have their own benefits. The `UIPropertyMetadata` class directly extends the `PropertyMetadata` class and adds the ability to disable all animations of the property value via its `IsAnimationProhibited` property.

Additionally, the `FrameworkPropertyMetadata` class further extends the `UIPropertyMetadata` class and provides us with the ability to set property inheritance, the default `Binding.Mode` and `Binding.UpdateSourceTrigger` values of the property and a variety of `FrameworkPropertyMetadataOptions` flags that affect layout.

Let's take a look at some of the `FrameworkPropertyMetadataOptions` members. If we think that most users will want to use Two-Way data binding with our property, then we can declare it with the `BindsTwoWayByDefault` instance. This has the effect of switching the `Binding.Mode` from the default `OneWay` member to the `TwoWay` member on all bindings to our property.

```
public static readonly DependencyProperty HoursProperty =
    DependencyProperty.Register(nameof(Hours), typeof(int),
    typeof(DurationPicker), new FrameworkPropertyMetadata(0,
    FrameworkPropertyMetadataOptions.BindsTwoWayByDefault, OnHoursChanged,
    CoerceHoursValue));
```

Another commonly used flag is the `Inherits` instance, that specifies that the property value can be inherited by child elements. Think of the `FontSize` or `Foreground` properties that can be set on a `Window` and inherited by each control inside it.

Note that if we want to create a Dependency Property using this `Inherits` member, then we should declare it as an Attached Property, as property value inheritance works better with Attached Properties. We will find out more about this soon, in a subsequent section, but now let's continue. Next is the `SubPropertiesDoNotAffectRender` member, which can be used to streamline performance, and we'll find out more about this particular instance in `Chapter 11`, *Deploying Your Masterpiece Application*.

The last commonly used options are the `AffectsArrange`, `AffectsMeasure`, `AffectsParentArrange` and `AffectsParentMeasure` members. These are typically used with Dependency Properties that have been declared in custom panels, or other UI controls, where the property value affects the look of the control and changes to it need to cause a visual update.

It should also be noted that this `FrameworkPropertyMetadataOptions` enumeration is declared with the `FlagsAttribute` attribute, which signifies that we can also allocate a bitwise combination of its instance values, and therefore set multiple options for each of our Dependency Properties.

```
public static readonly DependencyProperty HoursProperty =
    DependencyProperty.Register(nameof(Hours), typeof(int),
    typeof(DurationPicker), new FrameworkPropertyMetadata(0,
    FrameworkPropertyMetadataOptions.BindsTwoWayByDefault |
    FrameworkPropertyMetadataOptions.AffectsMeasure, OnHoursChanged,
    CoerceHoursValue));
```

In order to set the default value for the `Binding.UpdateSourceTrigger` property, we need to use the most heavily populated constructor, passing all six input parameters. It is however, perfectly fine to pass null values for the callback handlers, if we don't need to use them.

```
public static readonly DependencyProperty HoursProperty =
    DependencyProperty.Register(nameof(Hours), typeof(int),
    typeof(DurationPicker), new FrameworkPropertyMetadata(0,
    FrameworkPropertyMetadataOptions.BindsTwoWayByDefault, OnHoursChanged,
    CoerceHoursValue, false, UpdateSourceTrigger.PropertyChanged));
```

The `false` before the `UpdateSourceTrigger` value sets the `IsAnimationProhibited` property of the `UIPropertyMetadata` class. The `UpdateSourceTrigger` value set here will be used on all bindings to this property that have not explicitly set the `UpdateSourceTrigger` property on the binding, or have set the `UpdateSourceTrigger.Default` member to the binding property.

Now that we have fully investigated the various options that we have when we declare Dependency Properties using the `Register` method of the `DependencyProperty` class, let's take a look at the another registration method from this class.

Declaring read-only Dependency Properties

Typically, read-only Dependency Properties are most commonly found in custom controls in situations where we need to data bind to a value, but do not want it to be publicly accessible. It might be a property that holds some relation to an on screen visual, mid calculation point, or previous value, but generally, we don't want the users of our framework to be able to data bind to it.

Let's imagine a scenario where we want to create a button that will enable us to set a tooltip message to display when the control is disabled, in addition to the normal tooltip message. In this case, we could declare one Dependency Property to hold the disabled tooltip message and another to store the value of the original tooltip when displaying the disabled tooltip. This original tooltip property is a perfect candidate to be a read-only Dependency Property. Let's see what this property looks like.

```
private static readonly DependencyPropertyKey originalToolTipPropertyKey =
    DependencyProperty.RegisterReadOnly("OriginalToolTip", typeof(string),
    typeof(TooltipTextBox), new PropertyMetadata());

public static readonly DependencyProperty OriginalToolTipProperty =
    originalToolTipPropertyKey.DependencyProperty;

public static string GetOriginalToolTip(DependencyObject dependencyObject)
{
    return (string)dependencyObject.GetValue(OriginalToolTipProperty);
}
```

As you can see, we use a different syntax to declare read-only Dependency Properties. Instead of returning the `DependencyProperty` identifier that is returned from the `Register` method, the `RegisterReadOnly` method returns a `DependencyPropertyKey` object.

This object is typically declared with a `private` access modifier, to stop it from being externally used with the `DependencyObject.SetValue` method. However, this method can be used within the class that registered the read-only property to set its value.

The `DependencyProperty` property of the `DependencyPropertyKey` object is used to return the actual `DependencyProperty` identifier that is used to access the property value from the dictionary that we discussed earlier.

The input parameters of the `RegisterReadOnly` methods offer the same options as those of the standard `Register` method, although there is one less overload. Unlike the `Register` method, when calling the `RegisterReadOnly` methods, we always need to provide the `PropertyMetadata` object, although we can pass a null value if we do not need what it provides.

One very important point to note is that when data binding to a read-only Dependency Property, we *must* set the binding `Mode` property to the `OneWay` enumeration member. Failure to do so will result in an error at runtime. We've now covered the creation of normal Dependency Properties in some detail, so let's move on to take a look at a different kind Dependency Property.

Registering Attached Properties

The `DependencyProperty` class enables us to register one further, special type of Dependency Property. These properties are like the Extension methods of XAML, as they enable us to extend existing classes with our own functionality. They are of course, Attached Properties.

We've already seen some examples of them earlier in this book and we'll see further examples later, but in this chapter, we'll cover their registration. We can declare Attached Properties in exactly the same ways that we can create Dependency Properties and have all of the same various options of setting metadata and attaching handlers.

There are several overloads of the `RegisterAttached` and `RegisterAttachedReadOnly` methods that mirror the `Register` and `RegisterReadOnly` methods in input parameters and functionality. However, instead of declaring a CLR wrapper for our Attached Properties, we are required to declare a pair of getter and setter methods to access and set their values. Let's see another example from the `TextBoxProperties` class.

```
public static DependencyProperty IsFocusedProperty =
  DependencyProperty.RegisterAttached("IsFocused",
  typeof(bool), typeof(TextBoxProperties),
  new PropertyMetadata(false, OnIsFocusedChanged));

public static bool GetIsFocused(DependencyObject dependencyObject)
{
  return (bool)dependencyObject.GetValue(IsFocusedProperty);
}

public static void SetIsFocused(DependencyObject dependencyObject,
  bool value)
{
```

```
      dependencyObject.SetValue(IsFocusedProperty, value);
   }

   public static void OnIsFocusedChanged(DependencyObject dependencyObject,
      DependencyPropertyChangedEventArgs e)
   {
      TextBox textBox = dependencyObject as TextBox;
      if ((bool)e.NewValue && !(bool)e.OldValue && !textBox.IsFocused)
         textBox.Focus();
   }
```

Here, we have the declaration of a `bool` Attached Property named `IsFocused` with a `PropertyMetadata` element that specifies a default value and a `PropertyChangedCallback` handler. Like the CLR property wrappers for Dependency Properties, these getter and setter methods will not be called by the WPF Framework. They are typically declared both public and static.

However, there is one situation where we do not need to declare these methods public. If we want to create a Dependency Property whose value can be inherited by its children, then we should declare it using the `RegisterAttached` method, even if we don't require an Attached Property. In this situation, we are not required to publicly expose our property getter and setter.

Although we can specify the `FrameworkPropertyMetadataOptions.Inherits` metadata option upon the declaration of Dependency Properties and their value inheritance might work in some situations, it is not guaranteed in other situations. As Attached Properties are global properties in the property system, we can be assured that their property value inheritance will work in all situations.

Returning to our example, our `PropertyChangedCallback` handler is a simple affair. It casts the `dependencyObject` property to the type of control that the property is attached to, in this case, a `TextBox`. It then verifies that the data bound `bool` value has been set from `false` to `true` and that the control is not already focused. If these conditions are verified, the control is then focused.

This Attached Property can be data bound to a `bool` property in a View Model like this.

```
   xmlns:Attached="clr-namespace:CompanyName.ApplicationName.Views.Attached"
   ...
   <TextBox Attached:TextBoxProperties.IsFocused="{Binding IsFocused}"
      Text="{Binding User.Name}" />
```

The attached textbox control can then be focused from the View Model at any time using this following method:

```
private void Focus()
{
  IsFocused = false;
  IsFocused = true;
}
```

Note that we need to ensure that the variable is `false` before setting it to `true`, as it is the actual changing of the value that will trigger the control to become focused. Now that we know how to declare our own custom Dependency Properties, let's turn our attention to the rules that govern the way they are set.

Prioritizing value setting sources

As we have already seen, there are a number of ways of setting the values of Dependency Properties; we can set them directly in code, locally in XAML, or through the use of our `CoerceValueCallback` handlers for example. However, there are many more ways that they can be set. For example, they can also be set in styles, animations, or through property inheritance to name but a few.

When we data bind our View Model properties to Dependency Properties and find that the displayed value is not what we are expecting, one reason for this can be because another method of setting the property has a higher precedence and so overrides our expected value. This is because all of the methods of setting the values of Dependency Properties are ordered in terms of importance in a list called the Dependency Property Setting Precedence List.

1. Property system coercion.
2. Animated properties.
3. Local value.
4. Template properties.
5. Implicit style (only applies to the `Style` property).
6. Style triggers.
7. Template triggers.
8. Style setters.
9. Default (theme) style.
10. Inheritance.
11. Default value from Dependency Property metadata.

Last on the list, with the lowest precedence at position eleven, are the default values that are specified in the Dependency Property declarations. Next up the list are changes caused by property inheritance. Remember that this can be defined in our Dependency Properties using the `Inherits` instance of the `FrameworkPropertyMetadataOptions` enumeration in the `FrameworkPropertyMetadata` input parameter of the `DependencyProperty.Register` method. Let's see an example of this to highlight this order of precedence.

```
<StackPanel TextElement.FontSize="20">
  <TextBlock Text="Black Text" />
  <StackPanel Orientation="Horizontal" TextElement.Foreground="Red">
    <TextBlock Text="Red Text" />
  </StackPanel>
</StackPanel>
```

In this first example, the `TextBlock` control in the outer `StackPanel` has its `Foreground` color set to black by the default value that was set in the data bound `Text` property. However, the `TextBlock` control inside the inner `StackPanel` has its default `Foreground` property value overridden by the `TextElement.Foreground` Attached Property value that is set on its parent control. It inherits the value of this property from the `StackPanel` and this demonstrates that properties set through property inheritance have a higher precedence than properties set with default values.

However, default property values that are set in theme styles follow on the precedence list, with the next lowest priority, and override property values set through inheritance. As it is quite difficult to come up with a short XAML example for this, we'll skip over this item and move onto the next. At number eight on the list, we have property values that have been set by style setters. Let's adjust our earlier example to demonstrate this.

```
<StackPanel TextElement.FontSize="20">
  <TextBlock Text="Black Text" />
  <StackPanel Orientation="Horizontal" TextElement.Foreground="Red">
    <TextBlock Text="Red Text" Margin="0,0,10,0" />
    <TextBlock Text="Green Text">
      <TextBlock.Style>
        <Style TargetType="{x:Type TextBlock}">
          <Setter Property="Foreground" Value="Green" />
        </Style>
      </TextBlock.Style>
    </TextBlock>
  </StackPanel>
</StackPanel>
```

In this example, the `TextBlock` control in the outer `StackPanel` still has its `Foreground` color set to black by the default value of the data bound `Text` property. The top `TextBlock` control inside the inner `StackPanel` still has its default `Foreground` property value overridden by the `TextElement.Foreground` value from its parent control. However, now we can also see that values that are set in a `Style` will override inherited property values. This is the output of this code snippet:

```
Black Text
Red Text  Green Text
```

Next, at number seven on the precedence list, we have template triggers, which override property values that are set with style setters and all other previously mentioned methods of setting values. Note that this specifically deals with triggers that are declared within templates, such as the `ControlTemplate`, and does not relate to triggers that are declared within any `Style.Triggers` collections. Let's look at an example.

```
<Button Content="Blue Text" FontSize="20">
  <Button.Style>
    <Style TargetType="{x:Type Button}">
      <Setter Property="Foreground" Value="Green" />
      <Setter Property="Control.Template">
        <Setter.Value>
          <ControlTemplate TargetType="{x:Type Button}">
            <ContentPresenter />
            <ControlTemplate.Triggers>
              <Trigger Property="IsEnabled" Value="True">
                <Setter Property="Foreground" Value="Blue" />
              </Trigger>
            </ControlTemplate.Triggers>
          </ControlTemplate>
        </Setter.Value>
      </Setter>
    </Style>
  </Button.Style>
</Button>
```

In this example, we have declared a button and overridden its `ControlTemplate`, defining a new, minimal markup for it. In the style, we have set the `Foreground` property value to green in a setter. However, in our `ControlTemplate`, we have a `Trigger` that will override this value and set it to blue when its condition is met. Note that if we changed the trigger condition to `false`, or removed the whole trigger, the button text would then become green, as set by the style.

Next up the list at position six are triggers that are declared within `Style.Triggers` collections. One important point to note here is that this only relates to styles that are either declared inline locally, in the current control's `Resources` section, or in the application resources file and not to default styles, which have a lower precedence value. We can extend our previous example by adding a new trigger into the `Style.Triggers` collection to highlight this new priority.

```xml
<Button Content="Orange Text" FontSize="20">
  <Button.Style>
    <Style TargetType="{x:Type Button}">
      <Setter Property="Foreground" Value="Green" />
      <Setter Property="Control.Template">
        <Setter.Value>
          <ControlTemplate TargetType="{x:Type Button}">
            <ContentPresenter />
            <ControlTemplate.Triggers>
              <Trigger Property="IsEnabled" Value="True">
                <Setter Property="Foreground" Value="Blue" />
              </Trigger>
            </ControlTemplate.Triggers>
          </ControlTemplate>
        </Setter.Value>
      </Setter>
      <Style.Triggers>
        <Trigger Property="IsEnabled" Value="True">
          <Setter Property="Foreground" Value="Orange" />
        </Trigger>
      </Style.Triggers>
    </Style>
  </Button.Style>
</Button>
```

When running this example, our text is now orange. The `Foreground` property value that is set by the trigger in the `Triggers` collection of the style has overridden the value set by the template trigger, which itself has overridden the value set by the style setter. Let's move on.

At number five on the list, we have implicit styles. Note that this special level of precedence only applies to the `Style` property and no others. A style can be implicitly set to all members of a type, by specifying the target type and being declared without an `x:Key` directive set. Here is an example.

```
<Style TargetType="{x:Type Button}">
  <Setter Property="Foreground" Value="Green" />
</Style>
```

The relevant style must either be declared in the current XAML page, or the `Application.Resources` section of the `App.xaml` file. Styles from themes are not included here, as they have a lower value precedence. Note that this special position in the list was only added in .NET 4 and is omitted from the .NET 3 documentation on the MSDN website.

Next up the list at position four are properties that are set within either a `ControlTemplate` or a `DataTemplate`. If we set a property directly on any element within a template, that value will override all values set by methods with lower precedence. For example, if we directly set the `Foreground` property on the `ContentPresenter` from our previous example, then it's value will override all other settings in that example and the button text will be red.

```
<ControlTemplate TargetType="{x:Type Button}">
  <ContentPresenter TextElement.Foreground="Red" />
  <ControlTemplate.Triggers>
    <Trigger Property="IsEnabled" Value="True">
      <Setter Property="Foreground" Value="Blue" />
    </Trigger>
  </ControlTemplate.Triggers>
</ControlTemplate>
```

At position three on the list, we have locally set values. To demonstrate this, we could just set the `Foreground` property on the actual button from the last full example, but instead let's highlight an extremely common mistake that a lot of developers make. Imagine a situation where we want to output a value predominantly in one color, but in another color under certain circumstances. Some developers might try something like this.

```
<TextBlock Text="{Binding Account.Amount, StringFormat={}{0:C}}"
  Foreground="Green">
  <TextBlock.Style>
    <Style TargetType="{x:Type TextBlock}">
      <Style.Triggers>
        <DataTrigger Binding="{Binding Account.IsOverdrawn}" Value="True">
          <Setter Property="Foreground" Value="Red" />
        </DataTrigger>
```

```
      </Style.Triggers>
    </Style>
  </TextBlock.Style>
</TextBlock>
```

Upon running this example, some might expect this to work and be stumped when it doesn't. The reason why this doesn't work is because local property settings have a higher value setting precedence than properties set by style triggers. The solution to correcting this mistake is to use our new found knowledge of this value setting precedence list and move the local property setting to a style setter, which has a lower precedence than the trigger.

```
<TextBlock Text="{Binding Account.Amount, StringFormat={}{0:C}}">
  <TextBlock.Style>
    <Style TargetType="{x:Type TextBlock}">
      <Setter Property="Foreground" Value="Green" />
      <Style.Triggers>
        <DataTrigger Binding="{Binding Account.IsOverdrawn}" Value="True">
          <Setter Property="Foreground" Value="Red" />
        </DataTrigger>
      </Style.Triggers>
    </Style>
  </TextBlock.Style>
</TextBlock>
```

Now, the `TextBlock.Foreground` property will be set to green from the style setter and overridden by the trigger when the condition is true, as expected. Let's continue up the list to position two. In the penultimate position, we have property values that are set by animations. A very simple example can demonstrate this nicely for us.

```
<Rectangle Width="300" Height="300" Fill="Orange">
  <Rectangle.Triggers>
    <EventTrigger RoutedEvent="Loaded">
      <BeginStoryboard>
        <Storyboard Storyboard.TargetProperty="Width">
          <DoubleAnimation Duration="0:0:1" To="50" AutoReverse="True"
            RepeatBehavior="Forever" />
        </Storyboard>
      </BeginStoryboard>
    </EventTrigger>
  </Rectangle.Triggers>
</Rectangle>
```

In this example, the animation overrides the locally set value of the `Width` property and the rectangle grows and shrinks as planned. If we think logically about this, then it is clear that the animation system had to feature at a very high position on the property setting precedence list. Otherwise, if it was much lower down the list, we wouldn't be able to animate anything.

However, properties that are set by animations are at number two of the list, which means that there is one place that a property can be set that will override even values set by animations. At number one on the list of Dependency Property Setting Precedence, with the absolutely highest priority setting, is the property coercion system that we discussed in the *Dependency Properties* section.

This could only really happen if we built a custom control that animated a custom Dependency Property that had particular requirements placed upon it, such as specifying that it should have a certain maximum or minimum value. In this case, we could enforce these rules in a `CoerceValueCallback` handler that is attached to the Dependency Property.

If we had these requirements that were enforced by the property coercion system, yet wanted to animate them in the UI, it again makes perfect sense that we would want our coerced values to override the values set by the animation. In this way, we could rest assured that our coerced property values will remain within the bounds that we set for them at all times.

Data templates

We've already seen a number of simple examples of the `DataTemplate`, but they are such an important part of WPF that we're going to have a much more thorough look at them now. In short, we use a `DataTemplate` to define how we want particular data objects to be rendered in the UI.

If we were to data bind a particular type of object to a UI control without providing a `DataTemplate` for it, the WPF Framework would not know how to display it. In these cases, the best job that it can do is to display a string representation of it.

```
<ItemsControl ItemsSource="{Binding Users}" />
```

It achieves this by calling the `object.ToString` method on the data object and setting that value to the `Text` property of a `TextBlock`, which it uses to display the object. If this method has not been overridden in the object's class, this will result in the name of the type of the object being displayed in its place.

```
CompanyName.ApplicationName.DataModels.User
CompanyName.ApplicationName.DataModels.User
CompanyName.ApplicationName.DataModels.User
```

Knowing that the WPF Framework will call the `ToString` method on our data objects before displaying them enables us to take a shortcut, or a simple alternative to defining a `DataTemplate`, if we only need a textual output in the UI. Therefore, it is always a good idea for us to override the `object.ToString` method to output some meaningful display.

```
public override string ToString()
{
   return Name;
}
```

This will result in the following output:

```
James Smith
Robert Johnson
Maria Garcia
```

Note that Visual Studio IntelliSense also calls the `ToString` method on our data objects before displaying them, so the benefit of providing a custom implementation for it is doubled. As such, we often add an abstract method into our base class to ensure that all derived classes will implement this method.

```
namespace CompanyName.ApplicationName.DataModels
{
   public abstract class BaseDataModel : INotifyPropertyChanged
   {
      ...
```

```
    public abstract override string ToString();
  }
}
```

Returning to the topic of data templates now, let's first take a look at a better example for our `User` objects and then investigate where we can declare our data templates.

```
<DataTemplate x:Key="UserTemplate" DataType="{x:Type DataModels:User}">
  <Border BorderBrush="Black" BorderThickness="1" CornerRadius="5"
    Padding="5" Margin="0,0,0,5">
    <StackPanel Orientation="Horizontal">
      <TextBlock Text="{Binding Name}" Margin="0,0,3,0" />
      <TextBlock Text="{Binding Age, StringFormat={}({0})}" />
    </StackPanel>
  </Border>
</DataTemplate>
```

In this example, we simply output the user's name in one `TextBlock` and their age in another. Note the use of the `StringFormat` property to surround the age in brackets in the output. Let's now see how this `DataTemplate` renders our `User` objects.

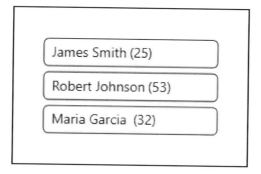

Primarily, we can declare our data templates in one of four main places. The first is in line with the control that the related data object or objects will be displayed in. We have two main options for this too, depending on the number of data objects that we have to display.

If we have a single object to display, we can utilize the `ContentControl` element to display it and the `ContentControl.ContentTemplate` property to define the `DataTemplate` element that it should use to render the data object.

```
<ContentControl Content="{Binding Users[0]}">
  <ContentControl.ContentTemplate>
    <DataTemplate DataType="{x:Type DataModels:User}">
      ...
    </DataTemplate>
  </ContentControl.ContentTemplate>
</ContentControl>
```

Similarly, in a collection control, or `ItemsControl`, such as the `ListBox` control, we can declare our `DataTemplate` directly in the `ItemTemplate` property.

```
<ListBox ItemsSource="{Binding Users}">
  <ListBox.ItemTemplate>
    <DataTemplate DataType="{x:Type DataModels:User}">
      ...
    </DataTemplate>
  </ListBox.ItemTemplate>
</ListBox>
```

The next place that we can declare our data templates is in the `Resources` section of the control that will display the data object or objects. Here is our `ContentControl` now.

```
<ContentControl Content="{Binding Users[0]}"
  ContentTemplate="{StaticResource UserTemplate}">
  <ContentControl.Resources>
    <DataTemplate x:Key="UserTemplate" DataType="{x:Type DataModels:User}">
      ...
    </DataTemplate>
  </ContentControl.Resources>
</ContentControl>
```

The next place that we can declare our data templates is in the `Resources` section of the `Window` or `UserControl` that contains the control that displays the data objects. If we have multiple data objects, then we can set our data template to the resource, like this.

```
<UserControl.Resources>
  <DataTemplate x:Key="UserTemplate" DataType="{x:Type DataModels:User}">
    ...
  </DataTemplate>
</UserControl.Resources>
<ListBox ItemsSource="{Binding Users}"
  ItemTemplate="{StaticResource UserTemplate}" />
```

The last place that we can define our data templates is in the `Application.Resources` section of the `App.xaml` file. When the WPF Framework searches for a data template for a data object, it first searches the local `Resources` section of the control that is applying the template.

If it finds no match for the type of the data object, it then searches the `Resources` collection of the parent control and then the parent of that control and so on. If it still does not find a data template with a matching type, then it will search through the `Application.Resources` section of the `App.xaml` page.

We can use this order of lookup to our advantage. We often declare our default data templates in the `Application.Resources` section of the `App.xaml` page, as these resources are available application wide. If we need to override our default data templates, to display a particular output in a particular View, we can declare a new data template with the same `x:Key` directive locally in the View's `Resources` section.

As the local `Resources` section is searched before the application resources, it will use the locally declared data template instead of the default one. Another way of overriding our default templates is to declare them without setting their `x:Key` directives.

```
<DataTemplate DataType="{x:Type DataModels:User}">
  ...
</DataTemplate>
```

Resources that are declared in this way are implicitly applied to all data objects of the appropriate type that do not have a data template explicitly applied. Therefore, in order to override these default data templates, we can simply declare a new data template and explicitly set it to the relative template property using its `x:Key` directive. Let's now look at one further way of specifying a data template.

Taking complete control

At times, we might want to display different objects of the same type in different ways, depending on the values of their properties. For example, with a collection of objects that represent vehicles, you might want to have different displays for different types of vehicle, as trucks have different specifications to motor boats. The `DataTemplateSelector` class enables us to do just that.

When extending the `DataTemplateSelector` class, we can override its single `SelectTemplate` method. In this method, we are provided with both the data object and the data bound object and can select different data templates to return, dependent on the data object's property values.

Let's see a very simple example, where we return one of two data templates based on the User's age. We'll first need to declare another DataTemplate for our User type.

```
<DataTemplate x:Key="InverseUserTemplate"
  DataType="{x:Type DataModels:User}">
  <Border BorderBrush="White" BorderThickness="1" Background="Black"
    TextElement.Foreground="White" CornerRadius="5" Padding="8,3,5,5"
    Margin="0,0,0,5">
    <StackPanel Orientation="Horizontal">
      <TextBlock Text="{Binding Name}" Margin="0,0,3,0" />
      <TextBlock Text="{Binding Age, StringFormat={}({0})}" />
    </StackPanel>
  </Border>
</DataTemplate>
```

In this template, we have simply inverted the colors of the background and foreground from those in the first template. Let's now see our DataTemplateSelector class that will reference both this and the other DataTemplate element.

```
using System.Windows;
using System.Windows.Controls;
using CompanyName.ApplicationName.DataModels;

namespace CompanyName.ApplicationName.Views.DataTemplateSelectors
{
  public class UserAgeDataTemplateSelector : DataTemplateSelector
  {
    public override DataTemplate SelectTemplate(object item,
      DependencyObject container)
    {
      FrameworkElement element = container as FrameworkElement;
      if (element != null && item != null && item is User)
      {
        User user = (User)item;
        if (user.Age < 35) return
          (DataTemplate)element.FindResource("InverseUserTemplate");
        else return (DataTemplate)element.FindResource("UserTemplate");
      }
      return null;
    }
  }
}
```

In this example, we perform the standard null checks for the two input parameters and a further check to ensure that the current data object is of the expected type. If the input parameters pass the checks, we cast the `item` parameter to a `User` object and use the `FindResource` method to return the appropriate data template dependent upon the value of the `Age` property.

The `FrameworkElement.FindResource` method first searches the calling object for the data template and then it's parent element and so on, up the logical tree. If it doesn't find it in any parent element in the application window, it then looks through the `App.xaml` file. If it still does not find it there, it then searches in the themes and system resources.

The `container` input parameter is used to access the `FindResource` method. Note that it will typically be of type `ContentPresenter` if we're using a normal collection control, so we could have cast it to that type in order to access the data templates.

However, the default container could be overridden to use one of the parent classes that the `ContentPresenter` class is derived from. Therefore, to avoid the possibility of exceptions, it is safer to cast it to the `FrameworkElement` class that actually declares the `FindResource` method.

Let's see how we can use this class now. First, we need to add the XML namespace prefix for our `DataTemplateSelectors` namespace.

```
xmlns:DataTemplateSelectors=
    "clr-namespace:CompanyName.ApplicationName.Views.DataTemplateSelectors"
```

Then we need to add an instance of our `UserAgeDataTemplateSelector` class to a Resources section.

```
<DataTemplateSelectors:UserAgeDataTemplateSelector
    x:Key="UserAgeDataTemplateSelector" />
```

Finally, we set our resource selector to the `ItemTemplateSelector` property.

```
<ItemsControl ItemsSource="{Binding Users}" Padding="10"
    ItemTemplateSelector="{StaticResource UserAgeDataTemplateSelector}" />
```

When running the application now, we'll see this new output.

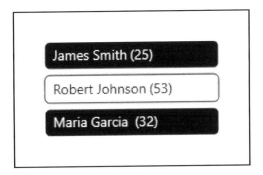

Note that `DataTemplateSelector` classes are typically used with very different templates, such as those that make up the different editing or viewing modes of a custom control. Slight differences like those in our simple example can be far easier achieved using style triggers and we'll find out more about triggers and styles in the next chapter.

Displaying hierarchical data

There is one class in the .NET Framework that extends the `DataTemplate` class in order to support UI controls that extend the `HeaderedItemsControl` class. As it sounds, the `HeaderedItemsControl` class represents a particular kind of `ItemsControl` element that has a header. Examples include the `MenuItem`, `TreeViewItem` and `ToolBar` classes.

The `HierarchicalDataTemplate` class was created to display hierarchical Data Models. To clarify a little further, a hierarchical data model is a data model that contains a collection property with items of the same type as the parent object. Think of the folder view in the Windows Explorer window; each folder can contain further folders.

The main difference between the `HierarchicalDataTemplate` and the `DataTemplate` class is that the `HierarchicalDataTemplate` class has an `ItemsSource` property that we can use to bind the children of each item to.

In addition to the `ItemsSource` property, there are a number of other item-related properties, such as the `ItemContainerStyle`, `ItemStringFormat` and `ItemTemplate` properties. We'll find out more about what these other properties do in the next chapter, but for now, let's look at an example.

There are plenty of `HierarchicalDataTemplate` examples that demonstrate the use of `TreeViewItem` elements to be found online, so for this example, we'll see how we can build an application menu using data binding. First, we'll need a View Model to data bind to each `MenuItem` control. Let's take a look at our `MenuItemViewModel` class.

```
using System.Collections.ObjectModel;
using System.Windows.Input;

namespace CompanyName.ApplicationName.ViewModels
{
  public class MenuItemViewModel : BaseViewModel
  {
    private string header = string.Empty;
    private ICommand command = null;
    private ObservableCollection<MenuItemViewModel> menuItems =
      new ObservableCollection<MenuItemViewModel>();

    public string Header
    {
      get { return header; }
      set { if (header != value) { header = value;
        NotifyPropertyChanged(); } }
    }

    public ICommand Command
    {
      get { return command; }
      set { if (command != value) { command = value;
        NotifyPropertyChanged(); } }
    }

    public ObservableCollection<MenuItemViewModel> MenuItems
    {
      get { return menuItems; }
      set { if (menuItems != value) { menuItems = value;
        NotifyPropertyChanged(); } }
    }
  }
}
```

In this simplified example, our View Model only declares three properties to data bind to the `MenuItem` control's properties. In a real application, we would typically add further properties, so that we could define the icon, or maybe the style of each menu item as well. However, continuing the example with our View Model, let's look at the class that would declare these View Models.

If an application has a menu control, it would typically reside in the `MainWindow.xaml` file. Therefore, the data bound `MenuItemViewModel` elements would be declared in the View Model that is data bound to the data context of that View. Let's look at the required properties.

```
private ObservableCollection<MenuItemViewModel> menuItems =
  new ObservableCollection<MenuItemViewModel>();

public ObservableCollection<MenuItemViewModel> MenuItems
{
  get { return menuItems; }
  set { if (menuItems != value) { menuItems = value;
    NotifyPropertyChanged(); } }
}
```

An alternative to programmatically declaring the various menu item View Models would be to define the items in an XML file, read it in and generate the items from that at runtime. However, for the purpose of this simple example, let's just hard code some values to use, omitting the commands for brevity.

```
MenuItems.Add(new MenuItemViewModel() { Header = "Users",
  MenuItems = new ObservableCollection<MenuItemViewModel>() {
  new MenuItemViewModel() { Header = "Details",
  MenuItems = new ObservableCollection<MenuItemViewModel>() {
  new MenuItemViewModel() { Header = "Banking" },
  new MenuItemViewModel() { Header = "Personal" } } },
  new MenuItemViewModel() { Header = "Security" } } });
MenuItems.Add(new MenuItemViewModel() { Header = "Administration" });
MenuItems.Add(new MenuItemViewModel() { Header = "View" });
MenuItems.Add(new MenuItemViewModel() { Header = "Help",
  MenuItems = new ObservableCollection<MenuItemViewModel>() {
  new MenuItemViewModel() { Header = "About" } } });
```

While this code is somewhat difficult to read, it is far more compact than declaring each child item separately and then building up the hierarchy afterwards. The end result is the same, so let's now see what the required XAML looks like.

```
<Menu ItemsSource="{Binding MenuItems}" FontSize="14" Background="White">
  <Menu.ItemContainerStyle>
    <Style TargetType="{x:Type MenuItem}">
```

```
        <Setter Property="Command" Value="{Binding Command}" />
      </Style>
    </Menu.ItemContainerStyle>
    <Menu.ItemTemplate>
      <HierarchicalDataTemplate
        DataType="{x:Type ViewModels:MenuItemViewModel}"
        ItemsSource="{Binding MenuItems}">
        <TextBlock Text="{Binding Header}" />
      </HierarchicalDataTemplate>
    </Menu.ItemTemplate>
  </Menu>
```

Here, we declare a `Menu` control and data bind our `MenuItems` collection to its `ItemsSource` property. The `ItemContainerStyle` enables us to define the style of the UI container that surrounds each of our data items. In this case, that control is a `MenuItem` control.

All we need to do in this style is to bind the `Command` property of our View Model to the `Command` property of the menu item. If we had declared any other properties in our View Model to map to the `MenuItem` class properties, then this style would be the place to data bind them.

As discussed earlier, the `ItemTemplate` property enables us to provide a data template, or in this case, our `HierarchicalDataTemplate` element, that will define how each item will be rendered. In the template declaration, we state the type of our data items and specify the collection property that contains the child items.

Inside the template, we simply output the value of the `Header` property in a `TextBlock` element. This will represent the name of each menu item. Let's see what this will all look like when the application is running now.

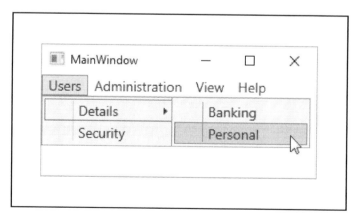

Data binding to enumeration collections

We've already seen a number of examples of data binding to enumeration instances. We've seen converters that we can use to convert our enumeration values and Extension methods that we can use to extract additional information from each member. Earlier in this chapter, we even saw a full but basic example using our `BitRate` enumeration. Now, with our new-found knowledge, let's see how we can improve that earlier example.

As noted, in the previous example, we manually declared a `RadioButton` control for each of our enumerations. While that is fine for our three member enumeration, it wouldn't make so much sense to use this method if we had a large number of members. Instead, let's think about how we could use a `DataTemplate` to declare how each member should be rendered. Let's remind ourselves how we declared each `RadioButton` in the previous example.

```
<RadioButton Content="16 bits" IsChecked="{Binding BitRate,
    Converter={StaticResource EnumToBoolConverter},
    ConverterParameter=Sixteen}" VerticalContentAlignment="Center" />
```

The first thing that we notice is the hard coded `Content` value. Obviously, we can't do this in a `DataTemplate`, otherwise every member would be given the same label. This is a perfect place for us to use the `EnumToDescriptionStringConverter` converter that we created earlier, so let's update that now.

```
<UserControl.Resources>
  ...
  <Converters:EnumToDescriptionStringConverter
    x:Key="EnumToDescriptionStringConverter" />
  ...
</UserControl.Resources>
...
<RadioButton Content="{Binding .,
  Converter={StaticResource EnumToDescriptionStringConverter}}"
  IsChecked="{Binding BitRate,
  Converter={StaticResource EnumToBoolConverter},
  ConverterParameter=Sixteen}" VerticalContentAlignment="Center" />
```

Next, we see that we have also hard coded the `Sixteen` enumeration member to the `ConverterParameter` property, so we'll need to change that in our data template too. Our first attempt might be to simply data bind the whole data context from the data template, which in our case, is one of the enumeration instances.

```
<RadioButton Content="{Binding .,
   Converter={StaticResource EnumToDescriptionStringConverter}}"
   IsChecked="{Binding BitRate,
   Converter={StaticResource EnumToBoolConverter},
   ConverterParameter={Binding}}" VerticalContentAlignment="Center" />
```

However, if we do this and run the application, we will receive the following exception.

```
A 'Binding' cannot be set on the 'ConverterParameter' property of
type 'Binding'. A 'Binding' can only be set on a DependencyProperty
of a DependencyObject.
```

Unfortunately, we cannot data bind to the `ConverterParameter` property, as it was not declared as a Dependency Property. As we cannot data bind to this property from within our data template and no longer use the `EnumToBoolConverter` class to specify the selected enumeration instance, this will complicate our example somewhat.

One trick that we can use is to utilize the `SelectedItem` property of the `ListBoxItem` class to hold the value of our selected enumeration member instead. We can achieve this by data binding this property to the `IsChecked` property of each `RadioButton` using a `RelativeSource.FindAncestor` binding in our `DataTemplate`.

```
<RadioButton Content="{Binding .,
   Converter={StaticResource EnumToDescriptionStringConverter}}"
   IsChecked="{Binding IsSelected,
   RelativeSource={RelativeSource AncestorType={x:Type ListBoxItem}},
   FallbackValue=False}" VerticalContentAlignment="Center" />
```

Note that each data item in a collection control will be implicitly wrapped in a UI container element. In our case, we'll use a `ListBox` control and so our enumeration instances will be wrapped in `ListBoxItem` elements, but if we had chosen a `ComboBox` for example, then our items' containers would be `ComboBoxItem` elements. We'll find out more about this in the next chapter, but for now, let's continue looking at this example.

So, now we have data bound the `Content` property of the `RadioButton` to the description of each member from the `DescriptionAttribute` attribute declared in the enumeration and the `IsChecked` property to the `IsSelected` property of the `ListBoxItem` element. However, we have lost the connection to our selected enumeration property from the View Model.

In order to restore this connection, we can data bind the `BitRate` property to the `SelectedItem` property of the `ListBox` control. The WPF Framework implicitly connects this property with the `IsSelected` property of each `ListBoxItem` element and so our connection between the `BitRate` property and the `IsChecked` property of each button is now restored. Let's see the updated XAML.

```
<UserControl x:Class="CompanyName.ApplicationName.Views.BitRateView"
  xmlns="http://schemas.microsoft.com/winfx/2006/xaml/presentation"
  xmlns:x="http://schemas.microsoft.com/winfx/2006/xaml"
  xmlns:mc="http://schemas.openxmlformats.org/markup-compatibility/2006"
  xmlns:d="http://schemas.microsoft.com/expression/blend/2008"
  xmlns:Converters="clr-namespace:CompanyName.ApplicationName.Converters;
    assembly=CompanyName.ApplicationName.Converters"
  xmlns:Enums="clr-namespace:CompanyName.ApplicationName.DataModels.
    Enums;assembly=CompanyName.ApplicationName.DataModels"
  mc:Ignorable="d" d:DesignHeight="90" d:DesignWidth="300">
  <UserControl.Resources>
    <Converters:EnumToBoolConverter x:Key="EnumToBoolConverter" />
  </UserControl.Resources>
  <GroupBox Header="Audio Quality" FontSize="14" Margin="20"
    HorizontalAlignment="Left" VerticalAlignment="Top" Padding="5">
    <ListBox ItemsSource="{Binding BitRates}"
      SelectedItem="{Binding BitRate}">
      <ListBox.ItemTemplate>
        <DataTemplate DataType="{x:Type Enums:BitRate}">
          <RadioButton Content="{Binding ., Converter={StaticResource
            EnumToDescriptionStringConverter}}"
            IsChecked="{Binding IsSelected,
            RelativeSource={RelativeSource
            AncestorType={x:Type ListBoxItem}}, FallbackValue=False}"
            VerticalContentAlignment="Center" />
        </DataTemplate>
      </ListBox.ItemTemplate>
    </ListBox>
  </GroupBox>
</UserControl>
```

To update our earlier example, we need to add the new `Enums` XML namespace prefix, so that we can specify our `BitRate` enumeration type in the data template. Next, we need to update the content of our `GroupBox` element. Now we're using a `ListBox` control so that we can take advantage of its item selection capabilities.

We data bind our `BitRates` collection to the `ItemsSource` property and our selected `BitRate` property to the `SelectedItem` property of the `ListBox`. The one problem with this method is that as we're now using a `ListBox` element in our example, we can see it and its contained `ListBoxItem` objects. This is not how radio buttons are typically displayed.

It's not a terrible problem and it can be easily fixed by declaring a few styles. We'll return to this example in the following chapter and demonstrate how we can style the listbox and its items to completely hide their use from the end users.

Summary

We've covered a lot of important information in this chapter, from examining the binding path syntax mini-language to exploring a number of different binding scenarios. We've investigated the plethora of options that we're afforded when declaring our own Dependency Properties and looked into the creation of Attached Properties, using some interesting examples. Finally, we examined the finer details of data templating and explored a number of ways of data binding to enumerations.

In the next chapter, we'll have an in-depth look at the various UI elements in the WPF Framework and their most relevant properties. We'll investigate when to customize them and when we need to create our own controls. We'll then explore the various ways of modifying existing controls in WPF and finally, take a detailed look at how to create our own custom controls.

5
Using the Right Controls for the Job

In this chapter, we'll first consider the existing controls that WPF offers us and look at how we can use them to create the layouts that we require. We'll investigate the many ways that we can modify these controls to avoid the need to create new controls.

We'll examine the various levels of functionality that are built into the existing controls and then discover how to best declare our own controls when required. We'll take an in-depth look at the various options that we have and determine when best to use each. Let's jump straight in and take a look at the various layout controls.

Investigating the built-in controls

There are a wide range of controls included in the .NET Framework. They cover most common scenarios and it is rare that we will need to create our own controls in a typical form-based application. All of the UI controls tend to have their functionality built up from a large number of common base classes.

All controls will share the same core-level base classes that provide the core-level functionalities and then a number of derived framework-level classes that provide the functionality that is associated with the WPF Framework, such as data binding, styling and templating. Let's take a look at an example.

Inheriting framework abilities

As with the base classes in our application framework, the built-in WPF controls also have an inheritance hierarchy, with each successive base class offering some additional functionality. Let's look at the `Button` class as an example. Here is the inheritance hierarchy of the `Button` control:

```
System.Object
   System.Windows.Threading.DispatcherObject
     System.Windows.DependencyObject
       System.Windows.Media.Visual
         System.Windows.UIElement
           System.Windows.FrameworkElement
             System.Windows.Controls.Control
               System.Windows.Controls.ContentControl
                 System.Windows.Controls.Primitives.ButtonBase
                   System.Windows.Controls.Button
```

As with every object in the .NET Framework, we start with the `Object` class, which provides low-level services to all classes. These include object comparison, finalization, and the ability to output a customizable string representation of each object.

Next is the `DispatcherObject` class, which provides each object with thread affinity and associates them with a `Dispatcher` object. The `Dispatcher` class manages a prioritized queue of work items for individual threads. Only the thread that the associated `Dispatcher` object was created on can access each `DispatcherObject` directly and this enables derived classes to enforce thread safety.

After the `DispatcherObject` class, we have the `DependencyObject` class, which enables all derived classes to use the WPF property system and declare Dependency Properties. The `GetValue` and `SetValue` methods that we call to access and set their values are also provided by the `DependencyObject` class.

Next up is the `Visual` class, which has the primary role of providing rendering support. All elements that are displayed in the UI will extend the `Visual` class. In addition to rendering each object, it also calculates their bounding box and provides support for hit testing, clipping, and transformations.

Extending the `Visual` class is the `UIElement` class, which provides a number of core services to all of its derived classes. These include the event and user input systems and the ability to determine the element's layout appearance and rendering behavior.

Following on from that is the `FrameworkElement` class, which provides the first framework-level members, building upon the foundation of the core-level classes that it extends. It is the `FrameworkElement` class that enables data binding through the `DataContext` property and styling through the `Style` property.

It also provides events that relate to an object's lifetime, an upgrade of the core-level layout system to a full layout system and improved support for animations, among other things. This is typically the lowest level class that we might want to extend if we were creating our own basic elements, as it enables derived classes to partake in the majority of the WPF UI capabilities.

The `Control` class extends the `FrameworkElement` class and is the base class for most of the WPF UI elements. It provides appearance templating through the use of its `ControlTemplate` functionality and a host of appearance-related properties. These include coloring properties, such as `Background`, `Foreground`, and `BorderBrush`, along with alignment and typeface properties.

Extending the `Control` class is the `ContentControl` class, which enables controls to have one object of any CLR type as its content. This means that we can either set data objects or UI elements as the content, although we may need to provide a `DataTemplate` for the data objects if they are of a custom type.

The final class in the long line of parent classes that the `Button` class extends is the `ButtonBase` class. In fact, this is the base class for all buttons in WPF and it adds useful functionality for buttons. This includes automatically converting certain keyboard events to mouse events, so that users can interact with the buttons without using a mouse.

The `Button` class itself adds little to its inherited members, with only three related `bool` properties; two that specify whether a button is the default button and one that specifies whether the button is a cancel button. We'll see an example of this shortly. It has an additional two protected overridden methods that get called, when the button is clicked, or when an automation peer is created for it.

While WPF enables us to modify existing controls to such a degree that we rarely need to create our own, it is important to be aware of this inheritance hierarchy, so that we can extend the appropriate and most lightweight base class that fulfils our requirements, when we need to.

For example, if we wanted to create our own custom button, it would typically make more sense to extend the `ButtonBase` class, rather than the `Button` class, and if we wanted to create a totally unique control, we could extend the `FrameworkElement` class. Now that we have a good understanding of the make-up of the available controls, let's see how they are displayed by the WPF layout system.

Laying it on the line

In WPF, the layout system is responsible for attaining the sizes of each element to be displayed, positioning them on the screen and then drawing them. As controls can be contained within other controls, the layout system works recursively, with each child control's overall position being determined by the position of its parent panel control.

The layout system first measures each child in each panel in what is known as a measure pass. During this pass, each panel calls the `Measure` method of each child element and they specify how much space they would ideally like to have; this determines the `UIElement.DesiredSize` property value. Note that this is not necessarily how much space they will be given.

After the measure pass comes the arrange pass, when each panel calls the `Arrange` method of each child element. During this pass, the panels generate the bounding boxes of each of their child elements, dependent upon their `DesiredSize` values. The layout system will adjust these sizes to add any required margins or additional adjustments that may be needed.

It returns a value to the input parameter of the panels' `ArrangeOverride` method and each panel performs its own specific layout behavior before returning the possibly adjusted value. The layout system performs any remaining required adjustments before returning execution to the panel and completing the layout process.

We need to be careful when developing our applications, to ensure that we do not unnecessarily trigger additional passes of the layout system, as this can lead to poor performance. This can occur when adding or removing items in a collection, applying transforms on the elements, or by calling the `UIElement.UpdateLayout` method, which forces a new layout pass.

Containing controls

The existing controls can mostly be split into two main categories; those that provide layout support for other controls and those that make up the visible UI, and are arranged in it by the first category of controls. The first category of controls are of course panels and they provide a variety of ways to arrange their child controls in the UI.

Some provide resizing capabilities, while others don't, and some are more efficient than others, so it's important to use the right panel for the job at hand. Additionally, different panels offer different layout behavior, so it is good to know what the available panels are and what they each offer us in terms of layout.

All panels extend the abstract `Panel` class and that extends the `FrameworkElement` class, so it has all of the members and functionality of that class. However, it doesn't extend the `Control` class and so it cannot inherit its properties. It therefore adds its own `Background` property to enable users to color the gaps between the panel's various items.

The `Panel` class also provides a `Children` property that represents the items in each panel, although we do not typically interact with this property unless creating a custom panel. Instead, we can populate this collection by simply declaring our child elements directly within the panel element in XAML.

We are able to do this because the `Panel` class specifies the `Children` property in a `ContentPropertyAttribute` attribute in its class definition. While the `Content` property of a `ContentControl` normally enables us to add a single item of content, we are able to add multiple items into panels because their `Children` property, which is set as the content, is a collection.

Another `Panel` class property that we might need to use is the `IsItemsHost` property, which specifies whether a panel is to be used as a container for the items of an `ItemsControl` element, or not. The default value is `false`, and it makes no sense to use this property set to `false`. In fact, it is only ever required in a very particular situation.

That situation is when we are replacing the default panel of an `ItemsControl`, or one of its derived classes, such as a `ListBox`, in a `ControlTemplate`. By setting this property to `true` on a panel element in a `ControlTemplate`, we are telling WPF to place the generated collection elements in the panel. Let's see a quick example of this:

```
<ItemsControl ItemsSource="{Binding Users}">
  <ItemsControl.Template>
    <ControlTemplate TargetType="{x:Type ItemsControl}">
      <StackPanel Orientation="Horizontal" IsItemsHost="True" />
    </ControlTemplate>
```

```
    </ItemsControl.Template>
  </ItemsControl>
```

In this simple example, we are replacing the default internal items panel of the `ItemsControl` element with a horizontal `StackPanel`. Note that this is a permanent replacement and no one can make further changes to this without providing a new `ControlTemplate`. There is however, a far easier way to achieve the same result and we saw an example of this in the previous chapter.

```
<ItemsControl ItemsSource="{Binding Users}">
  <ItemsControl.ItemsPanel>
    <ItemsPanelTemplate>
      <StackPanel Orientation="Horizontal" />
    </ItemsPanelTemplate>
  </ItemsControl.ItemsPanel>
</ItemsControl>
```

In this alternative example, we simply provide a new `ItemsPanelTemplate` for the `ItemsControl` through its `ItemsPanel` property. Using this code, the internal panel can still be easily changed without the need to provide a new `ControlTemplate` and so when we don't want other users to be able to swap out the inner panel, we use the first method, otherwise we use this method.

The `Panel` class also declares a `ZIndex` Attached Property, which can be used by child elements to specify a layered order within the panel. Child elements with higher values will appear above, or in front of, elements setting lower values, although this property is ignored in panels that do not overlap their children. We'll see an example of this in the next section, so let's now focus on the panels that derive from the `Panel` class and what they offer us.

Canvas

The `Canvas` class enables us to explicitly position child elements using combinations of the `Canvas.Top`, `Canvas.Left`, `Canvas.Bottom`, and `Canvas.Right` Attached Properties. This is vaguely similar to the old Windows Forms system of control placement.

However, when using WPF, we don't typically layout UI controls in a `Canvas`. Instead, we tend to use them more for displaying shapes, constructing graphs, showing animations, or drawing applications. Take the following example:

```
<Canvas Width="256" Height="109" Background="Black">
  <Canvas.Resources>
    <Style TargetType="{x:Type Ellipse}">
      <Setter Property="Width" Value="50" />
      <Setter Property="Height" Value="50" />
      <Setter Property="Stroke" Value="Black" />
      <Setter Property="StrokeThickness" Value="3" />
    </Style>
  </Canvas.Resources>
  <Canvas Canvas.Left="3" Canvas.Top="3" Background="Orange"
    Width="123.5" Height="50">
    <Ellipse Canvas.Top="25" Canvas.Left="25" Fill="Cyan" />
  </Canvas>
  <Canvas Canvas.Left="129.5" Canvas.Top="3" Background="Orange"
    Width="123.5" Height="50" Panel.ZIndex="1" />
  <Canvas Canvas.Left="3" Canvas.Top="56" Background="Red" Width="250"
    Height="50" ClipToBounds="True">
    <Ellipse Canvas.Top="-25" Canvas.Left="175" Fill="Lime" />
  </Canvas>
  <Ellipse Canvas.Top="29.5" Canvas.Left="103" Fill="Yellow" />
</Canvas>
```

This example demonstrates a number of important points, so let's first see the visual output of this code before discussing it:

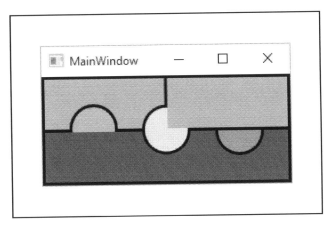

The top-left rectangle is the output from one canvas, the top-right and bottom ones are from two others and they are all contained within a parent canvas element with a black background. The three inner canvases are spaced to give the effect that they each have a border. They have been declared in the order top-left, top-right, bottom, and the last element to be declared is the middle circle.

The left circle is being drawn in the top-left canvas and we can see where it is overlapping the canvas' apparent bottom border, which shows that it is not being clipped by its parent canvas. However, it is being clipped by the lower canvas element and this demonstrates that UI elements that are declared later will be displayed over the top of earlier declared elements.

Nevertheless, the second canvas to be declared is clipping the middle circle, which was the last declared element. This demonstrates that setting the `Panel.ZIndex` property on an element to any positive number will position that element above all others that have not explicitly set this property. The default value for this property is zero, so an element that has this property set to `1` will be rendered on top of all elements that have not explicitly set a value for it.

The next element to be declared is the bottom rectangle and the right circle is declared within it. Now, as this element is declared after the top canvases, you might expect that the right circle would overlap the upper-right canvas. While this would normally be the case, this won't happen with our example for two reasons.

The first, as we've just found out, is because the upper-right panel has a higher `ZIndex` property value than the lower panel and the second reason is because we have set the `UIElement.ClipToBounds` property to `true`, which is used by the `Canvas` panel to determine whether it should clip the visual content of any children that may lie outside the bounds of the panel.

This is commonly used with animations, to enable a visual to be hidden out of the panel bounds and then slid into view in reaction to some event. We can tell that the right circle has been clipped by its parent panel because we can see its apparent top border, which is outside its bounds.

The last element to be declared is the middle circle and we can see that apart from the overlapping canvas element with the higher `ZIndex` property value, it overlaps all of the other elements. Note that the `Canvas` panel does not perform any kind of resizing on its children, so it is not typically used for generating form type UI.

DockPanel

The `DockPanel` class is primarily used in the top levels of the control hierarchy to lay out the top-level controls. It provides us with the ability to dock controls to various parts of the screen, for example, a menu to the top, a context menu to the left, a status bar to the bottom and our main View content control to the remainder of the screen.

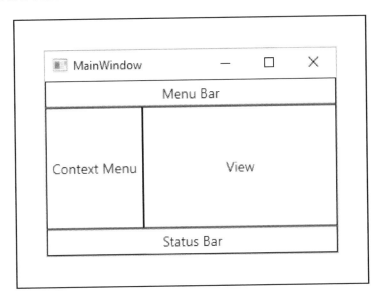

This layout shown in the preceding image can be easily achieved with just the following XAML:

```xaml
<DockPanel>
  <DockPanel.Resources>
    <Style TargetType="{x:Type TextBlock}">
      <Setter Property="HorizontalAlignment" Value="Center" />
      <Setter Property="VerticalAlignment" Value="Center" />
      <Setter Property="FontSize" Value="14" />
    </Style>
    <Style TargetType="{x:Type Border}">
      <Setter Property="BorderBrush" Value="Black" />
      <Setter Property="BorderThickness" Value="1" />
    </Style>
  </DockPanel.Resources>
  <Border Padding="0,3" DockPanel.Dock="Top">
    <TextBlock Text="Menu Bar" />
  </Border>
  <Border Padding="0,3" DockPanel.Dock="Bottom">
    <TextBlock Text="Status Bar" />
```

```
    </Border>
    <Border Width="100" DockPanel.Dock="Left">
      <TextBlock Text="Context Menu" TextWrapping="Wrap" />
    </Border>
    <Border>
      <TextBlock Text="View" />
    </Border>
  </DockPanel>
```

We specify where we want each element within the panel to be docked using the `DockPanel.Dock` Attached Property. We can specify the left, right, top, and bottom of the panel. The remaining space is normally filled by the last child that does not explicitly set one of the `Dock` property. However, if that is not the behavior that we want, then we can set the `LastChildFill` property to `false`.

The `DockPanel` will automatically resize itself to fit its content, unless its dimensions are specified, either explicitly using the `Width` and `Height` properties, or implicitly by a parent panel. If it and its children both have dimensions specified for them, there is a chance that certain children will not be provided with enough space and not be displayed correctly, as the last child is the only child that can be resized by the `DockPanel`. It should also be noted that this panel does not overlap its child elements.

Also note that the order that the children are declared in will affect the space and position that they are each provided with. For example, if we wanted the menu bar to fill the top of the screen, the context menu to take the remaining left side and the View and the status bar to take the remaining space, we could just declare the context menu before the status bar.

```
  ...
  <Border Padding="0,3" DockPanel.Dock="Top">
    <TextBlock Text="Menu Bar" />
  </Border>
  <Border Width="100" DockPanel.Dock="Left">
    <TextBlock Text="Context Menu" TextWrapping="Wrap" />
  </Border>
  <Border Padding="0,3" DockPanel.Dock="Bottom">
    <TextBlock Text="Status Bar" />
  </Border>
  <Border>
    <TextBlock Text="View" />
  </Border>
  ...
```

This slight change would result in the required layout.

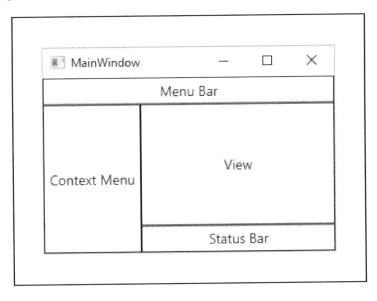

Grid

The Grid panel is by far the most commonly used when it comes to laying out typical UI controls. It is the most versatile and enables us to perform a number of tricks to end up with the layout that we require. It offers a flexible row and column based layout system that we can use to build UIs with a fluid layout. Fluid layouts are able to react and change size when users resize their application windows.

The Grid is one of the few panels that can resize all of its child elements, depending on the available size and so that makes it one of the most performance-intensive panels. Therefore, if we don't need the functionality that it provides, we should use a more performant panel, such as a Canvas, or StackPanel.

The children of a `Grid` panel can each set their `Margin` property to be laid out using absolute coordinates, in a similar fashion to the `Canvas` panel. However, this should be avoided wherever possible, because that will break the fluidity of our UI. Instead, we typically define our desired layout using the grid's `RowDefinitions` and `ColumnDefinitions` collections and the `Grid.Row` and `Grid.Column` Attached Properties.

While we can again hard code exact widths and heights for our rows and columns, we usually try to avoid doing so for the same reason. Instead, we generally take advantage of the grid's sizing behavior and declare our rows and columns, predominantly using one of two values.

The first is the `Auto` value, which takes its size from its content and the second is the default `*` star-sized value, which takes all of the remaining space. Typically, we set all columns or rows to `Auto` except the one(s) that contain(s) the most important data, which is/are set to `*`.

Note that if we have more than one star-sized column, then the space is normally divided equally between them. However, if we need unequal divisions of the remaining space, then we can specify a multiplier number with the asterisk, which will multiply the proportion of space that that row or column will be provided with. Let's see an example to help to clarify this:

```
<Grid TextElement.FontSize="14" Margin="10">
  <Grid.ColumnDefinitions>
    <ColumnDefinition Width="2.5*" />
    <ColumnDefinition />
    <ColumnDefinition />
  </Grid.ColumnDefinitions>
  <Grid.RowDefinitions>
    <RowDefinition />
    <RowDefinition Height="Auto" />
  </Grid.RowDefinitions>
  <TextBlock Grid.ColumnSpan="3" HorizontalAlignment="Center"
    VerticalAlignment="Center" Text="Are you sure you want to continue?"
    Margin="40" />
  <Button Grid.Row="1" Grid.Column="1" Content="Cancel" IsCancel="True"
    Height="26" Margin="0,0,2.5,0" />
  <Button Grid.Row="1" Grid.Column="2" Content="Ok" IsDefault="True"
    Height="26" Margin="2.5,0,0,0" />
</Grid>
```

This example demonstrates a number of points, so let's see the rendered output before continuing.

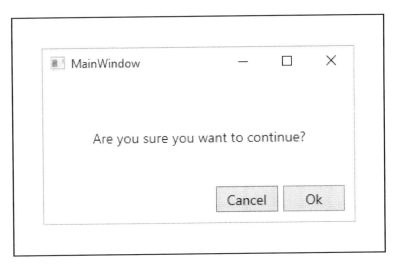

Here, we have a very basic confirmation dialog control. It is formed with a `Grid` panel with three columns and two rows. Note that as single star-sizing is used as the default width and height values for the `ColumnDefinition` and `RowDefinition` elements respectively, we do not need to explicitly set them and can simply declare empty elements.

Therefore, in our example, the second and third columns and the first row will use star-sizing and take all of the remaining space. The first column also uses star-sizing, however it specifies a multiplier value of `2.5`. As such, it will be provided with two and a half times the amount of space that the other two columns will each have.

Note that this first column is only used to push the buttons in the other two columns to the correct position. While the `TextBlock` element is declared in the first column, it does not only reside in that column, because it has also specified the `Grid.ColumnSpan` Attached Property, which allows it to spread out across multiple columns. The `Grid.RowSpan` Attached Property does the same for rows.

The `Grid.Row` and `Grid.Column` Attached Properties are used by each element to specify which cell they should be rendered in. However, the default value for these properties is zero and so, when we want to declare an element within the first column or row of the panel, we can omit the setting of these properties, as has been done for the `TextBlock` in our example.

The **Cancel** button has been declared in the second row and column and sets the `IsCancel` property to `true`, which enables the users to select it by pressing the *Esc* key on their keyboards. The **Ok** button sits next to it in the third column and sets the `IsDefault` key to `true`, which enables users to invoke it by pressing the *Enter* key on their keyboards.

Note that we could have set the lower `RowDefinition.Height` property to `26` instead of setting that on each button explicitly and the end result would have been the same, as the `Auto` value would be calculated from their height anyway. Also, note that the `Margin` property has been set on a few elements here for spacing purposes only, rather than for absolute positioning purposes.

There are two other useful properties declared by the `Grid` class. The first is the `ShowGridLines` property, which as you can imagine, shows the borders of the rows and columns in the panel when set to `true`. While not really required for simple layouts as in the previous example, this can be useful while developing more complicated layouts. However, due to its poor performance, this feature should never be utilized in production XAML.

```
<Grid TextElement.FontSize="14" Margin="10" ShowGridLines="True">
  ...
</Grid>
```

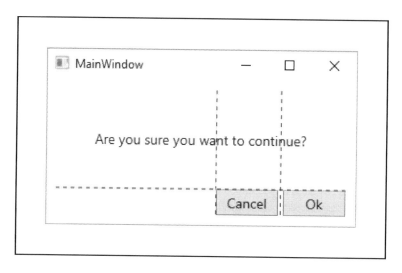

The other useful property is the `IsSharedSizeScope` Attached Property, which enables us to share sizing information between two or more `Grid` panels. We can achieve this by setting this property to `true` on a parent panel and then specifying the `SharedSizeGroup` property on the relevant `ColumnDefinition` and/or `RowDefinition` elements of the inner `Grid` panels.

There are a few conditions that we need to adhere to in order to get this to work and the first relates to scope. The `IsSharedSizeScope` Property need to be set on a parent element, but if that parent element is within a resource template and the definition elements that specify the `SharedSizeGroup` property are outside that template then it will not work. It will however, work in the opposite direction.

The other point to be aware of is that star-sizing is not respected when sharing sizing information. In these cases, the star values of any definition elements will be read as `Auto`, so we do not typically set the `SharedSizeGroup` property on our star-sized column. However, if we set it on the other columns, then we will be left with our desired layout. Let's see an example of this:

```xml
<Grid TextElement.FontSize="14" Margin="10" IsSharedSizeScope="True">
  <Grid.RowDefinitions>
    <RowDefinition Height="Auto" />
    <RowDefinition Height="Auto" />
    <RowDefinition />
  </Grid.RowDefinitions>
  <Grid TextElement.FontWeight="SemiBold" Margin="0,0,0,3"
    ShowGridLines="True">
    <Grid.ColumnDefinitions>
      <ColumnDefinition Width="Auto" SharedSizeGroup="Name" />
      <ColumnDefinition />
      <ColumnDefinition Width="Auto" SharedSizeGroup="Age" />
    </Grid.ColumnDefinitions>
    <TextBlock Text="Name" />
    <TextBlock Grid.Column="1" Text="Comments" Margin="10,0" />
    <TextBlock Grid.Column="2" Text="Age" />
  </Grid>
  <Separator Grid.Row="1" />
  <ItemsControl Grid.Row="2" ItemsSource="{Binding Users}">
    <ItemsControl.ItemTemplate>
      <DataTemplate DataType="{x:Type DataModels:User}">
        <Grid ShowGridLines="True">
          <Grid.ColumnDefinitions>
            <ColumnDefinition Width="Auto" SharedSizeGroup="Name" />
            <ColumnDefinition />
            <ColumnDefinition Width="Auto" SharedSizeGroup="Age" />
          </Grid.ColumnDefinitions>
```

```
                  <TextBlock Text="{Binding Name}" />
                  <TextBlock Grid.Column="1" Text="Star-sized column takes all
                    remaining space" Margin="10,0" />
                  <TextBlock Grid.Column="2" Text="{Binding Age}" />
               </Grid>
            </DataTemplate>
         </ItemsControl.ItemTemplate>
      </ItemsControl>
   </Grid>
```

In this example, we have an `ItemsControl` that is data bound to a slightly edited version of our `Users` collection from our earlier examples. Previously, all of the user names were of a similar length, so one has been edited to demonstrate this point more clearly. The `ShowGridLines` property has also been set to `true` on the inner panels for the same reason.

In the example, we first set the `IsSharedSizeScope` Attached Property to `true` on the parent `Grid` panel and then apply the `SharedSizeGroup` property to the definitions of the inner `Grid` controls, that are declared inside the outer panel and within the `DataTemplate` element. Let's see the rendered output of this code before continuing:

Note that we have provided the same number of columns and group names for the columns inside and outside of the `DataTemplate` element, which is essential for this functionality to work. Also note that we have not set the `SharedSizeGroup` property on the middle column, which is star-sized.

Grouping just the other two columns will have the same visual effect as grouping all three, but without losing the star-sizing on the middle column. However, let's see what would happen if we also set the `SharedSizeGroup` property on the middle column definitions.

```
   <ColumnDefinition SharedSizeGroup="Comments" />
```

As expected, we have lost the star-sizing on our middle column and the remaining space has now been applied to the last column.

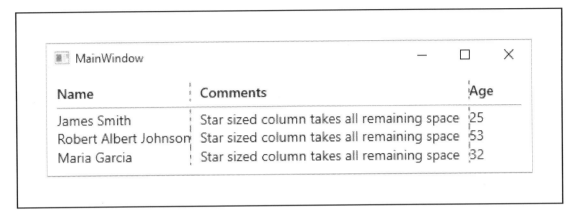

The `Grid` panel within the template will be rendered for each item in the collection and so this will actually result in several panels, each with the same group names and therefore, also column spacing. It is important that we set the `IsSharedSizeScope` property to `true` on the `Grid` panel that is the common parent to all of the inner panels that we wish to share sizing information between.

StackPanel

The `StackPanel` is one of the WPF panels that only provides limited resizing abilities to its child items. It will automatically set the `HorizontalAlignment` and `VerticalAlignment` properties of each of its children to `Stretch`, as long as they don't have explicit sizes specified. In these cases alone, the child elements will be stretched to fit the size of the containing panel. This can be easily demonstrated.

```
<Border Background="Black" Padding="5">
  <Border.Resources>
    <Style TargetType="{x:Type TextBlock}">
      <Setter Property="Padding" Value="5" />
      <Setter Property="Background" Value="Yellow" />
      <Setter Property="TextAlignment" Value="Center" />
    </Style>
  </Border.Resources>
  <StackPanel TextElement.FontSize="14">
    <TextBlock Text="Stretched Horizontally" />
    <TextBlock Text="With Margin" Margin="20" />
    <TextBlock Text="Centered&#x000A;Horizontally"
      HorizontalAlignment="Center" />
```

```
        <Border BorderBrush="Cyan" BorderThickness="1" Margin="0,5,0,0"
          Padding="5" SnapsToDevicePixels="True">
          <StackPanel Orientation="Horizontal">
            <TextBlock Text="Stretched&#x000A;Vertically" />
            <TextBlock Text="With Margin" Margin="20" />
            <TextBlock Text="Centered&#x000A;Vertically"
              VerticalAlignment="Center" />
          </StackPanel>
        </Border>
      </StackPanel>
    </Border>
```

This panel literally lays each child element out one after the other, vertically by default, or horizontally when its `Orientation` property is set to `Horizontal`. Our example uses both orientations, so let's take a quick look at its output before continuing:

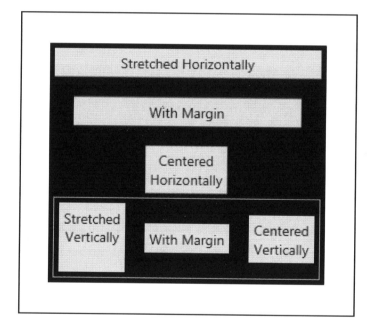

Our whole example is wrapped in a `Border` element with a black background. In its `Resources` section, we declared a few style properties for the `TextBlock` elements in our example. Inside the border, we declare our first `StackPanel` control, with its default vertical orientation. In this first panel, we have three `TextBlock` elements and another `StackPanel` wrapped in a border.

The first `TextBlock` element is automatically stretched to fit the width of the panel. The second adds a margin, but would otherwise also be stretched across the width of the panel. The third however, has its `HorizontalAlignment` property explicitly set to `Center` and so it is not stretched to fit by the panel.

The inner panel has three `TextBlock` elements declared inside it and has its `Orientation` property set to `Horizontal`. Its children are therefore laid out horizontally. Its border is colored, so that it is easier to see its bounds. Note the use of the `SnapsToDevicePixels` property set on it.

As WPF uses device-independent pixel settings, thin straight lines can sometimes lie across individual pixel boundaries and appear anti-aliased. Setting this property to `true` will force the element to be rendered exactly in line with the physical pixels, using device-specific pixel settings and forming a clearer, sharper line.

The first `TextBlock` element in the lower panel is automatically stretched to fit the height of the panel. As with the elements in the upper panel, the second adds a margin, but would otherwise also be stretched across the height of the panel. The third however, has its `VerticalAlignment` property explicitly set to `Center` and so it is not stretched vertically to fit by the panel.

As a side note, we have used the hexadecimal `&#x000A;` entity to add a new line in some of our text strings. This could also have been achieved using the `TextBlock.TextWrapping` property and hard coding a `Width` for each element, but this way is obviously far simpler.

UniformGrid

The `UniformGrid` panel is a lightweight panel that provides a simple way to create a grid of items, where each item is of the same size. We can set its `Row` and `Column` properties to specify how many rows and columns that we want our grid to have. If we do not set one or both of these properties, the panel will implicitly set them for us, dependent upon the available space it has and the size of its children.

It also provides us with a `FirstColumn` property that will affect the column that the first child item will be rendered in. For example, if we set this property to 2 then the first child will be rendered in the third column. This is perfect for a calendar control, so let's take a look at how we might create the following output using the `UniformGrid`.

Mon	Tue	Wed	Thu	Fri	Sat	Sun
▉		1	2	3	4	5
6	7	8	9	10	11	12
13	14	15	16	17	18	19
20	21	22	23	24	25	26
27	28	29	30	31	▉	

As you can see, a calendar control often needs to have blank spaces in the first few columns and so the `FirstColumn` property achieves this requirement simply. Let's see the XAML that defines this calendar example:

```
<StackPanel TextElement.FontSize="14" Background="White">
  <UniformGrid Columns="7" Rows="1">
    <UniformGrid.Resources>
      <Style TargetType="{x:Type TextBlock}">
        <Setter Property="Height" Value="35" />
        <Setter Property="HorizontalAlignment" Value="Center" />
        <Setter Property="Padding" Value="0,5,0,0" />
      </Style>
    </UniformGrid.Resources>
    <TextBlock Text="Mon" />
    <TextBlock Text="Tue" />
    <TextBlock Text="Wed" />
    <TextBlock Text="Thu" />
    <TextBlock Text="Fri" />
    <TextBlock Text="Sat" />
```

```
      <TextBlock Text="Sun" />
    </UniformGrid>
    <ItemsControl ItemsSource="{Binding Days}" Background="Black">
      <ItemsControl.ItemsPanel>
        <ItemsPanelTemplate>
          <UniformGrid Columns="7" FirstColumn="2" />
        </ItemsPanelTemplate>
      </ItemsControl.ItemsPanel>
      <ItemsControl.ItemTemplate>
        <DataTemplate>
          <Border BorderBrush="Black" BorderThickness="1,1,0,0"
            Background="White">
            <TextBlock Text="{Binding}" Height="35"
              HorizontalAlignment="Center" Padding="0,7.5,0,0" />
          </Border>
        </DataTemplate>
      </ItemsControl.ItemTemplate>
    </ItemsControl>
  </StackPanel>
```

We start with a `StackPanel` that is used to stack one `UniformGrid` panel directly above an `ItemsControl` that uses another one as its `ItemsPanel` and specifies a font size to use within the control. The top `UniformGrid` panel declares a single row of seven columns and some basic `TextBlock` styles. It has seven child `TextBlock` items, that output the names of the days in a week.

The `ItemsControl.ItemsSource` is data bound to a `Days` property in our View Model.

```
private List<int> days = Enumerable.Range(1, 31).ToList();

...

public List<int> Days
{
  get { return days; }
  set { days = value; NotifyPropertyChanged(); }
}
```

Note the use of the `Enumerable.Range` method to populate the collection. It provides a simple way to generate a contiguous sequence of integers from the supplied start and length input parameters. As a LINQ method, it is implemented using deferred execution and the actual values are not generated until actually accessed.

The second `UniformGrid` panel, that is set as the `ItemsControl.ItemsPanel`, only specifies that it should have seven columns, but leaves the number of rows to be calculated from the number of data bound items. Note also, that we have hard coded a value of 2 to the `FirstColumn` property, although in a proper control, we would typically data bind the value for the relevant month to it instead.

Finally, we use a `DataTemplate` to define what each day on the calendar should look like. Note that we do not need to specify a value for its `DataType` property in this example, because we are data binding to the whole data source object, which in this case, is just an integer. Let's now move on to investigate the `WrapPanel` panel.

WrapPanel

The `WrapPanel` is similar to the `StackPanel`, except that it will stack its children in both directions by default. It starts by laying out the child items horizontally and when it runs out of space on the first row, it automatically wraps the next item onto a new row and continues to lay out the remaining controls. It repeats this process using as many rows as are required, until all of the items are rendered.

However, it also provides an `Orientation` property like the `StackPanel`, and this will affect its layout behavior. If the `Orientation` property is changed from the default value of `Horizontal` to `Vertical`, then the panel's child items will be laid out vertically, from top to bottom until there is no more room in the first column. The items will then wrap to the next column and will continue in this way until all of the items have been rendered.

This panel also declares `ItemHeight` and `ItemWidth` properties that enable it to restrict items' dimensions and to produce a layout behavior similar to the `UniformGrid` panel. Note that the values will not actually resize each child item, but merely restrict the available space that they are provided with in the panel. Let's see an example of this:

```
<WrapPanel ItemHeight="50" Width="150" TextElement.FontSize="14">
  <WrapPanel.Resources>
    <Style TargetType="{x:Type Button}">
      <Setter Property="Width" Value="50" />
    </Style>
  </WrapPanel.Resources>
  <Button Content="7" />
  <Button Content="8" />
  <Button Content="9" />
  <Button Content="4" />
  <Button Content="5" />
  <Button Content="6" />
  <Button Content="1" />
```

```
        <Button Content="2" />
        <Button Content="3" />
        <Button Content="0" Width="100" />
        <Button Content="." />
    </WrapPanel>
```

Note that while similar to the output of a `UniformGrid` panel, the output of this example could not actually be achieved with that panel, because one of the child items is a different size to the others. Let's see the visual output of this example.

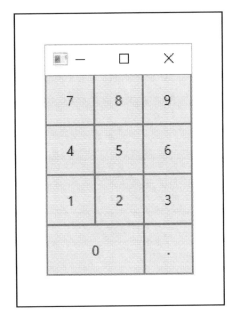

We first declare the `WrapPanel` and specify that each child should only be provided with a height of 50 pixels, while the panel itself should be 150 pixels wide. In the `Resources` section, we set the width of each button to be 50 pixels, therefore enabling three buttons to sit next to each other on each row, before wrapping items to the next row.

Next, we simply define the eleven buttons that make up the panel's children, specifying that the zero button should be twice as wide as the others. Note that this would not have worked if we had set the `ItemWidth` property to 50 pixels, along with the `ItemHeight` property. In that case, we would have seen half of the zero button, with the other half covered by the period button and a blank space where the period button currently is.

Providing custom layout behavior

When the layout behavior of the built-in panels do not meet our requirements, we can easily define a new panel with custom layout behavior. All we need to do is declare a class that extends the `Panel` class and override its `MeasureOverride` and `ArrangeOverride` methods.

In the `MeasureOverride` method, we simply call the `Measure` method on each child item from the `Children` collection, passing in a `Size` element set to `double.PositiveInfinity`. This is equivalent to saying "set your `DesriredSize` property as if you had all of the space that you could possibly need" to each child item.

In the `ArrangeOverride` method, we use the newly determined `DesriredSize` property value of each child item to calculate its required position and call its `Arrange` method to render it in that position. Let's look at an example of a custom panel that positions its items equally around the circumference of a circle.

```
using System;
using System.Windows;
using System.Windows.Controls;

namespace CompanyName.ApplicationName.Views.Panels
{
  public class CircumferencePanel : Panel
  {
    public Thickness Padding { get; set; }

    protected override Size MeasureOverride(Size availableSize)
    {
      foreach (UIElement element in Children)
      {
        element.Measure(
          new Size(double.PositiveInfinity, double.PositiveInfinity));
      }
      return availableSize;
    }

    protected override Size ArrangeOverride(Size finalSize)
    {
      if (Children.Count == 0) return finalSize;
      double currentAngle = 90 * (Math.PI / 180);
      double radiansPerElement =
        (360 / Children.Count) * (Math.PI / 180.0);
      double radiusX = finalSize.Width / 2.0 - Padding.Left;
      double radiusY = finalSize.Height / 2.0 - Padding.Top;
      foreach (UIElement element in Children)
```

```
      {
        Point childPoint = new Point(Math.Cos(currentAngle) * radiusX,
          -Math.Sin(currentAngle) * radiusY);
        Point centeredChildPoint = new Point(childPoint.X +
          finalSize.Width / 2 - element.DesiredSize.Width / 2, childPoint.Y
          + finalSize.Height / 2 - element.DesiredSize.Height / 2);
        Rect boundingBox =
          new Rect(centeredChildPoint, element.DesiredSize);
        element.Arrange(boundingBox);
        currentAngle -= radiansPerElement;
      }
      return finalSize;
    }
  }
}
```

In our `CircumferencePanel` class, we first declare our own `Padding` property of type `Thickness`, which will be used to enable the users of the panel to lengthen or shorten the radius of the circle and therefore, adjust the position of the rendered items within the panel. The `MeasureOverride` method is a simple affair, as previously explained.

In the `ArrangeOverride` method, we calculate the relevant angles to position the child items with, depending upon how many of them there are. We take the value of our `Padding` property into consideration when calculating the X and Y radiuses, so that users of our custom panel will be better able to control the position of the rendered items.

For each child item in the panel's `Children` collection, we first calculate the point on the circle where it should be displayed. We then offset that value using the value of the element's `DesiredSize` property, so that the bounding box of each item is centered on that point.

We then create the element's bounding box using a `Rect` element, with the offset point and the element's `DesiredSize` property, and pass that to its `Arrange` method to render it. After each element is rendered, the current angle is changed for the next item. Remember that we can utilize this panel by setting the `ItemsPanel` property of an `ItemsControl` or one of its derived classes.

```
<ItemsControl ItemsSource="{Binding Hours}" TextElement.FontSize="24">
  <ItemsControl.ItemsPanel>
    <ItemsPanelTemplate>
      <Panels:CircumferencePanel Padding="15" />
    </ItemsPanelTemplate>
  </ItemsControl.ItemsPanel>
</ItemsControl>
```

Given some suitable data, we could use this panel to display the numbers on a clock control, for example. Let's see the `Hours` property that the `ItemsSource` property of our example `ItemsControl` is data bound to.

```
private List<int> hours = new List<int>() { 12 };

public List<int> Hours
{
  get { return hours; }
  set { hours = value; NotifyPropertyChanged(); }
}

. . .

hours.AddRange(Enumerable.Range(1, 11));
```

As the hour numerals must start with twelve and then go back to one, we declare the collection with the twelve element initially. At some later stage, possibly during construction, we then add the remaining numbers to the collection and this is what it looks like when using our new panel.

This concludes our coverage of the main panels that are available in WPF. While we don't have the space to have an in-depth look at every other WPF control, we'll find tips and tricks for a number of them throughout this book. Instead, let's now focus on a few essential controls and what they can do for us.

Content controls

While this control is not often used directly, one use for it is to render a single data item according to a particular template. In fact, we often use a ContentControl to display our View Models and use a DataTemplate object that renders the associated View. We might use some form of ItemsControl to display a group of items and a ContentControl to display the selected item.

As we found out earlier, when looking at the inheritance hierarchy of the Button control, the ContentControl class extends the Control class and adds the ability for derived classes to contain any single CLR object. Note that if we need to specify more than a single object of content, we can use a single panel object that contains further objects.

```
<Button Width="80" Height="30" TextElement.FontSize="14">
  <StackPanel Orientation="Horizontal">
    <Rectangle Fill="Cyan" Stroke="Black" StrokeThickness="1" Width="16"
      Height="16" />
    <TextBlock Text="Cyan" Margin="5,0,0,0" />
  </StackPanel>
</Button>
```

We can specify this content through the use of the Content property. However, the ContentControl class specifies the Content property in a ContentPropertyAttribute attribute in its class definition and this enables us to set the content by simply adding a child element to the control. This attribute is used by the XAML processor when it processes XAML child elements.

If the content is of type `string`, then we can use the `ContentStringFormat` property to specify a particular format for it. Otherwise, we can use the `ContentTemplate` property to specify a `DataTemplate` to use while rendering the content. Alternatively, the `ContentTemplateSelector` property is of type `DataTemplateSelector` and also enables us to select a `DataTemplate`, but based upon some custom condition that we may have. All derived classes have access to these properties in order to shape the output of their content.

However, this control is also able to display many primitive types without us having to specify a custom template. Let's move on to the next section now, where we'll find out exactly how it manages to accomplish this.

Presenting content

In WPF, there is a special element that is essential, but often little understood. The `ContentPresenter` class basically presents content, as its name suggests. It is actually internally used within `ContentControl` objects to present their content.

That is its sole job and it should not be used for other purposes. The only time that we should declare these elements is within a `ControlTemplate` of a `ContentControl`, or one of its many derived classes. In these cases, we declare them where we want the actual content to appear.

Note that specifying the `TargetType` property on a `ControlTemplate` when using a `ContentPresenter` will result in its `Content` property being implicitly data bound to the `Content` property of the relevant `ContentControl` element. We are however, free to data bind it explicitly to whatever we like.

```
<ControlTemplate x:Key="ButtonTemplate" TargetType="{x:Type Button}">
  <ContentPresenter Content="{TemplateBinding ToolTip}" />
</ControlTemplate>
```

The `ContentTemplate` and `ContentTemplateSelector` properties both mirror those of the `ContentControl` class and also enable us to select a `DataTemplate` based upon a custom condition. Like the `Content` property, both of these properties will also be implicitly data bound to the properties of the same names in the templated parent if the `TargetType` property of the `ControlTemplate` has been set.

This usually saves us from having to explicitly data bind these properties, although there are a few controls where the names of the relevant properties do not match up. In these cases, we can use the `ContentSource` property as a shortcut to data bind the `Content`, `ContentTemplate` and `ContentTemplateSelector` properties.

If we set this property to `Header` for example, the Framework will look for a property named `Header` on the `ContentControl` object to implicitly data bind to the `Content` property of the presenter. Likewise, it will look for properties named `HeaderTemplate` and `HeaderTemplateSelector` to implicitly data bind to the `ContentTemplate` and `ContentTemplateSelector` properties.

This is primarily used in a `ControlTemplate` for a `HeaderedContentControl` element, or one of its derived classes.

```
<ControlTemplate x:Key="TabItemTemplate" TargetType="{x:Type TabItem}">
  <StackPanel>
    <ContentPresenter ContentSource="Header" />
    <ContentPresenter ContentSource="Content" />
  </StackPanel>
</ControlTemplate>
```

There are specific rules that determine what the `ContentPresenter` will display. If the `ContentTemplate` or `ContentTemplateSelector` property is set, then the data object specified by the `Content` property will have the resulting data template applied to it. Likewise, if a data template of the relevant type is found within scope of the `ContentPresenter` element, it will be applied.

If the content object is a UI element, or one is returned from a type converter, then the element is displayed directly. If the object is a string, or a string is returned from a type converter, then it will be set as the `Text` property of a `TextBlock` control and that will be displayed. Likewise, all other objects simply have the `ToString` method called on them and this output is rendered in a `TextBlock`.

Items controls

We've already seen a fair number of examples of the `ItemsControl` class, but we'll now take a closer look at this control. In the simplest terms, an `ItemsControl` contains a variable number of `ContentPresenter` elements and enables us to display a collection of items. It is the base class for most common collection controls, such as the `ListBox`, `ComboBox` and `TreeView` controls.

Each of these derived classes adds a specific look and set of capabilities, such as a border and the notion of a selected item. If we do not require these additional features and simply want to display a number of items, then we should just use the `ItemsControl`, because it is more efficient than its derived classes.

When using MVVM, we typically data bind a collection that implements the `IEnumerable` interface from our View Model to the `ItemsControl.ItemsSource` property. However, there is also an `Items` property that will reflect the items in the data bound collection.

To clarify this further, either property can be used to populate the collection of items to display. However, only one can be used at a time, so if you have data bound a collection to the `ItemsSource` property, then you cannot add items using the `Items` property. In this case, the `Items` collection will become read-only.

If we need to display a collection of items that does not implement the `IEnumerable` interface, then we will need to add them using the `Items` property. Note that the `Items` property is implicitly used when items are declared as the content of an `ItemsControl` element in XAML. However, when using MVVM, we generally use the `ItemsSource` property.

When displaying items in an `ItemsControl`, each item in the collection will implicitly be wrapped in a `ContentPresenter` container element. The type of this container element will depend upon the type of collection control used. For example, a `ComboBox` would wrap its items in `ComboBoxItem` elements.

The `ItemContainerStyle` and `ItemContainerStyleSelector` properties enable us to provide a style for these container items. We must ensure that the styles that we provide are targeted to the correct type of container control. For example, if we were using a `ListBox`, then we would need to provide a style targeting the `ListBoxItem` type, as in the following example.

Note that we can explicitly declare these container items, although there is little point in doing so, as it will otherwise be done for us. Furthermore, when using MVVM, we do not typically work with UI elements, preferring to work with data objects in the View Models and data bind to the `ItemsSource` property instead.

As we have already seen, the `ItemsControl` class has an `ItemsPanel` property of type `ItemsPanelTemplate`, that enables us to change the type of panel that the collection control uses to layout its items. When we want to customize the template of an `ItemsControl`, we have two choices regarding how we render the control's child items.

```
<ControlTemplate x:Key="Template1" TargetType="{x:Type ItemsControl}">
  <StackPanel Orientation="Horizontal" IsItemsHost="True" />
</ControlTemplate>
```

We already saw an example of the preceding method in the previous section. In this way, we specify the actual items panel itself and set the `IsItemsHost` property to `true` on it to indicate that it is indeed to be used as the control's items panel. Using the alternative method, we need to declare an `ItemsPresenter` element, which specifies where the actual items panel will be rendered. Note that this element will be replaced by the actual items panel being used at runtime.

```
<ControlTemplate x:Key="Template2" TargetType="{x:Type ItemsControl}">
  <ItemsPresenter />
</ControlTemplate>
```

As with the `ContentControl` class, the `ItemsControl` class also provides properties that enable us to shape its data items. The `ItemTemplate` and `ItemTemplateSelector` properties let us apply a data template for the items. However, if we just need a simple textual output, we can use the `DisplayMemberPath` property to specify the name of the property from the object to display and avoid defining a data template at all. Alternatively, we can set the `ItemStringFormat` property to format the output as a string.

Another interesting property is the `AlternationCount` property, which enables us to style alternating containers differently. We can set it to any number and the alternating sequence will repeat after that many items have been rendered. As a simple example, let's use a `ListBox`, because the `ListBoxItem` controls that will be wrapped around our items have appearance properties that we can alternate.

```
<ListBox ItemsSource="{Binding Users}" AlternationCount="3">
  <ListBox.ItemContainerStyle>
    <Style TargetType="{x:Type ListBoxItem}">
      <Setter Property="FontSize" Value="14" />
      <Setter Property="Foreground" Value="White" />
      <Setter Property="Padding" Value="5" />
      <Style.Triggers>
        <Trigger Property="ListBox.AlternationIndex" Value="0">
          <Setter Property="Background" Value="Red" />
        </Trigger>
        <Trigger Property="ListBox.AlternationIndex" Value="1">
          <Setter Property="Background" Value="Green" />
        </Trigger>
        <Trigger Property="ListBox.AlternationIndex" Value="2">
          <Setter Property="Background" Value="Blue" />
        </Trigger>
      </Style.Triggers>
    </Style>
  </ListBox.ItemContainerStyle>
</ListBox>
```

Here, we set the `AlternationCount` property to 3, so we can have three different styles for our items and this pattern will be repeated for every three further items. We make a style for the item containers using the `ItemContainerStyle` property.

In this style, we use some simple triggers to change the color of the container background, depending on the value of the `AlternationIndex` property. Notice that the `AlternationCount` property starts at 0, so the first item will have a red background, the second will have green, the third will have blue, then the pattern will repeat and the fourth will have red and so on.

Alternatively, we could have declared an `AlternationConverter` instance for each property that we wanted to alter and data bind them to the `AlternationIndex` property and the converter. We could create the same visual output using this XAML instead.

```
<ListBox ItemsSource="{Binding Users}" AlternationCount="3">
  <ListBox.Resources>
    <AlternationConverter x:Key="BackgroundConverter">
      <SolidColorBrush>Red</SolidColorBrush>
      <SolidColorBrush>Green</SolidColorBrush>
      <SolidColorBrush>Blue</SolidColorBrush>
    </AlternationConverter>
  </ListBox.Resources>
  <ListBox.ItemContainerStyle>
    <Style TargetType="{x:Type ListBoxItem}">
      <Setter Property="FontSize" Value="14" />
      <Setter Property="Foreground" Value="White" />
      <Setter Property="Padding" Value="5" />
      <Setter Property="Background"
        Value="{Binding (ItemsControl.AlternationIndex),
        RelativeSource={RelativeSource Self},
        Converter={StaticResource BackgroundConverter}}" />
    </Style>
  </ListBox.ItemContainerStyle>
</ListBox>
```

The `AlternationConverter` class works by simply returning the item from its collection that relates to the specified `AlternationIndex` value, where the first item is returned for index zero. Note that we need to include the parenthesis around the data bound class and property name because it is an Attached Property and we need to use a `RelativeSource.Self` binding because the property is set on the item container object itself. Let's see the output of these two code examples.

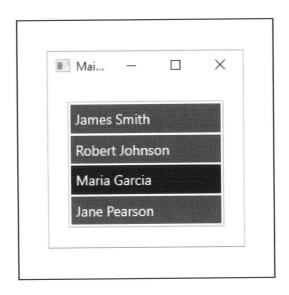

There is one more useful property that the `ItemsControl` class provides and that is the `GroupStyle` property, which is used to display the child items in groups. To group items in the UI, we need to accomplish a few simple tasks.

We first need to data bind a `CollectionViewSource` with one or more `PropertyGroupDescription` elements to our `Users` collection from the last example. We then need to set that as the `ItemsSource` value for the `ItemsControl` and then set up its `GroupStyle`. Let's see the `CollectionViewSource` object that we need to declare in the local `Resources` section.

```
<CollectionViewSource x:Key="GroupedUsers" Source="{Binding Users}">
  <CollectionViewSource.GroupDescriptions>
    <PropertyGroupDescription PropertyName="Name"
      Converter="{StaticResource StringToFirstLetterConverter}" />
  </CollectionViewSource.GroupDescriptions>
</CollectionViewSource>
```

We specify the property that we want to use to group items by using the `PropertyName` property of the `PropertyGroupDescription` element. Note that in our case, we only have a few `User` objects and so, there would be no groups if we simply grouped by name. Therefore, we added a converter to return the first letter from each name to group on and specified it using the `Converter` property.

```
using System;
using System.Globalization;
using System.Windows;
using System.Windows.Data;

namespace CompanyName.ApplicationName.Converters
{
  [ValueConversion(typeof(string), typeof(string))]
  public class StringToFirstLetterConverter : IValueConverter
  {
    public object Convert(object value, Type targetType, object parameter,
      CultureInfo culture)
    {
      if (value == null) return DependencyProperty.UnsetValue;
      return value.ToString()[0];
    }

    public object ConvertBack(object value, Type targetType,
      object parameter, CultureInfo culture)
    {
      return DependencyProperty.UnsetValue;
    }
  }
}
```

In this converter, we specify the data types that are involved in the implementation of the converter in the `ValueConversion` attribute, even though they are the same type. In the `Convert` method, we check the validity of our `value` input parameter and return the `DependencyProperty.UnsetValue` value if it is null. For valid values, we simply return the first letter of their string representations.

As we do not need, or would not be able to convert anything back using this converter, the `ConvertBack` method simply returns the `DependencyProperty.UnsetValue` value. By attaching this converter to the `PropertyGroupDescription` element, we are now able to group by the first letter of each name. Let's now see how we can declare the `GroupStyle` object.

```
<ItemsControl ItemsSource="{Binding Source={StaticResource GroupedUsers}}"
  FontSize="14">
  <ItemsControl.GroupStyle>
    <GroupStyle>
      <GroupStyle.HeaderTemplate>
        <DataTemplate>
          <TextBlock Text="{Binding Name,
            Converter={StaticResource StringToFirstLetterConverter}}"
            Background="Black" Foreground="White" FontWeight="Bold"
            Padding="5,4" />
        </DataTemplate>
      </GroupStyle.HeaderTemplate>
    </GroupStyle>
  </ItemsControl.GroupStyle>
  <ItemsControl.ItemTemplate>
    <DataTemplate DataType="{x:Type DataModels:User}">
     <TextBlock Text="{Binding Name}" Background="White" Foreground="Black"
       Padding="0,2" />
    </DataTemplate>
  </ItemsControl.ItemTemplate>
</ItemsControl>
```

Note that we need to use the `Binding.Source` property to access the `CollectionViewSource` object named `GroupedUsers` from the local `Resources` section. We then declare the data template that defines what each group header will look like in the `HeaderTemplate` property. Here we make use of the `StringToFirstLetterConverter` instance that has also been declared in a suitable resource collection, and set a few basic style properties.

Next, we specify a second data template, but one that defines what each item in each group should look like. We provide a very simple template that merely spaces the elements slightly and sets a few style properties. Let's see the output of this example.

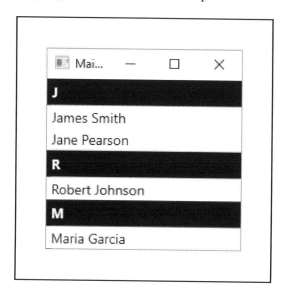

Adorners

An adorner is a special kind of class that is rendered above all UI controls, in what is known as an adorner layer. Adorner elements in this layer will always be rendered, on top of the normal WPF controls, regardless of their `Panel.ZIndex` property setting. Each adorner is bound to an element of type `UIElement` and independently rendered in a position that is relative to the adorned element.

The purpose of the adorner is to provide certain visual cues to the application user. For example, we could use an adorner to display a visual representation of UI elements that are being dragged in a drag and drop operation. Alternatively, we could use an adorner to add "handles" to a UI control to enable users to resize the element.

As the adorner is added to the adorner layer, it is the adorner layer that is the parent of the adorner, rather than the adorned element. In order to create a custom adorner, we need to declare a class that extends the `Adorner` class.

When creating a custom adorner, we need to be aware that we are responsible for writing the code to render its visuals. However, there are a few different ways to construct our adorner graphics; we can use the `OnRender` or `OnRenderSizeChanged` methods and a drawing context to draw basic lines and shapes, or we can use the `ArrangeOverride` method to arrange .NET controls.

Adorners receive events like other .NET controls, although if we don't need to handle them, we can arrange for them to be passed straight through to the adorned element. In these cases, we can set the `IsHitTestVisible` property to `false` and this will enable pass-through hit-testing of the adorned element. Let's see an example of a resizing adorner that lets us resize shapes on a canvas.

```
using System;
using System.Windows;
using System.Windows.Controls;
using System.Windows.Controls.Primitives;
using System.Windows.Documents;
using System.Windows.Input;
using System.Windows.Media;

namespace CompanyName.ApplicationName.Views.Adorners
{
  public class ResizeAdorner : Adorner
  {
    private VisualCollection visualChildren;
    private Thumb top, left, bottom, right;

    public ResizeAdorner(UIElement adornedElement) : base(adornedElement)
    {
      visualChildren = new VisualCollection(this);
      top = InitializeThumb(Cursors.SizeNS, Top_DragDelta);
      left = InitializeThumb(Cursors.SizeWE, Left_DragDelta);
      bottom = InitializeThumb(Cursors.SizeNS, Bottom_DragDelta);
      right = InitializeThumb(Cursors.SizeWE, Right_DragDelta);
    }

    private Thumb InitializeThumb(Cursor cursor,
      DragDeltaEventHandler eventHandler)
    {
      Thumb thumb = new Thumb();
      thumb.BorderBrush = Brushes.Black;
      thumb.BorderThickness = new Thickness(1);
      thumb.Cursor = cursor;
      thumb.DragDelta += eventHandler;
      thumb.Height = thumb.Width = 6.0;
      visualChildren.Add(thumb);
      return thumb;
```

```
  }

  private void Top_DragDelta(object sender, DragDeltaEventArgs e)
  {
    FrameworkElement adornedElement = (FrameworkElement)AdornedElement;
    adornedElement.Height =
      Math.Max(adornedElement.Height - e.VerticalChange, 6);
    Canvas.SetTop(adornedElement,
      Canvas.GetTop(adornedElement) + e.VerticalChange);
  }

  private void Left_DragDelta(object sender, DragDeltaEventArgs e)
  {
    FrameworkElement adornedElement = (FrameworkElement)AdornedElement;
    adornedElement.Width =
      Math.Max(adornedElement.Width - e.HorizontalChange, 6);
    Canvas.SetLeft(adornedElement,
      Canvas.GetLeft(adornedElement) + e.HorizontalChange);
  }

  private void Bottom_DragDelta(object sender, DragDeltaEventArgs e)
  {
    FrameworkElement adornedElement = (FrameworkElement)AdornedElement;
    adornedElement.Height =
      Math.Max(adornedElement.Height + e.VerticalChange, 6);
  }

  private void Right_DragDelta(object sender, DragDeltaEventArgs e)
  {
    FrameworkElement adornedElement = (FrameworkElement)AdornedElement;
    adornedElement.Width =
      Math.Max(adornedElement.Width + e.HorizontalChange, 6);
  }

  protected override void OnRender(DrawingContext drawingContext)
  {
    SolidColorBrush brush = new SolidColorBrush(Colors.Transparent);
    Pen pen = new Pen(new SolidColorBrush(Colors.DeepSkyBlue), 1.0);
    drawingContext.DrawRectangle(brush, pen,
      new Rect(-2, -2, AdornedElement.DesiredSize.Width + 4,
      AdornedElement.DesiredSize.Height + 4));
  }

  protected override Size ArrangeOverride(Size finalSize)
  {
    top.Arrange(
      new Rect(AdornedElement.DesiredSize.Width / 2 - 3, -8, 6, 6));
    left.Arrange(
```

```
      new Rect(-8, AdornedElement.DesiredSize.Height / 2 - 3, 6, 6));
    bottom.Arrange(new Rect(AdornedElement.DesiredSize.Width / 2 - 3,
      AdornedElement.DesiredSize.Height + 2, 6, 6));
    right.Arrange(new Rect(AdornedElement.DesiredSize.Width + 2,
      AdornedElement.DesiredSize.Height / 2 - 3, 6, 6));
    return finalSize;
  }

  protected override int VisualChildrenCount
  {
    get { return visualChildren.Count; }
  }

  protected override Visual GetVisualChild(int index)
  {
    return visualChildren[index];
  }
 }
}
```

Before we investigate this class, let's first see how we can use it. Adorners need to be initialized in code and so, a good place to do this is in the `UserControl.Loaded` method, when we can be certain that the canvas and its items will have been initialized. Note that as adorners are purely UI related, initializing them in the control's code behind does not present any conflict when using MVVM.

```
Loaded += View_Loaded;

...

private void View_Loaded(object sender, RoutedEventArgs e)
{
  AdornerLayer adornerLayer = AdornerLayer.GetAdornerLayer(Canvas);
  foreach (UIElement uiElement in Canvas.Children)
  {
    adornerLayer.Add(new ResizeAdorner(uiElement));
  }
}
```

We access the adorner layer for the canvas that we will add the adorners to using the `AdornerLayer.GetAdornerLayer` method, passing in the canvas as the `Visual` input parameter. In this example, we attach an instance of our `ResizeAdorner` to each element in the canvas' `Children` collection and add then add it to the adorner layer.

Now, we just need a `Canvas` panel named `Canvas` and some shapes to resize.

```
<Canvas Name="Canvas">
  <Rectangle Canvas.Top="50" Canvas.Left="50" Fill="Lime"
    Stroke="Black" StrokeThickness="3" Width="150" Height="50" />
  <Rectangle Canvas.Top="25" Canvas.Left="250" Fill="Yellow"
    Stroke="Black" StrokeThickness="3" Width="50" Height="150" />
</Canvas>
```

Let's now return to examine our `ResizeAdorner` class. Note that we have declared the `Adorners` namespace within the `Views` project, as this is the only place that it will be used. Inside the class, we declare the `VisualCollection` object that will contain the visuals that we want to render and then the visuals themselves, in the shape of `Thumb` controls.

We've chosen `Thumb` elements because they have built-in functionality that we want to take advantage of. They provide a `DragDelta` event that we will use to register the users' mouse movements when they drag each `Thumb`. These controls are normally used internally in the `Slider` and `ScrollBar` controls to enable users to alter values, so they're perfect for our purposes here.

We initialize these objects in the constructor, specifying a custom cursor and a different `DragDelta` event handler for each `Thumb` control. In these separate event handlers, we use the `HorizontalChange` or `VerticalChange` properties of the `DragDeltaEventArgs` object to specify the distance and direction of the mouse movement that triggered the event.

We use these values to move and/or resize the adorned element by the appropriate amount and direction. Note that we use the `Math.Max` method and the value 6 in our example to ensure that the adorned element cannot be resized smaller than the size of each `Thumb` element and the `Stroke` size of each adorned element.

After the four `DragDelta` event handlers, we find two different ways to render our adorner visuals. In the first method, we use the `DrawingContext` object that is passed into the `OnRender` method by the base class to manually draw shapes. This is somewhat similar to the way that we used to draw in the `Control.Paint` event handler methods when using `Windows.Forms`.

In this overridden method, we draw a rectangle that surrounds our element and is four pixels bigger than it in both dimensions. Note that we define a transparent background for the drawing brush, as we only want to see the rectangle border. Remember that adorner graphics are rendered on top of the adorned element, but we do not want to cover it.

In the `ArrangeOverride` method, we use the .NET Framework to render our `Visual` elements using their `Arrange` methods, as we would in a custom panel. Note that we could just as easily render our rectangle border in this method using a `Rectangle` element; the `OnRender` method was used in this example merely as a demonstration.

In this method, we simply arrange each `Visual` element at the relevant position and size in turn. Calculating the appropriate positions can be achieved simply by dividing the width or height of each adorned element in half and subtracting half of the width or height of each thumb element.

Finally, we get to the protected overridden `VisualChildrenCount` property and `GetVisualChild` method. The `Adorner` class extends the `FrameworkElement` class and that will normally return either zero or one from the `VisualChildrenCount` property, as each instance is normally represented by either no visual, or a single rendered visual.

In our case and other situations when a derived class has multiple visuals to render, it is a requirement of the layout system that the correct number of visuals is specified. For example, if we always returned the value 2 from this property, then only two of our thumbs would be rendered on the screen.

Likewise, we also need to return the correct item from our visual collection when requested to from the `GetVisualChild` method. If, for example, we always returned the first visual from our collection, then only that visual would be rendered, as the same visual cannot be rendered more than once. Let's see what our adorners look like when rendered above each of our shapes.

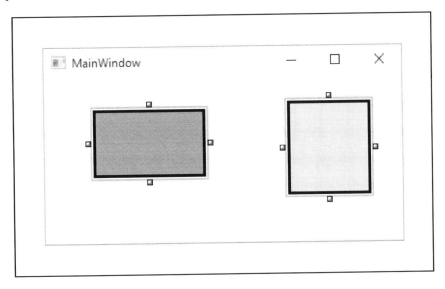

Modifying existing controls

When we find that the wide range of existing controls do not quite meet our needs, we might think that we need to create some new ones, as we would with other technologies. When using other UI languages, this might be the case, but with WPF, this is not necessarily correct, as it provides a number of ways to modify the existing controls to suit our requirements.

As we found out earlier, all classes that extend the `FrameworkElement` class have access to the framework's styling capabilities and those that extend the `Control` class can have their appearance totally changed through their `ControlTemplate` property. All of the existing WPF controls extend these base cases and so, possess these abilities.

In addition to these capabilities that enable us to change the look of the pre-existing WPF controls, we are also able to leverage the power of Attached Properties to add additional functionality to them too. In this section, we will investigate these different ways of modifying the existing controls.

Styling

Setting the various properties of a control is the simplest way to alter its look and enables us to make either minor, or more dramatic changes to it. As most UI elements extend the `Control` class, they mostly share the same properties that affect their appearance and alignment. When defining styles for controls, we should specify their type in the `TargetType` property, as this helps the compiler to verify that the properties that we are setting actually exist in the class.

```
<Button Content="Go">
  <Button.Style>
    <Style TargetType="{x:Type Button}">
      <Setter Property="Foreground" Value="Green" />
      <Setter Property="Background" Value="White" />
    </Style>
  </Button.Style>
</Button>
```

Failing to do so will result in the compiler stating that the member is not recognized or is not accessible. In these cases, we will need to specify the class type as well, in the format `ClassName.PropertyName`.

```
<Button Content="Go">
  <Button.Style>
    <Style>
```

```
      <Setter Property="Button.Foreground" Value="Green" />
      <Setter Property="Button.Background" Value="White" />
    </Style>
  </Button.Style>
</Button>
```

One really useful property that the `Style` class declares is the `BasedOn` property. Using this property, we can base our styles on other styles and this enables us to create a number of incrementally different versions. Let's highlight this with an example.

```
<Style x:Key="TextBoxStyle" TargetType="{x:Type TextBox}">
  <Setter Property="SnapsToDevicePixels" Value="True" />
  <Setter Property="Margin" Value="0,0,0,5" />
  <Setter Property="Padding" Value="1.5,2" />
  <Setter Property="TextWrapping" Value="Wrap" />
</Style>
<Style x:Key="ReadOnlyTextBoxStyle" TargetType="{x:Type TextBox}"
  BasedOn="{StaticResource TextBoxStyle}">
  <Setter Property="IsReadOnly" Value="True" />
  <Setter Property="Cursor" Value="Arrow" />
</Style>
```

Here, we define a simple style for the textboxes in our application. We name it `TextBoxStyle` and then reference it in the `BasedOn` property of the second style. This means that all of the property setters and triggers declared in the first style will also apply to the bottom style. In the second style, we add a few further setters to make the applied textbox read-only.

One last point to note is that if we wanted to base a style on the default style of a control, we can use the value that we normally enter into the `TargetType` property as the key to identify the style that we want to base the new style on.

```
<Style x:Key="ExtendedTextBoxStyle" TargetType="{x:Type TextBox}"
  BasedOn="{StaticResource {x:Type TextBox}}">
  ...
</Style>
```

Being resourceful

Styles are most often declared in the various `Resources` dictionaries of the application, along with various templates and application colors and brushes. The `Resources` property is of type `ResourceDictionary` and declared in the `FrameworkElement` class and so virtually all UI elements inherit it and can therefore host our styles and other resources.

Although the `Resources` property is of type `ResourceDictionary`, we do not need to explicitly declare this element.

```
<Application.Resources>
  <ResourceDictionary>
    <!-- Add resources here -->
  </ResourceDictionary>
</Application.Resources>
```

While there are some occasions when we do need to explicitly declare the `ResourceDictionary`, it will be implicitly declared for us if we do not.

```
<Application.Resources>
  <!-- Add Resources here -->
</Application.Resources>
```

Every resource in each collection must have a key that uniquely identifies them. We use the `x:Key` directive to explicitly set this key, however it can also be set implicitly as well. When we declare styles in any `Resources` section, we can specify the `TargetType` value, in which case the style will be implicitly applied to elements of the correct type that are in scope of the style.

```
<Resources>
  <Style TargetType="{x:Type Button}">
    <Setter Property="Foreground" Value="Green" />
    <Setter Property="Background" Value="White" />
  </Style>
</Resources>
```

In this case, the value for the `x:Key` directive is implicitly set to `{x:Type Button}`. Alternatively, we can set the `x:Key` directive explicitly, so that the style must also be applied explicitly.

```
<Resources>
  <Style x:Key="ButtonStyle">
    <Setter Property="Button.Foreground" Value="Green" />
    <Setter Property="Button.Background" Value="White" />
  </Style>
</Resources>
...
<Button Style="{StaticResource ButtonStyle}" Content="Go" />
```

Styles can have both values set as well, as shown in the following code:

```
<Resources>
  <Style x:Key="ButtonStyle" TargetType="{x:Type Button}">
    <Setter Property="Foreground" Value="Green" />
    <Setter Property="Background" Value="White" />
  </Style>
</Resources>
```

But a compilation error will be thrown if neither value is set:

```
<Resources>
  <Style>
    <Setter Property="Foreground" Value="Green" />
    <Setter Property="Background" Value="White" />
  </Style>
</Resources>
```

The preceding XAML would result in the following compilation error:

```
The member "Foreground" is not recognized or is not accessible.
The member "Background" is not recognized or is not accessible.
```

When a `StaticResource` with a specific key is requested, the lookup process first looks in the local control; if it has a style and that style has a resource dictionary, it checks that first; if there is no item with a matching key, it next looks in the resource collection of the control itself.

If there is still no match, the lookup process checks the resource dictionaries of each parent control until it reaches the `MainWindow.xaml` file. If it still does not find a match, then it will look in the application `Resources` section in the `App.xaml` file.

`StaticResource` lookups occur once upon initialization and will suit our requirements for most of the time. When using a `StaticResource` to reference one resource that is to be used within another resource, the resource being used must be declared beforehand. That is to say that a `StaticResource` lookup from one resource cannot reference another resource that is declared after it in the resource dictionary.

```
<Style TargetType="{x:Type Button}">
  <Setter Property="Foreground" Value="{StaticResource RedBrush}" />
</Style>
<SolidColorBrush x:Key="RedBrush" Color="Red" />
```

The preceding XAML would result in the following error:

```
The resource "RedBrush" could not be resolved.
```

Simply moving the declaration of the brush before the style would clear this error and get the application running again. However, there are certain situations when using a `StaticResource` to reference a resource isn't suitable. For example, we might need our styles to update during runtime in response to some programmatic or user interaction, such as a changing of the computer theme.

In these cases, we can use a `DynamicResource` to reference our resources and can rest assured that our styles will update when the relevant resources are changed. Note that the resource value is not actually looked up until it is actually requested, so this is perfect for resources that will not be ready until after the application start. Note the following altered example.

```
<Style TargetType="{x:Type Button}">
  <Setter Property="Foreground" Value="{DynamicResource RedBrush}" />
</Style>
<SolidColorBrush x:Key="RedBrush" Color="Red" />
```

In this case, there will be no compilation error, as the `DynamicResource` will retrieve the value whenever it is set. While it's great to have this ability, it's important not to abuse it, as using the `DynamicResource` will negatively affect performance. This is because they repeatedly lookup the value each time it is requested, whether the values have changed or not. For this reason, we should only ever use a `DynamicResource` if we really need to.

One final point about resource styles to mention here relates to scope. While this topic has been mentioned elsewhere in this book, it is outlined again here as it is essential to understand the resource lookup procedure. Application resources that are declared in the `App.xaml` file are available application wide, so this is a great place to declare our common styles.

However, this is one of the furthest removed places that we can declare our styles, ignoring external resource dictionaries and theme styles. In general, the rule is that given a resource identifier conflict, the most local resources override those that are declared further away. Therefore, we can define our default styles in the application resources, but retain the ability to override them locally.

Conversely, locally declared styles without an `x:Key` directive will be implicitly applied locally, but will not be applied to elements of the relevant type that are declared externally. We can therefore declare implicit styles in the `Resources` section of a panel for example and they will only be applied to elements of the relative type within the panel.

Merging resources

If we have a large application and our application resources are becoming overcrowded, we have the option of splitting our default colors, brushes, styles, templates and other resources into different files. In addition to organizational and maintenance benefits, this also enables our main resource files to be shared amongst our other applications and so, this promotes reusability too.

In order to do this, we first need one or more additional resource files. We can add an additional resource file using Visual Studio, by right-clicking on the relevant project and selecting the **Add** option and then the **Resource Dictionary...** option. Upon executing this command, we will be provided with a file like this.

```
<ResourceDictionary
    xmlns="http://schemas.microsoft.com/winfx/2006/xaml/presentation"
    xmlns:x="http://schemas.microsoft.com/winfx/2006/xaml">
</ResourceDictionary>
```

This is one of the occasions when we do need to explicitly declare the `ResourceDictionary` element. Once we have transferred our styles or other resources to this file, we can merge it into our main application resources file like this:

```
<Application.Resources>
  <ResourceDictionary>
    <!-- Add Resources here... -->
    <ResourceDictionary.MergedDictionaries>
      <ResourceDictionary Source="Default Styles.xaml" />
      <ResourceDictionary Source="Default Templates.xaml" />
    </ResourceDictionary.MergedDictionaries>
    <!-- ... or add resources here, but not in both locations -->
  </ResourceDictionary>
</Application.Resources>
```

Note that we do not specify the `x:Key` directive for this resource dictionary. In fact, if we did specify this value on the dictionary, we would receive a compilation error:

```
The "Key" attribute can only be used on an element that is contained
    in "IDictionary".
```

Note also that we can set the `ResourceDictionary.MergedDictionaries` value either above or below our locally declared resources, but not anywhere in the middle of them. Within this property, we can declare another `ResourceDictionary` element for each external resource file that we want to merge and specify its location using a **Uniform Resource Identifier (URI)** in the `Source` property.

If our external resource files reside in our startup project with our `App.xaml` file, we can reference them with relative paths, as shown in the preceding example. Otherwise, we will need to use the Pack URI notation. To reference a resource file from a referenced assembly, we would need to use the following format:

```
pack://application:,,,/ReferencedAssembly;component/ResourceFile.xaml
```

In our case, assuming that we had some resource files in a folder named `Styles` in a separate project, or other referenced assembly, we would merge the file using the following path.

```
<ResourceDictionary
  Source="pack://application:,,,/CompanyName.ApplicationName.Resources;
  component/Styles/Control Styles.xaml" />
```

When merging resource files, it is important to understand how naming conflicts will be resolved. Although the `x:Key` directives that we set on our resources must each be unique within their declared resource dictionary, it is perfectly legal to have duplicated key values within separate resource files. As such, there is an order of priority that will be followed in these cases. Let's see an example.

Imagine that we have the aforementioned referenced resource file in a separate project and in that file, we have this resource.

```
<SolidColorBrush x:Key="Brush" Color="Red" />
```

Note that we would need to add a reference to the `System.Xaml` assembly in that project in order to avoid errors. Now imagine that we also have the locally declared `Default Styles.xaml` resource file that was referenced in the previous example and in that file, we have this resource.

```
<SolidColorBrush x:Key="Brush" Color="Blue" />
```

Let's add a `Default Styles 2.xaml` resource file with this resource in it.

```
<SolidColorBrush x:Key="Brush" Color="Orange" />
```

Now, let's say that we merge all of these resource files and add this additional resource in our application resource file.

```
<Application.Resources>
  <ResourceDictionary>
    <ResourceDictionary.MergedDictionaries>
      <ResourceDictionary Source="Default Styles.xaml" />
      <ResourceDictionary Source="Default Styles 2.xaml" />
      <ResourceDictionary Source="pack://application:,,,/
```

```
            CompanyName.ApplicationName.Resources;
            component/Styles/Control Styles.xaml" />
      </ResourceDictionary.MergedDictionaries>
      <SolidColorBrush x:Key="Brush" Color="Green" />
      ...
   </ResourceDictionary>
</Application.Resources>
```

Finally, let's imagine that we have this in the XAML of one of our Views:

```
<Button Content="Go">
  <Button.Resources>
    <SolidColorBrush x:Key="Brush" Color="Cyan" />
  </Button.Resources>
  <Button.Style>
    <Style TargetType="{x:Type Button}">
      <Setter Property="Foreground" Value="{StaticResource Brush}" />
    </Style>
  </Button.Style>
</Button>
```

Also, let's assume that we have this in the local resources of that file:

```
<UserControl.Resources>
  <SolidColorBrush x:Key="Brush" Color="Purple" />
</UserControl.Resources>
```

When running the application, our button text will be cyan, because the main rule of resource scope is that the highest priority resource that will be used will always be the most locally declared resource. If we removed or commented out the local brush declaration, the button text would then become purple when the application was next run.

If we removed the local purple brush resource from the control's Resources section, the application resources would be searched next in an attempt to resolve the Brush resource key. The next general rule is that the latest declared resource will be resolved. In this way, the button text would then become green, because of the locally declared resource in the App.xaml file, which would override the values from the merged dictionaries.

However, if this green brush resource was now removed, an interesting thing will happen. Given the recently stated rules, we might expect that the button text would then be set to red by the resource file from the referenced assembly. Instead, it will be set to orange by the resource in the Default Styles 2.xaml file.

This is the result of a combination of the two rules together. The two locally declared resource files have a higher priority than the resource file from the referenced assembly because they have been declared more locally than it. The second of the two locally declared resource files takes precedence over the first because it was declared after the first.

If we removed the reference to the second of the locally declared resource files, the text would then be set to blue by the resource in the `Default Styles.xaml` file. If we then removed the reference to this file, we would finally see the red button text that would be set by the `Control Styles.xaml` file from the referenced assembly.

Triggering changes

In WPF, we have a number of `Trigger` classes that enable us to modify controls, albeit most commonly just temporarily. All of them extend the `TriggerBase` base class and therefore inherit its `EnterActions` and `ExitActions` properties. These two properties enable us to specify one or more `TriggerAction` objects to apply when the trigger becomes active and/or inactive respectively.

While most trigger types also contain a `Setters` property that we can use to define one or more property setters that should occur when a certain condition is met, the `EventTrigger` class does not. Instead, it provides an `Actions` property that enables us to set one or more `TriggerAction` objects to be applied when the trigger becomes active.

Furthermore, unlike the other triggers, the `EventTrigger` class has no concept of state termination. This means that the action applied by the `EventTrigger` will not be undone when the triggering condition is no longer true. If you hadn't already guessed this, the conditions that trigger the `EventTrigger` instances are events, or `RoutedEvent` objects more specifically. Let's investigate this type of trigger first with a simple example that we saw in the previous chapter.

```
<Rectangle Width="300" Height="300" Fill="Orange">
  <Rectangle.Triggers>
    <EventTrigger RoutedEvent="Loaded">
      <BeginStoryboard>
        <Storyboard Storyboard.TargetProperty="Width">
          <DoubleAnimation Duration="0:0:1" To="50" AutoReverse="True"
            RepeatBehavior="Forever" />
        </Storyboard>
      </BeginStoryboard>
    </EventTrigger>
  </Rectangle.Triggers>
</Rectangle>
```

In this example, the trigger condition is met when the `FrameworkElement.Loaded` event is raised. The action that is applied is the starting of the declared animation. Note that the `BeginStoryboard` class actually extends the `TriggerAction` class and this explains how we are able to declare it within the trigger. This action will be implicitly added into the `TriggerActionCollection` of the `EventTrigger` object, although we could have explicitly set it as follows:

```
<EventTrigger RoutedEvent="Loaded">
  <EventTrigger.Actions>
    <BeginStoryboard>
      <Storyboard Storyboard.TargetProperty="Width">
        <DoubleAnimation Duration="0:0:1" To="50" AutoReverse="True"
          RepeatBehavior="Forever" />
      </Storyboard>
    </BeginStoryboard>
  </EventTrigger.Actions>
</EventTrigger>
```

In addition to the `EventTrigger` class, there are also `Trigger`, `DataTrigger`, `MultiTrigger` and `MultiDataTrigger` classes that enable us to set properties or control animations when a certain condition, or multiple conditions in the case of the multi triggers, are met. Each have their own merits, but apart from the `EventTrigger` class, which can be used in any trigger collection, there are some restrictions on where we can use them.

Each control that extends the `FrameworkElement` class has a `Triggers` property of type `TriggerCollection`, that enable us to specify our triggers. However, if you've ever tried to declare a trigger there, then you're probably aware that we are only allowed to define triggers of type `EventTrigger` there.

However, there are further trigger collections that we can use to declare our other types of triggers. When defining a `ControlTemplate`, we have access to the `ControlTemplate.Triggers` collection. For all other requirements, we can declare our other triggers in the `Style.Triggers` collection. Remember that triggers defined in styles have a higher priority than those declared in templates.

Let's now take a look at the remaining types of triggers and what they can do for us. We start with the most simple, the `Trigger` class. Note that anything that the property trigger can do, the `DataTrigger` class can also do. However, the property trigger syntax is simpler and does not involve data binding and so it is more efficient.

There are however, a few requirements to using a property trigger and they are as follows. The relevant property must be a Dependency Property. Unlike the `EventTrigger` class, the other triggers do not specify actions to be applied when the trigger condition is met, but property setters instead.

We are able to specify one or more `Setter` objects within each `Trigger` object and they will also be implicitly added to the trigger's `Setters` property collection if we do not explicitly specify it. Note that also unlike the `EventTrigger` class, all other triggers will return the original property value when the trigger condition is no longer satisfied. Let's look at a simple example:

```
<Button Content="Go">
  <Button.Style>
    <Style TargetType="{x:Type Button}">
      <Setter Property="Foreground" Value="Black" />
      <Style.Triggers>
        <Trigger Property="IsMouseOver" Value="True">
          <Setter Property="Foreground" Value="Red" />
        </Trigger>
      </Style.Triggers>
    </Style>
  </Button.Style>
</Button>
```

Here we have a button that will change the color of its text when the user's mouse is over it. Unlike the `EventTrigger` however, it's text color will return to its previously set color when the mouse is no longer over the button. Note also that property triggers use the properties of the controls that they are declared in for their conditions, as they have no way of specifying any other target.

As previously mentioned, the `DataTrigger` class can also perform this same binding. Let's see what that might look like:

```
<Button Content="Go">
  <Button.Style>
    <Style TargetType="{x:Type Button}">
      <Setter Property="Foreground" Value="Black" />
      <Style.Triggers>
        <DataTrigger Binding="{Binding IsMouseOver,
          RelativeSource={RelativeSource Self}}" Value="True">
          <Setter Property="Foreground" Value="Red" />
        </DataTrigger>
      </Style.Triggers>
    </Style>
  </Button.Style>
</Button>
```

As you can see, when using a `DataTrigger`, instead of setting the `Property` property of the `Trigger` class, we need to set the `Binding` property instead. In order to achieve the same functionality as the property trigger, we also need to specify the `RelativeSource.Self` enumeration member to set the binding source to the control that is declaring the trigger.

The general rule of thumb is that when we are able to use a simple property trigger that uses a property of the host control in its condition, we should use the `Trigger` class. When we need to use a property of another control, or a data object in our trigger condition, we should use a `DataTrigger`. Let's look at an interesting practical example now.

```
<Style x:Key="TextBoxStyle" TargetType="{x:Type TextBox}">
  <Style.Triggers>
    <DataTrigger Binding="{Binding DataContext.IsEditable,
      RelativeSource={RelativeSource AncestorType={x:Type UserControl}}},
      FallbackValue=True}" Value="False">
      <Setter Property="IsReadOnly" Value="True" />
    </DataTrigger>
  </Style.Triggers>
</Style>
```

In this style, we added a `DataTrigger` element that data binds to an `IsEditable` property that we could declare in a View Model class, that would determine whether the users could edit the data in the controls on the screen or not. This would assume that the an instance of the View Model was correctly set as the `UserControl.DataContext` property.

If the value of the `IsEditable` property was `false`, then the `TextBox.IsReadOnly` property would be set to `true` and the control would become un-editable. Using this technique, we could make all of the controls in a form editable or un-editable by setting this property from the View Model.

The triggers that we have looked at so far have all used a single condition to trigger their actions or property changes. However, there are occasionally situations when we might need more than a single condition to trigger our property changes. For example, in one situation, we might want one particular style, and in another situation, we might want a different look. Let's see an example:

```
<Style x:Key="ButtonStyle" TargetType="{x:Type Button}">
  <Setter Property="Foreground" Value="Black" />
  <Style.Triggers>
    <Trigger Property="IsMouseOver" Value="True">
      <Setter Property="Foreground" Value="Red" />
    </Trigger>
    <MultiTrigger>
      <MultiTrigger.Conditions>
        <Condition Property="IsFocused" Value="True" />
        <Condition Property="IsMouseOver" Value="True" />
      </MultiTrigger.Conditions>
      <Setter Property="Foreground" Value="Green" />
    </MultiTrigger>
  </Style.Triggers>
</Style>
```

In this example, we have two triggers. The first will change the button text to red when the mouse is over it. The second will change the button text to green if the mouse is over it and the button is focused.

Note that we had to declare the two triggers in this order, as triggers are applied from top to bottom. Had we swapped their order, then the text would never change to green because the single trigger would always override the value set by the first one.

We can specify as many `Condition` elements as we need within the `Conditions` collection and as many setters we need within the `MultiTrigger` element itself. However, every condition must return true in order for the setters or other trigger actions to be applied.

The same can be said for the last trigger type to be introduced here, the `MultiDataTrigger`. The difference between this trigger and the previous one is the same as that between the property trigger and the data trigger. That is, the data and multi-data triggers have a much wider range of target sources, while triggers and multi triggers only work with properties of the local control.

```
<StackPanel>
  <CheckBox Name="ShowErrors" Content="Show Errors" Margin="0,0,0,10" />
  <TextBlock>
    <TextBlock.Style>
      <Style TargetType="{x:Type TextBlock}">
        <Setter Property="Text" Value="No Errors" />
```

```
            <Style.Triggers>
              <MultiDataTrigger>
                <MultiDataTrigger.Conditions>
                  <Condition Binding="{Binding IsValid}" Value="False" />
                  <Condition Binding="{Binding IsChecked,
                    ElementName=ShowErrors}" Value="True" />
                </MultiDataTrigger.Conditions>
                <MultiDataTrigger.Setters>
                  <Setter Property="Text" Value="{Binding ErrorList}" />
                </MultiDataTrigger.Setters>
              </MultiDataTrigger>
            </Style.Triggers>
          </Style>
        </TextBlock.Style>
      </TextBlock>
      ...
  </StackPanel>
```

This example demonstrates the wider reach of the `MultiDataTrigger` class, due to its access to the wide range of binding sources. We have a `Show Errors` checkbox, a `No Errors` textblock, and let's say some other form fields that are not displayed here. One of the conditions of this trigger uses the `ElementName` property to set the binding source to this checkbox and requires it to be checked.

The other condition binds to an `IsValid` property from our View Model that would be set to `true` if there were no validation errors. The idea is that when the checkbox is checked and there are validation errors, the `Text` property of the `TextBlock` element will be data bound to another View Model property named `ErrorList`, that could output a description of the validation errors.

Also note that in this example, we explicitly declared the `Setters` collection property and defined our setter within it. However, that is optional and we could have implicitly added the setter to the same collection without declaring the collection, as shown in the previous `MultiTrigger` example.

Before moving onto the next topic, let's take a moment to investigate the `EnterActions` and `ExitActions` properties of the `TriggerBase` class, that enable us to specify one or more `TriggerAction` objects to apply when the trigger becomes active and/or inactive respectively.

Note that we cannot specify style setters in these collections, as they are not
`TriggerAction` objects; setters can be added to the `Setters` collection. Instead, we use
these properties to start animations when the trigger becomes active and/or inactive. To do
that, we need to add a `BeginStoryboard` element, which does extend the `TriggerAction`
class. Let's see an example:

```
<TextBox Width="200" Height="28">
  <TextBox.Style>
    <Style TargetType="{x:Type TextBox}">
      <Setter Property="Opacity" Value="0.25" />
      <Style.Triggers>
        <Trigger Property="IsMouseOver" Value="True">
          <Trigger.EnterActions>
            <BeginStoryboard>
              <Storyboard Storyboard.TargetProperty="Opacity">
                <DoubleAnimation Duration="0:0:0.25" To="1.0" />
              </Storyboard>
            </BeginStoryboard>
          </Trigger.EnterActions>
          <Trigger.ExitActions>
            <BeginStoryboard>
              <Storyboard Storyboard.TargetProperty="Opacity">
                <DoubleAnimation Duration="0:0:0.25" To="0.25" />
              </Storyboard>
            </BeginStoryboard>
          </Trigger.ExitActions>
        </Trigger>
      </Style.Triggers>
    </Style>
  </TextBox.Style>
</TextBox>
```

In this example, the `Trigger` condition relates to the `IsMouseOver` property of the
`TextBox` control. Note that declaring our animations in the `EnterActions` and
`ExitActions` properties when using the `IsMouseOver` property is effectively the same as
having two `EventTrigger` elements, one for the `MouseEnter` event and one for
`MouseLeave` event.

In this example, the animation in the `EnterActions` collection will start as the user's mouse
cursor enters the control and the animation in the `ExitActions` collection will start as the
user's mouse cursor leaves the control.

We'll thoroughly cover animations later, in `Chapter 6`, *Mastering Practical Animations* but in short, the animation that starts as the user's mouse cursor enters the control will fade in the control from being almost transparent, to being opaque.

The other animation will return the `TextBox` control to an almost transparent state when the user's mouse cursor leaves the control. This creates a nice effect when a mouse is dragged over a number of controls with this style. Now that we have a good understanding of triggers, let's move on to find other ways of customizing the standard .NET controls.

Templating controls

While we can greatly vary the look of each control using styles alone, there are occasionally situations when we need to alter their template to achieve our goal. For example, there is no direct way to change the background color of a button through styles alone. In these situations, we need to alter the control's default template.

All UI elements that extend the `Control` class provide access to its `Template` property. This property is of type `ControlTemplate` and enables us to completely replace the originally declared template that defines the normal look of the control. We saw a simple example in the previous chapter, but let's now have a look at another example:

```
<Button Content="Go" Width="100" HorizontalAlignment="Center">
  <Button.Template>
    <ControlTemplate TargetType="{x:Type Button}">
      <Grid>
        <Ellipse Fill="Orange" Stroke="Black" StrokeThickness="3"
          Height="{Binding ActualWidth,
          RelativeSource={RelativeSource Self}}" />
        <ContentPresenter HorizontalAlignment="Center"
          VerticalAlignment="Center" TextElement.FontSize="18"
          TextElement.FontWeight="Bold" />
      </Grid>
    </ControlTemplate>
  </Button.Template>
</Button>
```

Here, we have a button that we have altered to look like a circle. It is very basic, as we have not bothered to define any mouseover or click effects, but it shows that there is nothing scary about overriding the default template of a control and that it is simple to achieve.

Note that the `ContentPresenter` element is declared after the `Ellipse` element because the ellipse is not a content control and cannot have another element set as its content. This results in the content being drawn on top of the ellipse. A side effect of this is that we therefore need to add a panel inside the template, to enable us to provide more than a single piece of content.

Also note that as with styles, we need to specify the `TargetType` property of the template. To clarify this a little, we need to specify it if the template contains a `ContentPresenter` element. Note that omitting this value will not raise a compilation error, but the content will simply not appear in our templated control. It is therefore good practice to always set this `TargetType` property.

However, unlike styles, if we declared a `ControlTemplate` and set its `TargetType` property in a `Resources` collection without specifying the `x:Key` directive, it will not be implicitly applied to all buttons in the application. Indeed, we will receive a compilation error.

```
Each dictionary entry must have an associated key.
```

Instead, we need to set the x:Key directive and explicitly apply the template to the Template property of the control in a style. If we want our template to be applied to every control of that type then we need to set it in the default style for that type. In this case, we need to not set the x:Key directive of the style, so that it will be implicitly applied.

```
<ControlTemplate x:Key="ButtonTemplate" TargetType="{x:Type Button}">
  ...
</ControlTemplate>
<Style TargetType="{x:Type Button}">
  <Setter Property="Template" Value="{StaticResource ButtonTemplate}" />
</Style>
```

Note that we would not typically hard code property values like we did in this template example, unless we did not want the users of our framework to be able to set their own colors on our templated controls. More often than not, we would make proper use of the TemplateBinding class to apply the values set from outside the control to the inner controls defined within our template.

```
<Button Content="Go" Width="100" HorizontalAlignment="Center"
    Background="Orange" HorizontalContentAlignment="Center"
    VerticalContentAlignment="Center" FontSize="18">
  <Button.Template>
    <ControlTemplate TargetType="{x:Type Button}">
      <Grid>
        <Ellipse Fill="{TemplateBinding Background}"
          Stroke="{TemplateBinding Foreground}" StrokeThickness="3"
          Height="{Binding ActualWidth,
          RelativeSource={RelativeSource Self}}" />
        <ContentPresenter HorizontalAlignment="{TemplateBinding
          HorizontalContentAlignment}"
          VerticalAlignment="{TemplateBinding
          VerticalContentAlignment}"
          TextElement.FontWeight="{TemplateBinding FontWeight}"
          TextElement.FontSize="{TemplateBinding FontSize}" />
      </Grid>
    </ControlTemplate>
  </Button.Template>
</Button>
```

While this example is now far more verbose, it is also more practical and would enable users to set their own button properties. Setting this template in a default style would make the templated control far more reusable. Note that now, the hard coded values are made on the button control itself, with the exception of the StrokeThickness property.

There is no suitable property on the Button class that we could use to expose this inner control property. If this was a problem for us, we could expose the value of that property in a custom Attached Property and data bind to it on the button as follows:

```
<Button Attached:ButtonProperties.StrokeThickness="3" ... />
```

And we could do the following inside the control template:

```
<Ellipse
    Stroke="{Binding (Attached:ButtonProperties.StrokeThickness)}" ... />
```

However, even though we have improved our template, there are certain elements defined in the default templates that affect the way their containing controls look, or work. If we remove these elements, as we have done in the preceding example, we will break that default functionality. For example, our example button no longer has focusing or interaction effects.

Sometimes, we may only need to slightly adjust the original template, in which case, we would typically start with the default ControlTemplate and then make our slight adjustment to it. If we had done this with our button example and simply replaced the visual aspects, then we could have retained the original interactivity with it.

In days gone by, it could be quite difficult to find the default control templates for the various controls. We would previously need to try and track them down on the MSDN website, or use Blend, however now, we can use Visual Studio to provide it for us.

In the WPF designer, select the relevant control, or click on it with the mouse in a XAML file. With the relevant control selected, or focused, press the *F4* key on your keyboard to open the **Properties** window. Next, open the **Miscellaneous** category to find the **Template** property, or type Template in the search field at the top of the **Properties** window.

Click on the little square to the right of the **Template** value field and select the **Convert to New Resource...** item in the template options tooltip. In the popup dialog window that appears, name the new `ControlTemplate` to be added and decide where you want it to be defined.

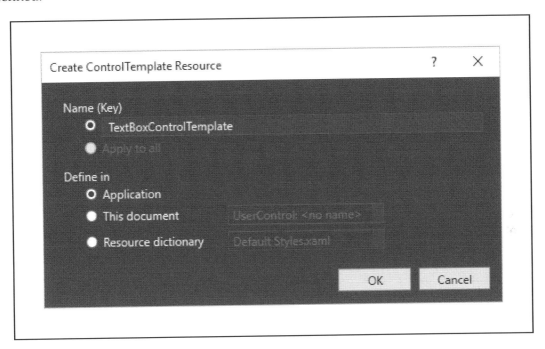

Once you have entered the required details, click the **OK** button to create a copy of the default template of your selected control in your desired location. As an example, let's take a look at the default control template of the `TextBox` control.

```
<ControlTemplate TargetType="{x:Type TextBox}">
  <Border Name="border" BorderBrush="{TemplateBinding BorderBrush}"
    BorderThickness="{TemplateBinding BorderThickness}"
    Background="{TemplateBinding Background}"
    SnapsToDevicePixels="True">
    <ScrollViewer Name="PART_ContentHost" Focusable="False"
      HorizontalScrollBarVisibility="Hidden"
      VerticalScrollBarVisibility="Hidden" />
  </Border>
  <ControlTemplate.Triggers>
    <Trigger Property="IsEnabled" Value="False">
      <Setter Property="Opacity" TargetName="border" Value="0.56" />
    </Trigger>
    <Trigger Property="IsMouseOver" Value="True">
```

```
        <Setter Property="BorderBrush" TargetName="border"
          Value="#FF7EB4EA" />
      </Trigger>
      <Trigger Property="IsKeyboardFocused" Value="True">
        <Setter Property="BorderBrush" TargetName="border"
          Value="#FF569DE5" />
      </Trigger>
    </ControlTemplate.Triggers>
  </ControlTemplate>
```

As we can see, most of the properties set on the inner controls have been exposed to the `TextBox` control through the use of the `TemplateBinding` class. At the end of the template are the triggers that react to various states, such as focus, mouseover and enabled states.

However, inside the `Border` element, we see a `ScrollViewer` named `PART_ContentHost`. The fact that this is named with the `PART_` prefix specifies that this control is required within this template. All named parts of each UI element will be listed on the *[ControlType] Styles and Templates* pages of MSDN.

This named part control is required in the textbox because when the textbox is initialized, it programmatically adds the `TextBoxView` and `CaretElement` objects into the `ScrollViewer` object and these are the predominant elements that make up the textbox's functionality.

These specially named elements also need to be registered within the declaring class and we'll find out more about that later in the chapter as well. It is therefore important that we include these named controls in our custom templates if we want to keep the existing functionality.

Note that we will not receive any compilation errors, or even trace warnings if we do not include these named controls and we are free to leave them out if we do not require their relevant functionality. This following example, while hardly functional, it still perfectly valid.

```
<TextBox Text="Hidden Text Box">
  <TextBox.Template>
    <ControlTemplate TargetType="{x:Type TextBox}">
      <ContentPresenter Content="{TemplateBinding Text}" />
    </ControlTemplate>
  </TextBox.Template>
</TextBox>
```

Although this textbox will indeed display the specified text value, it will have no containing box, like a normal textbox would. What will happen when this template is rendered is that the `ContentPresenter` element will see a string and default to displaying it in a `TextBlock` element.

Its `Text` property will still be data bound to the `Text` property of our textbox and so when focused, it will still act like a textbox and enable us to enter text. Of course, we won't see when it's focused, because we didn't add any triggers to make that happen and there won't be a caret as the `CaretElement` object will no longer be added.

Instead, if we simply supply the required named control, even without anything else, we'll still regain most of the original functionality.

```
<TextBox Name="Text" Text="Does this work?"
    TextChanged="TextBox_TextChanged">
  <TextBox.Template>
    <ControlTemplate TargetType="{x:Type TextBox}">
      <ScrollViewer Margin="0" Name="PART_ContentHost" />
    </ControlTemplate>
  </TextBox.Template>
</TextBox>
```

Now when we run our application, we have the textbox caret and text cursor when the mouse is over the textbox and so we have some of the functionality, but not the look. However usually, the best option is to keep as much of the original template as we can and only change the parts that we really need to.

Attaching properties

When using WPF, we have one further tool at our disposal to enable us to manipulate the built-in controls and avoid the need to create new ones. We are of course, discussing Attached Properties, so let's extend an example that we started looking at in the previous chapter.

In order to create a button that will enable us to set a second tooltip message to display when the control is disabled, we'll need to declare two Attached Properties. One will hold the disabled tooltip message and the other will be the previously mentioned read-only property that temporarily holds onto the original tooltip value. Let's look at our full `ButtonProperties` class now:

```
using System.Windows;
using System.Windows.Controls;

namespace CompanyName.ApplicationName.Views.Attached
{
  public class ButtonProperties : DependencyObject
```

```
{
  private static readonly DependencyPropertyKey
    originalToolTipPropertyKey =
    DependencyProperty.RegisterAttachedReadOnly("OriginalToolTip",
    typeof(string), typeof(ButtonProperties),
    new FrameworkPropertyMetadata(default(string)));

  public static readonly DependencyProperty OriginalToolTipProperty =
    originalToolTipPropertyKey.DependencyProperty;

  public static string GetOriginalToolTip(
    DependencyObject dependencyObject)
  {
    return
      (string)dependencyObject.GetValue(OriginalToolTipProperty);
  }

  public static DependencyProperty DisabledToolTipProperty =
    DependencyProperty.RegisterAttached("DisabledToolTip",
    typeof(string), typeof(ButtonProperties),
    new UIPropertyMetadata(string.Empty, OnDisabledToolTipChanged));

  public static string GetDisabledToolTip(
    DependencyObject dependencyObject)
  {
    return (string)dependencyObject.GetValue(
      DisabledToolTipProperty);
  }

  public static void SetDisabledToolTip(
    DependencyObject dependencyObject, string value)
  {
    dependencyObject.SetValue(DisabledToolTipProperty, value);
  }

  public static void OnDisabledToolTipChanged(DependencyObject
    dependencyObject, DependencyPropertyChangedEventArgs e)
  {
    Button button = dependencyObject as Button;
    ToolTipService.SetShowOnDisabled(button, true);
    if (e.OldValue == null && e.NewValue != null)
      button.IsEnabledChanged += Button_IsEnabledChanged;
    else if (e.OldValue != null && e.NewValue == null)
      button.IsEnabledChanged -= Button_IsEnabledChanged;
  }

  private static void Button_IsEnabledChanged(object sender,
    DependencyPropertyChangedEventArgs e)
```

```
    {
      Button button = sender as Button;
      if (GetOriginalToolTip(button) == null)
        button.SetValue(originalToolTipPropertyKey,
        button.ToolTip.ToString());
      button.ToolTip = (bool)e.NewValue ?
        GetOriginalToolTip(button) : GetDisabledToolTip(button);
    }
  }
}
```

As with all Attached Properties, we start with a class that extends the DependencyObject class. In this class, we first declare the read-only originalToolTipPropertyKey field using the RegisterAttachedReadOnly method and the OriginalToolTipProperty property and its associated CLR getter.

Next, we use the RegisterAttached method to register the DisabledToolTip property that will hold the value of the tooltip to be displayed when the control is disabled. We then see its CLR getter and setter methods and its all-important PropertyChangedCallback handling method.

In the OnDisabledToolTipChanged method, we first cast the dependencyObject input parameter to its actual type of Button. We then use it to set the ToolTipService.SetShowOnDisabled Attached Property to true, which is required because we want the button's tooltip to be displayed when the button is disabled. The default value is false, so our Attached Property would not work without this step.

Next, we determine whether we need to attach or detach the Button_IsEnabledChanged event handling method dependent upon the NewValue and OldValue property values of the DependencyPropertyChangedEventArgs object. If the old value is null, then the property has not been set before and we need to attach the handler and if the new value is null, then we need to detach the handler.

In the Button_IsEnabledChanged event handling method, we first cast the sender input parameter to the Button type. We then use it to access the OriginalToolTip property and if it is null, we set it with the current value from the control's normal ToolTip property. Note that we need to pass the originalToolTipPropertyKey field into the SetValue method, as it is a read-only property.

Finally, we utilize the `e.NewValue` property value to determine whether to set the original tooltip or the disabled tooltip into the control's normal `ToolTip` property. Therefore, if the control is enabled, the `e.NewValue` property value will be `true` and the original tooltip will be returned and if the button is disabled, the disabled tooltip will be displayed. We could use this Attached Property as follows:

```
<Button Content="Save" Attached:ButtonProperties.DisabledToolTip="You must
   correct validation errors before saving" ToolTip="Saves the user" />
```

As can be seen from this simple example, Attached Properties enable us to easily add new functionality to the existing suite of UI controls. This again highlights how versatile WPF is and demonstrates that we often have no need to create completely new controls.

Combining controls

When we need to arrange a number of existing controls in a particular way, we typically use a `UserControl` object. This is why we normally use this type of control to build our Views. However, when we need to build a reusable control, such as an address control, we tend to separate these from our Views, by declaring them in a `Controls` folder and namespace within our Views project.

When declaring these reusable controls, it is customary to define Dependency Properties in the code behind and as long as there is no business-related functionality in the control, it is also ok to use the code behind to handle events. If the control is business-related, then we can use a View Model, as we do with normal Views. Let's take a look at an example of an address control.

```
<UserControl x:Class=
  "CompanyName.ApplicationName.Views.Controls.AddressControl"
  xmlns="http://schemas.microsoft.com/winfx/2006/xaml/presentation"
  xmlns:x="http://schemas.microsoft.com/winfx/2006/xaml"
  xmlns:mc="http://schemas.openxmlformats.org/markup-compatibility/2006"
  xmlns:d="http://schemas.microsoft.com/expression/blend/2008"
  xmlns:Controls=
    "clr-namespace:CompanyName.ApplicationName.Views.Controls"
  mc:Ignorable="d" d:DesignHeight="300" d:DesignWidth="300">
  <Grid>
    <Grid.ColumnDefinitions>
      <ColumnDefinition Width="Auto" SharedSizeGroup="Label" />
      <ColumnDefinition />
    </Grid.ColumnDefinitions>
    <Grid.RowDefinitions>
      <RowDefinition Height="Auto" />
```

```
    <RowDefinition Height="Auto" />
    <RowDefinition Height="Auto" />
    <RowDefinition Height="Auto" />
    <RowDefinition Height="Auto" />
  </Grid.RowDefinitions>
  <TextBlock Text="House/Street" />
  <TextBox Grid.Column="1" Text="{Binding Address.HouseAndStreet,
    RelativeSource={RelativeSource
    AncestorType={x:Type Controls:AddressControl}}}" />
  <TextBlock Grid.Row="1" Text="Town" />
  <TextBox Grid.Row="1" Grid.Column="1"
    Text="{Binding Address.Town, RelativeSource={RelativeSource
    AncestorType={x:Type Controls:AddressControl}}}" />
  <TextBlock Grid.Row="2" Text="City" />
  <TextBox Grid.Row="2" Grid.Column="1"
    Text="{Binding Address.City, RelativeSource={RelativeSource
    AncestorType={x:Type Controls:AddressControl}}}" />
  <TextBlock Grid.Row="3" Text="Post Code" />
  <TextBox Grid.Row="3" Grid.Column="1"
    Text="{Binding Address.PostCode, RelativeSource={RelativeSource
    AncestorType={x:Type Controls:AddressControl}}}" />
  <TextBlock Grid.Row="4" Text="Country" />
  <TextBox Grid.Row="4" Grid.Column="1"
    Text="{Binding Address.Country, RelativeSource={RelativeSource
    AncestorType={x:Type Controls:AddressControl}}}" />
  </Grid>
</UserControl>
```

In this example, we declare this class within the `Controls` namespace and set up a XAML namespace prefix for it. We then see the `Grid` panel that is used to layout the address controls and notice that the `SharedSizeGroup` property is set on the `ColumnDefinition` element that defines the label column. This will enable the column sizes within this control to be shared with externally declared controls.

We then see all of the `TextBlock` and `TextBox` controls that are data bound to the control's address fields. There's not much to note here except that the data bound properties are all accessed through a `RelativeSource` binding to an `Address` Dependency Property that is declared in the code behind file of the `AddressControl`.

Remember that it's fine to do this when using MVVM as long as we are not encapsulating any business rules here. Our control merely enables the users to input or add address information, which will be used by various Views and View Models. Let's see this property now.

```
using System.Windows;
using System.Windows.Controls;
```

```
using CompanyName.ApplicationName.DataModels;

namespace CompanyName.ApplicationName.Views.Controls
{
  public partial class AddressControl : UserControl
  {
    public AddressControl()
    {
      InitializeComponent();
    }

    public static readonly DependencyProperty AddressProperty =
      DependencyProperty.Register(nameof(Address),
      typeof(Address), typeof(AddressControl),
      new PropertyMetadata(new Address()));

    public Address Address
    {
      get { return (Address)GetValue(AddressProperty); }
      set { SetValue(AddressProperty, value); }
    }
  }
}
```

This is a very simple control with just one Dependency Property. We can see that the Address property is of type Address, so let's have a quick look at that class next:

```
namespace CompanyName.ApplicationName.DataModels
{
  public class Address : BaseDataModel
  {
    private string houseAndStreet, town, city, postCode, country;

    public string HouseAndStreet
    {
      get { return houseAndStreet; }
      set { if (houseAndStreet != value) { houseAndStreet = value;
        NotifyPropertyChanged(); } }
    }

    public string Town
    {
      get { return town; }
      set { if (town != value) { town = value; NotifyPropertyChanged(); } }
    }

    public string City
    {
```

```
      get { return city; }
      set { if (city != value) { city = value; NotifyPropertyChanged(); } }
    }

    public string PostCode
    {
      get { return postCode; }
      set { if (postCode != value) { postCode = value;
        NotifyPropertyChanged(); } }
    }

    public string Country
    {
      get { return country; }
      set { if (country != value) { country = value;
        NotifyPropertyChanged(); } }
    }

    public override string ToString()
    {
      return $"{HouseAndStreet}, {Town}, {City}, {PostCode}, {Country}";
    }
  }
}
```

Again, we have a very simple class that is primarily made up from the address related properties. Note the use of the string interpolation in the overridden `ToString` method to output a useful display of the class contents. Now we've seen the control, let's take a look at how we can use it in our application. We can edit a View that we saw earlier, so let's see the updated `UserView` XAML now.

```
<Grid TextElement.FontSize="14" Grid.IsSharedSizeScope="True" Margin="10">
  <Grid.Resources>
    <Style TargetType="{x:Type TextBlock}">
      <Setter Property="HorizontalAlignment" Value="Right" />
      <Setter Property="VerticalAlignment" Value="Center" />
      <Setter Property="Margin" Value="0,0,5,5" />
    </Style>
    <Style TargetType="{x:Type TextBox}">
      <Setter Property="VerticalAlignment" Value="Center" />
      <Setter Property="Margin" Value="0,0,0,5" />
    </Style>
  </Grid.Resources>
  <Grid.ColumnDefinitions>
    <ColumnDefinition Width="Auto" SharedSizeGroup="Label" />
    <ColumnDefinition />
  </Grid.ColumnDefinitions>
```

```
        <Grid.RowDefinitions>
          <RowDefinition Height="Auto" />
          <RowDefinition Height="Auto" />
          <RowDefinition Height="Auto" />
        </Grid.RowDefinitions>
        <TextBlock Text="Name" />
        <TextBox Grid.Column="1" Text="{Binding User.Name}" />
        <TextBlock Grid.Row="1" Text="Age" />
        <TextBox Grid.Row="1" Grid.Column="1" Text="{Binding User.Age}" />
        <Controls:AddressControl Grid.Row="2" Grid.ColumnSpan="2"
          Address="{Binding User.Address}" />
      </Grid>
```

In this example, we can see the use of the `Grid.IsSharedSizeScope` property on the outermost `Grid` panel. Remember that the `SharedSizeGroup` property was set in the `AddressControl` XAML, although without this setting on the outer `Grid`, that does nothing by itself.

Looking at the outer panel's column definitions, we can see that we have also set the `SharedSizeGroup` property to the same value on the left column, so that the two panels' columns will be aligned.

We can skip over the two styles that are declared in the panel's `Resources` section, as in a proper application, these would most likely reside in the application resources file. In the remainder of the View, we simply have a couple of rows of user properties and then the `AddressControl`.

This code assumes that we have declared an `Address` property of type `Address` in our `User` class and populated it with suitable values in the `UserViewModel` class. Note how we data bind the `Address` property of the `User` class to the `Address` property of the control, rather than setting the `DataContext` property. As the control's internal controls are data bound using `RelativeSource` bindings which specify their own binding source, they do not require any `DataContext` to be set. In fact, doing so in this example would stop it from working.

Creating custom controls

When using WPF, we can generally create the UI that we want using the many techniques already discussed in this book. However, in the cases when we require a totally unique control with both a custom drawn appearance and custom functionality, then we may need to declare a custom control.

Developing custom controls is very different to creating `UserControl` elements and it can take some time to master this. To start with, we will need to add a new project of type **WPF Custom Control Library** to declare them in. Also, instead of having a XAML page and a code behind file, we only have the code file. At this point, you may be wondering where we define what our control should look like.

In fact, when defining a custom control, we declare our XAML in a separate file named `Generic.xaml`, which is added by Visual Studio when we add our controls project. To clarify, the XAML for all of the custom controls that we declare in this project will go into this file. This does not relate to controls that extend the `UserControl` class and we should not declare those in this project.

This `Generic.xaml` file gets added into a folder named `Themes` in the root directory of our **WPF Custom Control Library** project, as this is where the Framework will look for the default styles of our custom controls. As such, we must declare the UI design of our control in a `ControlTemplate` and set it to the `Template` property in a style that targets the type of our control in this file.

The style must be applied to all instances of our control and so the style is defined with the `TargetType` set, but without the `x:Key` directive. If you remember, this will ensure that it is implicitly applied to all instances of our control that haven't an alternative template explicitly applied.

A further difference is that we cannot directly reference any of the controls that are defined within the style in the `Generic.xaml` file. If you recall, when we provided a new template for the built-in controls, we were under no obligation to provide the same controls that were originally used. Therefore, if we tried to access a control from our original template that had been replaced, it would cause an error.

Instead, we generally need to access them by overriding the `FrameworkElement.OnApplyTemplate` method, which is raised once our default template has been applied to the instance of our control. In this method, we need to almost expect that our required control(s) will be missing and ensure that no errors occur if that is the case.

Let's look at a simple example of a custom control that creates a meter that can be used to monitor CPU activity, RAM usage, audio loudness, or any other regularly changing value. We'll first need to create a new project of type **WPF Custom Control Library** and rename the `CustomControl1.cs` class that Visual Studio adds for us to `Meter.cs`.

Note that we can only add a custom control to a project of this type and that when the project is added, Visual Studio will also add our Themes folder and Generic.xaml file, with a style for our control already declared inside it. Let's see the code in the Meter.cs file.

```
using System;
using System.Windows;
using System.Windows.Controls;

namespace CompanyName.ApplicationName.CustomControls
{
  public class Meter : Control
  {
    static Meter()
    {
      DefaultStyleKeyProperty.OverrideMetadata(typeof(Meter),
        new FrameworkPropertyMetadata(typeof(Meter)));
    }

    public static readonly DependencyProperty ValueProperty =
      DependencyProperty.Register(nameof(Value),
      typeof(double), typeof(Meter),
      new PropertyMetadata(0.0, OnValueChanged, CoerceValue));

    private static object CoerceValue(DependencyObject dependencyObject,
      object value)
    {
      return Math.Min(Math.Max((double)value, 0.0), 1.0);
    }

    private static void OnValueChanged(DependencyObject dependencyObject,
      DependencyPropertyChangedEventArgs e)
    {
      Meter meter = (Meter)dependencyObject;
      meter.SetClipRect(meter);
    }

    public double Value
    {
      get { return (double)GetValue(ValueProperty); }
      set { SetValue(ValueProperty, value); }
    }

    public static readonly DependencyPropertyKey clipRectPropertyKey =
      DependencyProperty.RegisterReadOnly(nameof(ClipRect), typeof(Rect),
      typeof(Meter), new PropertyMetadata(new Rect()));
```

```
    public static readonly DependencyProperty ClipRectProperty =
        clipRectPropertyKey.DependencyProperty;

    public Rect ClipRect
    {
        get { return (Rect)GetValue(ClipRectProperty); }
        private set { SetValue(clipRectPropertyKey, value); }
    }

    public override void OnApplyTemplate()
    {
        SetClipRect(this);
    }

    private void SetClipRect(Meter meter)
    {
        double barSize = meter.Value * meter.Height;
        meter.ClipRect =
            new Rect(0, meter.Height - barSize, meter.Width, barSize);
    }
  }
}
```

This is a relatively small class, with only two Dependency Properties and their associated CLR property wrappers and callback handlers. Of particular note is the class's static constructor and the use of the DefaultStyleKeyProperty.OverrideMetadata method.

This is also added by Visual Studio when adding the class and is required to override the type specific metadata of the DefaultStyleKey Dependency Property when we derive a custom class from the FrameworkElement class.

Specifically, this key is used by the Framework to find the default theme style for our control and so, by passing the type of our class into the OverrideMetadata method, we are telling the Framework to look for a default style for this type in our Themes folder.

If you remember, the theme styles are the last place that the Framework will look for the style of a specific type and declaring styles just about anywhere else in the application will override the default styles defined here.

The first Dependency Property is the main Value property of the control and this is used to determine the size of the visible meter bar. This property defines a default value of 0.0 and attaches the CoerceValue and OnValueChanged callback handlers.

In the `CoerceValue` handling method, we ensure that the output value always remains between `0.0` and `1.0`, as that is the scale that we will be using. In the `OnValueChanged` handler, we update the value of the other Dependency Property, `ClipRect`, dependent upon the input value.

To do this, we first cast the `dependencyObject` input parameter to our `Meter` type and then pass that instance to the `SetClipRect` method. In this method, we calculate the relative size of the meter bar and define the `Rect` element for the `ClipRect` Dependency Property accordingly.

Next, we see the CLR property wrapper for the `Value` Dependency Property and then the declaration of the `ClipRect` Dependency Property. Note that we declare it using a `DependencyPropertyKey` element, thus making it a read-only property, because it is only for internal use and has no value being exposed publicly. The actual `ClipRect` Dependency Property comes from this key element.

After this, we see the CLR property wrapper for the `ClipRect` Dependency Property and then we come to the aforementioned `OnApplyTemplate` method. In our case, the purpose of overriding this method is because often, data bound values will be set before the control's template has been applied and so we would not be able to correctly set the size of the meter bar from those values.

Therefore, when the template has been applied and the control has been arranged and sized, we call the `SetClipRect` method in order to set the `Rect` element for the `ClipRect` Dependency Property to the appropriate value. Before this point in time, the `Height` and `Weight` properties of the `meter` instance will be `double.NaN` (Not a Number) and cannot be used to size the `Rect` element correctly.

When this method is called, we can rest assured that the `Height` and `Weight` properties of the `meter` instance will have valid values. Note that had we needed to access any elements from our template, we could have called the `FrameworkTemplate.FindName` method from this method, on the `ControlTemplate` object that is specified by our control's `Template` property.

Imagine that we had named a `Rectangle` element in our XAML to `PART_Rectangle`, we could access it from the `OnApplyTemplate` method like this.

```
Rectangle rectangle = (Rectangle)Template.FindName("PART_Rectangle", this);
if (rectangle != null)
{
  // Do something with rectangle
}
```

Note that we always need to check for null, because the applied template may be a custom template that does not contain the `Rectangle` element at all. Note also that when we require the existence of a particular element in the template, we can decorate our custom control class declaration with a `TemplatePartAttribute`, that specifies the details of the required control.

```
[TemplatePart(Name = "PART_Rectangle", Type = typeof(Rectangle))]
public class Meter : Control
{
  ...
}
```

This will not enforce anything and will not raise any compilation errors if the named part is not included in a custom template, but it will be used in documentation and by various XAML tools. It helps users of our custom controls to find out which elements are required when they provide custom templates.

Now that we've seen the inner workings of this control, let's take a look at the XAML of the default style of our control in the `Generic.xaml` file to see how the `ClipRect` property is used.

```
<ResourceDictionary
  xmlns="http://schemas.microsoft.com/winfx/2006/xaml/presentation"
  xmlns:x="http://schemas.microsoft.com/winfx/2006/xaml"
  xmlns:CustomControls=
    "clr-namespace:CompanyName.ApplicationName.CustomControls">
  <Style TargetType="{x:Type CustomControls:Meter}">
    <Setter Property="Template">
      <Setter.Value>
        <ControlTemplate TargetType="{x:Type
          CustomControls:Meter}">
          <ControlTemplate.Resources>
            <LinearGradientBrush x:Key="ScaleColours"
              StartPoint="0,1" EndPoint="0,0">
              <GradientStop Color="LightGreen" />
              <GradientStop Color="Yellow" Offset="0.5" />
              <GradientStop Color="Orange" Offset="0.75" />
              <GradientStop Color="Red" Offset="1.0" />
            </LinearGradientBrush>
          </ControlTemplate.Resources>
          <Border Background="{TemplateBinding Background}"
            BorderBrush="{TemplateBinding BorderBrush}"
            BorderThickness="{TemplateBinding BorderThickness}">
            <Border.ToolTip>
              <TextBlock Text="{Binding Value, StringFormat={}{0:P0}}" />
            </Border.ToolTip>
            <Rectangle Fill="{StaticResource ScaleColours}"
```

```
              HorizontalAlignment="Stretch" VerticalAlignment="Stretch"
              SnapsToDevicePixels="True" Name="PART_Rectangle">
              <Rectangle.Clip>
                <RectangleGeometry Rect="{Binding ClipRect,
                  RelativeSource={RelativeSource
                  AncestorType={x:Type CustomControls:Meter}}}" />
              </Rectangle.Clip>
            </Rectangle>
          </Border>
        </ControlTemplate>
      </Setter.Value>
    </Setter>
  </Style>
</ResourceDictionary>
```

When each custom control class is created in a **WPF Custom Control Library** project, Visual Studio adds an almost empty default style that sets a basic ControlTemplate and targets the type of the class into the Generic.xaml file. We just need to define our custom XAML within this template.

We start by declaring the ScaleColours gradient brush resource within the template. Note that the default value for the Offset property of a GradientStop element is 0 and so, we can omit the setting of this property, if that is the value that we want it set to. Therefore, when we see a declared GradientStop, like the one with the Color property set to LightGreen, we know its Offset property is set to 0.

Our meter control is basically made up from a Border element that surrounds a Rectangle element. We use a TemplateBinding to data bind the Background, BorderBrush and BorderThickness properties of the Border element.

This enables users of the control to specify the border and background colors of the internal Border element of the meter control from outside the control. We could just as easily have exposed an additional brush property to replace the ScaleColours resource and enable users to define their own meter scale brush.

Note that we couldn't use a TemplateBinding to data bind the Value property in the ToolTip element. This is not because we don't have access to it through the template, but because we need to use the Binding.StringFormat property and the P format specifier to transform our double property value to a percentage value.

If you remember, a TemplateBinding is a lightweight binding and does not offer this functionality. While it is beneficial to use it when we can, this example highlights the fact that we cannot use it in every circumstance.

Finally, we come to the all-important `Rectangle` element that is responsible for displaying the actual meter bar of our control. The `ScaleColours` brush resource is used here to paint the background of the rectangle. We set the `SnapsToDevicePixels` property to `true` on this element to ensure that the level that it displays is accurate and well-defined.

The magic in this control is formed by the use of the `UIElement.Clip` property. Essentially, this enables us to provide any type of `Geometry` element to alter the shape and size of the visible portion of a UI element. The geometry shape that we assign here will specify the visible portion of the control.

In our case, we declare a `RectangleGeometry` class, whose size and location are specified by its `Rect` property. We therefore data bind our `ClipRect` Dependency Property to this `Rect` property, so that the sizes calculated from the incoming data values are represented by this `RectangleGeometry` instance and therefore, the visible part of the `Rectangle` element.

Note that we do this so that the gradient that is painted on the meter bar remains constant and does not change with the height of the bar as its value changes. If we had simply painted the background of the rectangle with the brush resource and adjusted its height, the background gradient would move with the size of the meter bar and spoil the effect.

Therefore, the whole rectangle is always painted with the gradient brush and we simply use its `Clip` property to just display the appropriate part of it. In order to use it in one of our Views, we'd first need to specify the `CustomControls` XAML namespace prefix.

```
xmlns:CustomControls="clr-namespace:CompanyName.ApplicationName.
    CustomControls;assembly=CompanyName.ApplicationName.CustomControls"
```

We could then declare a number of them, data bind some appropriate properties to their `Value` property and set styles for them, just like any other control.

```
<StackPanel Orientation="Horizontal" HorizontalAlignment="Center">
  <StackPanel.Resources>
    <Style TargetType="{x:Type CustomControls:Meter}">
      <Setter Property="Background" Value="Black" />
      <Setter Property="BorderBrush" Value="Black" />
      <Setter Property="BorderThickness" Value="2" />
      <Setter Property="HorizontalAlignment" Value="Center" />
      <Setter Property="Width" Value="20" />
      <Setter Property="Height" Value="100" />
    </Style>
  </StackPanel.Resources>
  <CustomControls:Meter Value="{Binding CpuActivity}" />
  <CustomControls:Meter Value="{Binding DiskActivity}" Margin="10,0" />
  <CustomControls:Meter Value="{Binding NetworkActivity}" />
```

```
</StackPanel>
```

Given some valid properties to data bind to, the preceding example would produce an output similar to the following:

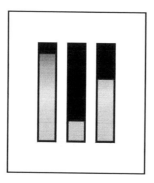

Summary

In this chapter, we've investigated the rich inheritance hierarchy of the built-in WPF controls, determining which abilities comes from which base classes and seen how each control is laid out by their containing panels. We've examined the differences between the different panels and understand that some work better in certain conditions than others.

We've also uncovered the mysteries of the ContentControl and ItemsControl elements and now have a good understanding of ContentPresenter and ItemsPresenter objects. We moved on to discover a wide variety of ways for us to customize the built-in controls. Finally, we considered how best to make our own controls.

In the next chapter, we will take a thorough look at the WPF animation system and discover how we can utilize it in every day applications. We'll also find out a number of techniques to fine-tune animations to get that perfect effect and discover how we can build animation functionality into our application framework.

6
Mastering Practical Animations

WPF offers a wide range of animation possibilities, from the simple to the really quite complex. We will thoroughly explore the WPF property animation system, yet focus primarily on those parts that can be suitably applied to real-world business applications. We'll investigate how to control running applications in real time and predominantly concentrate on XAML-based syntax. We'll then see how we can build animations right into our application framework.

In WPF, animations are created by repeatedly altering individual property values at regular intervals. Animations are comprised of a number of components; we need a timing system, an animation object that is responsible for updating the values of a particular type of object and a suitable property to animate.

In order to be able to animate a property, it must be a Dependency Property of a `DependencyObject` and its type must implement the `IAnimatable` interface. As most UI controls extend the `DependencyObject` class, this enables us to animate the properties of most controls.

Furthermore, an animation object for the relevant type of the property must exist. In WPF, the animation objects also double up as the timing system, as they extend the `Timeline` class. Before investigating the various animation objects, let's first examine the timing system.

Investigating timelines

Animations require some kind of timing mechanism that is responsible for updating the relevant property values at the right time. In WPF, this timing mechanism is catered for by the abstract `Timeline` class, which in short, represents a period of time. All of the available animation classes extend this class and add their own animation functionality.

When a `Timeline` class is used for animations, an internal copy is made and frozen, so that it is immutable. Additionally, a `Clock` object is created to preserve the runtime timing state of the `Timeline` object and is responsible for the actual timing of the animated property updates. The `Timeline` object itself does little other than define the relevant period of time.

The `Clock` object will be automatically created for us when we define a `Storyboard` object, or call one of the `Animatable.BeginAnimation` methods. Note that we do not typically need to concern ourselves with these `Clock` objects directly, but it can be helpful to know about them in order to understand the bigger picture.

There are a number of different types of `Timeline` objects, from the `AnimationTimeline` class to the `TimelineGroup` and `ParallelTimeline` classes. However, for animation purposes, we predominantly utilize the `Storyboard` class, which extends the `ParallelTimeline` and the `TimelineGroup` classes and adds animation-targeting properties and methods for controlling the timeline. Let's first investigate the main properties of the base `Timeline` class.

The `Duration` property specifies the time that is represented by the associated `Timeline` object. However, a timeline can have repetitions, so a more accurate description of the `Duration` property might be that it specifies the time of a single iteration of the associated `Timeline` object.

The duration property is of type `Duration`, which contains a `TimeSpan` property that contains the actual time that specifies the value of the duration. However, WPF includes a type converter that enables us to specify this `TimeSpan` value in XAML in the following formats, where the square brackets highlight optional segments.

```
Duration="[Days.]Hours:Minutes:Seconds[.FractionalSeconds]"
Duration="[Days.]Hours:Minutes"
```

However, the `Duration` structure also accepts other values in addition to the `TimeSpan` duration. There is a value of `Automatic`, which is the default value for component timelines that contain other timelines. In these cases, this value simply means that the parent timeline's duration will be as long as the longest duration of its children timelines. There is little purpose for us to explicitly use this value.

However, there is one further value that is very useful to us. The `Duration` structure also defines a `Forever` property that represents an infinite period of time. We can use this value to make an animation continue indefinitely, or more accurately, as long as its related View is being displayed.

```
Duration="Forever"
```

A `Timeline` object will stop playing when it reaches the end of its duration. If it has any child timelines associated with it, then they will also stop playing at this point. However, the natural duration of a timeline can be extended or shortened using other properties, as we will see shortly.

Some timelines, such as the `ParallelTimeline` and `Storyboard` classes, are able to contain other timelines and can affect their durations by setting their own values for the `Duration` property, which will override those set by the child timelines. Let's alter an earlier animation example from the previous chapter to demonstrate this.

```
<Rectangle Width="0" Height="0" Fill="Orange">
  <Rectangle.Triggers>
    <EventTrigger RoutedEvent="Loaded">
      <BeginStoryboard>
        <Storyboard Duration="0:0:2.5">
          <DoubleAnimation Storyboard.TargetProperty="Width" To="300.0"
            Duration="0:0:2.5" />
          <DoubleAnimation Storyboard.TargetProperty="Height" To="300.0"
            Duration="0:0:5" />
        </Storyboard>
      </BeginStoryboard>
    </EventTrigger>
  </Rectangle.Triggers>
</Rectangle>
```

In this preceding example, we have a `Rectangle` object with its dimensions initially set to zero. The `Storyboard` object contains two separate animation objects that will animate its dimensions from zero to three hundred pixels. The animation object that will animate the rectangle's width has a duration of two and a half seconds, while the animation object that will animate the height has a duration of five seconds.

However, the containing `Storyboard` object has a duration of two and a half seconds and so this will stop the timelines of the two child animation objects after two and a half seconds, regardless of their declared durations. The result of this will be that after the animation is complete, our `Rectangle` object will appear as a rectangle, instead of a square with equal height and width values.

If we had changed the duration of the storyboard to match that of the longer child animation, or changed that animation duration to match that of the shorter child animation, then our animated shape would end as a square, rather than as a rectangle.

Another way to adjust the assigned duration of an animation element is to set its
`AutoReverse` property. In effect, setting this property to `true` will usually double the
length of time that is specified by the `Duration` property, as the timeline will play in
reverse after it has completed its normal forwards iteration. Let's alter the storyboard from
the previous example to demonstrate this.

```
<Storyboard Duration="0:0:5">
  <DoubleAnimation Storyboard.TargetProperty="Width" To="300.0"
    Duration="0:0:2.5" AutoReverse="True" />
  <DoubleAnimation Storyboard.TargetProperty="Height" To="300.0"
    Duration="0:0:5" />
</Storyboard>
```

Now, both child timelines will have the same overall duration, as the first, previously
shorter, timeline has effectively been doubled in length. However, this will result in the first
timeline animating the width of the rectangle to three hundred pixels and then back to zero,
so it will be invisible when the animations have completed. Also note that we had to set the
parent storyboard duration to five seconds in order to see the difference in the child
timelines.

Note again that properties set on timelines that contain other timelines will affect the values
of those properties on the child timelines. As such, setting the `AutoReverse` property to
`true` on the parent timeline (the `Storyboard` object) will double the total length of time
that the child animations will run for; in our case, using the following example, the
rectangle will now be animated for ten seconds in total.

```
<Storyboard Duration="0:0:5" AutoReverse="True">
  <DoubleAnimation Storyboard.TargetProperty="Width" To="300.0"
    Duration="0:0:2.5" AutoReverse="True" />
  <DoubleAnimation Storyboard.TargetProperty="Height" To="300.0"
    Duration="0:0:5" />
</Storyboard>
```

The `RepeatBehavior` property is of type `RepeatBehavior` and can also affect the overall
duration of a timeline. Unlike the `AutoReverse` property, it can also shorten the overall
duration as well as lengthen it. Using the `RepeatBehavior` property, we can specify the
value in a number of ways using different behaviors.

The most simple is to provide a count of how many times we would like to multiply the original duration of the timeline. A pre-existing XAML type converter enables us to set the repeat count in XAML by specifying an x after the count, as can be seen in the following example. Note that we can also specify numbers with decimal places here, including values less than one.

```
<Storyboard Duration="0:0:5" AutoReverse="True" RepeatBehavior="2x">
  <DoubleAnimation Storyboard.TargetProperty="Width" To="300.0"
    Duration="0:0:2.5" AutoReverse="True" />
  <DoubleAnimation Storyboard.TargetProperty="Height" To="300.0"
    Duration="0:0:5" />
</Storyboard>
```

In this example, the normal duration would be five seconds, but the AutoReverse property is set to true and so that duration is doubled. However, the RepeatBehavior property is set to 2x and this will multiply the doubled ten seconds to twenty seconds. This value of two will be stored in the Count property of the RepeatBehavior structure.

An alternative to using the count option is to simply set the duration that we would like the animation to last for. The same XAML syntax that is used to set the Duration property can also be used to set the RepeatBehavior property. Similarly, the RepeatBehavior structure also defines a Forever property that represents an infinite period of time and we can use this value to make an animation continue indefinitely.

One further property that can affect the duration of an animation is the SpeedRatio property. This value is multiplied by the other related duration properties and so can both speed up and slow down the associated timeline. Let's update our example again to help to explain this property now.

```
<Storyboard Duration="0:0:5" AutoReverse="True" SpeedRatio="0.5">
  <DoubleAnimation Storyboard.TargetProperty="Width" To="300.0"
    Duration="0:0:2.5" AutoReverse="True" />
  <DoubleAnimation Storyboard.TargetProperty="Height" To="300.0"
    Duration="0:0:5" SpeedRatio="2" />
</Storyboard>
```

Again, the normal duration here would be five seconds and the AutoReverse property is set to true, so the duration is doubled. However, the SpeedRatio property is set to 0.5 and so the doubled duration is again doubled to twenty seconds. Note that a SpeedRatio value of 0.5 represents half the normal speed and therefore twice the normal duration.

The second child timeline also sets the `SpeedRatio` property, but its is set to 2 and so its speed is doubled and its duration halved. As its specified duration is twice that of its sibling timeline and its speed now twice as fast, this has the effect of re-synchronizing the two child animations, so that the two dimensions now grow together, as a square, rather than as a rectangle.

There are two more speed-related properties that we can use to fine-tune our animations; the `AccelerationRatio` and `DecelerationRatio` properties. These properties adjust the proportion of time that the related animation takes to speed up and slow down respectively. While this effect can be subtle at times, it can also give our animations that professional touch when used correctly.

Acceptable values for both of these properties exist between zero and one. Furthermore, if both of these properties are used, then the total sum of their values must remain at or below one. Failure to do so will result in the following exception being thrown at runtime:

```
The sum of AccelerationRatio and DecelerationRatio must be less than
or equal to one.
```

Entering values out of the acceptable range on either of these properties will also result in an error, although doing this will cause a compilation error instead.

```
Property value must be between 0.0 and 1.0.
```

Let's look at an example that highlights the difference between the different values of these two properties:

```xml
<StackPanel Margin="20">
  <StackPanel.Triggers>
    <EventTrigger RoutedEvent="Loaded">
      <BeginStoryboard>
        <Storyboard RepeatBehavior="Forever" Duration="0:0:1.5"
          SpeedRatio="0.5" Storyboard.TargetProperty="Width">
          <DoubleAnimation Storyboard.TargetName="RectangleA"
            AccelerationRatio="1.0" From="0" To="300" />
          <DoubleAnimation Storyboard.TargetName="RectangleB"
            AccelerationRatio="0.8" DecelerationRatio="0.2" From="0"
            To="300" />
          <DoubleAnimation Storyboard.TargetName="RectangleC"
            AccelerationRatio="0.6" DecelerationRatio="0.4" From="0"
            To="300" />
          <DoubleAnimation Storyboard.TargetName="RectangleD"
            AccelerationRatio="0.5" DecelerationRatio="0.5" From="0"
            To="300" />
          <DoubleAnimation Storyboard.TargetName="RectangleE"
            AccelerationRatio="0.4" DecelerationRatio="0.6" From="0"
```

```
            To="300" />
        <DoubleAnimation Storyboard.TargetName="RectangleF"
          AccelerationRatio="0.2" DecelerationRatio="0.8" From="0"
          To="300" />
        <DoubleAnimation Storyboard.TargetName="RectangleG"
          DecelerationRatio="1.0" From="0" To="300" />
      </Storyboard>
    </BeginStoryboard>
  </EventTrigger>
</StackPanel.Triggers>
<Rectangle Name="RectangleA" Fill="#FF0000" Height="30" />
<Rectangle Name="RectangleB" Fill="#D5002B" Height="30" />
<Rectangle Name="RectangleC" Fill="#AB0055" Height="30" />
<Rectangle Name="RectangleD" Fill="#800080" Height="30" />
<Rectangle Name="RectangleE" Fill="#5500AB" Height="30" />
<Rectangle Name="RectangleF" Fill="#2B00D5" Height="30" />
<Rectangle Name="RectangleG" Fill="#0000FF" Height="30" />
</StackPanel>
```

This code defines a number of `Rectangle` objects in a `StackPanel` control, each with its own associated `DoubleAnimation` element, that increases its width from zero to three hundred pixels over one and a half seconds.

Here, we've used the `Storyboard.TargetName` and `Storyboard.TargetProperty` properties to target the rectangles from a single `EventTrigger` to reduce the amount of code in the preceding example. We'll cover these Attached Properties in detail shortly, but for now, we'll just say that they are used to specify the target element and property to animate.

Each animation targets a different rectangle and has different values set for the `AccelerationRatio` and `DecelerationRatio` properties. The top rectangle's animation has its `AccelerationRatio` property set to `1.0` and the animation for the bottom rectangle has its `DecelerationRatio` property set to `1.0`.

The animations for the rectangles in between have varying values. The higher the rectangle, the higher the values for the `AccelerationRatio` property and the lower the values for the `DecelerationRatio` property and the lower the rectangle, the lower the values of the `AccelerationRatio` property and the higher the values for the `DecelerationRatio` property.

When this example is run, we can clearly see the differences between the various ratio values. At one point near the start of each iteration, we can see that the top rectangles that are animated with higher `AccelerationRatio` values have not grown in size as much as the lower rectangles that are animated with higher `DecelerationRatio` values however, all rectangles reach 300 pixels at approximately the same time.

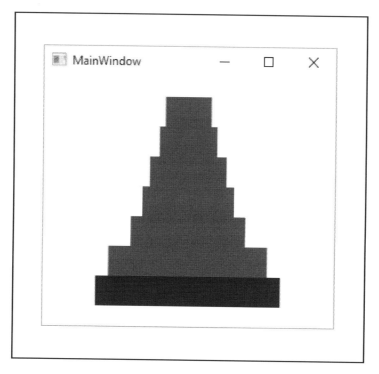

Another useful property in the `Timeline` class is the `BeginTime` property. As the name suggests, it sets the time to begin the animation; it can be thought of as a delay time that delays the start of its animation with relation to parent and sibling timelines.

The default value of this property is zero seconds and when it is set with a positive value, the delay occurs just once at the start of the timeline and is not affected by other properties that may be set on it. It is often used to delay the start of one or more animations until another animation has completed. Let's adjust our earlier example again to demonstrate this.

```
<Rectangle Width="0" Height="1" Fill="Orange">
  <Rectangle.Triggers>
    <EventTrigger RoutedEvent="Loaded">
      <BeginStoryboard>
```

```
            <Storyboard>
              <DoubleAnimation Storyboard.TargetProperty="Width" To="300.0"
                Duration="0:0:2" />
              <DoubleAnimation Storyboard.TargetProperty="Height" To="300.0"
                Duration="0:0:2" BeginTime="0:0:2" />
              <DoubleAnimation Storyboard.TargetProperty="Width" To="0.0"
                Duration="0:0:2" BeginTime="0:0:4" />
              <DoubleAnimation Storyboard.TargetProperty="Height" To="0.0"
                Duration="0:0:2" BeginTime="0:0:4" />
            </Storyboard>
          </BeginStoryboard>
        </EventTrigger>
      </Rectangle.Triggers>
    </Rectangle>
```

In this example, we have a single pixel high rectangle with a width that grows outward until it is three hundred pixels wide and then grows vertically until it is three hundred pixels high. At that point, its dimensions equally reduce in size until the shape shrinks to nothing.

This is achieved by delaying the last three animations while the width-increasing animation runs and then delaying the last two animations while the height-increasing animation runs. The BeginTime properties of the last two animations are set to the same value, so that they both start and run in synchronization with each other.

The last really useful timeline property is the FillBehavior property, which specifies what should happen to the data bound property value when the timeline reaches the end of its total duration, or its fill period. This property is of type FillBehavior and has just two values.

If we set this property to a value of HoldEnd, the data bound property value will remain at the final value that was reached just before the animation ended. Conversely, if we set this property to a value of Stop, which is the default value, the data bound property value will revert to the value that the property originally had before the animation started. Let's illustrate this with a simple example.

```
    <StackPanel Margin="20">
      <StackPanel.Triggers>
        <EventTrigger RoutedEvent="Loaded">
          <BeginStoryboard>
            <Storyboard Duration="0:0:1.5" SpeedRatio="0.5"
              Storyboard.TargetProperty="Opacity">
              <DoubleAnimation Storyboard.TargetName="RectangleA" To="0.0"
                FillBehavior="HoldEnd" />
              <DoubleAnimation Storyboard.TargetName="RectangleB" To="0.0"
                FillBehavior="Stop" />
```

```
          </Storyboard>
        </BeginStoryboard>
      </EventTrigger>
    </StackPanel.Triggers>
    <Rectangle Name="RectangleA" Fill="Orange" Height="100"
      HorizontalAlignment="Stretch" Margin="0,0,0,20" />
    <Rectangle Name="RectangleB" Fill="Orange" Height="100"
      HorizontalAlignment="Stretch" />
</StackPanel>
```

In this example, the difference between the two `FillBehavior` enumeration instances is clearly demonstrated. We have two rectangles of identical size that have identical timelines set up to animate their `Opacity` property values, with the exception of their `FillBehavior` property values.

Both rectangles fade from being opaque to being invisible in the same amount of time, but once the two timelines are complete, the rectangle with the `FillBehavior` property set to `Stop` immediately becomes visible again, as it was prior to the start of the animation, while the other with the `FillBehavior` property set to `HoldEnd` remains invisible, as it was at the end of the animation.

While this covers the main properties that are exposed by the `Timeline` class directly, there are a few more properties that are declared by many of the animation classes that extend the `Timeline` class and are essential to fully understand. They are the `From`, `By` and `To` properties, which specify the start and end points of the animations.

Because the animation classes generate property values, there are different types of animation classes for different property types. For example, the animation class that generates `Point` values is called the `PointAnimation` class and all of the normal animation classes follow the same naming pattern, using the name of the related type in the form `<TypeName>Animation`, for example `ColorAnimation`.

The normal animation classes, often referred to as the `From`, `By` and `To` animations, usually require two values to be specified, although one of these can sometimes be implicitly provided. The relevant property will then be animated along a path of automatically interpolated values between the two specified values.

It is most common to provide a starting value using the `From` property and an ending value using the `To` property. However, we can also specify a single starting, ending, or offset value and the second value will be taken from the current value of the animated property. We can set the offset value using the `By` property and this represents the exact amount the property value will change over the duration.

Specifying values for these different properties can have dramatically different effects on the resulting animations. Using the `From` property alone will start the animation at the desired value and will animate the property until it reaches the property's base value.

Using the `To` property alone will start animating the property from its current value and end at the specified value. Using only the `By` property will animate the property from its current value until the sum of that value with the specified offset amount has been reached.

Combinations of the three properties can be used to target just the right range of property values. Setting the `From` and `By` properties will start the animations from the value specified by the `From` property and animate the property until the offset specified by the `By` property has been reached.

Setting the `From` and `To` properties together will start the animations from the value specified by the `From` property and animate the property until the value specified by the `To` property. As the `By` and `To` properties both specify the ending value of the animation, the value specified by the `By` property will be ignored if they are both set on an animation element.

While these more common animations use one or two of the `From`, `By`, and `To` properties together to specify the range of values of the related property to be animated, there is another way to specify the target values. Let's now take a look at key-frame animations.

Introducing key-frames

Key-frame animations enable us to do a number of things that we cannot do with the `From`, `By`, and `To` animations. Unlike those animations, with key-frame animations, we are able to specify more than two target values and animate objects in discrete steps that cannot normally be animated. As such, there are more `<TypeName>AnimationUsingKeyFrames` classes than `<TypeName>Animation` classes, for example: `RectAnimationUsingKeyFrames`, `SizeAnimationUsingKeyFrames`.

Each `<TypeName>AnimationUsingKeyFrames` class has a `KeyFrames` property that we populate with key-frames to specify various values that must be passed during the animation. Each key-frame has a `KeyTime` and a `Value` property to specify the value and the relative time that it should be reached.

If no key-frame is declared with a key time of zero seconds, the animation will start from the relevant property's current value. The animation will order the key-frames by the values of their `KeyTime` property, rather than the order that they were declared in, and will create transitions between the various values according to their interpolation methods, which we'll find out about momentarily.

Note that the `KeyTime` property is of type `KeyTime` and this enables us to set it using types of values, other than `TimeSpan` values. We are also able to specify percentage values, which determine the percentage of the specified animation duration that each key-frame will be allotted. Note that we need to use cumulative values, so that the final key-frame key time value will always be `100%`.

Alternatively, there are a number of special values that we can use. When we want an animation with a constant velocity, regardless of the specified values, we can specify the `Paced` value for each of the key-frames. This takes the change between each key-frame's value into consideration before spacing them across the duration of the parent timeline and creating a smooth, even transition.

In contrast to this method, we can also specify the `Uniform` value for each key-frame, which basically spaces the key-frames out evenly across the duration of the parent animation. To do this, it simply counts the number of key-frames and divides that number by the total duration length, so that each key-frame will last for the same amount of time.

There are different kinds of key-frames for different `<TypeName>AnimationUsingKeyFrames` classes and there are also different kinds of interpolation methods used. The naming convention of these key-frames follows the format, `<InterpolationMethod><TypeName>KeyFrame`, for example: `LinearDoubleKeyFrame`.

There are three kinds of interpolation methods. The first is `Discrete`, which performs no interpolation and simply jumps from one value to another. This method is useful for setting Boolean or object values.

The next method is `Linear`, which performs a linear interpolation between the key-frame's value and the previous key-frame's value. This means that the animation will appear smooth, but speed up and slow down if your key-frame times are not evenly spaced out.

The last and most complicated interpolation method is `Spline`, but it also provides the user with the most control over the animation timing. It adds a further property named `KeySpline`, which enables us to specify two control points on a Bezier curve that extends from `0.0, 0.0` to `1.0, 1.0`. The first control point affects the first half of the curve, while the second point affects the second half.

Using these two control points, we can adjust the speed of the animation over its duration. As an example, using the first control point set to 0.0, 1,0 and the second set to 1.0, 0.0 will cause maximum distortion to the original linear curve and result in an animation that will quickly accelerate, before slowing almost to a stop in the middle and then dramatically speeding up again at the end.

With these two points, we can have full control over the speed of value change between each pair of key-frame values. This type of interpolation is most useful when attempting to create animations that are more realistic looking. Note that we are free to mix and match key-frames with different interpolation methods within each key-frame animation.

As an example, let's say that we wanted to animate a `Point` element. In this case we'd need to use the `PointAnimationUsingKeyFrames` class and would then have a choice of key-frame classes that represent the different interpolation methods. With this example, we could use any combination of the `DiscretePointKeyFrame`, `LinearPointKeyFrame`, and `SplinePointKeyFrame` classes.

Note that, as the `KeyFrames` property is set as the `name` input parameter in the `ContentPropertyAttribute` attribute that forms part of the declared class signature in each of the `<TypeName>AnimationUsingKeyFrames` classes, we do not need to explicitly declare this property in XAML and can declare the various key-frames directly inside these elements as shown in the following code:

```
<Ellipse Width="100" Height="100" Stroke="Black" StrokeThickness="3">
  <Ellipse.Fill>
    <RadialGradientBrush>
      <GradientStop Color="Yellow" Offset="0" />
      <GradientStop Color="Orange" Offset="1" />
    </RadialGradientBrush>
  </Ellipse.Fill>
  <Ellipse.Triggers>
    <EventTrigger RoutedEvent="Loaded">
      <BeginStoryboard>
        <Storyboard RepeatBehavior="Forever"
          Storyboard.TargetProperty="Fill.GradientOrigin">
          <PointAnimationUsingKeyFrames>
            <DiscretePointKeyFrame Value="0.5, 0.5" KeyTime="0:0:0" />
            <LinearPointKeyFrame Value="1.0, 1.0" KeyTime="0:0:2" />
            <SplinePointKeyFrame KeySpline="0,0.25 0.75,0" Value="1.0, 0.0"
              KeyTime="0:0:4" />
            <LinearPointKeyFrame Value="0.0, 0.0" KeyTime="0:0:5" />
            <SplinePointKeyFrame KeySpline="0,0.75 0.25,0" Value="0.5, 0.5"
              KeyTime="0:0:8" />
          </PointAnimationUsingKeyFrames>
        </Storyboard>
```

```
        </BeginStoryboard>
      </EventTrigger>
    </Ellipse.Triggers>
  </Ellipse>
```

In this example, we declare an `Ellipse` shape with its `Fill` property set to an instance of the `RadialGradientBrush` class. The brush has a yellow center and is orange around the edges. Note that these brushes have a property named `GradientOrigin` that specifies the center point of the gradient and defaults to the point `0.5, 0.5`. In this example, we animate this property, which has a similar effect to moving a light source around a 3D ball.

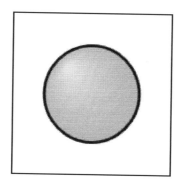

We use an `EventTrigger` with the `Loaded` event to start our animation and set the `RepeatBehavior` property to `Forever` on the associated storyboard. As mentioned, we set the `TargetProperty` property to the `GradientOrigin` property of the brush that is set as the `Fill` property.

Inside the storyboard, we declare a `PointAnimationUsingKeyFrames` element and directly inside it, we declare a number of various `<InterpolationMethod><Type>KeyFrame` objects. As mentioned, we do not need to explicitly declare the `KeyFrames` property in order to declare these key-frame elements within it.

Note that the `DiscretePointKeyFrame` element that is used here is entirely optional and would not change anything if removed. This is because the point `0.5, 0.5` is both the starting value of the animation and default value of the gradient brush and also the ending value of the animation. Furthermore, if we omit a zero time key-frame, one will be implicitly added for us with this value.

Next, we declare a `LinearPointKeyFrame` element, that will animate the gradient origin from the point `0.5, 0.5` to the point `1.0, 1.0` in a linear, even fashion. Following that, we have a `SplinePointKeyFrame` element that will animate the gradient origin from the previous point to the point `1.0, 0.0`. Note the `KeySpline` property that adjusts the speed of the animation as it progresses.

From there, we use another `LinearPointKeyFrame` element to smoothly and evenly transition to the point `0.0, 0.0` over one second. Finally, we use a second `SplinePointKeyFrame` element to animate the gradient origin back to the center of the circle and its starting position, taking the last three seconds of the total duration.

When this example is run, we can clearly see it animating the gradient origin point evenly during the periods of the two `LinearPointKeyFrame` elements and change speed during the periods of the two `SplinePointKeyFrame` elements.

Telling stories

While the various animation classes that extend the `Timeline` class can be used to animate control properties directly in code, in order to declare and trigger animations using XAML alone, we need to use the `Storyboard` class. This is what is known as a container timeline, as it extends the abstract `TimelineGroup` class that enables it to contain child timelines.

Another container timeline class that the `Storyboard` class extends is the `ParallelTimeline` class and these classes enable us to group child timelines and to set properties on them as a group. When creating more complex animations, if all we need to do is to delay the start of a group of child timelines, we should use the `ParallelTimeline` class rather than the `Storyboard` class, as it is more efficient.

We could rewrite our earlier `BeginTime` example to use a `ParallelTimeline` element to delay the start of our last two timelines. Let's see what that might look like.

```
<Storyboard>
  <DoubleAnimation Storyboard.TargetProperty="Width" To="300.0"
    Duration="0:0:2" />
  <DoubleAnimation Storyboard.TargetProperty="Height" To="300.0"
    Duration="0:0:2" BeginTime="0:0:2" />
  <ParallelTimeline BeginTime="0:0:4">
    <DoubleAnimation Storyboard.TargetProperty="Width" To="0.0"
      Duration="0:0:2" />
    <DoubleAnimation Storyboard.TargetProperty="Height" To="0.0"
      Duration="0:0:2" />
  </ParallelTimeline>
```

```
    </Storyboard>
```

As the `Storyboard` class is a `Timeline` object, it also has the same properties as the various animation objects. One additional property that it inherits from the `ParallelTimeline` class is the `SlipBehavior` property. This property is only really useful when we want to synchronize an animation timeline with the playback of a `MediaTimeline` element, but it's worth knowing about.

This property is of the enumeration type `SlipBehavior` and it only has two members. A value of `Grow` specifies that we do not need our animation timelines to be synchronized with our media timeline(s) and is the default value of this property.

Conversely, a value of `Slip` indicates that we want our animation timelines to slip, either forwards or backwards, whenever necessary in order to keep them in sync with the playing media. If the media takes time to load when using this setting, then the animation timelines within the storyboard will wait until the media is ready and continue at that point.

In addition to the properties that have been inherited from the various base classes, the `Storyboard` class also declares three important Attached Properties that are essential for targeting animations to individual UI elements and/or their properties.

The `Storyboard.Target` Attached Property specifies the UI control that should be animated, although setting this property alone is not enough, as it does not specify the target property. This property is of type `object`, although it can only be used with objects of type `DependencyObject`.

In order to use this property, we need to specify a binding path that references the target UI control. If the target element extends the `FrameworkElement` or `FrameworkContentElement` classes, then one way would be to name the target element and to use an `ElementName` binding to reference it.

```
    Storyboard.Target="{Binding ElementName=TargetControlName}"
```

Most UI elements extend one of these two classes that declare the `Name` property. However, if we provide a name for the target control, then there is a simpler way to target it. Instead of using the `Storyboard.Target` property, we could use the `Storyboard.TargetName` Attached Property to specify the target element using just their declared name, without any binding.

```
    Storyboard.TargetName="TargetControlName"
```

We do not always need to specify this property value, as on occasion, the target element can be worked out implicitly. If the relevant storyboard was started with a `BeginStoryboard` element, the UI element that declared it will be targeted. Additionally, if the relevant storyboard is a child of another timeline, then the target of the parent timeline will be inherited.

The most important property that the `Storyboard` class declares is the `TargetProperty` Attached Property. We use this property to specify which property on the target element that we want to animate. Note that in order for this to work, the target property must be a Dependency Property.

Occasionally, we may want to target objects that do not extend either of the framework classes mentioned earlier; in WPF, we are also able to target freezable classes that extend the `Freezable` class. In order to target one of these classes in XAML, we need to specify the name of the object using the `x:Name` directive instead, as they have no `Name` property.

As a side note, WPF classes that declare their own `Name` property actually map the name value through to the `x:Name` directive, which is part of the XAML specification. In these cases, we are free to use either of these to register a name for an element, but we must not set both. Note that unnamed elements can still be referenced by our animations, although they need to be indirectly referenced. Instead of referencing them directly, we need to specify the name of the parent property or freezable object and then chain properties in the `TargetProperty` Attached Property, until we reach the desired element. We used this method in the last example of the previous section.

```
Storyboard.TargetProperty="Fill.GradientOrigin"
```

In this case, we reference the `Fill` property, which is of type `RadialGradientBrush` and then we chain to the `GradientOrigin` property of the brush from there. Note that if we had used an instance of the `SolidColorBrush` class here instead, this reference would fail, because there is no `GradientOrigin` property in that brush. However, while the animation would fail to work, this would not cause any errors to be raised.

Controlling storyboards

In order to start a storyboard in XAML, we need to use a `BeginStoryboard` element. This class extends the `TriggerAction` class and if you remember, that is the type that we need to use in the `TriggerActionCollection` of the `EventTrigger` class and the `TriggerBase.EnterActions` and `TriggerBase.ExitActions` properties.

We specify the storyboard to use with the `BeginStoryboard` element by setting it to the `Storyboard` property in code. When using XAML, the `Storyboard` property is implicitly set to the storyboard that is declared within the `BeginStoryboard` element.

The `BeginStoryboard` action is responsible for connecting the animation timelines with the animation targets and their targeted properties and is also responsible for starting the various animation timelines within its storyboard. It does this by calling the `Begin` method of the associated `Storyboard` object, once its parent's trigger condition has been met.

If an already running storyboard is asked to begin again, either indirectly, using a `BeginStoryboard` action, or directly, using the `Begin` method, what happens will depend upon the value set by the `HandoffBehavior` property.

This property is of the enumeration type `HandoffBehavior` and has two values. The default value is `SnapshotAndReplace` and this will renew the internal clocks and essentially have the effect of replacing one copy of the timeline with another. The other value is more interesting; the `Compose` value will retain the original clocks when restarting the animation and append the new animation after the current one, performing some interpolation between them, resulting in a smoother join.

One problem with this method is that the retained clocks will continue to use system resources and this can end in memory problems if not handled correctly. However, this method produces much smoother and more natural and fluid animations that can be worth the extra resources. This is best demonstrated with a small example.

```xml
<Canvas>
  <Rectangle Canvas.Top="200" Canvas.Left="25" Width="100" Height="100"
    Fill="Orange" Stroke="Black" StrokeThickness="3">
    <Rectangle.Style>
      <Style TargetType="{x:Type Rectangle}">
        <Style.Triggers>
          <Trigger Property="IsMouseOver" Value="True">
            <Trigger.EnterActions>
              <BeginStoryboard>
                <Storyboard>
                  <DoubleAnimation Duration="0:0:2"
                    Storyboard.TargetProperty="(Canvas.Top)" To="0" />
                </Storyboard>
              </BeginStoryboard>
            </Trigger.EnterActions>
            <Trigger.ExitActions>
              <BeginStoryboard>
                <Storyboard>
                  <DoubleAnimation Duration="0:0:2"
                    Storyboard.TargetProperty="(Canvas.Top)" To="200" />
```

```
                </Storyboard>
              </BeginStoryboard>
            </Trigger.ExitActions>
          </Trigger>
        </Style.Triggers>
      </Style>
    </Rectangle.Style>
  </Rectangle>
  <Rectangle Canvas.Top="200" Canvas.Left="150" Width="100" Height="100"
    Fill="Orange" Stroke="Black" StrokeThickness="3">
    <Rectangle.Style>
      <Style TargetType="{x:Type Rectangle}">
        <Style.Triggers>
          <Trigger Property="IsMouseOver" Value="True">
            <Trigger.EnterActions>
              <BeginStoryboard>
                <Storyboard>
                  <DoubleAnimation Duration="0:0:2"
                    Storyboard.TargetProperty="(Canvas.Top)" To="0" />
                </Storyboard>
              </BeginStoryboard>
            </Trigger.EnterActions>
            <Trigger.ExitActions>
              <BeginStoryboard HandoffBehavior="Compose">
                <Storyboard>
                  <DoubleAnimation Duration="0:0:2"
                    Storyboard.TargetProperty="(Canvas.Top)" To="200" />
                </Storyboard>
              </BeginStoryboard>
            </Trigger.ExitActions>
          </Trigger>
        </Style.Triggers>
      </Style>
    </Rectangle.Style>
  </Rectangle>
</Canvas>
```

In this example, we have two rectangles, each with its own animation. The only difference between them is that the `BeginStoryboard` element that starts the animation for the right rectangle has a `HandoffBehavior` of `Compose`, while the other uses the default value of `SnapshotAndReplace`.

When the example is run, each rectangle will move upwards when the mouse cursor is placed over it and move back downwards when the cursor is moved away from it. If we keep the mouse cursor within the bounds of each rectangle, moving it up to the top of the screen with the rectangle and then move the cursor away to let the rectangle fall, the two animations will appear identical.

However, if we move the mouse cursor from side to side across the two rectangles, we will start to see a difference between the two animations. We'll see that as the cursor enters the bounds of each rectangle, they each start their upward movement. But once the cursor leaves the rectangle bounds, we see the difference.

The rectangle on the left with the default value of `SnapshotAndReplace`, will stop moving up and immediately begin its downward animation, while the other rectangle will continue to move upward for a short time before commencing its downward animation. This results in a much smoother, more natural looking transition between the two animations.

The difference between these two handoff behaviors though, is most clearly demonstrated by simply placing the mouse cursor on one of the rectangles and leaving it there. Doing this to the rectangle on the left will cause the rectangle to move upward until the mouse cursor is no longer within its bounds and then it will immediately begin to move downwards again.

However, as the mouse cursor will then be within the bounds of the rectangle again, it will begin the upwards animation once more. This will cause the rectangle to move away from the mouse cursor again and so we will end with a repetitive loop of this behavior and it will result in what looks like a quick shaking, or stuttering, of the rectangle just above the position of the mouse.

On the other hand, the rectangle on the right, with the `HandoffBehavior` of `Compose` will move upward until the mouse cursor is no longer within its bounds, but will then continue to move upwards for a short time before starting to move downwards again. Once more, this creates a far smoother animation and will result in the rectangle bouncing gently above the mouse cursor, in sharp contrast to the other, stuttering rectangle.

There are several related `TriggerAction` derived classes that are suffixed with the word `Storyboard` and enable us to control various aspects of the related `Storyboard` element. By specifying the `Name` property value of the `BeginStoryboard` element in the `BeginStoryboardName` property of the other actions, we are able to further control the running storyboard.

We can use the `PauseStoryboard` element to pause a running storyboard and the `ResumeStoryboard` to resume a paused storyboard. The `PauseStoryboard` element does nothing if the related storyboard is not running and similarly, the `ResumeStoryboard` action does nothing if the related storyboard is not already paused. Therefore, a storyboard cannot be started with a `ResumeStoryboard` trigger action.

The `StopStoryboard` action will stop a running storyboard, but does nothing if the related storyboard is not already running. Finally, there is a `RemoveStoryboard` trigger action that will remove a storyboard when its parent's trigger condition has been met. As storyboards consume resources, we should remove them when they are no longer required.

For example, if we use an `EventTrigger` with the `Loaded` event to start a timeline that has its `RepeatBehavior` property set to `Forever`, then we should use another `EventTrigger` element with a `RemoveStoryboard` action in the `Unloaded` event to remove the storyboard. This is somewhat analogous to calling the `Dispose` method on an `IDisposable` implementation.

Note that it is essential to remove a storyboard that was started by a `BeginStoryboard` action with its `HandoffBehavior` property set to `Compose`, as it could end with many internal clocks being instantiated, but not disposed of. Removing the storyboard will also result in the internally used clocks being disposed of. Let's see a practical example of how we might use these elements.

```xml
<StackPanel TextElement.FontSize="14">
  <TextBox Text="{Binding Name, UpdateSourceTrigger=PropertyChanged}"
    Margin="20">
    <TextBox.Effect>
      <DropShadowEffect Color="Red" ShadowDepth="0" BlurRadius="0"
        Opacity="0.5" />
    </TextBox.Effect>
    <TextBox.Style>
      <Style TargetType="{x:Type TextBox}">
        <Style.Triggers>
          <DataTrigger Binding="{Binding IsValid}" Value="False">
            <DataTrigger.EnterActions>
              <BeginStoryboard Name="GlowStoryboard">
                <Storyboard RepeatBehavior="Forever">
                  <DoubleAnimation Storyboard.
                    TargetProperty="Effect.(DropShadowEffect.BlurRadius)"
                    To="25" Duration="0:0:1.0" AutoReverse="True" />
                </Storyboard>
              </BeginStoryboard>
            </DataTrigger.EnterActions>
          </DataTrigger>
          <MultiDataTrigger>
            <MultiDataTrigger.Conditions>
              <Condition Binding="{Binding IsValid}" Value="False" />
              <Condition Binding="{Binding IsFocused,
                RelativeSource={RelativeSource Self}}" Value="True" />
            </MultiDataTrigger.Conditions>
            <MultiDataTrigger.EnterActions>
              <PauseStoryboard BeginStoryboardName="GlowStoryboard" />
```

```
              </MultiDataTrigger.EnterActions>
            </MultiDataTrigger>
            <Trigger Property="IsFocused" Value="True">
              <Trigger.EnterActions>
                <PauseStoryboard BeginStoryboardName="GlowStoryboard" />
              </Trigger.EnterActions>
              <Trigger.ExitActions>
                <ResumeStoryboard BeginStoryboardName="GlowStoryboard" />
              </Trigger.ExitActions>
            </Trigger>
            <DataTrigger Binding="{Binding IsValid}" Value="True">
              <DataTrigger.EnterActions>
                <StopStoryboard BeginStoryboardName="GlowStoryboard" />
              </DataTrigger.EnterActions>
            </DataTrigger>
            <EventTrigger RoutedEvent="Unloaded">
              <EventTrigger.Actions>
                <RemoveStoryboard BeginStoryboardName="GlowStoryboard" />
              </EventTrigger.Actions>
            </EventTrigger>
          </Style.Triggers>
        </Style>
      </TextBox.Style>
    </TextBox>
    <TextBox Margin="20 0" />
</StackPanel>
```

This example has two textboxes, with the lower one existing solely to enable us to remove focus from the first one. The first textbox is data bound to a Name property in our View Model. Let's imagine that we have some validation code that will update a property named IsValid when the Name property is changed. We'll cover validation in depth in Chapter 8, *Implementing Responsive Data Validation*, but for now, let's keep it simple.

```
private string name = string.Empty;
private bool isValid = false;

...

public string Name
{
  get { return name; }
  set
  {
    if (name != value)
    {
      name = value;
      NotifyPropertyChanged();
```

```
      if (name.Length > 2) IsValid = true;
    }
  }
}

public bool IsValid
{
  get { return isValid; }
  set { if (isValid != value) { isValid = value;
    NotifyPropertyChanged(); } }
}
```

Here, we simply verify that the `Name` property has a value that has three or more characters in it. The basic idea in this example is that we have an animation that highlights the fact that a particular form field requires a valid value.

It could be a shaking, or growing and shrinking of the form field, or the animation of an adjacent element, but in our case, we have used a `DropShadowEffect` element to create a glowing effect around it.

In the `Triggers` collection of our style, we have declared a number of triggers. The first one is a `DataTrigger` and it data binds to the `IsValid` property in the View Model and uses the `BeginStoryboard` trigger action element named `GlowStoryboard` to make the glowing effect around the textbox grow and shrink when the property value is `false`.

While animations are great at attracting the eye, they can also be quite distracting. Skipping over the `MultiDataTrigger` momentarily, our animation will therefore be paused when the textbox is focused, so that the user can enter the details without distraction. We achieve this by declaring a `PauseStoryboard` action in the trigger with the condition that the `IsFocused` property is `true`.

Using the `EnterActions` collection of the trigger ensures that the `PauseStoryboard` action is run as the `IsFocused` property is set to `true`. Declaring the `ResumeStoryboard` action in the `ExitActions` collection of the trigger ensures that it will be run as the `IsFocused` property is set to `false`, or in other words, when the control loses focus.

When the user has entered a value, our View Model validates whether the provided value is indeed valid and if so, it sets the `IsValid` property to `true`. In our example, we just verify that the entered string contains three or more characters in order for it to be valid. Setting the `UpdateSourceTrigger` property to `PropertyChanged` on the binding ensures this validation occurs on each keystroke.

Our example uses a `DataTrigger` to data bind to this property and when it is `true`, it triggers the `StopStoryboard` action, which stops the storyboard from running any further. As the `FillBehavior` property of our storyboard is not explicitly set, it will default to the `Stop` value and the animated property value will return to the original value that it had prior to being animated.

However, what should happen if the user entered three or more characters and then deleted them? The data trigger would trigger the `StopStoryboard` action and the storyboard would be stopped. As they deleted the characters and the `IsValid` property would be set to `false` and the condition of the first `DataTrigger` would then trigger the initial `BeginStoryboard` action to start the storyboard again.

But this would occur while the focus was still on the textbox and while the animation on the effect should not be running. It is for this reason that we declared the `MultiDataTrigger` element that we skipped over earlier. In this trigger, we have two conditions. One is that the `IsFocused` property should be `true` and for this alone, we could have used a `MultiTrigger` instead.

However, the other condition requires that we data bind to the `IsValid` property from the View Model and for that, we need to use the `MultiDataTrigger` element. So, this trigger will run its `PauseStoryboard` action when the textbox is focused and as soon as the data bound value becomes invalid, or in other words, as the user deletes the third character.

The triggers are evaluated from top to bottom in the declared order in the XAML and as the user deletes the third character, the first trigger begins the animation. The `MultiDataTrigger` has to be declared after the first trigger, so that the storyboard will be started before it pauses it. In this case, the glow effect will start again once the user has moved focus from the first textbox as required.

Finally, this example demonstrates how we can use a `RemoveStoryboard` trigger action to remove the storyboard when it is no longer needed, freeing up its resources. The usual way to do this is by utilizing an `EventTrigger` in the `Unloaded` event of the relevant control.

While these are the only trigger action elements that control the running state of their associated storyboard elements, there are a further three actions that can control other aspects of, or set other properties of the storyboard.

The `SetStoryboardSpeedRatio` trigger action can set the `SpeedRatio` of the associated storyboard. We specify the desired ratio in its `SpeedRatio` property and this value will be applied when the action's related trigger condition is met. Note that this element can only work on a storyboard that has already been started, although it can work at any time after this point.

The `SkipStoryboardToFill` trigger action will move the current position of a storyboard to its fill period, if it has one. Remember that the `FillBehavior` property determines what should happen during the fill period. If the storyboard has child timelines, then their positions will also be forwarded to their fill periods at this point.

Last, but not least, there is a `SeekStoryboard` trigger action, which enables us to move the current position of storyboard to a location, relative to the position specified by the `Origin` property, which has a begin time of zero seconds by default. When declaring the `SeekStoryboard` action, we specify the desired seek position in the `Offset` property and optionally set the `Origin` property.

The `Offset` property is of type `TimeSpan` and we can use the time notation highlighted earlier to specify its value in XAML. The `Origin` property is of type `TimeSeekOrigin` and we can specify one of two values.

The first is the default value of `BeginTime`, which places the origin at the start of the timeline, while the second is `Duration`, which places it at the end of a single iteration of the timeline's natural duration. Note that the various speed ratio values are not taken into consideration when seeking through a timeline's duration.

That completes our look at the range of trigger actions that we can use to control our storyboards. Each of these trigger actions have corresponding methods in the `Storyboard` class that they call when their related trigger conditions are met.

Easing functions

When declaring animations with WPF, we are able to utilize a powerful capability that helps us to define more specialized animations. While we normally provide a start and end value for our animations and let WPF interpolate the intermediate values, there is a way that we can affect this interpolation process.

There are a number of mathematical functions that provide complex animation paths and are known as easing functions. For example, these can accurately replicate the movement of a spring, or the bounce of a ball.

We can simply declare the appropriate easing function within the `EasingFunction` property of the animation. Each easing function extends the `EasingFunctionBase` class and has its own specific properties. For example, the `BounceEase` element provides `Bounces` and `Bounciness` properties, while the `ElasticEase` class declare the `Oscillations` and `Springiness` properties.

All easing functions inherit the `EasingMode` property from the base class. This property is of the enumeration type `EasingMode` and gives us three options. The `EaseIn` option follows the normal mathematical formula associated with each easing function. The `EaseOut` option uses the inverse of the mathematical formula.

The `EaseInOut` option uses the standard formula for the first half and the inverse formula for the second half. While not strictly true, this can be somewhat thought of as `EaseIn` affects the start of the animation, `EaseOut` affects the end of the animation and `EaseInOut` affects both the start and the end of the animation. Let's see an example of a bouncing ball animation to demonstrate this ability.

```
<Canvas>
  <Ellipse Width="50" Height="50" Fill="Orange" Stroke="Black"
    StrokeThickness="3">
    <Ellipse.Triggers>
      <EventTrigger RoutedEvent="Loaded">
        <BeginStoryboard>
          <Storyboard RepeatBehavior="Forever">
            <Storyboard Storyboard.TargetProperty="(Canvas.Top)">
              <DoubleAnimation Duration="00:00:3" From="0" To="200">
                <DoubleAnimation.EasingFunction>
                  <BounceEase EasingMode="EaseOut" Bounces="10"
                    Bounciness="1.5" />
                </DoubleAnimation.EasingFunction>
              </DoubleAnimation>
            </Storyboard>
            <Storyboard Storyboard.TargetProperty="(Canvas.Left)">
              <DoubleAnimation Duration="00:00:3.5" From="0" To="200"
                DecelerationRatio="0.2" />
            </Storyboard>
          </Storyboard>
        </BeginStoryboard>
      </EventTrigger>
    </Ellipse.Triggers>
  </Ellipse>
  <Line Canvas.Top="250" Canvas.Left="25" X1="0" Y1="1.5" X2="225" Y2="1.5"
    Stroke="Black" StrokeThickness="3" />
</Canvas>
```

Here, we have a `Canvas` panel that contains two shapes; an ellipse and a line. The line is simply to give the impression of the ground. The `Ellipse` element defines some basic appearance properties and then an `EventTrigger` element that starts our eased animation when the shape object is loaded. We have an outer `Storyboard` element that is set to repeat forever and contains two inner storyboards.

The first of these inner storyboards targets the `Canvas.Top` Attached Property using the `Storyboard.TargetProperty`, while the second targets its `Canvas.Left` Attached Property. Note that we do not need to specify the `Storyboard.TargetProperty` value here, as the storyboard resides within the target element, which will be implicitly set as the target for us. Also, remember that we need to wrap the Attached Property name with its class name in brackets for this to work.

The first storyboard is responsible for the vertical movement of our ball and so this is the animation that we want to use the `BounceEase` function with. In order to utilize this functionality, we simply declare the `BounceEase` object within the `DoubleAnimation.EasingFunction` property and set the desired property values.

The `Bounces` property determines how many times the ball should bounce, or rebound off the lower extent of the animation. Note that this does not include the final half-bounce that this easing function will perform. The `Bounciness` property specifies how bouncy the ball is. Strangely, the higher this value is, the less bouncy the ball will be. Also note that this value must be positive.

As physics determines that the horizontal velocity of the ball should remain constant for the most part, we do not need to apply an easing function to the second animation. Instead, we have added a small value for its `DecelerationRatio` property, which nicely simulates the sideways friction on the ball.

As can be seen, it is very easy to take advantage of these mathematical formulae to greatly increase the movement of our animations. While there is not enough space in this book for us to cover all of these easing functions, it is well worth investigating them yourselves. Let's take a look at another example, to see how we can simulate the movement of a spring using the `ElasticEase` class:

```xml
<Rectangle Canvas.Top="250" Canvas.Left="25" Width="25" Height="50"
  Fill="Orange" Stroke="Black" StrokeThickness="3">
  <Rectangle.Triggers>
    <EventTrigger RoutedEvent="Loaded">
      <BeginStoryboard>
        <Storyboard RepeatBehavior="Forever">
          <Storyboard Storyboard.TargetProperty="Height">
            <DoubleAnimation Duration="00:00:3" From="50" To="200">
```

```
            <DoubleAnimation.EasingFunction>
              <ElasticEase EasingMode="EaseOut" Oscillations="6"
                Springiness="2" />
            </DoubleAnimation.EasingFunction>
          </DoubleAnimation>
        </Storyboard>
      </Storyboard>
    </BeginStoryboard>
  </EventTrigger>
  </Rectangle.Triggers>
</Rectangle>
```

In this example, we have a thin `Rectangle` element that simulates the movement of a coiled spring using an `ElasticEase` function. The `Oscillations` property specifies the number of times that the rectangle will grow and shrink over the lifetime of the animation effect and the `Springiness` property determines the stiffness of the spring, where larger values equal more springiness.

While the two demonstrated easing functions are rather specialized and unsuitable to use in many cases, the vast majority of the remaining functions are all variations on standard circular, or exponential curves, or curves that use the formula $f(t) = t^n$, where n is either determined by the exact easing function used, or by the `Power` property of the `PowerEase` function.

For example, the `QuadraticEase` function uses the formula $f(t) = t^2$, the `CubicEase` function uses the formula $f(t) = t^3$, the `QuarticEase` function uses the formula $f(t) = t^4$, the `QuinticEase` function uses the formula $f(t) = t^5$, while the `PowerEase` function uses the formula $f(t) = t^n$, where n is determined by its `Power` property.

Apart from these variations of the standard acceleration/deceleration curve, there is one final useful easing function named `BackEase`. This has the effect of overshooting its starting or ending `From` or `To` values, dependent upon the value of the `EasingMode` property, and then reversing back to it. This is one of the more usable easing functions, so let's see an example of a `TextBox` element sliding on screen.

```
<Canvas ClipToBounds="True">
  <TextBox Canvas.Top="50" Canvas.Left="-150" Width="150" Height="25">
    <TextBox.Triggers>
      <EventTrigger RoutedEvent="Loaded">
        <BeginStoryboard>
          <Storyboard Storyboard.TargetProperty="(Canvas.Left)"
            Duration="00:00:2" RepeatBehavior="Forever">
            <DoubleAnimation Duration="00:00:1" From="-150" To="50">
              <DoubleAnimation.EasingFunction>
                <BackEase EasingMode="EaseOut" Amplitude="0.75" />
```

```
                </DoubleAnimation.EasingFunction>
              </DoubleAnimation>
            </Storyboard>
          </BeginStoryboard>
        </EventTrigger>
      </TextBox.Triggers>
    </TextBox>
  </Canvas>
```

In this example, we start with a `Canvas` object that has its `ClipToBounds` property set to `true`. This ensures that elements that are outside the bounds of the canvas will not be visible. Inside the canvas, we have declared a `TextBox` control that is initially placed totally outside the bounds of the canvas and so it will be invisible.

When the control is loaded, the `EventTrigger` element will start the animation that targets the `Canvas.Left` Attached Property. Note that the duration on the storyboard is one second longer than the duration on the animation and so the storyboard will wait for one second after the animation has completed before restarting. This gives us time to appreciate the effect of the applied easing function.

The animation will slide the textbox to its ending position from its initial off-screen position. By using the `BackEase` function, the textbox will slightly slide past its ending position and then reverse back into it. The amount past its ending position that it will slide to is determined by the value of its `Amplitude` property, with higher values extending the overshoot distance.

While we have only discussed using these easing functions with `From`, `By` and `To` animations so far, it is also possible to use them with key-frame animations as well. There are a number of classes that follow the `Easing<Type>KeyFrame` naming convention, such as the `EasingColorKeyFrame` class. These classes have an `EasingFunction` property that enables us to specify which function to use.

```
<TextBlock Text="The operation was successful" Margin="20">
  <TextBlock.Triggers>
    <EventTrigger RoutedEvent="Loaded">
      <BeginStoryboard>
        <Storyboard Storyboard.TargetProperty="FontSize">
          <DoubleAnimationUsingKeyFrames Duration="00:00:2.5">
            <DiscreteDoubleKeyFrame KeyTime="0:0:0" Value="8" />
            <EasingDoubleKeyFrame KeyTime="0:0:1" Value="36">
              <EasingDoubleKeyFrame.EasingFunction>
                <BounceEase EasingMode="EaseOut" Bounces="2"
                  Bounciness="1.5" />
              </EasingDoubleKeyFrame.EasingFunction>
            </EasingDoubleKeyFrame>
```

```
        <EasingDoubleKeyFrame KeyTime="0:0:2" Value="8">
          <EasingDoubleKeyFrame.EasingFunction>
            <ElasticEase EasingMode="EaseIn" Oscillations="2"
              Springiness="1.5" />
          </EasingDoubleKeyFrame.EasingFunction>
        </EasingDoubleKeyFrame>
        <EasingDoubleKeyFrame KeyTime="0:0:2.5" Value="36">
          <EasingDoubleKeyFrame.EasingFunction>
            <BackEase EasingMode="EaseOut" Amplitude="2" />
          </EasingDoubleKeyFrame.EasingFunction>
        </EasingDoubleKeyFrame>
      </DoubleAnimationUsingKeyFrames>
    </Storyboard>
  </BeginStoryboard>
  </EventTrigger>
 </TextBlock.Triggers>
</TextBlock>
```

In this example, we animate the size of the text in a `TextBlock` element using a number of key-frames. This creates the kind of transition effect that we might see on lines of text in Microsoft PowerPoint presentations and could be suitable to use in an application that presents textual information to the user.

We start by targeting the `FontSize` property and specifying a total duration of two and a half seconds. Our first key-frame simply sets our starting font size at zero seconds and so we can use a `DiscreteDoubleKeyFrame` for that. The second key-frame is an `EasingDoubleKeyFrame` element with a `BounceEase` easing function and a duration, or key time, of one second.

Following that, we have another `EasingDoubleKeyFrame` element that lasts for one second, but this one uses an `ElasticEase` function. Finally, we finish with one further `EasingDoubleKeyFrame` element with a `BackEase` easing function and a duration of half a second. Note that we have used small values for the `Bounces` and `Oscillations` properties, to keep the animation more usable.

Using these easing functions with key-frames enable us to chain any number of them together to create more complicated animated effects. However, it is easy to go overboard and create effects that are too much, as can be seen by increasing the values set for the `Bounces` and `Oscillations` properties in this example. In reality, even the modest nvalues used here could be considered to be too much for practical use.

Animating along a path

There is one further method of animating property values in WPF. Using `PathFigure` and `PathSegment` objects, we can construct a `PathGeometry` object and then animate a property value according to the X, Y and/or rotation angle values of the path.

As this method is primarily used for animating objects along a complex path and therefore not aimed at typical business applications, we will cover only the basics of this functionality here. As with the other kinds of animation classes, there are different path animation types that manipulate different CLR types. Path animation classes follow the naming convention `<Type>AnimationUsingPath`.

Each `<Type>AnimationUsingPath` class has a `PathGeometry` property that we can use to specify a path to animate along, using an object of type `PathGeometry`. In order to take advantage of the ability to animate the path X and Y values in addition to the rotation angle, we need to use a `MatrixTransform` element. Let's see an example of this.

```xml
<TextBlock Margin="100,125" Text="Hello World" FontSize="18">
  <TextBlock.RenderTransform>
    <MatrixTransform x:Name="MatrixTransform">
      <MatrixTransform.Matrix>
        <Matrix />
      </MatrixTransform.Matrix>
    </MatrixTransform>
  </TextBlock.RenderTransform>
  <TextBlock.Triggers>
    <EventTrigger RoutedEvent="TextBlock.Loaded">
      <BeginStoryboard>
        <Storyboard>
          <MatrixAnimationUsingPath
            Storyboard.TargetName="MatrixTransform"
            Storyboard.TargetProperty="Matrix" Duration="0:0:4"
            RepeatBehavior="Forever" DoesRotateWithTangent="True">
            <MatrixAnimationUsingPath.PathGeometry>
              <PathGeometry>
                <PathFigure StartPoint="49.99,49.99">
                  <ArcSegment Point="50,50" Size="50,50"
                    SweepDirection="Clockwise" IsLargeArc="True" />
                </PathFigure>
              </PathGeometry>
            </MatrixAnimationUsingPath.PathGeometry>
          </MatrixAnimationUsingPath>
        </Storyboard>
      </BeginStoryboard>
    </EventTrigger>
  </TextBlock.Triggers>
```

```
</TextBlock>
```

In this example, we animate a `TextBlock` element around a circular path using a `MatrixAnimationUsingPath` element. The circular path is defined by a single `ArcSegment` element within a single `PathFigure` element. We set the `PathFigure.StartPoint` property value to almost match the `ArcSegment.Point` value so that the two ends of the ellipse meet.

In order to animate the rotation of the text element from the `MatrixAnimationUsingPath` element, we need to set its `DoesRotateWithTangent` property to `true`. If this property was set to `false`, or simply omitted, then the text element would still be animated in a circular motion, but it would no longer rotate in line with the tangent of the circular path, instead remaining upright.

In addition to the `MatrixAnimationUsingPath` class, we can also use either of the `DoubleAnimationUsingPath` or `PointAnimationUsingPath` classes to animate objects on a path. However, rather than providing examples for these alternative methods, let's now move on to find out how we can include every day animations in our application framework.

Creating everyday animations

After covering the wide range of animations that WPF provides, we can see that many of them were designed to enable us to perform animations that emulate real-world situations, rather than to animate form fields in a standard business application. As such, some of the techniques discussed in this chapter are inappropriate for use in our application framework.

However, this does not mean that we cannot create animations to use in our everyday applications. As long as we remember that less is more when it comes to animations in business applications, we can certainly build simple animations into our application framework. One of the best ways to encapsulate these basic animations in our framework is to write one or more custom-animated panels. Let's look at a simple example of an animated `StackPanel`.

```
using System;
using System.Windows;
using System.Windows.Controls;
using System.Windows.Media;
using System.Windows.Media.Animation;

namespace CompanyName.ApplicationName.Views.Panels
{
```

```
public class AnimatedStackPanel : Panel
{
  public static DependencyProperty OrientationProperty =
    DependencyProperty.Register(nameof(Orientation),
    typeof(Orientation), typeof(AnimatedStackPanel),
    new PropertyMetadata(Orientation.Vertical));

  public Orientation Orientation
  {
    get { return (Orientation)GetValue(OrientationProperty); }
    set { SetValue(OrientationProperty, value); }
  }

  protected override Size MeasureOverride(Size availableSize)
  {
    double x = 0, y = 0;
    foreach (UIElement child in Children)
    {
      child.Measure(availableSize);
      if (Orientation == Orientation.Horizontal)
      {
        x += child.DesiredSize.Width;
        y = Math.Max(y, child.DesiredSize.Height);
      }
      else
      {
        x = Math.Max(x, child.DesiredSize.Width);
        y += child.DesiredSize.Height;
      }
    }
    return new Size(x, y);
  }

  protected override Size ArrangeOverride(Size finalSize)
  {
    Point endPosition = new Point();
    foreach (UIElement child in Children)
    {
      child.Arrange(Orientation == Orientation.Horizontal ?
        new Rect(child.DesiredSize) :
        new Rect(0, 0, finalSize.Width, child.DesiredSize.Height));
      AnimatePosition(child, endPosition,
        TimeSpan.FromMilliseconds(300));
      if (Orientation == Orientation.Horizontal)
        endPosition.X += child.DesiredSize.Width;
      else endPosition.Y += child.DesiredSize.Height;
    }
    return finalSize;
  }
```

```
        }

      private void AnimatePosition(UIElement child, Point endPosition,
        TimeSpan animationDuration)
      {
        if (Orientation == Orientation. Vertical)
          GetTranslateTransform(child).BeginAnimation(
          TranslateTransform.YProperty,
          new DoubleAnimation(endPosition.Y, animationDuration));
        else GetTranslateTransform(child).BeginAnimation(
          TranslateTransform.XProperty,
          new DoubleAnimation(endPosition.X, animationDuration));
      }

      private TranslateTransform GetTranslateTransform(UIElement child)
      {
        return child.RenderTransform as TranslateTransform ??
          AddTranslateTransform(child);
      }

      private TranslateTransform AddTranslateTransform(UIElement child)
      {
        TranslateTransform translateTransform = new TranslateTransform();
        child.RenderTransform = translateTransform;
        return translateTransform;
      }
    }
  }
```

As with all custom panels, we just need to provide the implementation for the `MeasureOverride` and `ArrangeOverride` methods. However, in our case, we want to recreate the functionality of the original `StackPanel` control and so we have also declared an `Orientation` Dependency Property of type `System.Windows.Controls.Orientation`, with a default value of `Vertical`.

In the `MeasureOverride` method, we iterate through each of the panel's children, calling their `Measure` method, passing in the `availableSize` input parameter. Note that this sets their `DesiredSize` property, which will be set to a size of 0, 0 until this point.

After calling the `Measure` method on each child, we are able to use their `DesiredSize` property values to calculate the total size required to properly display the rendered items, depending on the value of the `Orientation` property.

If the `Orientation` property is set to `Vertical`, we use the `Math.Max` method to ensure that we keep account of the size of the widest element and if it is set to `Horizontal`, then we use it to find height of the tallest element. Once each child has been measured and the overall required size of the panel has been calculated, we return this size value from the `MeasureOverride` method.

In the `ArrangeOverride` method, we again iterate through the collection of children, but this time we call the `Arrange` method on each child, positioning them at the origin point of `0, 0`, which will be the starting point of their animations. We pass the size of the child into this method if the `Orientation` property is set to `Vertical`, but use the width value of the `finalSize` input parameter as the child's width if it is set to `Horizontal`.

This has the effect of stretching each item across the width of the panel when the vertical option is being used, as neatly aligned items with uniform widths look more tidy and professional than items with uneven edges. In this way, we can build these kinds of decisions right into our framework controls.

Next, we call the `AnimatePosition` method, passing in the child, the desired end position of the child after animation and the duration of the animation. We then calculate the desired end position of the next child with the `endPosition` variable, again taking the value of the `Orientation` property into consideration. We end the method by returning the unchanged `finalSize` input parameter.

In the `AnimatePosition` method, we call the `GetTranslateTransform` method to get the `TranslateTransform` object that we will use to move each child across the panel. If the `Orientation` property is set to `Vertical`, we animate the `TranslateTransform.YProperty` property to the value of the `endPosition.Y` property, otherwise we animate the `TranslateTransform.XProperty` property to the value of the `endPosition.X` property.

In order to animate these property values, we use the `BeginAnimation` method on the `UIElement` object with the property to be added. There are two overloads of this method, but we are using one that accepts the key of the Dependency Property to animate and the animation object. The other overload enables us to specify the `HandoffBehavior` to use with the animation.

For our animation, we are using a `DoubleAnimation`, with a constructor that accepts the `To` value and the duration of the animation, although there are several other overloads that we could have used, had we needed to specify further properties, such as the `From` and `FillBehavior` values.

In order to animate the movement of the items in the panel, we need to ensure that they have a `TranslateTransform` element applied to the `RenderTransform` property of the container item of each child. Remember that different `ItemsControl` classes will use different container items, for example, a `ListBox` control will use `ListBoxItem` container elements.

Therefore, if an item does not already have a `TranslateTransform` element applied, we must add one. Once each element has a `TranslateTransform` element, we can use its `X` and `Y` properties to move the item.

In the `GetTranslateTransform` method, we simply return the existing `TranslateTransform` element from the `RenderTransform` property of each child if one exists, or call the `AddTranslateTransform` method to return a new one otherwise. In the `AddTranslateTransform` method, we just initialize a new `TranslateTransform` element and set it to the `RenderTransform` property of the `child` input parameter, before returning it.

We've now created a basic animated panel and with just around seventy lines of code. The developers that use our application framework can now animate the entry of items in any `ItemsControl`, or any of its derived collection controls, by simply specifying it in a `ItemsPanelTemplate` as the `ItemsPanel` value.

```
xmlns:Panels="clr-namespace:CompanyName.ApplicationName.Views.Panels"
...
<ListBox ItemsSource="{Binding Users}">
  <ListBox.ItemsPanel>
    <ItemsPanelTemplate>
      <Panels:AnimatedStackPanel />
    </ItemsPanelTemplate>
  </ListBox.ItemsPanel>
</ListBox>
```

However, our panel currently only provides one type of animation, albeit in two possible directions, and only works as new items are added. Animating objects' exit is somewhat trickier, because they are normally removed immediately from the panel's `Children` collection when the `Remove` method is called on the data bound collection.

In order to accomplish working exit animations, we'll need to implement a number of things. We'll need to update our data model classes to provide them with new properties to identify which stage of the animation that they're currently in and new events to raise when the current status changes.

We'll need an `IAnimatable` interface and an `Animatable` class that provides the implementation for each data model. Let's first see the interface.

```
namespace CompanyName.ApplicationName.DataModels.Interfaces
{
  public interface IAnimatable
  {
    Animatable Animatable { get; set; }
  }
}
```

Now let's see the implementation of the `Animatable` class:

```
using System;
using CompanyName.ApplicationName.DataModels.Enums;
using CompanyName.ApplicationName.DataModels.Interfaces;

namespace CompanyName.ApplicationName.DataModels
{
  public class Animatable
  {
    private AdditionStatus additionStatus = AdditionStatus.ReadyToAnimate;
    private RemovalStatus removalStatus = RemovalStatus.None;
    private TransitionStatus transitionStatus = TransitionStatus.None;
    private IAnimatable owner;

    public Animatable(IAnimatable owner)
    {
      Owner = owner;
    }

    public Animatable() { }

    public event EventHandler<EventArgs> OnRemovalStatusChanged;
    public event EventHandler<EventArgs> OnTransitionStatusChanged;

    public IAnimatable Owner
    {
      get { return owner; }
      set { owner = value; }
    }

    public AdditionStatus AdditionStatus
    {
      get { return additionStatus; }
      set { additionStatus = value; }
    }
```

```
      public TransitionStatus TransitionStatus
      {
        get { return transitionStatus; }
        set
        {
          transitionStatus = value;
          OnTransitionStatusChanged?.Invoke(this, new EventArgs());
        }
      }

      public RemovalStatus RemovalStatus
      {
        get { return removalStatus; }
        set
        {
          removalStatus = value;
          OnRemovalStatusChanged?.Invoke(this, new EventArgs());
        }
      }
    }
  }
```

This class needs little explanation, other than to note that the
OnTransitionStatusChanged and OnRemovalStatusChanged events get raised when
the values of the TransitionStatus and RemovalStatus properties are changed
respectively and that the class passes itself in as the sender input parameter in each case.
Let's see the three new enumeration classes that are used in our Animatable class.

```
    namespace CompanyName.ApplicationName.DataModels.Enums
    {
      public enum AdditionStatus
      {
        None = -1, ReadyToAnimate = 0, DoNotAnimate = 1, Added = 2
      }

      public enum TransitionStatus
      {
        None = -1, ReadyToAnimate = 0, AnimationComplete = 1
      }

      public enum RemovalStatus
      {
        None = -1, ReadyToAnimate = 0, ReadyToRemove = 1
      }
    }
```

We then need to implement this interface in each data model class that we want to animate.

```
public class User : ... , IAnimatable
{
  private Animatable animatable;

  ...

  public User(Guid id, string name, int age)
  {
    Animatable = new Animatable(this);
    ...
  }

  public Animatable Animatable
  {
    get { return animatable; }
    set { animatable = value; }
  }

  ...
}
```

The next thing that we need to do, is to stop the `Remove` method from actually removing each item when called. We'll need to update our `BaseCollection<T>` class, or add a new `BaseAnimatableCollection<T>` class, so that it triggers the animation instead of removing the item directly. Here is a cut down example showing one way that we might do this.

```
using System;
using System.Collections.Generic;
using System.ComponentModel;
using System.Linq;
using CompanyName.ApplicationName.DataModels.Enums;
using CompanyName.ApplicationName.DataModels.Interfaces;

namespace CompanyName.ApplicationName.DataModels.Collections
{
  public class BaseAnimatableCollection<T> : BaseCollection<T>
    where T : class, IAnimatable, INotifyPropertyChanged, new()
  {
    private bool isAnimatable = true;

    public BaseAnimatableCollection(IEnumerable<T> collection)
    {
      foreach (T item in collection) Add(item);
    }
```

```
...

public bool IsAnimatable
{
  get { return isAnimatable; }
  set { isAnimatable = value; }
}

public new int Count => IsAnimatable ?
  this.Count(i => i.Animatable.RemovalStatus == RemovalStatus.None) :
  this.Count();

public new void Add(T item)
{
  item.Animatable.OnRemovalStatusChanged +=
    Item_OnRemovalStatusChanged;
  item.Animatable.AdditionStatus = AdditionStatus.ReadyToAnimate;
  base.Add(item);
}

public new virtual void Add(IEnumerable<T> collection)
{
  foreach (T item in collection) Add(item);
}

public new virtual void Add(params T[] items)
{
  Add(items as IEnumerable<T>);
}

public new void Insert(int index, T item)
{
  item.Animatable.OnRemovalStatusChanged +=
    Item_OnRemovalStatusChanged;
  item.Animatable.AdditionStatus = AdditionStatus.ReadyToAnimate;
  base.Insert(index, item);
}

protected override void ClearItems()
{
  foreach (T item in this) item.Animatable.OnRemovalStatusChanged -=
    Item_OnRemovalStatusChanged;
  base.ClearItems();
}

public new bool Remove(T item)
{
  item.Animatable.RemovalStatus = RemovalStatus.ReadyToAnimate;
```

```
          return true;
      }

      public void Item_OnRemovalStatusChanged(object sender, EventArgs e)
      {
          Animatable animatable = (Animatable)sender;
          if (animatable.RemovalStatus == RemovalStatus.ReadyToRemove ||
            (animatable.RemovalStatus == RemovalStatus.ReadyToAnimate &&
            !IsAnimatable))
          {
            base.Remove(animatable.Owner as T);
            animatable.RemovalStatus = RemovalStatus.None;
          }
      }
    }
  }
}
```

Bear in mind that this is a basic example that could be improved in many ways, such as adding checks for null, enabling addition, removal and insertion capabilities that do not trigger animations and adding other useful properties.

In this class, we start by specifying that the generic T type parameter must implement the IAnimatable interface. As with our other base collection classes, we ensure that all added and inserted items call a new Add method that attaches our animation related handlers. We show an example of this in the constructor, but skip the other constructor declarations to save space.

We then declare an IsAnimatable property that we can use to make this collection work without animation. This property is used in the overridden (or new) Count property, to ensure that items that are due to be removed are not included in the count of the collection's children.

In the new Add method, we attach a reference of our Item_OnRemovalStatusChanged handler to the OnRemovalStatusChanged event of the Animatable object of the item being added. We then set the AdditionStatus property of the Animatable object to the ReadyToAnimate member to signal that the object is ready to begin its entrance animation.

As this base collection is extending another base class, we need to remember to call its Add method, passing in the item, so that it can attach its own handler for the item's PropertyChanged event. The other Add overloads enable multiple items to be added to the collection, but both internally call the first Add method. The Insert method does the same as the first Add method.

The `ClearItems` method iterates through each item in the collection, detaching the reference to the `Item_OnRemovalStatusChanged` handler from each before calling the `ClearItems` method of the base class. As it is, this method could be reserved for removing all items from the collection without animation, but it would be easy to call the `Remove` method with each item to include animations.

The `Remove` method in this class enables us to animate the exit of each item; it doesn't actually remove the item from the collection, but instead sets the `RemovalStatus` property of the item's `Animatable` object to the `ReadyToAnimate` member to signal that the object is ready to begin its exit animation. It then returns true from the method to signify successful removal of the item.

Finally, we get to the `Item_OnRemovalStatusChanged` event handler, which is the next major part in enabling exit animations. In it, we cast the `sender` input parameter to an instance of our `Animatable` class. Remember that it passes itself as the `sender` parameter when raising the event.

We then use it to determine whether its `RemovalStatus` property is set to the `ReadyToRemove` member, or both its `RemovalStatus` property is set to `ReadyToAnimate` and the collection is not animatable. If either condition is true, we finally call the `Remove` method of the base class to actually remove the item from the collection and set the `RemovalStatus` property to `None`.

In this way, when the collection is set to be not animatable and the `Remove` method is called, the item is immediately removed and the `Animatable` object's `RemovalStatus` property is set to the `None` member in the `Item_OnRemovalStatusChanged` handler. If you remember, the `OnRemovalStatusChanged` event gets raised when the `RemovalStatus` property value is changed.

However, we're still missing part of this puzzle. What sets the `Animatable` object's `RemovalStatus` property to the `ReadyToRemove` member to remove each item? We will need to update our animated panel to accomplish this task and to do this, it will need to maintain a collection of the elements that need to be removed and signal the collection to remove them once their exit animations complete.

```
private List<UIElement> elementsToBeRemoved = new List<UIElement>();
```

We can use the `Storyboard.Completed` event to notify us when the animation is complete and then signal to remove the item at that point, by setting the `Animatable` object's `RemovalStatus` property to the `ReadyToRemove` member. Let's take a look at the required changes to our animated panel. First, we need to add the following using declarations.

```
using System.Collections.Generic;
using CompanyName.ApplicationName.DataModels.Enums;
using Animatable = CompanyName.ApplicationName.DataModels.Animatable;
using IAnimatable =
   CompanyName.ApplicationName.DataModels.Interfaces.IAnimatable;
```

Next, we need to replace the call to the `AnimatePosition` method from the original `ArrangeOverride` method with the following line.

```
BeginAnimations(child, finalSize, endPosition);
```

We then need to add the following additional methods after the `ArrangeOverride` method.

```
private void BeginAnimations(UIElement child, Size finalSize,
  Point endPosition)
{
  FrameworkElement frameworkChild = (FrameworkElement)child;
  if (frameworkChild.DataContext is IAnimatable)
  {
    Animatable animatable =
      ((IAnimatable)frameworkChild.DataContext).Animatable;
    animatable.OnRemovalStatusChanged -= Item_OnRemovalStatusChanged;
    animatable.OnRemovalStatusChanged += Item_OnRemovalStatusChanged;
    if (animatable.AdditionStatus == AdditionStatus.DoNotAnimate)
    {
      child.Arrange(new Rect(endPosition.X, endPosition.Y,
        frameworkChild.ActualWidth, frameworkChild.ActualHeight));
    }
    else if (animatable.AdditionStatus == AdditionStatus.ReadyToAnimate)
    {
      AnimateEntry(child, endPosition);
      animatable.AdditionStatus = AdditionStatus.Added;
      animatable.TransitionStatus = TransitionStatus.ReadyToAnimate;
    }
    else if (animatable.RemovalStatus == RemovalStatus.ReadyToAnimate)
      AnimateExit(child, endPosition, finalSize);
    else if (animatable.TransitionStatus ==
      TransitionStatus.ReadyToAnimate)
      AnimateTransition(child, endPosition);
  }
}
```

```
private void Item_OnRemovalStatusChanged(object sender, EventArgs e)
{
  if (((Animatable)sender).RemovalStatus == RemovalStatus.ReadyToAnimate)
    InvalidateArrange();
}

private void AnimateEntry(UIElement child, Point endPosition)
{
  AnimatePosition(child, endPosition, TimeSpan.FromMilliseconds(300));
}

private void AnimateTransition(UIElement child, Point endPosition)
{
  AnimatePosition(child, endPosition, TimeSpan.FromMilliseconds(300));
}

private void AnimateExit(UIElement child, Point startPosition,
  Size finalSize)
{
  SetZIndex(child, 100);
  Point endPosition =
    new Point(startPosition.X + finalSize.Width, startPosition.Y);
  AnimatePosition(child, startPosition, endPosition,
    TimeSpan.FromMilliseconds(300), RemovalAnimation_Completed);
  elementsToBeRemoved.Add(child);
}

private void AnimatePosition(UIElement child, Point startPosition,
  Point endPosition, TimeSpan animationDuration,
  EventHandler animationCompletedHandler)
{
  if (startPosition.X != endPosition.X)
  {
    DoubleAnimation xAnimation = new DoubleAnimation(startPosition.X,
      endPosition.X, animationDuration);
    xAnimation.AccelerationRatio = 1.0;
    if (animationCompletedHandler != null)
      xAnimation.Completed += animationCompletedHandler;
    GetTranslateTransform(child).BeginAnimation(
      TranslateTransform.XProperty, xAnimation);
  }
  if (startPosition.Y != endPosition.Y)
  {
    DoubleAnimation yAnimation = new DoubleAnimation(startPosition.Y,
      endPosition.Y, animationDuration);
    yAnimation.AccelerationRatio = 1.0;
    if (startPosition.X == endPosition.X && animationCompletedHandler !=
      null) yAnimation.Completed += animationCompletedHandler;
```

```
        GetTranslateTransform(child).BeginAnimation(
          TranslateTransform.YProperty, yAnimation);
    }
}

private void RemovalAnimation_Completed(object sender, EventArgs e)
{
  for (int index = elementsToBeRemoved.Count - 1; index >= 0; index--)
  {
    FrameworkElement frameworkElement =
      elementsToBeRemoved[index] as FrameworkElement;
    if (frameworkElement.DataContext is IAnimatable)
    {
      ((IAnimatable)frameworkElement.DataContext).Animatable.RemovalStatus
        = RemovalStatus.ReadyToRemove;
      elementsToBeRemoved.Remove(frameworkElement);
    }
  }
}
```

Let's examine this new code. First, we have the `BeginAnimations` method, in which we cast the container control to a `FrameworkElement`, so that we can access its `DataContext` property. Our data object is accessed from this property and we cast it to an `IAnimatable` instance, so that we can access the `Animatable` object via its `Animatable` property.

We then remove our `Item_OnRemovalStatusChanged` event handler from the `OnRemovalStatusChanged` event before re-attaching it, to ensure that only a single handler is attached, regardless of how many times each child passes through this method.

If the `AdditionStatus` property is set to `DoNotAnimate`, we arrange the item at its end position immediately and without animation, while if it is set to `ReadyToAnimate`, we call the `AnimateEntry` method and then set the `AdditionStatus` property to `Added`. Finally, if the `RemovalStatus` property is set to `ReadyToAnimate`, we call the `AnimateExit` method.

In the `Item_OnRemovalStatusChanged` event handler, we call the panel's `InvalidateArrange` method if the `RemovalStatus` property is set to `ReadyToAnimate`. This is another essential part of the exit animation strategy and it requests the layout system to call the `ArrangeOverride` method, thereby triggering the starting of the exit animation(s).

Remember that the OnRemovalStatusChanged event gets raised when the value of the RemovalStatus property is changed and that it is set to the ReadyToAnimate member in the Remove method of the BaseAnimatableCollection<T> class. That raises the event and this event handler starts the animations in response.

The AnimateEntry method simply calls the original, unchanged AnimatePosition method from our first animated panel attempt. The AnimateExit method takes an additional startPosition input parameter, which represents the current position of each item within the panel.

We start by setting the Panel.SetZIndex Attached Property to a value of 100 for each child, to ensure that their animated departure is rendered above, or over the top of, the remaining items. We then calculate the end position of the animation using the start position and the size of the panel.

Next, we call an overload of the AnimatePosition method, passing in our child, start and end positions, animation duration and an event handler as parameters. After the child item's position animation has been started, the child is added to the elementsToBeRemoved collection.

In the AnimatePosition method, we first check that our start and end positions are different, before creating and starting our DoubleAnimation objects. If the X values are different and the event handler input parameter is not null, then we attach it to the Completed event of the xAnimation object before starting its animation.

If the Y values are different and the event handler input parameter is not null and the event handler was not already attached to the xAnimation object, then we attach it to the Completed event of the yAnimation object before starting its animation. Note that we only need to attach one handler to this event, because we only have one object to remove from the collection.

Also note that we set the AccelerationRatio property to 1.0 in this overload, so that the item accelerates off screen. However, in a business application framework, we would want to keep our animation properties in sync and so, we would probably set the AccelerationRatio property to 1.0 on the animation objects in the original AnimatePosition method as well.

The last piece of the puzzle is the RemovalAnimation_Completed event handling method. This method gets called when the exit animation has completed and iterates through the elementsToBeRemoved collection. If any element to remove implements the IAnimatable interface, its Animatable object's RemovalStatus property is set to the ReadyToRemove member.

If you remember, this raises the `OnRemovalStatusChanged` event, which is handled by the `Item_OnRemovalStatusChanged` event handler in the `BaseAnimatableCollection` class. In that method, the `Animatable` object's `RemovalStatus` property is checked for the `ReadyToRemove` member and if found, the owning item is actually removed from the collection.

And so, to summarize; the `Remove` method of the animation collection is called, but instead of removing the item, it sets a property on it, which raises an event that is handled by the animated panel; the panel then starts the exit animation and when completed, it raises an event that is handled by the collection class and results in the item actually being removed from the collection.

While this animated panel is entirely usable as it is, there are many ways that it could be further improved. One important thing that we could do would be to extract all of the properties and animation code from this class and put them into a base `AnimatedPanel` class. In this way, we could reuse this class when creating other types of animated panel, such as an `AnimatedWrapPanel`.

We could then further extend the base class by exposing additional animation properties, so that users of our panel could have more control over the animations that it provides. For example, we could declare `VerticalContentAlignment` and `HorizontalContentAlignment` properties to dictate how our panel items should be aligned in the panel.

Additionally, we could add `EntryAnimationDirection` and `ExitAnimationDirection` properties to specify which direction to animate our panel items as they are added and removed from the panel. We could also enable different types of animation, such as fading or spinning, by animating the `Opacity` property, or the `Angle` property of a `RotationTransform` element.

Furthermore, we could add `EntryAnimationDuration` and `ExitAnimationDuration` properties to specify the length of time that each animation should take, rather than hardcoding values directly into our panel. There really is no limit to what functionality that we can provide with our application framework panels, other than the limitations dictated by the end users' computer hardware.

Summary

In this chapter, we've investigated the variety of animation possibilities that WPF provides us with, primarily focusing on XAML and the more usable options. We've discovered the finer details of timelines and also explored how we can incorporate animation into our application framework, so that its users can easily leverage the power of animations without having to know anything about them.

In the next chapter, we will look at a number of ways that we can improve the overall look and feel of our applications, from providing consistent application styles and icons to examining a number of techniques for creating rich graphics.

7
Creating Visually Appealing User Interfaces

While it is simple to add form elements to a View, it takes somewhat more to produce an application that looks visually appealing. Luckily, WPF provides us with many features that can help us to achieve this goal, such as gradient brushes, rounded corners, opacity control, layered visuals and animations.

In this chapter, we'll be looking at a number of ways of using these elements to greatly improve the visual aspect of our applications. We'll investigate solutions that are simple to implement, using style properties, and others that will take more work, such as animations and custom controls.

Styling applications consistently

One of the easiest ways to make our applications stand out is to make them look unique. This can be achieved by defining custom styles for the controls that we use in it. However, if we decide to style our controls, it is essential that we style all of the controls that we use, as a half styled application can often look worse than an application that merely uses the default styles.

It is therefore absolutely essential that we design our application control styles consistently, in order to attain a professional look for our application. In this section, we'll discuss a number of tips and tricks to help us to implement these application styles.

Overriding default control styles

When providing custom styles for our application controls, this typically requires us to define a new `ControlTemplate` element for each of them. As these can often be very large, it is customary to declare them in a separate resource file and merge it with the application resources in the `App.xaml` file, as shown in the previous chapter.

Before starting this task, we need to plan how we want our controls to look and then apply this same look to each control. Another mistake would be to customize different controls with different styles, as consistency is key to providing a professional look. For example, if we want our single line textboxes to be a certain height, then we should also define our other controls to be the same height.

The custom styles that we declare for our controls can be part of our application framework. If we define them without naming them via the `x:Key` directive, they will be implicitly applied and so the developers that utilize our application framework need not concern themselves with the look of each control, effectively freeing them up to concentrate on aggregating them into the various Views.

The first thing to do before starting to design our custom styles is to define a small range of colors that we will use in our application. Using too many colors in an application can make it look less professional, so we should chose a few shades of a small number of colors to use. There are a number of online tools that can help us to pick a color palette to use.

Once we have chosen our application colors, we should declare them first as `Color` objects in the `App.xaml` file and then declare brush elements that use them, as most controls use brushes rather than colors. This has two benefits; using only these colors will promote consistency and if we ever need to change a color, we only need to change it in a single place.

```
<Color x:Key="ReadOnlyColor" A="255" R="88" G="88" B="88" />
...
<SolidColorBrush x:Key="ReadOnlyBrush"
  Color="{StaticResource ReadOnlyColor}" />
```

It is often a good idea to also define multiple named styles for the most common types of controls. For example, having a `Label` style for `TextBlock` elements, that right aligns them and adds suitable margins, or a `Heading` style that sets a larger font size and heavier font weight. Providing the developers with a set of predefined styles helps to make the application as a whole look consistent.

When defining multiple named styles, it is common to reuse some of them in others. For example, if we have a default style for the `TextBox` control, we can base other style variations on it. Let's see some XAML examples.

```xaml
<Style x:Key="TextBoxStyle" TargetType="{x:Type TextBox}">
  <Setter Property="SnapsToDevicePixels" Value="True" />
  <Setter Property="Margin" Value="0,0,0,5" />
  <Setter Property="Padding" Value="1.5,2" />
  <Setter Property="MinHeight" Value="25" />
  <Setter Property="TextWrapping" Value="Wrap" />
  ...
</Style>
<Style x:Key="Max2LineTextBoxStyle" TargetType="{x:Type TextBox}"
  BasedOn="{StaticResource TextBoxStyle}">
  <Setter Property="MaxHeight" Value="44" />
  <Setter Property="VerticalScrollBarVisibility" Value="Auto" />
  <Setter Property="ToolTip"
    Value="{Binding Text, RelativeSource={RelativeSource Self}}" />
</Style>
<Style x:Key="Max3LineTextBoxStyle" TargetType="{x:Type TextBox}"
  BasedOn="{StaticResource Max2LineTextBoxStyle}">
  <Setter Property="MaxHeight" Value="64" />
</Style>
<Style x:Key="ReadOnlyTextBoxStyle" TargetType="{x:Type TextBox}"
  BasedOn="{StaticResource TextBoxStyle}">
  <Setter Property="Background" Value="{StaticResource ReadOnlyBrush}" />
  <Setter Property="IsReadOnly" Value="True" />
  <Setter Property="Cursor" Value="Arrow" />
</Style>
```

Here, the simplified `TextBoxStyle` style defines the majority of the properties for all `TextBox` controls. The `Max2LineTextBoxStyle` style inherits all of the property settings from this style and sets a few more that ensure that the vertical scrollbar can appear when required and enforce a maximum height for the control.

The `Max3LineTextBoxStyle` style extends the `Max2LineTextBoxStyle` style and so, inherits all of its property settings, as well as those of the `TextBoxStyle` style. It overrides the `MaxHeight` property that was set in the previous style. The `ReadOnlyTextBoxStyle` style also extends the `TextBoxStyle` style and sets properties to ensure that the control is read-only. Defining styles in this way ensures that controls in each View will remain consistent.

As well as defining default styles for our application controls, it is often also a good idea to provide default data template resources for each data model in the application. In a similar way to the controls, predefining these data templates can result in improved consistency. We can also define a number of named templates to override the default ones with and use in different scenarios.

If there are a large number of data models in an application, it can be helpful to also declare their data templates in a separate resource file and merge it with the application resources in the `App.xaml` file, like the default control templates. It is therefore not unusual to see multiple resource files being merged in the application resources file.

Using professional icons

One thing that can often be underestimated when developing applications is the overall impact that a consistent set of decent icons can have. Using miss-matched icons that have been sourced from a number of different places can really make an otherwise professional looking application look far less professional.

If you or your company cannot afford to, or will not for any other reason buy a set of custom icons, all is not lost. Visual Studio has long since offered sets of professional icons in a number of different formats, that we can utilize in our applications free of charge. These are the actual icons that are used in Visual Studio, Office and other Microsoft applications, so many users will already be familiar with them.

In older versions of Visual Studio, such as the 2010, or even 2008 versions, the provided image library was installed with the application and could be found at one of the following paths:

- `C:\Program Files\Microsoft Visual Studio 9.0\Common7\VS2008ImageLibrary\1033`
- `C:\Program Files\Microsoft Visual Studio 10.0\Common7\VS2010ImageLibrary\1033`

Note that on a 64 bit machine, this path would change to the following:

- `C:\Program Files (x86)\Microsoft Visual Studio 10.0\Common7\VS2010ImageLibrary\1033`

However, Microsoft changed how the image library could be accessed in newer versions of Visual Studio, from the 2012 version onwards. In these later versions, the image library was no longer included in the installation of Visual Studio. Instead, we have to manually download it from the **Microsoft Developer Network** (**MSDN**) website.

We can find them all by navigating to the MSDN website and searching for `Visual Studio Image Library`. All versions of these icon sets can be accessed from there, although the newer versions also contain the older versions, so downloading the latest set is normally the best option.

The newer icon sets also contain searchable Adobe Reader files that list the contents of the icon sets and provide links to the relevant folders of each of the icons. Most of the icons are also included in multiple sizes and so the newer libraries are much larger than the previous ones. A few examples of the 2010 icons can be seen in the following image:

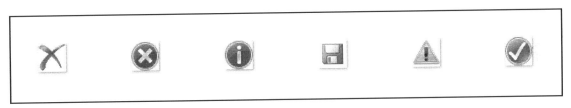

The following image shows the latest flat style icons for comparison:

Layering visuals

So far, we've just looked at simple redefinitions of the standard controls, by altering shapes, sizes, borders and other common properties. However, we can do much more than that with WPF. Before continuing with this section, it is important to know that the more visuals that each control is comprised of, the longer it will take to render them and so, this can negatively affect performance.

As such, it's important not to overdo the visual aspect of our controls if our application will be run on slow, old computers. Conversely, if we know that our end users will have plenty of RAM and/or graphics cards, then we can go the extra distance and develop visually stunning controls. Let's look at some techniques that we can use to improve the look of our controls.

Throwing shadows

One of the easiest ways to make our UI elements pop out of the screen is to add a shadow to them. Each control has an `Effect` property that is inherited from the `UIElement` class. We can set an object of type `DropShadowEffect` to this property to add a shadow to our controls.

However, we must be conservative with the settings that we use on the `DropShadowEffect` element, because this effect can be easily overdone. We also do not want to apply this effect to every control, as that would spoil the overall effect. It is most useful when set on a panel that contains other controls, or on a border that surrounds such a panel. Let's see a simple example of applying this effect.

```
<Button Content="Click Me" Width="140" Height="34" FontSize="18">
  <Button.Effect>
    <DropShadowEffect Color="Black" ShadowDepth="6" BlurRadius="6"
      Direction="270" Opacity="0.5" />
  </Button.Effect>
</Button>
```

Let's see what the output of this code looks like:

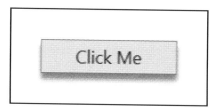

In this example, we have a standard button with a `DropShadowEffect` element that is set as its `Effect` property. As we'll see later in this chapter, the `DropShadowEffect` class has a number of uses, but its primary use is to create shadow effects.

When using this element for shadow effects, we generally want to set its `Color` property to black and its `Opacity` property to a value that is at least semi-transparent for best, or most realistic, results. The `ShadowDepth` property dictates how far from the element the shadow should fall. Along with the `BlurRadius` property, this property is used to add a sense of height to the element.

The `BlurRadius` property spreads out the shadow area, while also making it less dense. Like the `ShadowDepth` property, this property has a default value of five. The `Direction` property specifies which direction the shadow should fall in, with a value of zero degrees making the shadow fall to the right and increasing values moving the shadow angle anti-clockwise.

Note that a value of `270` makes the shadow fall directly below the applied control and is often most suitable for use in business applications. Using this angle results in what appears to be an element that is hovering slightly above, or in front of, the screen, with a light source coming from above, which is the most natural direction for light to come from.

In contrast to this, an angle of `45` degrees for example, would place the shadow to the top right of the element and this would have the effect of telling the brain that there is a light source to the bottom left. However, this particular effect is unnatural looking and can detract from, rather than add to the styling of an application.

Declaring multiple borders

One simple technique that we can use to make our controls stand out is to use multiple `Border` elements for each control. By declaring one or more borders within an outer border, we can give our controls that professional look. We'll see how we can animate these borders differently when the user's mouse cursor is over the button later, but for now, let's see how we can create this effect.

```
<Grid Width="160" Height="68">
  <Grid.Background>
    <LinearGradientBrush StartPoint="0,0" EndPoint="1,1">
      <GradientStop Color="Red" />
      <GradientStop Color="Yellow" Offset="1" />
    </LinearGradientBrush>
  </Grid.Background>
  <Button Content="Click Me" Width="120" Height="28" FontSize="14"
    Margin="20">
    <Button.Template>
      <ControlTemplate TargetType="{x:Type Button}">
        <Border BorderBrush="Black" BorderThickness="1"
          Background="#7FFFFFFF" Padding="1" CornerRadius="5"
```

```
            SnapsToDevicePixels="True">
            <Border BorderBrush="#7F000000" BorderThickness="1"
              Background="White" CornerRadius="3.5"
              SnapsToDevicePixels="True">
              <ContentPresenter HorizontalAlignment="Center"
                VerticalAlignment="Center" />
            </Border>
          </Border>
        </ControlTemplate>
      </Button.Template>
    </Button>
  </Grid>
```

In this example, we have declared a simple `ControlTemplate` element for our `Button` control to demonstrate the double border technique. Note that we would typically declare this template in the `Application.Resources` section of the `App.xaml` file, so that it could be reused, but we have declared it locally to save space here.

Note that we need to adjust the corner radius of the inner border to accurately fit within the outer border. If we had used the same size for both, they would not have correctly fit together. Also, we have set the `SnapsToDevicePixels` property to `true` on the two borders to ensure that they are not blurred by anti-aliasing artefacts.

One further point to note is that we have used `#7FFFFFFF` as the value for the background of the outer border and the border brush of the inner border. The alpha channel in this value is set to `7F`, which equates to an opacity value of `0.5`. This means that these elements will be partly transparent and so the colors from the background will partly show through the border edges.

We added our button into a `Grid` panel and set a `LinearGradientBrush` object as its background to demonstrate this semi-transparent effect. When rendered, our background gradient and button will look like the following image:

Reusing composite visuals

The next technique involves defining a particular motif that will be rendered in the background of our controls. This could be all or part of a company logo, a particular shape, or even just a simple, well-placed curve. This will form the bottom most level of our control visuals, and can have additional levels of visuals on top. Let's take a look at one way that we could implement such a design, starting with defining some resources.

```
<RadialGradientBrush x:Key="LayeredButtonBackgroundBrush" RadiusX="1.85"
  RadiusY="0.796" Center="1.018,-0.115" GradientOrigin="0.65,- 0.139">
  <GradientStop Color="#FFCACACD" />
  <GradientStop Color="#FF3B3D42" Offset="1" />
</RadialGradientBrush>
<LinearGradientBrush x:Key="LayeredButtonCurveBrush" StartPoint="0,0"
  EndPoint="1,1">
  <GradientStop Color="#FF747475" Offset="0" />
  <GradientStop Color="#FF3B3D42" Offset="1" />
</LinearGradientBrush>
<Grid x:Key="LayeredButtonBackgroundElements">
  <Rectangle Fill="{StaticResource LayeredButtonBackgroundBrush}" />
  <Path StrokeThickness="0"
    Fill="{StaticResource LayeredButtonCurveBrush}">
    <Path.Data>
      <CombinedGeometry GeometryCombineMode="Intersect">
        <CombinedGeometry.Geometry1>
          <EllipseGeometry Center="-20,50.7" RadiusX="185" RadiusY="46" />
        </CombinedGeometry.Geometry1>
        <CombinedGeometry.Geometry2>
          <RectangleGeometry Rect="0,0,106,24" />
        </CombinedGeometry.Geometry2>
      </CombinedGeometry>
    </Path.Data>
  </Path>
</Grid>
<VisualBrush x:Key="LayeredButtonBackground"
  Visual="{StaticResource LayeredButtonBackgroundElements}" />
```

Once we have added these resources into the `Application.Resources` section in the `App.xaml` file, we can use them through the `VisualBrush` element, like this:

```
<Button Background="{StaticResource LayeredButtonBackground}" Width="200"
  Height="40" SnapsToDevicePixels="True" />
```

This will render the gradients in the button background, like this.

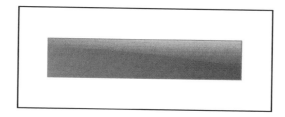

There are a few elements to this design, so let's look at each one individually. We started by declaring a RadialGradientBrush element with the key LayeredButtonBackgroundBrush and a LinearGradientBrush with a key of LayeredButtonCurveBrush.

The RadiusX and RadiusY properties of the RadialGradientBrush element specify the X and Y radii of the outermost ellipse that encompasses the radial gradient, while the Center and GradientOrigin properties dictate the center and focal point of the radial gradient and enable us to position it precisely within our rectangle.

The LinearGradientBrush element has a StartPoint value of 0, 0 and an EndPoint value of 1, 1, which results in a diagonal gradient. With this particular design, the idea is to have a sharp contrast between the two gradients at the center and to somewhat blend them together at the edges.

Next, we declare a Grid panel with the key LayeredButtonBackgroundElements, that contains a Rectangle and a Path element. The rectangle is stretched to fill the panel by default and is painted with the LayeredButtonBackgroundBrush resource. The Path element is painted with the LayeredButtonCurveBrush resource.

The Data property of the Path object is where we define the shape of the path. There are a number of ways that we can specify the path data, but in this example, we use a CombinedGeometry element with a GeometryCombineMode value of Intersect, which outputs a single shape that represents the intersection of the two specified geometry shapes.

Inside the CombinedGeometry element, we have the Geometry1 and Geometry2 properties, where we combine the two geometry shapes, according to the Intersect mode specified by the GeometryCombineMode property.

Our first shape defines the curve in our design and comes from an `EllipseGeometry` element, using the `Center` property to position the ellipse and the `RadiusX` and `RadiusY` properties to shape it. The second shape is a rectangle that comes from a `RectangleGeometry` element and is defined by its `Rect` property.

The intersection of these two shapes is the result of this path and approximately covers the bottom section of our overall shape, up to the curve. The partly obscured rectangle element behind completes the remainder of the overall shape.

The `Visual` property of the `VisualBrush` element with key `LayeredButtonBackground` is set to the `LayeredButtonBackgroundElements` panel and so, any UI element that is painted with this brush will now have this design imprinted on it. In our example, we manually specify the reference to the visual brush to paint the `Button` object's background.

However, setting the background in this way would require the developers that use our application framework to do this each time they add a button. A better solution would be to redesign the default button template, so that the visual brush is automatically applied to each button. We'll see an example of this later in this chapter, when we pull together a number of these techniques.

Reflecting light

Another technique involves adding a semi-opaque layer with a gradient that fades to transparency over the top of our controls to give the appearance of the reflection of a light source. This can easily be achieved using a simple `Border` element and a `LinearGradientBrush` instance. Let's see how we can accomplish this:

```
<Button Content="Click Me" Width="140" Height="34" FontSize="18"
  Foreground="White" Margin="20">
  <Button.Template>
    <ControlTemplate TargetType="{x:Type Button}">
      <Border Background="#FF007767" CornerRadius="5"
        SnapsToDevicePixels="True">
        <Grid>
          <Rectangle RadiusX="4" RadiusY="4" Margin="1,1,1,7"
            SnapsToDevicePixels="True">
            <Rectangle.Fill>
              <LinearGradientBrush StartPoint="0,0" EndPoint="0,1">
                <GradientStop Color="#BFFFFFFF" />
                <GradientStop Color="#00FFFFFF" Offset="0.8" />
              </LinearGradientBrush>
            </Rectangle.Fill>
          </Rectangle>
```

```
            <ContentPresenter HorizontalAlignment="Center"
              VerticalAlignment="Center" />
          </Grid>
        </Border>
      </ControlTemplate>
    </Button.Template>
  </Button>
```

When run, this example will produce a button that looks like this:

Let's examine this example. We start by declaring the `Button` element with a few style properties. Rather than defining a separate style or control template in a resources section as we would in a real world application, we again declare the template inline to save space here.

In the control template, we first declare a `Border` element with a jade green background and a `CornerRadius` value of 5. We again set the `SnapsToDevicePixels` property to `true` go ensure that the edges remain sharp.

Inside the border, we define two elements within a `Grid` panel. The first is the `Rectangle` element that produces the reflection effect and the second is the required `ContentPresenter` object. The rectangle uses a value of 4 in the `RadiusX` and `RadiusY` properties and sets the `Margin` property appropriately to ensure that there is a tiny gap around the edge of the reflection.

It also sets its `SnapsToDevicePixels` property to true to ensure that this tiny gap is not blurred. Note that the value for the bottom margin is 7, because we do not want the reflection effect to cover the bottom half of the button. The `Fill` property is where the reflection effect is actually created.

In the rectangle's `Fill` property, we define a vertical `LinearGradientBrush` element by setting both of the `X` values of the `StartPoint` and `EndPoint` properties and the `StartPoint.Y` property to 0 and the `Endpoint.Y` property to 1; plotting these points on a graph will produce a vertical line and so, this produces a vertical gradient.

In the `GradientStops` collection of the `LinearGradientBrush` object, we have defined two `GradientStop` elements. The first has an offset of zero and is set to a white color, with a hexadecimal alpha channel value of `BF`, which approximates an opacity value of `0.7`. The second has an offset of `0.8` and is set to a white color that has a hexadecimal alpha channel value of `00`, which results in a completely transparent color and could be replaced with the `Transparent` color.

The resulting gradient therefore starts slightly transparent at the top and is fully transparent at the bottom which, with the bottom margin and offset values, is actually around the middle of the button. As with our other examples, the `ContentPresenter` object is declared afterwards, so that it is rendered on top of the reflection effect.

Creating glowing effects

Another effect that we can create for our controls is that of a glowing appearance, as if a light were shining outwards from inside the control. We'll need another `LinearGradientBrush` instance and UI element to paint it on. A `Rectangle` element suits this role well, as it's very light weight. We should define these resources in the application resources in the `App.xaml` file to enable every View to use them.

```xml
<TransformGroup x:Key="GlowTransformGroup">
  <ScaleTransform CenterX="0.5" CenterY="0.85" ScaleY="1.8" />
  <TranslateTransform Y="0.278" />
</TransformGroup>
<RadialGradientBrush x:Key="GreenGlow" Center="0.5,0.848"
  GradientOrigin="0.5,0.818" RadiusX="-1.424" RadiusY="-0.622"
  RelativeTransform="{StaticResource GlowTransformGroup}">
  <GradientStop Color="#CF65FF00" Offset="0.168" />
  <GradientStop Color="#4B65FF00" Offset="0.478" />
  <GradientStop Color="#0065FF00" Offset="1" />
</RadialGradientBrush>
<Style x:Key="GlowingButtonStyle" TargetType="{x:Type Button}">
  <Setter Property="SnapsToDevicePixels" Value="True" />
  <Setter Property="Template">
    <Setter.Value>
      <ControlTemplate TargetType="{x:Type Button}">
        <Border BorderBrush="White" BorderThickness="1"
          Background="DarkGray" CornerRadius="3">
          <Grid>
            <Rectangle IsHitTestVisible="False" RadiusX="2"
              RadiusY="2" Fill="{StaticResource GreenGlow}" />
            <ContentPresenter Content="{TemplateBinding Content}"
              HorizontalAlignment="Center" VerticalAlignment="Center" />
          </Grid>
```

```
            <Border.Effect>
              <DropShadowEffect Color="#FF65FF00" ShadowDepth="4"
                Opacity="0.4" Direction="270" BlurRadius="10" />
            </Border.Effect>
          </Border>
        </ControlTemplate>
      </Setter.Value>
    </Setter>
  </Style>
```

We start off by declaring a `TransformGroup` element that enables us to group one or more transform objects together. Inside it, we define a `ScaleTransform` element that scales applied elements vertically by the default factor of 1 and horizontally by a factor of `1.8`. We specify the center of this transformation using its `CenterX` and `CenterY` properties. Next, we declare a `TranslateTransform` element that moves applied elements downwards by a small amount.

After this, we define a `RadialGradientBrush` object that will represent the glow in our design. We use the `RadiusX` and `RadiusY` properties to shape the brush element and specify the `Center` and `GradientOrigin` properties to dictate the center and focal point of the radial gradient.

We then set the `TransformGroup` element to the `RelativeTransform` property of the brush to apply the transforms to it. Note that the three `GradientStop` elements all use the same R, G and B values, and just differ in alpha channel, or opacity values.

Next, we declare the `GlowingButtonStyle` style for the `Button` type, setting the `SnapsToDevicePixels` property to `true`. In the `Template` property, we define a `ControlTemplate` element, with a white `Border` element with slightly rounded corners.

Inside the border, we declare a `Grid` panel containing a `Rectangle` and a `ContentPresenter` element. Again, the `RadiusX` and `RadiusY` properties of the rectangle are set to a smaller value than that of the `CornerRadius` property of the parent border control to ensure that it fits evenly within it. Our `RadialGradientBrush` resource is assigned as the rectangle's `Fill` property.

The `ContentPresenter` object is centered to ensure that the content of the button will be rendered in its center. Returning to the `Border` element, we see a `DropShadowEffect` that is declared within its `Effect` property. However, this element is not here to create a shadow effect; this class is multi-functional and can also render glowing effects as well as shadow effects.

The trick is to set its `Color` property to a color other than black and to set its `BlurRadius` property to a larger value than we would typically use when creating a shadow effect. In our particular case, we set the `Direction` property to `270` and `ShadowDepth` property to `4` in order to position the glow effect towards the bottom of the border. where the light is supposed to be coming from.

Unfortunately, this effect does not translate to gray scale and paper well, so the glowing effect is somewhat lost when not viewed in color and on screen. For the readers of the e-book version of this book, here is what the glowing effect from our example looks like.

Putting it all together

While these various effects can improve the look of our controls on their own, the biggest improvement can be found when amalgamating a number of them into a single design. In this next example, we'll do just that. We first need to add a few more resources to use.

```
<SolidColorBrush x:Key="TransparentWhite" Color="#7FFFFFFF" />
<SolidColorBrush x:Key="VeryTransparentWhite" Color="#3FFFFFFF" />
<SolidColorBrush x:Key="TransparentBlack" Color="#7F000000" />
<SolidColorBrush x:Key="VeryTransparentBlack" Color="#3F000000" />
<VisualBrush x:Key="SemiTransparentLayeredButtonBackground"
    Visual="{StaticResource LayeredButtonBackgroundElements}"
    Opacity="0.65" />
```

There isn't anything too complicated here. We simply have a number of colors defined with varying levels of transparency and a slightly transparent version of our visual brush that references our layered background elements. Let's move on to the encompassing style now.

```
<Style TargetType="{x:Type Button}">
  <Setter Property="SnapsToDevicePixels" Value="True" />
  <Setter Property="Cursor" Value="Hand" />
  <Setter Property="Template">
    <Setter.Value>
      <ControlTemplate TargetType="{x:Type Button}">
        <Border CornerRadius="3"
          BorderBrush="{StaticResource TransparentBlack}"
          BorderThickness="1"
```

```
              Background="{StaticResource TransparentWhite}">
              <Border Name="InnerBorder" CornerRadius="2"
                Background="{StaticResource LayeredButtonBackground}"
                Margin="1">
                <Grid>
                  <Rectangle IsHitTestVisible="False" RadiusX="2"
                    RadiusY="2" Fill="{StaticResource GreenGlow}" />
                  <ContentPresenter Content="{TemplateBinding Content}"
                    Margin="{TemplateBinding Padding}"
                    HorizontalAlignment="{TemplateBinding
                    HorizontalContentAlignment}"
                    VerticalAlignment="{TemplateBinding
                    VerticalContentAlignment}" />
                </Grid>
              </Border>
              <Border.Effect>
                <DropShadowEffect Color="Black" ShadowDepth="6"
                  BlurRadius="6" Direction="270" Opacity="0.5" />
              </Border.Effect>
            </Border>
            <ControlTemplate.Triggers>
              <Trigger Property="IsMouseOver" Value="True">
                <Setter TargetName="InnerBorder"
                  Property="Background" Value="{StaticResource
                  SemiTransparentLayeredButtonBackground}" />
              </Trigger>
              <Trigger Property="IsPressed" Value="True">
                <Setter TargetName="InnerBorder" Property="Background"
                  Value="{StaticResource LayeredButtonBackground}" />
              </Trigger>
            </ControlTemplate.Triggers>
          </ControlTemplate>
        </Setter.Value>
      </Setter>
    </Style>
```

First note that we have omitted the x:Key directive on this style, so that it will be implicitly applied to all Button elements that do not explicitly apply a different style. We are therefore able to declare our Button elements without specifying the style, like the following code snippet:

```
<Button Content="Click Me" Width="200" Height="40" FontSize="20"
  Foreground="White" />
```

This results in the following visual output:

Looking at the example XAML, we see that the `SnapsToDevicePixels` property is set to `true`, to avoid anti-aliasing artefacts blurring the edges of the button, and the `Cursor` property is set to display the pointing finger cursor when the user's mouse is over the button.

Within the control template, we see the two nested `Border` elements. Note that the outer border uses the `TransparentBlack` and `TransparentWhite` brush resources, so that it is semi-transparent. Also note that the white inner border actually comes from the background of the outer border, rather than the inner border, which sets the `Margin` property to 1 to give the impression of an inner border.

In this example, the inner border element is only responsible for displaying the layered button elements from the visual brush and has no displayed border of its own. Again, we have adjusted its `CornerRadius` property so that it fits neatly within the outer border. We can zoom in the magnification level in the WPF designer to help us to decide what values we should use here.

Inside the inner border, we declare a `Grid` panel, so that we can add both the required `ContentPresenter` and the `Rectangle` element that is painted with the `GreenGlow` brush from resources. Again, we set its `IsHitTestVisible` property to `false`, so that users cannot interact with it and set the `RadiusX` and `RadiusY` properties to match the `CornerRadius` value of the inner border.

We use `TemplateBinding` elements to map properties of the `ContentPresenter` object to suitable properties from the templated object, so that setting properties on our button can affect its positioning and content. Next, we set the previously displayed `DropShadowEffect` element to the `Effect` property of the outer border and that sums up the contained UI elements in the template.

To make the template more useful, we have set some `Trigger` objects in the `ControlTemplate.Triggers` collection, that will add mouse over effects for our button. The first trigger targets the `IsMouseOver` property and sets the background of the inner border to the slightly more transparent version of the layered button elements visual brush when true.

The second trigger targets the `IsPressed` property and re-applies the original visual brush when the property is true. Note that these two triggers must be defined in this order, so that the one that targets the `IsPressed` property will override the other when both conditions are true. It is of course, a matter of taste, whether the button lights up or goes out when clicked, or perhaps even changes color.

We could take this glowing idea further too, by defining a number of different color resources and using data triggers inside a data template to change the color of the glow to indicate different states of a data object. This enables us to provide further visual information to the users, in addition to the usual textual feedback methods.

For example, a blue glow on a data model object could specify an unchanged object, while green could signify an object with valid changes and red could highlight an object in error. We'll see how we can implement this idea in the next chapter, but for now, let's continue looking at different ways to make our applications stand out from the crowd.

Moving away from the ordinary

The vast majority of business applications in general, look fairly ordinary, with various form pages containing banks of standard rectangular form fields. Visually appealing applications on the other hand, stand out from the crowd. Therefore, in order to create visually appealing applications, we need to move away from the ordinary.

Whether this means simply adding control templates with rounded corners for our controls, or something more is up to you. There are many different ways that we can enhance the look of our controls and we'll take a look at a number of these ideas in this section. Let's start with a refection effect that is best suited for use with logos, or startup or background images.

Casting reflections

All `FrameworkElement`-derived classes have a `RenderTransform` property that we can utilize to transform their rendered output in a variety of ways. A `ScaleTransform` element enables us to scale each object in both horizontal and vertical directions. One useful facet about the `ScaleTransform` object is that we can also scale negatively, and therefore reverse the visual output.

One visually pleasing effect that we can create with this particular facet is a mirror image, or reflection of the object. In order to enhance this effect, we can use an opacity mask to fade out the reflection as it recedes from the object. This can give the visual impression of an object sitting on a table, being reflected in the shiny surface, as shown in the following image:

Let's see how we can achieve this result.

```
<StackPanel HorizontalAlignment="Center" VerticalAlignment="Center"
  Width="348">
  <TextBlock Name="TextBlock" FontFamily="Candara"
    Text="APPLICATION NAME" FontSize="40" FontWeight="Bold">
    <TextBlock.Foreground>
      <LinearGradientBrush StartPoint="0,0" EndPoint="1,0">
        <GradientStop Color="Orange" />
        <GradientStop Color="Red" Offset="0.5" />
        <GradientStop Color="Orange" Offset="1" />
      </LinearGradientBrush>
    </TextBlock.Foreground>
  </TextBlock>
  <Rectangle Height="31" Margin="0,-11.6,0,0">
    <Rectangle.Fill>
      <VisualBrush Visual="{Binding ElementName=TextBlock}">
        <VisualBrush.RelativeTransform>
          <ScaleTransform ScaleY="-1.0" CenterX="0.5" CenterY="0.5" />
        </VisualBrush.RelativeTransform>
      </VisualBrush>
    </Rectangle.Fill>
    <Rectangle.OpacityMask>
```

```
            <LinearGradientBrush StartPoint="0,0" EndPoint="0,1">
              <GradientStop Color="#DF000000" />
              <GradientStop Color="Transparent" Offset="0.8" />
            </LinearGradientBrush>
          </Rectangle.OpacityMask>
        </Rectangle>
      </StackPanel>
```

In this example, we use a `StackPanel` object to position a `TextBlock` element above a `Rectangle` element. The text will be the object to reflect and the reflection will be generated in the rectangle. The panel's width is constrained to ensure that the reflection fits the text element exactly. We start by naming the `TextBlock` element and setting some typeface properties, along with the text to output.

We've set a `LinearGradientBrush` object as the color for the text to make it more interesting, although this plays no part in creating the reflection effect. Next, note that the `Rectangle` element is sized and positioned exactly to fit the size of the text from the `TextBlock` element. We can of course use this technique to reflect anything and are not restricted to just reflecting text elements.

The background of the rectangle is painted with a `VisualBrush` object, where the `Visual` property is data bound to the visual output of the `TextBlock` element, using the `ElementName` property. Note the `RelativeTransform` property of the `VisualBrush` object, enables us to transform the visual in some way and is set to an instance of the `ScaleTransform` class.

This is one of the most important constituents for creating this effect, as this element is what inverts the related visual in the vertical plain. Setting the `ScaleY` property to −1 will invert the visual vertically for us, while setting the `ScaleX` property to −1 would invert the visual horizontally. Note that we omit the `ScaleX` property here because we want it set at its default value of 1.

Next, we see the `OpacityMask` property, which lets us set a gradient brush to be mapped to the opacity of the rectangle. When the alpha channel of the brush is 1, the rectangle will be opaque, when it is 0, the rectangle will be transparent and when it is in between, the rectangle will be semi-transparent. This is the other essential part of this effect and creates the fade of the reflected image.

In our example, we have a vertical gradient that is almost solid black at the top and gets increasingly transparent until it reaches four fifths of the way down, when it becomes fully transparent. When set as the rectangle's OpacityMask, only the alpha channel values are used and this results in it being totally visible at the top and fading to invisibility four fifths of the way down, as shown in the preceding image.

Exploring borderless windows

Using WPF, it is possible to create windows without borders, a title bar and the standard minimize, restore and close buttons. It is also possible to create irregular shaped windows and windows with transparent areas that display whatever lies beneath. Although it would be somewhat unconventional to make our main application window borderless, we can still take advantage of this ability.

For example, we could create a borderless window for custom message boxes, or perhaps for extended tooltips, or any other popup control that provides information to the end user. Creating borderless windows can be achieved within a few simple steps. Let's start with the basics and assume that we're adding this to our existing application framework.

In this case, we've already got our MainWindow class and need to add an additional window. Probably, one of the easiest way to do this in Visual Studio, is to add a WPF User Control class into our Controls folder and then simply replace the word UserControl with the word Window in both the XAML file and its associated code behind file.

All we need to do now is to set the window's WindowStyle property to None and its AllowsTransparency property to true. This will result in the white background of our window's declared size appearing.

```
<Window
  x:Class="CompanyName.ApplicationName.Views.Controls.BorderlessWindow"
  xmlns="http://schemas.microsoft.com/winfx/2006/xaml/presentation"
  xmlns:x="http://schemas.microsoft.com/winfx/2006/xaml"
  xmlns:mc="http://schemas.openxmlformats.org/markup-compatibility/2006"
  xmlns:d="http://schemas.microsoft.com/expression/blend/2008"
  mc:Ignorable="d"
  Height="150" Width="300" WindowStyle="None"AllowsTransparency="True">
</Window>

...

using System.Windows;

namespace CompanyName.ApplicationName.Views.Controls
```

```
  {
    public partial class BorderlessWindow : Window
    {
      public BorderlessWindow()
      {
        InitializeComponent();
      }
    }
  }
```

However, while this removes the default window chrome that we are all used to and provides us with a borderless window, it also removes the standard buttons, so we are unable to close, resize or even move the window directly. Luckily, making our window moveable is a very simple matter. We just need to add the following line of code into our window's constructor after the `InitializeComponent` method is called.

```
MouseLeftButtonDown += (o, e) => DragMove();
```

This `DragMove` method is declared within the `Window` class and enables us to click and drag the window from anywhere within its bounds. We could easily recreate the normal window functionality of only being able to move the window from the title bar by adding our own title bar and attaching this anonymous event handler to that object's `MouseLeftButtonDown` event instead.

If we want our borderless window to be resizable, there is a `ResizeMode` property in the `Window` class that provides us with a few options. One value that we can use with our borderless window is the `CanResizeWithGrip` value. This option adds a so-called resize grip, specified by a triangular pattern of dots in the bottom right corner of the window, that users can resize the window with.

If we set the `ResizeMode` property to this value and set the background to a color that will contrast with this resize grip, we will end with this visual output.

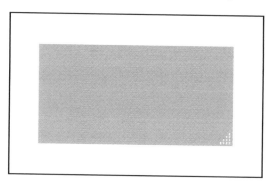

However, we still have no way to close the window. For this, we could add our own button, or perhaps enable the window to be closed by pressing the escape key (*Esc*), or some other key on the keyboard. Either way, whatever the trigger, closing the window is a simple matter of calling the window's `Close` method.

Rather than implementing a replacement window chrome, which could be easily achieved with a few borders, let's focus on developing a borderless window with an irregular shape, that we could use to popup helpful information for the users. Ordinarily, we would need to set the window's background to transparent to hide it, but we will be replacing its control template, so we don't need to do this.

For this example, we don't need a resize grip either, so let's set the `ResizeMode` property to `NoResize`. We also have no need to move this callout window by mouse, so we don't need to add the anonymous event handler that calls the `DragMove` method.

As this window will only offer information to the user, we should also set a few other window properties. One important property to set is the `ShowInTaskbar` property, which specifies whether the application icon should appear in the Windows Taskbar, or not. As this window will be an integral part of our main application, we set this property to `false`, so that its icon will be hidden.

Another useful property for this situation is the `WindowStartupLocation` property, which enables the window to be positioned using the `Window.Top` and `Window.Left` properties. In this way, the callout window can be programmatically positioned on screen anywhere that it is needed. Before continuing any further, let's see the code for this window.

```xml
<Window x:Class="CompanyName.ApplicationName.Views.Controls.CalloutWindow"
    xmlns="http://schemas.microsoft.com/winfx/2006/xaml/presentation"
    xmlns:x="http://schemas.microsoft.com/winfx/2006/xaml"
    xmlns:mc="http://schemas.openxmlformats.org/markup-compatibility/2006"
    xmlns:d="http://schemas.microsoft.com/expression/blend/2008"
    xmlns:Controls=
      "clr-namespace:CompanyName.ApplicationName.Views.Controls"
  mc:Ignorable="d" d:DesignHeight="150" d:DesignWidth="300"
    WindowStartupLocation="Manual">
  <Window.Resources>
    <Style TargetType="{x:Type Controls:CalloutWindow}">
      <Setter Property="ShowInTaskbar" Value="False" />
      <Setter Property="WindowStyle" Value="None" />
      <Setter Property="AllowsTransparency" Value="True" />
      <Setter Property="ResizeMode" Value="NoResize" />
      <Setter Property="Template">
        <Setter.Value>
          <ControlTemplate TargetType="{x:Type Controls:CalloutWindow}">
            <Grid Margin="0,0,0,12">
```

```
            <Grid.ColumnDefinitions>
              <ColumnDefinition Width="*" />
              <ColumnDefinition Width="5*" />
            </Grid.ColumnDefinitions>
            <Path Grid.ColumnSpan="2"
              Fill="{TemplateBinding Background}"
              Stroke="{TemplateBinding BorderBrush}"
              StrokeThickness="2" Stretch="Fill">
              <Path.Data>
                <CombinedGeometry GeometryCombineMode="Union">
                  <CombinedGeometry.Geometry1>
                    <PathGeometry>
                      <PathFigure StartPoint="0,60">
                        <LineSegment Point="50,45" />
                        <LineSegment Point="50,75" />
                      </PathFigure>
                    </PathGeometry>
                  </CombinedGeometry.Geometry1>
                  <CombinedGeometry.Geometry2>
                    <RectangleGeometry RadiusX="20" RadiusY="20"
                      Rect="50,0,250,150" />
                  </CombinedGeometry.Geometry2>
                </CombinedGeometry>
              </Path.Data>
            </Path>
            <ContentPresenter Grid.Column="1"
              Content="{TemplateBinding Content}"
              HorizontalAlignment="{TemplateBinding
              HorizontalContentAlignment}"
              VerticalAlignment="{TemplateBinding
              VerticalContentAlignment}"
              Margin="{TemplateBinding Padding}">
              <ContentPresenter.Resources>
                <Style TargetType="{x:Type TextBlock}">
                  <Setter Property="TextWrapping" Value="Wrap" />
                </Style>
              </ContentPresenter.Resources>
            </ContentPresenter>
            <Grid.Effect>
              <DropShadowEffect Color="Black"
                Direction="270" ShadowDepth="7" Opacity="0.3" />
            </Grid.Effect>
          </Grid>
        </ControlTemplate>
      </Setter.Value>
    </Setter>
  </Style>
</Window.Resources>
```

```
</Window>
```

While this example is not overly long, there is a lot to discuss here. In order to clarify the situation somewhat, let's also see the code behind before we examine this code:

```
using System.Windows;
using System.Windows.Media;

namespace CompanyName.ApplicationName.Views.Controls
{
  public partial class CalloutWindow : Window
  {
    static CalloutWindow()
    {
      BorderBrushProperty.OverrideMetadata (typeof(CalloutWindow),
        new FrameworkPropertyMetadata(
        new SolidColorBrush(Color.FromArgb(255, 238, 156, 88))));
      HorizontalContentAlignmentProperty.OverrideMetadata(
        typeof(CalloutWindow),
        new FrameworkPropertyMetadata(HorizontalAlignment.Center));
      VerticalContentAlignmentProperty.OverrideMetadata(
        typeof(CalloutWindow),
        new FrameworkPropertyMetadata(VerticalAlignment.Center));
    }

    public CalloutWindow()
    {
      InitializeComponent();
    }

    public new static readonly DependencyProperty BackgroundProperty =
      DependencyProperty.Register(nameof(Background), typeof(Brush),
      typeof(CalloutWindow),
      new PropertyMetadata(new LinearGradientBrush(Colors.White,
      Color.FromArgb(255, 250, 191, 143), 90)));

    public new Brush Background
    {
      get { return (Brush)GetValue(BackgroundProperty); }
      set { SetValue(BackgroundProperty, value); }
    }
  }
}
```

This code behind file is simpler than the XAML file, so let's quickly walk through it first. We added a static constructor in order to call the `OverrideMetadata` method on a few pre-existing Dependency Properties. This enables us to override the default settings of these properties and we do this in a static constructor because we want to run this code just once per class and because it is called before any other constructor or method in the class.

In this constructor, we override the metadata for the `BorderBrush` property, in order to set a default border color for our callout window. We do the same for both the `HorizontalContentAlignment` and `VerticalContentAlignment` properties to ensure that the window content will be centered by default. By doing this, we are re-using these existing properties.

However, we can also totally replace the pre-existing properties. As an example, we've replaced the `Background` property to paint our callout background. In this case, we declare our own `Background` property, specified by the `new` keyword, and set its own default brush color. We then use that to paint the background of our callout shape, although we could just as easily add another setter into our style to reuse the original `Background` property.

Looking at the XAML code now, we can see the `WindowStartupLocation` property set in the `Window` declaration, followed by a style in the window's `Resources` section. In this style, we set the aforementioned properties and define the window's control template. Inside the `ControlTemplate` object, we define a `Grid` panel. We'll return to this later, but for now, note that there is a nine pixel margin set on the bottom of the panel.

Next, note that the panel has two star-sized `ColumnDefinition` elements declared, one with a width of `*` and another with a width of `5*`. If we add these together, we end with a total width of six equal divisions. This means that the first column will be one sixth of the total width of the window and the second column will take up the remaining five sixths. We will soon see why this is set as it is.

Inside the `Grid` panel, we first declare the `Path` element that is used to define the shape of our callout. We set the `Grid.ColumnSpan` property on it to 2, to ensure that it takes all of the space of the parent window. Next, we set our new `Background` property to the `Fill` property, so that users of our window can set its `Background` property and have that brush paint just the background of our path.

We also set the `Stroke` property of the `Path` element to the overridden `BorderBrush` property and although we didn't, we could have exposed the `StrokeThickness` property by declaring another Dependency Property. Note that we use `TemplateBinding` elements to access the properties of the window, as they are the most efficient in this particular case.

Take special note of the `Path.Stretch` property, which we have set to `Fill` and defines how the shape should fill the space that it is provided with. Using this `Fill` value specifies that the content should fill all of the available space, rather than preserve its originally defined aspect ratio. However, if we want to preserve the aspect ratio, then we can change this property to the `Uniform` value instead.

The most important part of the path is found in the `Path.Data` section. This defines the shape of the rendered path and like our layered background example, we utilize a `CombinedGeometry` element here to combine two separate geometries. Unlike the previous example, here we use a `GeometryCombineMode` value of `Union`, which renders the output of both geometry shapes together.

In the `CombinedGeometry.Geometry1` element, we declare a `PathGeometry` object with a `PathFigure` element that has a starting point and two `LineSegment` elements. Together with the starting point, these two elements form the triangle section of our callout, that points to the area on screen that our window's information relates to. Note that this triangle is fifty pixels wide in the path.

In the `CombinedGeometry.Geometry2` element, we declare a `RectangleGeometry` object, with its size specified by the `Rect` property and the size of its rounded corners being specified by the `RadiusX` and `RadiusY` properties. The rectangle is positioned fifty pixels away from the left edge and its width is two hundred and fifty pixels wide.

The overall area taken up by the rectangle and the triangle is therefore three hundred pixels. One sixth of three hundred is fifty and this is how wide the triangle in our shape is. This explains why our first `Grid` column is set to take one sixth of the total space.

After the `Path` object, we declare the `ContentPresenter` element that is required to output the actual content of the window and set it to be in the second column of the panel. In short, this column is used to position the `ContentPresenter` element directly over the rectangle section of our shape, avoiding the triangular section.

In the `ContentPresenter` element, we data bind several positional properties to the relevant properties of the window using `TemplateBinding` elements. We also data bind its `Content` property to the `Content` property of the window using another `TemplateBinding` element.

Note that we could have declared our UI controls directly within the `Window` control. However, had we done that, then we would not be able to data bind to its `Content` property in this way, as setting it externally would replace all of our declared XAML controls, including the `ContentPresenter` object. By providing a new template, we are totally overriding the default behavior of the window.

Also note that we have declared a style in the `Resources` section of the `ContentPresenter` element. This style has been declared without the `x:Key` directive, so that it will be implicitly applied to all `TextBlock` objects within scope, specifically to affect the `TextBlock` objects that the `ContentPresenter` element will automatically generate for string values, while not affecting others.

The style sets the `TextBlock.TextWrapping` property to the `Wrap` member of the `TextWrapping` enumeration, which has the effect of wrapping long text lines onto the following lines. The default setting is `NoWrap`, which would result in long strings not being fully displayed in our window.

Finally, we come to the end of the XAML example and find a `DropShadowEffect` object set as the `Effect` property of the `Grid` panel. As with all shadow effects, we set the `Color` property to black and the `Opacity` property to a value less or equal to `0.5`. The `Direction` property is set to `270`, which produces a shadow that lies directly underneath our callout shape.

Note that we set the `ShadowDepth` property to a value of `7`. Now, do you remember the bottom margin that was set on the grid? That was set to a value just above this value and was to ensure that enough space was left in the window to display our shadow underneath our callout shape. Without this, the shadow would sit outside the bounding box of the window and not be displayed.

If we had set a different value for the `Direction` property, then we would need to adjust the `Grid` panel's margin to ensure that it left enough space around the window to display the shadow in its new location. Let's now take a look at how we could use our new window:

```
CalloutWindow calloutWindow = new CalloutWindow();
calloutWindow.Width = 225;
calloutWindow.Height = 120;
calloutWindow.FontSize = 18;
calloutWindow.Padding = new Thickness(20);
calloutWindow.Content = "Please fill in the first line of your address.";
calloutWindow.Show();
```

Running this code from a suitable location would result in the following rendered output:

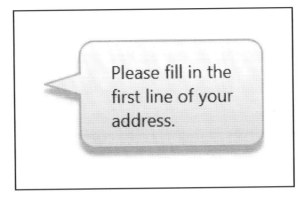

In our window-showing code, we set a string to the `Content` property of the window. However, this property is of type `object` and so we can add any object as its value. In the same way that we set our View Model instances to the `Content` property of a `ContentControl` earlier in this book, we can also do that with our window.

Given a suitable `DataTemplate` that defines some UI for a particular custom object type, we could set an instance of that object to our window's `Content` property and have the controls from that template rendered within our callout window, so we are not restricted to only using strings here. Let's use a previous example:

```
calloutWindow.DataContext = new UsersViewModel();
```

With a few slight adjustments to our `calloutWindow` dimension properties, we would see this:

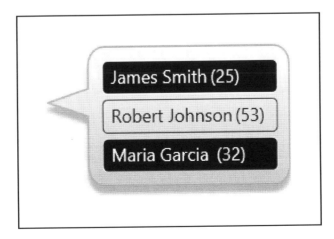

Visualizing data

While there are a number of pre-existing graph controls and third party data visualization controls available in WPF, we can create our own relatively easily. Expressing data in textual terms alone, while generally acceptable, is not optimal. Breaking the norm in an application always makes that application stand out from the rest that strictly adhere to the standard.

As an example, imagine a simple situation, where we have a dashboard that visualizes the number of work tasks that have come in and the number that have been completed. We could just output the numbers in a big, bold font, but that would be the normal kind of output. What about if we visualized each number as a shape, with its size being specified by the number?

Let's reuse our layering techniques from earlier and design some visually appealing spheres, that grow in size depending upon a particular value. To do this, we can create another custom control, with a `Value` Dependency Property to data bind to. Let's first look at the code of the `Sphere` class:

```
using System.Windows;
using System.Windows.Controls;
using System.Windows.Media;
using System.Windows.Shapes;
using CompanyName.ApplicationName.CustomControls.Enums;
using MediaColor = System.Windows.Media.Color;

namespace CompanyName.ApplicationName.CustomControls
{
  [TemplatePart(Name = "PART_Background", Type = typeof(Ellipse))]
  [TemplatePart(Name = "PART_Glow", Type = typeof(Ellipse))]
  public class Sphere : Control
  {
    private RadialGradientBrush greenBackground =
      new RadialGradientBrush(new GradientStopCollection() {
      new GradientStop(MediaColor.FromRgb(0, 254, 0), 0),
      new GradientStop(MediaColor.FromRgb(1, 27, 0), 0.974) });
    private RadialGradientBrush greenGlow =
      new RadialGradientBrush(new GradientStopCollection() {
      new GradientStop(MediaColor.FromArgb(205, 67, 255, 46), 0),
      new GradientStop(MediaColor.FromArgb(102, 88, 254, 72), 0.426),
      new GradientStop(MediaColor.FromArgb(0, 44, 191, 32), 1) });
    private RadialGradientBrush redBackground =
      new RadialGradientBrush(new GradientStopCollection() {
      new GradientStop(MediaColor.FromRgb(254, 0, 0), 0),
      new GradientStop(MediaColor.FromRgb(27, 0, 0), 0.974) });
    private RadialGradientBrush redGlow =
```

```
  new RadialGradientBrush(new GradientStopCollection() {
  new GradientStop(MediaColor.FromArgb(205, 255, 46, 46), 0),
  new GradientStop(MediaColor.FromArgb(102, 254, 72, 72), 0.426),
  new GradientStop(MediaColor.FromArgb(0, 191, 32, 32), 1) });

static Sphere()
{
  DefaultStyleKeyProperty.OverrideMetadata(typeof(Sphere),
    new FrameworkPropertyMetadata(typeof(Sphere)));
}

public static readonly DependencyProperty ValueProperty =
  DependencyProperty.Register(nameof(Value), typeof(double),
  typeof(Sphere), new PropertyMetadata(50.0));

public double Value
{
  get { return (double)GetValue(ValueProperty); }
  set { SetValue(ValueProperty, value); }
}

public static readonly DependencyProperty ColorProperty =
  DependencyProperty.Register(nameof(Color), typeof(SphereColor),
  typeof(Sphere), new PropertyMetadata(SphereColor.Green,
  OnColorChanged));

public SphereColor Color
{
  get { return (SphereColor)GetValue(ColorProperty); }
  set { SetValue(ColorProperty, value); }
}

private static void OnColorChanged(DependencyObject
  dependencyObject, DependencyPropertyChangedEventArgs e)
{
  ((Sphere)dependencyObject).SetEllipseColors();
}

public override void OnApplyTemplate()
{
  SetEllipseColors();
}

private void SetEllipseColors()
{
  Ellipse backgroundEllipse =
    GetTemplateChild("PART_Background") as Ellipse;
  Ellipse glowEllipse = GetTemplateChild("PART_Glow") as Ellipse;
```

```
      if (backgroundEllipse != null) backgroundEllipse.Fill =
        Color == SphereColor.Green ? greenBackground : redBackground;
      if (glowEllipse != null) glowEllipse.Fill =
        Color == SphereColor.Green ? greenGlow : redGlow;
      base.OnApplyTemplate();
    }
  }
}
```

As this class will declare its own `Color` property, we start by adding a `MediaColor` using alias directive, which we'll just use as a shortcut to accessing the methods of the `System.Windows.Media.Color` class, when declaring the brushes that will be used in the `Sphere` class.

From the class declaration, we can see that there are two named parts specified in `TemplatePartAttribute` attributes. These specify that the two mentioned `Ellipse` elements are required in our control's template in the `Generic.xaml` file. Inside the class, we define a number of `RadialGradientBrush` resources to paint our spheres with.

In the static constructor, we call the `OverrideMetadata` method to let the Framework know where our control's default style is. We then see the declaration of the `Value` and `Color` Dependency Properties, with the `Color` property's related `PropertyChangedCallback` hander method.

In this `OnColorChanged` method, we cast the `dependencyObject` input parameter to an instance of our `Sphere` class and call its `SetEllipseColors` method. In that method, we use the `FrameworkElement.GetTemplateChild` method to access the two main `Ellipse` objects from our `ControlTemplate` element.

Remember that we must always check these objects for null, as our `ControlTemplate` could have been replaced with one that does not contain these ellipse elements. If they are not null, we then set their `Fill` properties to one of our brush resources using the ternary operator and depending upon the value of our `Color` property.

One alternative for creating this functionality would be to declare a Dependency Property of type `Brush` to data bind to each ellipse's `Fill` property and to set the relevant brush resources to these properties, instead of accessing the XAML elements directly. Before viewing the control's default style, let's see the `SphereColor` enumeration that is used by the `Color` property.

```
namespace CompanyName.ApplicationName.CustomControls.Enums
{
  public enum SphereColor
  {
    Green, Red
  }
}
```

As you can see, this is a simple affair and could be easily extended. Note that this enumeration has been declared within the `CustomControls` namespace and project, so that the project is self-contained and can be reused in other applications without any external dependencies. Let's take a look at our control's default style from `Generic.xaml` now.

```
<Style TargetType="{x:Type CustomControls:Sphere}">
  <Setter Property="Template">
    <Setter.Value>
      <ControlTemplate TargetType="{x:Type CustomControls:Sphere}">
        <ControlTemplate.Resources>
          <DropShadowEffect x:Key="Shadow" BlurRadius="10"
            Direction="270" ShadowDepth="7" Opacity="0.5" />
          <LinearGradientBrush x:Key="Reflection"
            StartPoint="0,0" EndPoint="0,1">
            <GradientStop Color="#90FFFFFF" Offset="0.009" />
            <GradientStop Color="#2DFFFFFF" Offset="0.506" />
            <GradientStop Offset="0.991" />
          </LinearGradientBrush>
        </ControlTemplate.Resources>
        <Grid Height="{Binding Value,
          RelativeSource={RelativeSource TemplatedParent}}"
          Width="{Binding Value,
          RelativeSource={RelativeSource TemplatedParent}}">
          <Grid.RowDefinitions>
            <RowDefinition Height="5*" />
            <RowDefinition Height="2*" />
          </Grid.RowDefinitions>
          <Grid.ColumnDefinitions>
            <ColumnDefinition Width="*" />
            <ColumnDefinition Width="8*" />
            <ColumnDefinition Width="*" />
          </Grid.ColumnDefinitions>
          <Ellipse Name="PART_Background" Grid.RowSpan="2"
```

```
                  Grid.ColumnSpan="3" Stroke="#FF1B0000"
                  Effect="{StaticResource Shadow}" />
                <Ellipse Name="PART_Glow" Grid.RowSpan="2"
                  Grid.ColumnSpan="3" />
                <Ellipse Grid.Column="1" Margin="0,2,0,0"
                  Fill="{StaticResource Reflection}" />
              </Grid>
          </ControlTemplate>
        </Setter.Value>
      </Setter>
    </Style>
```

When looking at our control's default template, we can see some resources defined in the `ControlTemplate.Resources` section. We first declare a `DropShadowEffect` element, similar to our previous uses of this class. Next, we define a vertical `LinearGradientBrush` element, to use as a light reflection layer, in a similar way to our example in an earlier section of this chapter.

Previously, we saw that the default value of the `GradientStop.Offset` property is zero and so we can omit the setting of this property if that is the value that we need to use. In this brush resource, we see that the last `GradientStop` element has no `Color` value specified. This is because its default value of this property is `Transparent` and that is the value that we need to use here.

In the actual markup for our control, we declare three `Ellipse` objects within a `Grid` panel. Two of these elements are named and referenced in the control's code, while the third ellipse uses the brush from resources to create the 'shine' on top of the other ellipses. The panel's size properties are data bound to the `Value` Dependency Property, using a `TemplatedParent` source.

Note that we have used the star-sizing capabilities of the `Grid` panel to both position and size our ellipse elements, with the exception of the two pixels of top margin specified on the reflection ellipse. In this way, our control can be any size and the positioning of the various layers will remain visually correct. Note that we could not achieve this by hardcoding exact margin values for each element.

Let's see how we could use this in a simple view:

```
<Grid TextElement.FontSize="28" TextElement.FontWeight="Bold" Margin="20">
  <Grid.ColumnDefinitions>
    <ColumnDefinition />
    <ColumnDefinition />
  </Grid.ColumnDefinitions>
  <Grid.RowDefinitions>
    <RowDefinition />
```

```
    <RowDefinition Height="Auto" />
  </Grid.RowDefinitions>
  <CustomControls:Sphere Color="Red" Value="{Binding InCount}"
    VerticalAlignment="Bottom" />
  <CustomControls:Sphere Grid.Column="1" Value="{Binding OutCount}"
    VerticalAlignment="Bottom" />
  <TextBlock Grid.Row="1" Text="{Binding InCount}"
    HorizontalAlignment="Center" Margin="0,10,0,0" />
  <TextBlock Grid.Row="1" Grid.Column="1" Text="{Binding OutCount}"
    HorizontalAlignment="Center" Margin="0,10,0,0" />
</Grid>
```

This is how our example looks when rendered.

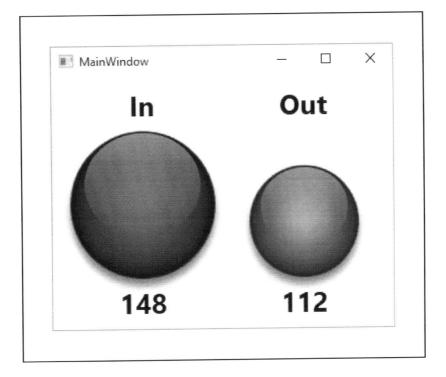

As you can see, WPF is very powerful and enables us to create completely original looking controls. However, we can also use it to recreate more commonly seen controls. As an example, let's see how we can create an alternative control to gauge how close we may be to our particular target value.

This example features a semi-circular arc, which is something that does not exist in a form that is usable from XAML, so we'll first create an `Arc` control to use internally within our `Gauge` control. Let's see how we can achieve this, by adding a new custom control:

```
using System;
using System.Windows;
using System.Windows.Media;
using System.Windows.Shapes;

namespace CompanyName.ApplicationName.CustomControls
{
  public class Arc : Shape
  {
    public static readonly DependencyProperty StartAngleProperty =
      DependencyProperty.Register(nameof(StartAngle), typeof(double),
```

```
    typeof(Arc), new PropertyMetadata(180.0));

public double StartAngle
{
  get { return (double)GetValue(StartAngleProperty); }
  set { SetValue(StartAngleProperty, value); }
}

public static readonly DependencyProperty EndAngleProperty =
  DependencyProperty.Register(nameof(EndAngle), typeof(double),
  typeof(Arc), new PropertyMetadata(0.0));

public double EndAngle
{
  get { return (double)GetValue(EndAngleProperty); }
  set { SetValue(EndAngleProperty, value); }
}

protected override Geometry DefiningGeometry
{
  get { return GetArcGeometry(); }
}

private Geometry GetArcGeometry()
{
  Point startPoint = ConvertToPoint(Math.Min(StartAngle, EndAngle));
  Point endPoint = ConvertToPoint(Math.Max(StartAngle, EndAngle));
  Size arcSize = new Size(Math.Max(0, (RenderSize.Width -
    StrokeThickness) / 2), Math.Max(0, (RenderSize.Height -
    StrokeThickness) / 2));
  bool isLargeArc = Math.Abs(EndAngle - StartAngle) > 180;
  StreamGeometry streamGeometry = new StreamGeometry();
  using (StreamGeometryContext context = streamGeometry.Open())
  {
    context.BeginFigure(startPoint, false, false);
    context.ArcTo(endPoint, arcSize, 0, isLargeArc,
      SweepDirection.Counterclockwise, true, false);
  }
  streamGeometry.Transform =
    new TranslateTransform(StrokeThickness / 2, StrokeThickness / 2);
  streamGeometry.Freeze();
  return streamGeometry;
}

private Point ConvertToPoint(double angleInDegrees)
{
  double angleInRadians = angleInDegrees * Math.PI / 180;
  double radiusX = (RenderSize.Width - StrokeThickness) / 2;
```

```
        double radiusY = (RenderSize.Height - StrokeThickness) / 2;
        return new Point(radiusX * Math.Cos(angleInRadians) + radiusX,
          radiusY * Math.Sin(-angleInRadians) + radiusY);
      }
    }
  }
```

Note that we extend the `Shape` class when creating our `Arc` class. We do this because it provides us with a wide variety of stroke and fill properties and also the apparatus to render our custom shape from a `Geometry` object. Additionally, users of our `Arc` control will also be able to take advantage of the `Shape` class' transformation abilities through its `Stretch` and `GeometryTransform` properties.

To draw our arc, we will use the `ArcTo` method of the `StreamGeometryContext` class and with it, we need to specify exact `Point` values for its start and end. However, in order to reflect the correct value in the size of our arc, it is easier to define it using angle values for its start and end. Therefore, we add `StartAngle` and `EndAngle` Dependency Properties to our `Arc` class.

After these property declarations, we see the overridden `DefiningGeometry` property, that enables us to return a `Geometry` object that defines the shape to be rendered. We simply return the result from the `GetArcGeometry` method from this property.

In the `GetArcGeometry` method, we obtain the required start and end `Point` elements from the `ConvertToPoint` method, passing in the `StartAngle` and `EndAngle` property values. Note that we use the `Min` and `Max` methods of the `Math` class here to ensure that the start point is calculated from the smaller angle and the end point is calculated from the larger angle.

Our arc shape's fill will actually come from the geometric arc's stroke and so we will not be able to add a stroke to it. In WPF, the stroke of a shape with a thickness of one pixel will extend no further than the shape's bounding box. However, at the furthest point, strokes with larger thickness values are rendered so that their center remains on the line of the bounding box and therefore, half of it will extend outside the bounds of the element and half will be rendered within the bounds.

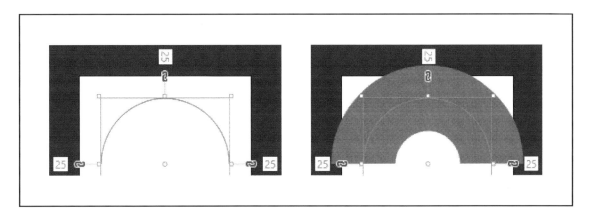

Therefore, we calculate the size of the arc by dividing the `RenderSize` value minus the `StrokeThickness` value by two. This will reduce the size of the arc so that it remains totally within the bounds of our control. We make use of the `Math.Max` method to ensure that the values that we pass to the `Size` class are never less than zero and avoid exceptions.

When using the `ArcTo` method, we need to specify a value that determines whether we want to connect our start and end points with a short arc or a long one. Our `isLargeArc` variable therefore determines whether the two specified angles would produce an arc of more than one hundred and eighty degrees or not.

Next, we create a `StreamGeometry` object and retrieve a `StreamGeometryContext` object from its `Open` method, with which to define our geometric shape. Note that we could equally use a `PathGeometry` object here, but as we do not need its data binding, animation, or other abilities, we use the more efficient `StreamGeometry` object instead.

We enter the arc's start point in the `BeginFigure` method and the remaining parameters in the `ArcTo` method. Note that we call these methods on our `StreamGeometryContext` object from within a `using` statement to ensure that it is closed and disposed of properly, once we are finished with it.

Next, we apply a `TranslateTransform` element to the `Transform` property of the `StreamGeometry` object in order to shift the arc so that it is fully contained within our control. Without this step, our arc would stick out of the bounding box of our control to the upper left, by the amount of half of the `StrokeThickness` property value.

Once we have finished manipulating our `StreamGeometry` object, we call its `Freeze` method, which makes it unmodifiable and rewards us with additional performance benefits. We'll find out more about this in `Chapter 10`, *Improving Application Performance*, but for now, let's continue looking through this example.

Finally, we get to the `ConvertToPoint` method, which converts the values of our two angle Dependency Properties to two-dimensional `Point` objects. Our first job is to convert each angle from degrees to radians, as the methods of the `Math` class that we need to use require radian values.

Next, we calculate the two radii of our arc, using half of the `RenderSize` value minus the `StrokeThickness` property value, so that the size of the arc does not exceed the bounding box of our `Arc` control. Finally, we perform some basic trigonometry using the `Math.Cos` and `Math.Sin` methods when calculating the `Point` element to return.

That completes our simple `Arc` control and so now we can utilize this new class in our `Gauge` control. We'll need to create another new custom control for it, so let's first see the properties and code in our new `Gauge` class:

```
using System.Windows;
using System.Windows.Controls;

namespace CompanyName.ApplicationName.CustomControls
{
  public class Gauge : Control
  {
    static Gauge()
    {
      DefaultStyleKeyProperty.OverrideMetadata (typeof(Gauge),
        new FrameworkPropertyMetadata(typeof(Gauge)));
    }

    public static readonly DependencyPropertyKey valueAnglePropertyKey =
      DependencyProperty.RegisterReadOnly(nameof(ValueAngle),
      typeof(double), typeof(Gauge), new PropertyMetadata(180.0));

    public static readonly DependencyProperty ValueAngleProperty =
      valueAnglePropertyKey.DependencyProperty;

    public double ValueAngle
    {
      get { return (double)GetValue(ValueAngleProperty); }
      private set { SetValue(valueAnglePropertyKey, value); }
    }
```

```
public static readonly DependencyPropertyKey
  rotationAnglePropertyKey = DependencyProperty.RegisterReadOnly(
  nameof(RotationAngle), typeof(double), typeof(Gauge),
  new PropertyMetadata(180.0));

public static readonly DependencyProperty RotationAngleProperty =
  rotationAnglePropertyKey.DependencyProperty;

public double RotationAngle
{
  get { return (double)GetValue(RotationAngleProperty); }
  private set { SetValue(rotationAnglePropertyKey, value); }
}

public static readonly DependencyProperty ValueProperty =
  DependencyProperty.Register(nameof(Value), typeof(double),
  typeof(Gauge), new PropertyMetadata(0.0, OnValueChanged));

private static void OnValueChanged(DependencyObject
  dependencyObject, DependencyPropertyChangedEventArgs e)
{
  Gauge gauge = (Gauge)dependencyObject;
  if (gauge.MaximumValue == 0.0)
    gauge.ValueAngle = gauge.RotationAngle = 180.0;
  else if ((double)e.NewValue > gauge.MaximumValue)
  {
    gauge.ValueAngle = 0.0;
    gauge.RotationAngle = 360.0;
  }
  else
  {
    double scaledPercentageValue =
      ((double)e.NewValue / gauge.MaximumValue) * 180.0;
    gauge.ValueAngle = 180.0 - scaledPercentageValue;
    gauge.RotationAngle = 180.0 + scaledPercentageValue;
  }
}

public double Value
{
  get { return (double)GetValue(ValueProperty); }
  set { SetValue(ValueProperty, value); }
}

public static readonly DependencyProperty MaximumValueProperty =
  DependencyProperty.Register(nameof(MaximumValue), typeof(double),
  typeof(Gauge), new PropertyMetadata(0.0));
```

```
      public double MaximumValue
      {
        get { return (double)GetValue(MaximumValueProperty); }
        set { SetValue(MaximumValueProperty, value); }
      }

      public static readonly DependencyProperty TitleProperty =
        DependencyProperty.Register(nameof(Title), typeof(string),
        typeof(Gauge), new PropertyMetadata(string.Empty));

      public string Title
      {
        get { return (string)GetValue(TitleProperty); }
        set { SetValue(TitleProperty, value); }
      }
    }
  }
```

As usual, we start by overriding the metadata of the `DefaultStyleKeyProperty` for our
control type in the static constructor, to help the Framework find where its default style is
defined. We then declare the internal, read-only `ValueAngle` and `RotationAngle`
Dependency Properties and the regular public `Value`, `MaximumValue` and `Title`
Dependency Properties.

We declare a `PropertyChangedCallback` hander for the `Value` property and in that
method, we first cast the `dependencyObject` input parameter to an instance of our `Gauge`
class. If the value of the `MaximumValue` property is zero, then we simply set both of the
`ValueAngle` and `RotationAngle` properties to `180.0`, which results in the arc and needle
displaying in their start positions, to the left.

If the new value of the data bound `Value` property is more than the value of the
`MaximumValue` property, then we make the arc and needle display in their end, or full,
positions to the right. We do this by setting the `ValueAngle` property to `0.0` and the
`RotationAngle` property to `360.0`.

If the new value of the `Value` property is valid, then we calculate the
`scaledPercentageValue` variable. We do this by first dividing the new value by the value
of the `MaximumValue` property, to get the percentage of the maximum value. We then
multiply that figure by `180.0`, because our gauge covers a range of one hundred and eighty
degrees.

We then subtract the `scaledPercentageValue` variable value from `180.0` for the `ValueAngle` property and add it to `180.0` for the `RotationAngle` property. This is because the `ValueAngle` property is used by our arc and needs to be between `180.0` and `0.0` and the `RotationAngle` property is used by our gauge needle and needs to be between `180.0` and `360.0`.

This will soon be made clearer, so let's now see how we use these properties and the `Arc` control in our `Gauge` control's default style from the `Generic.xaml` file:

```
<Style TargetType="{x:Type CustomControls:Gauge}">
  <Setter Property="Template">
    <Setter.Value>
      <ControlTemplate TargetType="{x:Type CustomControls:Gauge}">
        <Grid Background="{Binding Background,
          RelativeSource={RelativeSource TemplatedParent}}">
          <Grid Margin="{Binding Padding,
            RelativeSource={RelativeSource TemplatedParent}}">
            <Grid.RowDefinitions>
              <RowDefinition Height="Auto" />
              <RowDefinition />
              <RowDefinition Height="Auto" />
            </Grid.RowDefinitions>
            <TextBlock Text="{Binding Title,
              RelativeSource={RelativeSource TemplatedParent}}"
              HorizontalAlignment="Center" />
            <Canvas Grid.Row="1" Width="300" Height="150"
              HorizontalAlignment="Center" Margin="0,5">
              <CustomControls:Arc Width="300" Height="300"
                StrokeThickness="75"  Stroke="#FF444444" />
              <CustomControls:Arc Width="300" Height="300"
                StrokeThickness="75" Stroke="OrangeRed" StartAngle="180"
                EndAngle="{Binding AngleValue,
                RelativeSource={RelativeSource TemplatedParent}}" />
              <Path Canvas.Left="150" Canvas.Top="140"
                Fill="White" StrokeThickness="5" Stroke="White"
                StrokeLineJoin="Round" Data="M0,0 L125,10, 0,20Z"
                Stretch="Fill" Width="125" Height="20">
                <Path.RenderTransform>
                  <RotateTransform Angle="{Binding RotationAngle,
                    RelativeSource={RelativeSource TemplatedParent}}"
                    CenterX="0" CenterY="10" />
                </Path.RenderTransform>
              </Path>
            </Canvas>
            <TextBlock Grid.Row="2" Text="{Binding Value, StringFormat=N0,
              RelativeSource={RelativeSource TemplatedParent}}"
              HorizontalAlignment="Center" FontWeight="Bold" />
```

```
                </Grid>
              </Grid>
          </ControlTemplate>
        </Setter.Value>
     </Setter>
  </Style>
```

We start our default style as usual, by specifying the type of our control in both the style and the control template. Inside the template, we have two `Grid` panels and data bind the `Background` of the outer panel and the `Margin` property of the inner panel to properties of our templated control, so that users can set them externally.

We then define three rows in our inner panel. The control's `Title` property is data bound to a horizontally centered `TextBlock` element in the first row. In the second row, we declare a horizontally centered `Canvas` panel that contains two of our new `Arc` controls and a `Path` object.

The first `Arc` control is gray and represents the background track that the `Arc` that represents our `Gauge` control's `Value` property sits on. The second `Arc` control is colored `OrangeRed` and displays the current value of our `Gauge` control's `Value` property, by data binding its `EndAngle` property to the `AngleValue` Dependency Property of the `Gauge` control.

Note that the angles in our `Arc` control follow the common Cartesian coordinate system, with an angle of zero degrees falling to the right and increasing values moving anti-clockwise. Therefore, to draw a semi-circular arc from left to right, we start with an angle of `180` degrees and end at `0` degrees, as demonstrated by the background arc in our `Gauge` control.

Furthermore, our `Arc` controls have the same width and height values, but as we don't need their lower halves, we crop them using the height of the canvas panel. The `Path` object represents the gauge needle in our control and is painted white.

We set the `StrokeLineJoin` property to the `Round` value in order to curve the three corners, where the lines of the needle path meet. Note that the needle is positioned exactly half way across the width of the canvas and ten pixels above the bottom, to enable its center line to lie along the bottom of the canvas.

Rather than declaring `PathFigure` and `LineSegment` objects to define the needle, we have used the shorthand notation inline in the `Data` property. The `M` specifies that we should move to (or start from) the point `0, 0`, the `L` specifies that we want to draw a line to the point `125, 10` and then from there to the point `0, 20` and the `Z` means that we want to close the path by joining the first and last points.

We then set the width and height of the path to the same values that were declared within its `Data` property. Now, the essential part of enabling this needle to point to the relevant position to reflect the data bound `Value` property, is the `RotateTransform` object that is applied to the path's `RenderTransform` property. Note that its center point is set to be the center of the bottom of the needle, as that is the point that we want to rotate from.

As the `RotateTransform` object rotates clockwise with increasing `Angle` values, we cannot reuse the `AngleValue` Dependency Property with it. Therefore, in this particular example, we define the needle pointing to the right and use a range of `180.0` to `360.0` degrees in the `RotationAngle` read-only Dependency Property with the transform object to match the position of the value arc.

At the end of the example, we see another horizontally centered `TextBlock` element, that outputs the current, unaltered value of the data bound `Value` Dependency Property. Note that we use the `StringFormat` value of `N0` to remove the decimal places from the value before displaying it.

That completes our new `Gauge` control and so, all we need to do now is see how we can use it.

```
<CustomControls:Gauge Width="400" Height="300"
    MaximumValue="{Binding InCount}" Value="{Binding OutCount}"
    Title="Success Percentage" Foreground="White" FontSize="34"
    Padding="10" />
```

We could extend our new `Gauge` control to make it more usable in several ways. We could add a `MinimumValue` Dependency Property to enable its use with value ranges that do not start at zero, or we could expose further properties to enable users to color, size, or further customize the control. Alternatively, we could rewrite it to enable it to be any size, instead of hard coding sizes as we did.

Livening up UI controls

In addition to making our UI controls look visually appealing, we can also 'liven them up' by adding user interactivity in the form of mouse over effects. While most mouse over effects are created using `Trigger` and `Setter` objects, that immediately update the relevant style properties when the related trigger condition is met, we can alternatively use animations to produce these effects.

Having even subtle transitions between states, rather than instantly switching, can also provide a richer user experience. Let's reuse our initial double bordered example from earlier and add some mouse interactivity animations to it to demonstrate this point. We'll need to add a few more resources into a suitable resource collection and adjust a couple of our previously declared resources too.

```
<Color x:Key="TransparentWhiteColor" A="127" R="255" G="255" B="255" />
<Color x:Key="TransparentBlackColor" A="127" R="0" G="0" B="0" />
```

Now that we have declared our semi-transparent `Color` resources, we can adjust our earlier brush resources to utilize them.

```
<SolidColorBrush x:Key="TransparentWhite"
  Color="{StaticResource TransparentWhiteColor}" />
<SolidColorBrush x:Key="TransparentBlack"
  Color="{StaticResource TransparentBlackColor}" />
```

Let's see our full example now.

```
<Grid Width="160" Height="68">
  <Grid.Background>
    <LinearGradientBrush StartPoint="0,0" EndPoint="1,1">
      <GradientStop Color="Red" />
      <GradientStop Color="Yellow" Offset="1" />
    </LinearGradientBrush>
  </Grid.Background>
  <Button Content="Click Me" Width="120" Height="28" FontSize="14"
    Margin="20">
    <Button.Template>
      <ControlTemplate TargetType="{x:Type Button}">
        <Border Name="OuterBorder"
          BorderBrush="{StaticResource TransparentBlack}"
          BorderThickness="1" Padding="1"
          Background="{StaticResource TransparentWhite}"
          CornerRadius="5" SnapsToDevicePixels="True">
          <Border Name="InnerBorder"
            BorderBrush="{StaticResource TransparentBlack}"
            BorderThickness="1" Background="White"
            CornerRadius="3.5" SnapsToDevicePixels="True">
            <ContentPresenter HorizontalAlignment="Center"
              VerticalAlignment="Center" />
          </Border>
        </Border>
        <ControlTemplate.Triggers>
          <Trigger Property="IsMouseOver" Value="True">
            <Trigger.EnterActions>
              <BeginStoryboard>
```

```
      <Storyboard Storyboard.TargetName="OuterBorder"
        Storyboard.TargetProperty=
        "BorderBrush.(SolidColorBrush.Color)">
        <ColorAnimation To="Black" Duration="0:0:0.25" />
      </Storyboard>
    </BeginStoryboard>
    <BeginStoryboard>
      <Storyboard Storyboard.TargetName="InnerBorder"
        Storyboard.TargetProperty=
        "BorderBrush.(SolidColorBrush.Color)">
        <ColorAnimation To="Black" Duration="0:0:0.3" />
      </Storyboard>
    </BeginStoryboard>
    <BeginStoryboard Name="BackgroundFadeIn"
      HandoffBehavior="Compose">
      <Storyboard Storyboard.TargetName="InnerBorder"
        Storyboard.TargetProperty=
        "Background.(SolidColorBrush.Color)">
        <ColorAnimation To="{StaticResource
          TransparentWhiteColor}" Duration="0:0:0.2" />
      </Storyboard>
    </BeginStoryboard>
  </Trigger.EnterActions>
  <Trigger.ExitActions>
    <BeginStoryboard>
      <Storyboard Storyboard.TargetName="OuterBorder"
        Storyboard.TargetProperty=
        "BorderBrush.(SolidColorBrush.Color)">
        <ColorAnimation To="{StaticResource
          TransparentBlackColor}" Duration="0:0:0.5" />
      </Storyboard>
    </BeginStoryboard>
    <BeginStoryboard>
      <Storyboard Storyboard.TargetName="InnerBorder"
        Storyboard.TargetProperty=
        "BorderBrush.(SolidColorBrush.Color)">
        <ColorAnimation To="{StaticResource
          TransparentBlackColor}" Duration="0:0:0.3" />
      </Storyboard>
    </BeginStoryboard>
    <BeginStoryboard Name="BackgroundFadeOut"
      HandoffBehavior="Compose">
      <Storyboard Storyboard.TargetName="InnerBorder"
        Storyboard.TargetProperty=
        "Background.(SolidColorBrush.Color)">
        <ColorAnimation To="White" Duration="0:0:0.4" />
      </Storyboard>
    </BeginStoryboard>
```

```
              </Trigger.ExitActions>
            </Trigger>
            <Trigger Property="IsPressed" Value="True">
              <Trigger.EnterActions>
                <BeginStoryboard Name="MouseDownBackground"
                  HandoffBehavior="Compose">
                  <Storyboard Storyboard.TargetName="InnerBorder"
                    Storyboard.TargetProperty=
                    "Background.(SolidColorBrush.Color)">
                    <ColorAnimation From="#D6FF21" Duration="0:0:1"
                      DecelerationRatio="1.0" />
                  </Storyboard>
                </BeginStoryboard>
              </Trigger.EnterActions>
            </Trigger>
            <EventTrigger RoutedEvent="Unloaded">
              <RemoveStoryboard BeginStoryboardName="BackgroundFadeIn" />
              <RemoveStoryboard BeginStoryboardName="BackgroundFadeOut" />
              <RemoveStoryboard BeginStoryboardName="MouseDownBackground" />
            </EventTrigger>
          </ControlTemplate.Triggers>
        </ControlTemplate>
      </Button.Template>
    </Button>
  </Grid>
```

While this example might seem quite long, it is actually fairly simple. We start with our original control template, albeit with the previously hardcoded brush values being replaced by our newly defined resources. The main difference to the original example is found in the `ControlTemplate.Triggers` collection.

The first trigger will start its various storyboards when the `IsMouseOver` property of the `Button` element is true, or in other words, when the user moves the mouse cursor over the button. Our storyboards are split between the `Trigger.EnterActions` and `Trigger.ExitActions` collections.

Remember that the storyboards in the `Trigger.EnterActions` will be started as the mouse enters the bounds of the button, while the storyboards in the `Trigger.ExitActions` will be started as the mouse leaves the bounds of the button. We declare three `BeginStoryboard` objects with their associated `Storyboard` objects within each of these `TriggerActionCollection` objects.

The first animation targets the `BorderBrush` property of the `OuterBorder` element. Note that this property is of type `Brush`, but there is no `BrushAnimation` class in WPF. Therefore, we need to target the `Color` property of the `SolidColorBrush` that is actually applied to this property and use a `ColorAnimation` object instead.

In order to do this, we need to use indirect targeting to first reference the `BorderBrush` property and then to chain to the `Color` property using the syntax `BorderBrush.(SolidColorBrush.Color)`. Note that this will only work if we are in fact using a `SolidColorBrush` element, as we are in this example.

However, if we were using one of the gradient brushes instead of a `SolidColorBrush` element, we could target the various colors of its `GradientStop` elements with a slightly different syntax. For example, we could target the color of the first `GradientStop` element in a gradient brush like this:

```
BorderBrush.(GradientBrush.GradientStops)[0].(GradientStop.Color)
```

Returning to this example now, the second animation targets the `BorderBrush` property of the `InnerBorder` element and follows the syntactical example of the first animation. While the third animation also uses indirect targeting to reference the `Background` property of the `InnerBorder` element, it is somewhat different to the other two animations.

For this animation, we name the `BeginStoryboard` object `BackgroundFadeIn` and set its `HandoffBehavior` property to `Compose`, to enable smoother transitions between this and the other animations of this property. The specified name will be used later in the example.

Note that these three `ColorAnimation` objects only have their `To` and `Duration` properties set and that the three duration values are slightly different. This has the effect of slightly thickening the effect, although synchronizing the times also works well.

We have omitted the `From` values on these animations to avoid situations where the current animated colors do not match the `From` values and have to immediately jump to the starting values before animating to the `To` values. By omitting these values, the animations will start at their current color values and will result in smoother transitions.

The three animations in the `Trigger.ExitActions` collection are very similar to those in the `EnterActions` collection, albeit animating the colors back to their original starting colors, so we can skip their explanation here. However, it is worth highlighting the fact that the third animation is also declared in a named `BeginStoryboard` that has its `HandoffBehavior` property set to `Compose`.

The next `Trigger` object will start its associated storyboard when the `IsPressed` property of the `Button` element is true and as it is declared within the `EnterActions` collection, it will start when the user presses the mouse button down, rather than upon its release.

This animation also uses indirect targeting to reference the `Background` property of the `InnerBorder` element and also has a named `BeginStoryboard` object with its `HandoffBehavior` property set to `Compose`. Unlike the other animations, this one has an extended duration and also sets the `DecelerationRatio` property to `1.0`, which results in quick start and slow end.

Finally, we reach the last trigger, which is an `EventTrigger` object that will be triggered when the `Button` object is unloaded. In this trigger, we remove the three named storyboards, thereby freeing the extra resources that they consume when using the `Compose` handoff behavior. This was the sole purpose for naming the three `BeginStoryboard` objects that reference the `Background` property.

When animating mouse over effects on buttons, we are not restricted to simply changing the background and border colors. The more imaginative that we can be, the more our applications will stand out from the crowd.

For example, rather than simply changing the background colour of the button, we can instead move the focal point of the gradient with the mouse. We'll need to use some code to do this, so we'll need to create another custom control to demonstrate this point. Let's first look at the code from our new custom control:

```
using System.Windows;
using System.Windows.Controls;
using System.Windows.Controls.Primitives;
using System.Windows.Input;
using System.Windows.Media;
using CompanyName.ApplicationName.CustomControls.Enums;

namespace CompanyName.ApplicationName.CustomControls
{
  [TemplatePart(Name = "PART_Root", Type = typeof(Grid))]
  public class GlowButton : ButtonBase
  {
    private RadialGradientBrush glowBrush = null;

    static GlowButton()
    {
      DefaultStyleKeyProperty.OverrideMetadata(typeof(GlowButton),
        new FrameworkPropertyMetadata(typeof(GlowButton)));
    }
```

```
public GlowMode GlowMode { get; set; } = GlowMode.FullCenterMovement;

public static readonly DependencyProperty GlowColorProperty =
  DependencyProperty.Register(nameof(GlowColor), typeof(Color),
  typeof(GlowButton), new PropertyMetadata(
  Color.FromArgb(121, 71, 0, 255), OnGlowColorChanged));

public Color GlowColor
{
  get { return (Color)GetValue(GlowColorProperty); }
  set { SetValue(GlowColorProperty, value); }
}

private static void OnGlowColorChanged(
  DependencyObject dependencyObject,
  DependencyPropertyChangedEventArgs e)
{
  ((GlowButton)dependencyObject).SetGlowColor((Color)e.NewValue);
}

public override void OnApplyTemplate()
{
  Grid rootGrid = GetTemplateChild("PART_Root") as Grid;
  if (rootGrid != null)
  {
    rootGrid.MouseMove += Grid_MouseMove;
    glowBrush =
      (RadialGradientBrush)rootGrid.FindResource("GlowBrush");
    SetGlowColor(GlowColor);
  }
}

private void SetGlowColor(Color value)
{
  GlowColor = Color.FromArgb(121, value.R, value.G, value.B);
  if (glowBrush != null)
  {
    GradientStop gradientStop = glowBrush.GradientStops[2];
    gradientStop.Color = GlowColor;
  }
}

private void Grid_MouseMove(object sender, MouseEventArgs e)
{
  Grid grid = (Grid)sender;
  if (grid.IsMouseOver && glowBrush != null)
  {
    Point mousePosition = e.GetPosition(grid);
```

```
        double x = mousePosition.X / ActualWidth;
        double y = GlowMode != GlowMode.HorizontalCenterMovement ?
          mousePosition.Y / ActualHeight : glowBrush.Center.Y;
        glowBrush.Center = new Point(x, y);
        if (GlowMode == GlowMode.HorizontalCenterMovement)
          glowBrush.GradientOrigin =
          new Point(x, glowBrush.GradientOrigin.Y);
        else if (GlowMode == GlowMode.FullCenterMovement)
          glowBrush.GradientOrigin = new Point(x, y);
      }
    }
  }
}
```

We start as usual, by adding the relevant using references and declaring the
`PART_RootGrid` panel element as being a required part of the control template in the
`TemplatePartAttribute` attribute. As our custom control is a button, we extend the
`ButtonBase` class.

Next, we define the `glowBrush` field and set it to null. In the static constructor, we call the
`OverrideMetadata` method to inform the Framework of where our control's default style
is. We then declare a `GlowMode` CLR property of type `GlowMode` and set it to the default
`FullCenterMovement` member. Let's see the members of this `GlowMode` enumeration now.

```
namespace CompanyName.ApplicationName.CustomControls.Enums
{
  public enum GlowMode
  {
    NoCenterMovement, HorizontalCenterMovement, FullCenterMovement
  }
}
```

Returning to our `GlowButton` class, we also declare a `GlowColor` Dependency Property
and define a default purple color, a property changed handler and some CLR property
wrappers for it. In the `OnGlowColorChanged` handler method, we cast the
`dependencyObject` input parameter to our `GlowButton` class and call the `SetGlowColor`
method, passing in the new `Color` input value.

Next, we see the `OnApplyTemplate` method that is called when the button element's
control template has been applied. In this method, we attempt to access the `PART_Root`
panel element using the `GetTemplateChild` method and check it for null. If it is not null,
we do a number of things.

First, we attach the `Grid_MouseMove` event handler method to the grid's `MouseMove` event. Note that this is the way to attach event handlers to the UI elements that are declared in the `Generic.xaml` file, as it has no related code behind file.

Next, we call the grid's `FindResource` method in order to access the `GlowBrush` resource from its `Resources` section and set it to our local `glowBrush` field, as we will be referencing it regularly. After this, we call the `SetGlowColor` method and pass in the current `GlowColor` value.

We do this because the `OnApplyTemplate` method is generally called after the properties have been set, but we are unable to update the brush resource until the template has been applied. When writing custom controls, we often need to update properties from this method, once the template has been applied.

Next is the `SetGlowColor` method and in it, we first make the set color semi-transparent. If the `glowBrush` variable is not null, we then access the third `GradientStop` element from its `GradientStops` collection and set its `Color` property to the value of our `GlowColor` property.

Note that the third `GradientStop` element represents the dominant color in this gradient and so in this example, we are only updating this single element, in order to save space in this book. This gives the overall impression of a complete color change, but anyone that looks carefully will be able to see a dash of purple showing through from the other two unchanged `GradientStop` elements. You may wish to extend this example to update the whole `GradientStops` collection.

Next, we see the `Grid_MouseMove` event handling method that was attached to the `rootGrid` variable in the `OnApplyTemplate` method. In it, we check that the mouse is currently over the grid and that the `glowBrush` variable is not null. If these conditions are true, we call the `GetPosition` method on the `MouseEventArgs` input parameter to get the current position of the mouse.

Using the mouse position and the current value of the `GlowMode` property, we determine the movement mode and update the position of the `glowBrush` field's `Center` and/or `GradientOrigin` properties. This has the effect of moving the center and/or the focal point of the gradient with the mouse cursor when it is over our glow button. Let's see the XAML in the `Generic.xaml` file now:

```
<Style TargetType="{x:Type CustomControls:GlowButton}">
  <Setter Property="Template">
    <Setter.Value>
      <ControlTemplate TargetType="{x:Type CustomControls:GlowButton}">
        <Grid Name="PART_Root">
```

```xml
<Grid.Resources>
  <RadialGradientBrush x:Key="GlowBrush"
    RadiusY="0.622" Center="0.5,0.848"
    GradientOrigin="0.5,0.818" RadiusX="1.5">
    <RadialGradientBrush.RelativeTransform>
      <ScaleTransform x:Name="ScaleTransform"
        CenterX="0.5" CenterY="0.5" ScaleX="1.0" ScaleY="1.8" />
    </RadialGradientBrush.RelativeTransform>
    <GradientStop Color="#B9F6F2FF" />
    <GradientStop Color="#A9F4EFFF" Offset="0.099" />
    <GradientStop Color="{Binding GlowColor}" Offset="0.608" />
    <GradientStop Offset="1" Color="#004700FF" />
  </RadialGradientBrush>
  <RadialGradientBrush x:Key="LayeredButtonBackgroundBrush"
    RadiusX="1.85" RadiusY="0.796" Center="1.018, -0.115"
    GradientOrigin="0.65,-0.139">
    <GradientStop Color="#FFCACACD" />
    <GradientStop Color="#FF3B3D42"  Offset="1" />
  </RadialGradientBrush>
  <LinearGradientBrush x:Key="LayeredButtonCurveBrush"
    StartPoint="0,0" EndPoint="1,1">
    <GradientStop Color="#FF747475" Offset="0" />
    <GradientStop Color="#FF3B3D42" Offset="1" />
  </LinearGradientBrush>
  <Grid x:Key="LayeredButtonBackgroundElements">
    <Rectangle
      Fill="{StaticResource LayeredButtonBackgroundBrush}" />
    <Path StrokeThickness="0"
      Fill="{StaticResource LayeredButtonCurveBrush}">
      <Path.Data>
        <CombinedGeometry GeometryCombineMode="Intersect">
          <CombinedGeometry.Geometry1>
            <EllipseGeometry Center="-20,50.7" RadiusX="185"
              RadiusY="46" />
          </CombinedGeometry.Geometry1>
          <CombinedGeometry.Geometry2>
            <RectangleGeometry Rect="0,0,106,24" />
          </CombinedGeometry.Geometry2>
        </CombinedGeometry>
      </Path.Data>
    </Path>
  </Grid>
  <VisualBrush x:Key="LayeredButtonBackground"
    Visual="{StaticResource LayeredButtonBackgroundElements}" />
</Grid.Resources>
<Border CornerRadius="3" BorderBrush="#7F000000"
  BorderThickness="1" Background="#7FFFFFFF"
  SnapsToDevicePixels="True">
```

```
      <Border CornerRadius="2" Margin="1"
        Background="{StaticResource LayeredButtonBackground}"
        SnapsToDevicePixels="True">
        <Grid>
          <Rectangle x:Name="Glow" IsHitTestVisible="False"
            RadiusX="2" RadiusY="2"
            Fill="{StaticResource GlowBrush}" Opacity="0" />
          <ContentPresenter Content="{TemplateBinding Content}"
            Margin="{TemplateBinding Padding}"
            HorizontalAlignment="Center"
            VerticalAlignment="Center" />
        </Grid>
      </Border>
    </Border>
    <Grid.Triggers>
      <EventTrigger RoutedEvent="MouseEnter">
        <BeginStoryboard>
          <Storyboard>
            <DoubleAnimation Storyboard.TargetName="Glow"
              Storyboard.TargetProperty="Opacity" To="1.0"
              Duration="0:0:0.5" DecelerationRatio="1" />
          </Storyboard>
        </BeginStoryboard>
      </EventTrigger>
      <EventTrigger RoutedEvent="MouseLeave">
        <BeginStoryboard>
          <Storyboard>
            <DoubleAnimation Storyboard.TargetName="Glow"
              Storyboard.TargetProperty="Opacity" To="0.0"
              Duration="0:0:1" DecelerationRatio="1" />
          </Storyboard>
        </BeginStoryboard>
      </EventTrigger>
      <EventTrigger RoutedEvent="MouseDown">
        <BeginStoryboard>
          <Storyboard>
            <DoubleAnimation Storyboard.TargetName="ScaleTransform"
              Storyboard.TargetProperty="ScaleX" From="10.0"
              To="1.0" Duration="0:0:0.15" AccelerationRatio="0.5" />
            <DoubleAnimation Storyboard.TargetName="ScaleTransform"
              Storyboard.TargetProperty="ScaleY" From="10.0"
              To="1.8" Duration="0:0:0.15" AccelerationRatio="0.5" />
          </Storyboard>
        </BeginStoryboard>
      </EventTrigger>
    </Grid.Triggers>
  </Grid>
</ControlTemplate>
```

```
            </Setter.Value>
        </Setter>
    </Style>
```

Inside this `ControlTemplate`, we see the `Grid` named `PART_Root` and inside it, we see some resources declared within its `Resources` section. Much of this XAML is taken up by the same resources that we used in our layered button background example, so we can skip their explanation.

There is however, one new resource of type `RadialGradientBrush` and named `GlowBrush`. This is the brush that puts the color into our button. In particular, note that its `RelativeTransform` property is set to a `ScaleTransform` element named `ScaleTransform` and that its third `GradientStop` object is data bound to the `GlowColor` property from our control.

In the actual template, we see our double `Border` elements with their `SnapsToDevicePixels` properties set to true to ensure a sharp rendered image. Again, the outer border has a larger `CornerRadius` value than the inner border to ensure their tight fit together and the inner border's background is painted with the `LayeredButtonBackground` visual brush.

Inside the inner border, we have a `Grid` panel that contains a `Rectangle` element and the required `ContentPresenter` object. We use the `GlowBrush` resource to paint the background of the rectangle and set its `IsHitTestVisible` property to `false`, so that it takes no part in user interaction. Note that in this example, we set its `Opacity` property to zero to make it initially invisible.

We data bind the button's `Content` and `Padding` properties to the `Content` and `Margin` properties of the `ContentPresenter` element respectively, and center it within the control. That completes the visual markup for our glow button and now, we reach the all-important `Grid.Triggers` collection, where we declare three `EventTrigger` objects to trigger our mouse over effects.

The first trigger starts its associated storyboard when the `MouseEnter` event is raised. It's associated `DoubleAnimation` object animates the 'glowing' rectangle's `Opacity` property to `1.0` over half a second. Note that we omit the `From` property here, so that the `Opacity` value will start animating from its current value, rather than jumping back to `0.0` each time it starts the animation.

The second trigger starts its storyboard when the `MouseLeave` event is raised. It's `DoubleAnimation` object animates the rectangle's `Opacity` property back to `0.0` over a whole second. Note that we also omit the `From` property here, so that the `Opacity` value will start animating from its current value, rather than jumping to `1.0` each time it starts its animation. This ensures a smoother transition.

The third trigger starts its storyboard when the `MouseDown` event is raised and it contains two `DoubleAnimation` objects. They animate the `ScaleX` and `ScaleY` properties of the `ScaleTransform` object from `10.0` to their usual values over one hundred and fifty milliseconds, which produces an interesting effect when the user clicks the button.

Using the `GlowColor` and `GlowMode` properties, we can produce a wide range of buttons and interaction effects. After defining the relevant XAML namespace in our View, we can use this glow button example in the following way:

```
<CustomControls:GlowButton Content="Glowing button"
    GlowMode="NoCenterMovement" GlowColor="Red" FontSize="28"
    Foreground="White" Height="60" Width="275" />
```

When our example is run, it can produce mouse over effects, which vary depending on the position of the mouse cursor, as shown in the following examples:

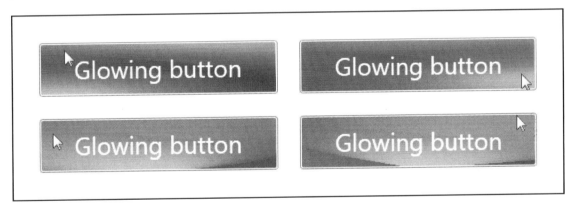

The top left image illustrates the `HorizontalCenterMovement` mode, the top right shows the `FullCenterMovement` mode and the bottom two highlight two mouse positions when using the `NoCenterMovement` mode. The top two use the default color and the bottom two were rendered using a `GlowColor` of `Red`. This reveals the differences between the various `GlowMode` values in our example.

Summary

In this chapter, we investigated a number of techniques that we can use to improve the look of our applications, from simply adding shadows to implementing far more complicated layered visuals. We saw the importance of remaining consistent throughout our application and how to get that professional look.

We then looked at more advanced techniques for making our application stand out from the crowd and saw further examples of how to create a variety of custom controls. We finished with a look at how we can incorporate animations into our everyday controls, in order to bring about a sense of exclusivity to our applications.

In the following chapter, we're going to investigate a number of ways that we can validate the data in our applications. We'll examine the various validation interfaces that are available to us in WPF and work on extending our application framework with a complete validation system using data annotations.

8

Implementing Responsive Data Validation

Data validation goes hand in hand with data input forms and is essential to promote clean, usable data. While the UI controls in WPF can automatically validate that entered values match the type of their data bound properties, they cannot validate for the correctness of the entered data.

For example, a `TextBox` control that is data bound to an integer may highlight an error if a user entered a non-numeric value, but it wouldn't validate that the entered number had the correct number of digits in, or that the first four digits were appropriate for the type of credit card specified.

In order to validate these types of data correctness when using MVVM, we'll need to implement one of the .NET validation interfaces. In this chapter, we'll thoroughly examine the available interfaces, looking at a number of implementations and explore the other validation related features that WPF provides us with. Let's start by looking at the validation system.

In WPF, the validation system very much revolves around the static `Validation` class. This class has several Attached Properties, methods and an Attached Event that support data validation. Each binding instance has a `ValidationRules` collection that can contain `ValidationRule` elements.

WPF provides three built-in rules; the `ExceptionValidationRule` object checks for any exceptions thrown as the binding source property is updated, the `DataErrorValidationRule` class checks for errors that may be raised by classes that implement the `IDataErrorInfo` interface and the `NotifyDataErrorValidationRule` class checks for errors raised by classes that implement the `INotifyDataErrorInfo` interface.

Each time an attempt is made to update a data source property, the binding engine first clears the `Validation.Errors` collection and then checks the binding's `ValidationRules` collection to see if it contains any `ValidationRule` elements. If it does, it calls each rule's `Validate` method in turn until they all pass, or one returns an error.

When a data bound value fails the condition in the `Validation` method of a `ValidationRule` element, the binding engine adds a new `ValidationError` object to the `Validation.Errors` collection of the data binding target control.

This in turn, will set the `Validation.HasError` Attached Property of the element to `true` and if the `NotifyOnValidationError` property of the binding is set to `true`, the binding engine will also raise the `Validation.Error` Attached Event on the data binding target.

Using validation rules – To do or not to do?

In WPF, there are two different approaches for dealing with data validation. On the one hand, we have the UI-based `ValidationRule` classes, the `Validation.Error` Attached Event and the `Binding.NotifyOnValidationError` and `UpdateSourceExceptionFilter` properties and on the other, we have two code-based validation interfaces.

While the `ValidationRule` classes and their related validation approach work perfectly well, they are specified in the XAML and as such, are tied to the UI. Furthermore, when using the `ValidationRule` classes, we are effectively separating the validation logic from the data models that they are validating and storing it in a completely different assembly.

When developing a WPF application using the MVVM methodology, we work with data, rather than UI elements and so, we tend to shy away from using the `ValidationRule` classes and their related validation strategy directly.

Additionally, the `NotifyOnValidationError` and `UpdateSourceExceptionFilter` properties of the `Binding` class also require event or delegate handlers respectively and as we have discovered, we prefer to avoid doing this when using MVVM. Therefore, we will not be looking at this UI-based validation approach in this book, instead focusing on the two code-based validation interfaces.

Getting to grips with validation interfaces

In WPF, we have access to two main validation interfaces; the original one is the IDataErrorInfo interface and in .NET 4.5, the INotifyDataErrorInfo interface was added. In this section, we'll first investigate the original validation interface and its shortcomings and see how we can make it more usable, before examining the latter.

Implementing the IDataErrorInfo interface

The IDataErrorInfo interface is a very simple affair, with only two required properties to implement. The Error property returns the error message that describes the validation error and the Item[string] indexer returns the error message for the specified property.

It certainly seems straight forward enough, so let's take a look at a basic implementation of this interface. Let's create another base class to implement this in and for now, omit all other unrelated base class members, so that we can concentrate on this interface.

```
using System.ComponentModel;
using System.Runtime.CompilerServices;

namespace CompanyName.ApplicationName.DataModels
{
  public abstract class BaseValidationModel : INotifyPropertyChanged,
    IDataErrorInfo
  {
    protected string error = string.Empty;

    #region IDataErrorInfo Members

    public string Error => error;

    public virtual string this[string propertyName] => error;

    #endregion

    #region INotifyPropertyChanged Members

    ...

    #endregion
  }
}
```

In this simplest of implementations, we have declared a protected `error` field, that will be accessible to derived classes. Note that the `Error` property that returns it uses the C# 6.0 expression bodied property syntax. This new syntax is nothing but a shorthand notation for simple methods or getter only properties that return something, where the member body is replaced with an inline expression.

We have declared the class indexer (the `this` property) as `virtual`, so that we can override it in the derived classes. Another option would be to declare it as `abstract`, so that derived classes were forced to override it. Whether you prefer to use `virtual` or `abstract` will depend on your particular circumstances, such as whether you expect every derived class to need validation or not.

Let's take a look at an example of a class that derives from our new base class:

```
using System;

namespace CompanyName.ApplicationName.DataModels
{
  public class Product : BaseValidationModel
  {
    private Guid id = Guid.Empty;
    private string name = string.Empty;
    private decimal price = 0;

    public Guid Id
    {
      get { return id; }
      set { if (id != value) { id = value; NotifyPropertyChanged(); } }
    }

    public string Name
    {
      get { return name; }
      set { if (name != value) { name = value; NotifyPropertyChanged(); } }
    }

    public decimal Price
    {
      get { return price; }
      set { if (price != value) { price = value;
        NotifyPropertyChanged(); } }
    }

    public override string this[string propertyName]
    {
      get
```

```
    {
      error = string.Empty;
      if (propertyName == nameof(Name))
      {
        if (string.IsNullOrEmpty(Name))
          error = "Please enter the product name.";
        else if (Name.Length > 25) error = "The product name cannot be
          longer than twenty-five characters.";
      }
      else if (propertyName == nameof(Price) && Price == 0)
        error = "Please enter a valid price for the product.";
      return error;
    }
  }
 }
}
```

Here we have a basic `Product` class that extends our new base class. The only job that each derived class that wants to participate in the validation process needs to do is to override the class indexer and supply details regarding their relevant validation logic.

In the indexer, we first set the `error` field to an empty string. Note that this is an essential part of this implementation, as without it, any triggered validation errors would never be cleared. There are a number of ways to implement this method, with several different abstractions being possible. However, all implementations require validation logic to be run when this property is called.

In our particular example, we simply use an `if` statement to check for errors in each property, although a `switch` statement works just as well here. The first condition checks the value of the `propertyName` input parameter, while multiple validation rules per property can be handled with inner `if` statements.

If the `propertyName` input parameter equals `Name`, then we first check to ensure that it has some value and provide an error message in case of failure. If the property value is not null or empty, then a second validation condition checks that the length is no longer than twenty-five characters, which simulates a particular database constraint that we may have.

If the `propertyName` input parameter equals `Price`, then we simply check that a valid, positive value has been entered and provide another error message in case of failure. If we had further properties in this class, then we would simply add further `if` conditions, checking their property names, and further relevant validation checks.

Now that we have our validatable class, let's add a new View and View Model and the `DataTemplate` in the `App.xaml` file that connects the two, to demonstrate what else we need to do to get our validation logic connected to the data in the UI. Let's first see the `ProductViewModel` class:

```
using CompanyName.ApplicationName.DataModels;

namespace CompanyName.ApplicationName.ViewModels
{
  public class ProductViewModel : BaseViewModel
  {
    private Product product = new Product();

    public Product Product
    {
      get { return product; }
      set { if (product != value) { product = value;
        NotifyPropertyChanged(); } }
    }
  }
}
```

The `ProductViewModel` class simply defines a single `Product` object and exposes it via the `Product` property. Let's now see the related View.

```
<UserControl x:Class="CompanyName.ApplicationName.Views.ProductView"
  xmlns="http://schemas.microsoft.com/winfx/2006/xaml/presentation"
  xmlns:x="http://schemas.microsoft.com/winfx/2006/xaml"
  xmlns:mc="http://schemas.openxmlformats.org/markup-compatibility/2006"
  xmlns:d="http://schemas.microsoft.com/expression/blend/2008"
  mc:Ignorable="d" FontSize="14" Width="600">
  <Grid Margin="20">
    <Grid.Resources>
      <Style x:Key="LabelStyle" TargetType="{x:Type TextBlock}">
        <Setter Property="HorizontalAlignment" Value="Right" />
        <Setter Property="VerticalAlignment" Value="Center" />
        <Setter Property="Margin" Value="0,0,10,10" />
      </Style>
      <Style x:Key="TextBoxStyle" TargetType="{x:Type TextBox}">
        <Setter Property="SnapsToDevicePixels" Value="True" />
        <Setter Property="VerticalAlignment" Value="Center" />
        <Setter Property="Margin" Value="0,0,0,10" />
        <Setter Property="Padding" Value="1.5,2" />
      </Style>
    </Grid.Resources>
    <Grid.RowDefinitions>
      <RowDefinition Height="Auto" />
```

```
          <RowDefinition Height="Auto" />
      </Grid.RowDefinitions>
      <Grid.ColumnDefinitions>
          <ColumnDefinition Width="Auto" />
          <ColumnDefinition />
      </Grid.ColumnDefinitions>
      <TextBlock Text="Name" Style="{StaticResource LabelStyle}" />
      <TextBox Grid.Column="1" Text="{Binding Product.Name,
          UpdateSourceTrigger=PropertyChanged, ValidatesOnDataErrors=True}"
          Style="{StaticResource TextBoxStyle}" />
      <TextBlock Grid.Row="1" Text="Price"
          Style="{StaticResource LabelStyle}" />
      <TextBox Grid.Row="1" Grid.Column="1" Text="{Binding Product.Price,
          UpdateSourceTrigger=PropertyChanged, ValidatesOnDataErrors=True}"
          Style="{StaticResource TextBoxStyle}" />
    </Grid>
  </UserControl>
```

In this example, note that we have added some styles into the `Grid.Resources` section for completeness, although in a production application, these styles would be declared in the application resources instead, where all Views would have access to them.

In the XAML, we have a typical two column `Grid` panel, with two rows. The two `TextBlock` labels have the `LabelStyle` style applied and the two `TextBox` input controls have the `TextBoxStyle` style applied. The binding applied to each `TextBox.Text` property has two important properties set on it.

The first is the `UpdateSourceTrigger` property and this controls when the data source is updated and therefore, also when validation occurs. If you remember, a value of `PropertyChanged` causes updates to occur as soon as the data bound property value changes. An alternative value would be `LostFocus`, which cause updates to occur when the UI control loses focus.

The other important property here is the `ValidatesOnDataErrors` property, without which, our current example would not work. Setting this property to `true` on a binding causes a built-in `DataErrorValidationRule` element to be implicitly added to the `Binding.ValidationRules` collection.

As the data bound value changes, this element will check for errors raised by the `IDataErrorInfo` interface. It does this by calling the indexer in our data model with the name of the data bound property each time the data source is updated. Therefore, in this basic example, the developers would be responsible for setting this property to `true` on each binding to make the validation work.

When using a value of `PropertyChanged` for the `UpdateSourceTrigger` property, along with the fact that we validate each time the properties change, we have the benefit of immediate updates of errors. However, this method of validation works in a pre-emptive manner, with all validation errors being shown before the user has a chance to enter any data. This can be somewhat off-putting to a user, so let's take a quick look at our example when it first starts.

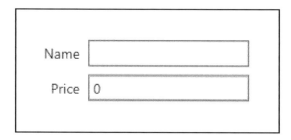

As you can see, it's clear that there are some problems, but it's unclear as to what they are. So far, we have no output for our error messages. One common output that we could use would be the tooltips of the various form controls.

We could add a trigger to our `TextBoxStyle` style that listened to the `Validation.HasError` Attached Property and set the textbox's tooltip to the `ErrorContent` property of the error whenever one was present. This is how Microsoft demonstrates how to do this on their MSDN website:

```
<Style.Triggers>
  <Trigger Property="Validation.HasError" Value="True">
    <Setter Property="ToolTip" Value="{Binding (Validation.Errors)[0].
      ErrorContent, RelativeSource={RelativeSource Self}}" />
  </Trigger>
</Style.Triggers>
```

Note that we use brackets in the binding path for the `Validation.Errors` collection because it is an Attached Property and that we use the `RelativeSource.Self` instance because we want to target the `Errors` collection of the `TextBox` control itself. Also note that this example only displays the first `ValidationError` object in the `Errors` collection.

Using this style on our data bound textboxes helps to provide the user with further information when they position their mouse cursor over the relevant control(s).

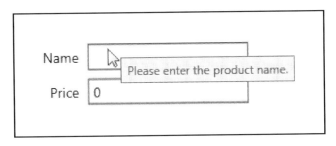

However, when there are no validation errors to display, an error will be seen in the **Output** window of Visual Studio, because we are attempting to view the first error from the `Validation.Errors` Attached Property collection and it does not exist:

```
System.Windows.Data Error: 17 : Cannot get 'Item[]' value (type
'ValidationError') from '(Validation.Errors)' (type
'ReadOnlyObservableCollection`1'). BindingExpression:
Path=(Validation.Errors)[0].ErrorContent; DataItem='TextBox' (Name='');
target element is 'TextBox' (Name=''); target property is 'ToolTip' (type
'Object') ArgumentOutOfRangeException: 'System.ArgumentOutOfRangeException:
Specified argument was out of the range of valid values.
Parameter name: index'
```

There are a number of ways to avoid this error, such as simply displaying the whole collection, and we'll see an example of this later in the chapter. However, the simplest way is to make use of the `CurrentItem` property of the `ICollectionView` object that is implicitly used to wrap `IEnumerable` data collections that are data bound to `ItemsControl` elements.

This is similar to the way that a `ListBox` will implicitly wrap our data bound data items in `ListBoxItem` elements. The implementation of the `ICollectionView` interface that wraps our data collection is primarily used to enable sorting, filtering and grouping of the data, without affecting the actual data, but its `CurrentItem` property is a bonus in this situation.

With it, we can replace the indexer that was causing us a problem when there were no validation errors. Now, when there are no errors, the `CurrentItem` property will return null, rather than throwing an exception and so, despite Microsoft's own examples showing the use of the indexer, this is a far better solution.

```
<Setter Property="ToolTip" Value="{Binding (Validation.Errors).
    CurrentItem.ErrorContent, RelativeSource={RelativeSource Self}}" />
```

Nevertheless, if an end user does not know to place their mouse cursor over the control to see the tooltip, then the situation is still not improved. Therefore, this initial implementation still has room for improvement. Another shortcoming of this interface is that it was designed to be atomic, as it only deals with a single error per property at a time.

In our example, we want to validate that the Name property is not only entered, but also has a valid length. In the order that we declared our two validation conditions for this property, the first error will be raised when the field in the UI is empty and the second will be raised if the entered value is too long. As the entered value cannot be both non-existent and too long at the same time, having only a single reported error at one time is not a problem in this particular example.

However, if we had a property that had multiple validation conditions, such as a maximum length and a particular format, then with the usual IDataErrorInfo interface implementation, we'd only be able to view one of these errors at once. However, despite this limitation, we can still improve this basic implementation. Let's see how we can do this:

```
using System.Collections.ObjectModel;
using System.Collections.Specialized;
using System.ComponentModel;
using System.Linq;
using System.Runtime.CompilerServices;
using System.Text;
using CompanyName.ApplicationName.Extensions;

namespace CompanyName.ApplicationName.DataModels
{
  public abstract class BaseValidationModelExtended :
    INotifyPropertyChanged, IDataErrorInfo
  {
    protected ObservableCollection<string> errors =
      new ObservableCollection<string>();
    protected ObservableCollection<string> externalErrors =
      new ObservableCollection<string>();

    protected BaseValidationModelExtended()
    {
      ExternalErrors.CollectionChanged += ExternalErrors_CollectionChanged;
    }

    public virtual ObservableCollection<string> Errors => errors;

    public ObservableCollection<string> ExternalErrors => externalErrors;

    public virtual bool HasError => errors != null && Errors.Any();
```

```
#region IDataErrorInfo Members

public string Error
{
  get
  {
    if (!HasError) return string.Empty;
    StringBuilder errors = new StringBuilder();
    Errors.ForEach(e => errors.AppendUniqueOnNewLineIfNotEmpty(e));
    return errors.ToString();
  }
}

public virtual string this[string propertyName] => string.Empty;

#endregion

#region INotifyPropertyChanged Members

public virtual event PropertyChangedEventHandler PropertyChanged;
protected virtual void NotifyPropertyChanged(
  params string[] propertyNames)
{
  if (PropertyChanged != null)
  {
    foreach (string propertyName in propertyNames)
    {
      if (propertyName != nameof(HasError)) PropertyChanged(this,
        new PropertyChangedEventArgs(propertyName));
    }
    PropertyChanged(this,
      new PropertyChangedEventArgs(nameof(HasError)));
  }
}

protected virtual void NotifyPropertyChanged(
  [CallerMemberName]string propertyName = "")
{
  if (PropertyChanged != null)
  {
    if (propertyName != nameof(HasError)) PropertyChanged(this,
      new PropertyChangedEventArgs(propertyName));
    PropertyChanged(this,
      new PropertyChangedEventArgs(nameof(HasError)));
  }
}

#endregion
```

```
    private void ExternalErrors_CollectionChanged(object sender,
      NotifyCollectionChangedEventArgs e) =>
      NotifyPropertyChanged(nameof(Errors));
  }
}
```

In this example, we add two collections to hold error messages; the `Errors` collection property contains validation errors that are generated within the derived class and the `ExternalErrors` collection property holds externally generated validation errors, typically from a parent View Model.

In the constructor, we attach the `ExternalErrors_CollectionChanged` event handler to the `CollectionChanged` event of the `ExternalErrors` collection property, so that it is notified whenever items are added or removed from it.

After the declaration of the error collection properties, we see the `HasError` expression bodied property, that checks whether the `Errors` collection contains any errors or not. Note that we check the `errors` field for null, rather than the `Errors` property, because we do not want to regenerate the error messages twice each time this property is called.

Next, we see the new implementation of the `IDataErrorInfo` interface. The class indexer remains the same as the one from the previous implementation, but we see a difference in the definition of the `Error` property, which now compiles a complete list of all errors, rather than returning a single error message at a time.

In it, we first check whether any errors exist and return an empty string if not. If errors do exist, we initialize a `StringBuilder` object and use our `ForEach` Extension method to iterate through the `Errors` collection and append each of them to it, if they haven't already been included. We do this using another Extension method before returning the output, so let's see what that looks like now.

```
public static void AppendUniqueOnNewLineIfNotEmpty(
  this StringBuilder stringBuilder, string text)
{
  if (text.Trim().Length > 0 && !stringBuilder.ToString().Contains(text))
    stringBuilder.AppendFormat("{0}{1}", stringBuilder.ToString().Trim().
    Length == 0 ? string.Empty : Environment.NewLine, text);
}
```

In our `AppendUniqueOnNewLineIfNotEmpty` Extension method, we first check that the input value is not an empty string and that it is not already present in the `StringBuilder` object. If the `text` input parameter is valid, we use the ternary operator to determine whether it is the first value to be added and whether we need to precede it with a new line or not, before adding the new, unique value.

Returning to our validation base class now, we see the new implementation of the `INotifyPropertyChanged` interface. Note that we repeat our earlier base class example, by raising the `PropertyChanged` event each time changes are registered for any other properties, but unlike the previous example, we raise the `HasError` property here rather than the `HasChanges` property.

We can combine both of these and raise the `PropertyChanged` event for both properties each time we receive notification of changes to other properties if we desire. In this case, the purpose is to call the `HasError` property, which will be used in the UI to display or hide the control that displays the error messages and so, it will be updated after every validatable property change.

At the bottom of our class, we see the expression bodied `ExternalErrors_CollectionChanged` method, which calls the `NotifyPropertyChanged` method for the `Errors` collection property. This notifies controls that are data bound to this property that its value has changed and that they should retrieve that new value. Let's see an example implementation of this from our `Product` class now:

```
public override ObservableCollection<string> Errors
{
  get
  {
    errors = new ObservableCollection<string>();
    errors.AddUniqueIfNotEmpty(this[nameof(Name)]);
    errors.AddUniqueIfNotEmpty(this[nameof(Price)]);
    errors.AddRange(ExternalErrors);
    return errors;
  }
}
```

Therefore, when an error is externally added to the `ExternalErrors` collection, the `ExternalErrors_CollectionChanged` method will be called and that notifies of changes to the `Errors` property. This results in the property being called and the external error(s) being added to the internal `errors` collection, along with any internal errors.

To get this particular implementation of the `IDataErrorInfo` interface to work, each data model class will need to override this `Errors` property to add error messages from each validated property. We provide a few Extension methods to make this task easier. As its name implies, the `AddUniqueIfNotEmpty` method adds strings to the collection if they do not already exist in it.

```
public static void AddUniqueIfNotEmpty(
  this ObservableCollection<string> collection, string text)
{
  if (!string.IsNullOrEmpty(text) && !collection.Contains(text))
    collection.Add(text);
}
```

The `AddRange` method is another useful Extension method that simply iterates through the `range` collection input parameter and adds them to the `collection` parameter one by one.

```
public static void AddRange<T>(this ICollection<T> collection,
  ICollection<T> range)
{
  foreach (T item in range) collection.Add(item);
}
```

In addition to implementing this new `Errors` collection property in their derived classes, developers will also need to ensure that they notify of changes to it each time a validatable property value is changed. We can do this using our overload of the `NotifyPropertyChanged` method that takes multiple values.

```
public string Name
{
  get { return name; }
  set { if (name != value) { name = value;
    NotifyPropertyChanged(nameof(Name), nameof(Errors)); } }
}

public decimal Price
{
  get { return price; }
  set { if (price != value) { price = value;
    NotifyPropertyChanged(nameof(Price), nameof(Errors)); } }
}
```

The `Errors` property is responsible for calling the class indexer with the name of each of the properties that we want to validate. Any error messages that are returned, including those from the `ExternalErrors` collection property, are then added to the internal `errors` collection.

In effect, we have replicated what the `Validation` class and the `DataErrorValidationRule` element does in the UI, but in our data model instead. This means that we no longer have to set the `ValidatesOnDataErrors` property to `true` on each binding. This is a better solution when using MVVM, as we prefer to work with data, rather than UI elements, and now also have full access to all of the data validation errors in our View Models.

Furthermore, we now have the ability to manually feed in error messages from our View Models to our data models via the `ExternalErrors` collection property. This can be very useful when we need to validate across a collection of data model objects.

For example, if we need to ensure that the name of each data model object is unique within a collection of related objects, we can use this feature. Let's update our `ProductViewModel` example to see how we can accomplish this:

```
using System;
using System.ComponentModel;
using System.Linq;
using CompanyName.ApplicationName.DataModels;
using CompanyName.ApplicationName.DataModels.Collections;

namespace CompanyName.ApplicationName.ViewModels
{
  public class ProductViewModel : BaseViewModel
  {
    private Products products = new Products();

    public ProductViewModel()
    {
      Products.Add(new Product() { Id = Guid.NewGuid(),
        Name = "Virtual Reality Headset", Price = 14.99m });
      Products.Add(new Product() { Id = Guid.NewGuid(),
        Name = "Virtual Reality Headset" });
      Products.CurrentItemChanged += Products_CurrentItemChanged;
      Products.CurrentItem = Products.Last();
      ValidateUniqueName(Products.CurrentItem);
    }

    public Products Products
    {
      get { return products; }
      set { if (products != value) { products = value;
        NotifyPropertyChanged(); } }
    }

    private void Products_CurrentItemChanged(Product oldProduct,
```

```
      Product newProduct)
    {
      if (newProduct != null)
        newProduct.PropertyChanged += Product_PropertyChanged;
      if (oldProduct != null)
        oldProduct.PropertyChanged -= Product_PropertyChanged;
    }

    private void Product_PropertyChanged(object sender,
      PropertyChangedEventArgs e)
    {
      if (e.PropertyName == "Name")
        ValidateUniqueName(Products.CurrentItem);
    }

    private void ValidateUniqueName(Product product)
    {
      string errorMessage = "The product name must be unique";
      if (!IsProductNameUnique(product))
        product.ExternalErrors.Add(errorMessage);
      else product.ExternalErrors.Remove(errorMessage);
    }

    private bool IsProductNameUnique(Product product) =>
      Products.Count(p => p.Id != product.Id && p.Name != string.Empty &&
      p.Name == product.Name) == 0;
  }
}
```

Our `ProductViewModel` class still extends the `BaseViewModel` class, but now it declares a `Products` collection and adds the original `Product` object to it in the constructor, along with an additional `Product` instance. The `Products` class simply extends our `BaseCollection` class.

```
namespace CompanyName.ApplicationName.DataModels.Collections
{
  public class Products : BaseCollection<Product> { }
}
```

In the class constructor, we first add a couple of test products to the `Products` collection and then attach the `Products_CurrentItemChanged` method to its `CurrentItemChanged` delegate. The `BaseCollection` class automatically sets the first item in each collection to the `CurrentItem` property, so in order to set the second item as the current item, we call the `Last` method on the `Products` collection and set that to its `CurrentItem` property.

This ensures that the `Products_CurrentItemChanged` method is called when setting the second item as the current item and the `Product_PropertyChanged` handler is attached to it. After this, we then call the `ValidateUniqueName` method that is described shortly, passing in the current item.

After the declaration of the `Products` property, we see the `Products_CurrentItemChanged` method, which will be called each time the value of the `CurrentItem` property is changed. In it, we attach the `Product_PropertyChanged` method to the `PropertyChanged` event of the new current `Product` object and detach it from the previous current `Product` item.

The `Product_PropertyChanged` method will be called each time any property of the related `Product` object changes. In it, we simply call the `ValidateUniqueName` method if the changed property was the `Name` property, as that is the property that we need to validate for uniqueness.

The `ValidateUniqueName` method is responsible for adding or removing the error from the `ExternalErrors` collection property of the `product` input parameter. It does this by checking the result of the `IsProductNameUnique` method, which does the actual check for uniqueness.

In the expression bodied `IsProductNameUnique` method, we use LINQ to query the `Products` collection and find out whether an existing item shares the same name or not. It does this by checking that each item does not have the same identification number, or in other words, is not the object being edited, but does have the same name and that the name is not an empty string.

If any other products that have the same name are found, then the method returns `false` and an error is added to the product's `ExternalErrors` collection in the `ValidateUniqueName` method. Let's update our earlier `ProductView` now to better display these errors:

```
<UserControl x:Class="CompanyName.ApplicationName.Views.ProductView"
  xmlns="http://schemas.microsoft.com/winfx/2006/xaml/presentation"
  xmlns:x="http://schemas.microsoft.com/winfx/2006/xaml"
  xmlns:mc="http://schemas.openxmlformats.org/markup-compatibility/2006"
  xmlns:d="http://schemas.microsoft.com/expression/blend/2008"
  xmlns:Converters="clr-namespace:CompanyName.ApplicationName.Converters;
    assembly=CompanyName.ApplicationName.Converters"
  mc:Ignorable="d" d:DesignHeight="300" Width="600" FontSize="14">
  <Grid Margin="20">
    <Grid.Resources>
      <Converters:BoolToVisibilityConverter
        x:Key="BoolToVisibilityConverter" />
```

```xml
      <DataTemplate x:Key="WrapTemplate">
        <TextBlock Text="{Binding}" TextWrapping="Wrap" />
      </DataTemplate>
      ...
    </Grid.Resources>
    <Grid.ColumnDefinitions>
      <ColumnDefinition />
      <ColumnDefinition />
    </Grid.ColumnDefinitions>
    <ListBox ItemsSource="{Binding Products}" SelectedItem="{Binding
      Products.CurrentItem}" DisplayMemberPath="Name" Margin="0,0,20,0" />
    <Grid Grid.Column="1">
      <Grid.RowDefinitions>
        <RowDefinition Height="Auto" />
        <RowDefinition Height="Auto" />
        <RowDefinition Height="Auto" />
      </Grid.RowDefinitions>
      <Grid.ColumnDefinitions>
        <ColumnDefinition Width="Auto" />
        <ColumnDefinition />
      </Grid.ColumnDefinitions>
      <Border Grid.ColumnSpan="2" BorderBrush="Red"
        BorderThickness="2" Background="#1FFF0000" CornerRadius="5"
        Visibility="{Binding Products.CurrentItem.HasError,
        Converter={StaticResource BoolToVisibilityConverter}}"
        Margin="0,0,0,10" Padding="10">
        <ItemsControl ItemsSource="{Binding Products.CurrentItem.Errors}"
          ItemTemplate="{StaticResource WrapTemplate}" />
      </Border>
      <TextBlock Grid.Row="1" Text="Name"
        Style="{StaticResource LabelStyle}" />
      <TextBox Grid.Row="1" Grid.Column="1"
        Text="{Binding Products.CurrentItem.Name,
        UpdateSourceTrigger=PropertyChanged}"
        Style="{StaticResource TextBoxStyle}" />
      <TextBlock Grid.Row="2" Text="Price"
        Style="{StaticResource LabelStyle}" />
      <TextBox Grid.Row="2" Grid.Column="1"
        Text="{Binding Products.CurrentItem.Price, Delay=250,
        UpdateSourceTrigger=PropertyChanged}"
        Style="{StaticResource TextBoxStyle}" />
    </Grid>
  </Grid>
</UserControl>
```

Note that the styles that were declared in the resources from the previous `ProductView` example have been omitted for brevity, although they are still used in this example. In addition, we defined a XAML namespace for our `Converters` project and declared a `BoolToVisibilityConverter` instance and a simple data template to wrap the text of the error items in our global error display.

In this example, we now have a `Grid` panel with two columns. In the left column, we have a `ListBox` control and in the right, we have another `Grid` panel with our form fields. The `ItemsSource` property of the `ListBox` control is data bound to the `Products` collection property from our View Model and the `SelectedItem` property is data bound to its `CurrentItem` property.

We set the `DisplayMemberPath` property to `Name` as a shortcut for creating a `DataTemplate` for our `Product` class that outputs the name of each product. Alternatively, we could have returned the value of the `Name` property from the `ToString` method in our `Product` class to achieve the same result.

In the `Grid` panel on the right, we declare three rows and in the top one, we define a `Border` element containing an `ItemsControl` object. Its `ItemsSource` property is data bound to the `Errors` collection property of the item that is set to the `CurrentItem` property of the `Products` collection and its `ItemTemplate` property is set to our new `WrapTemplate` data template. The `Visibility` property of the border is data bound to the item's `HasError` property using the `BoolToVisibilityConverter` instance from the resources.

Therefore, when a change is made to a validated property of the item and an error is raised in our validation base class, the `PropertyChanged` event is raised for the `HasError` property and this alerts this binding to check the latest value and update its visibility value via the applied `BoolToVisibilityConverter` instance accordingly.

Note that we use an `ItemsControl` here, because with this collection, we have no need for the extra features that the `ListBox` control provides us with, such as a border, or the notion of a selected item. The two rows underneath the error output contain the form fields from the original example.

When this example is run, we'll see two items that have the same name in our `ListBox` control. As such, there will already be a validation error displayed that highlights this fact and was added through the `ExternalErrors` collection in the View Model. In addition to this, we'll see another error, highlighting the fact that a valid price needs to be entered.

As the `UpdateSourceTrigger` property of the field bindings have been set to `PropertyChanged` and the data bound properties are validated straight away, the errors will immediately disappear and/or reappear as soon as we type in the relevant form fields. This setting, along with the fact that we validate each time the properties change, makes our validation work in a pre-emptive manner.

We can also change this to work only when a user presses a submit button, by setting the `UpdateSourceTrigger` property to the `Explicit` value. However, this requires that we access the data bound controls in the code behind files and so we tend to avoid this approach when using the MVVM methodology.

```
BindingExpression bindingExpression =
    NameOfTextBox.GetBindingExpression(TextBox.TextProperty);
bindingExpression.UpdateSource();
```

Alternatively, if we wanted to validate in this way when using MVVM, we could simply call the validation code when the command that is data bound to the submit or save button is executed instead. Let's now take a look at the `INotifyDataErrorInfo` interface, to see how it differs from the `IDataErrorInfo` interface.

Introducing the INotifyDataErrorInfo interface

The `INotifyDataErrorInfo` interface was added to the .NET Framework in .NET 4.5 to address concerns over the previous `IDataErrorInfo` interface. Like the `IDataErrorInfo` interface, the `INotifyDataErrorInfo` interface is also a simple affair, with only three members for us to implement.

With this interface, we now have a `HasErrors` property that indicates whether the relevant data model instance has any errors or not, a `GetErrors` method that replaces the indexer of the `IDataErrorInfo` interface and retrieves the object's error collection, and an `ErrorsChanged` event to raise when the entity's errors change.

We can see straight away that this interface was designed to work with multiple errors, unlike the `IDataErrorInfo` interface. However, past this fact, it is unclear how this interface should be implemented. Let's take a look at one possible implementation now.

```
using System;
using System.Collections;
using System.Collections.Generic;
using System.ComponentModel;
using System.Linq;
using System.Runtime.CompilerServices;
using CompanyName.ApplicationName.Extensions;
```

```
namespace CompanyName.ApplicationName.DataModels
{
  public abstract class BaseNotifyValidationModel : INotifyPropertyChanged,
    INotifyDataErrorInfo
  {
    private Dictionary<string, List<string>> allPropertyErrors =
      new Dictionary<string, List<string>>();

    protected Dictionary<string, List<string>> AllPropertyErrors =>
      allPropertyErrors;

    public abstract IEnumerable<string> this[string propertyName] { get; }

    public void NotifyPropertyChangedAndValidate(
      params string[] propertyNames)
    {
      foreach (string propertyName in propertyNames)
        NotifyPropertyChangedAndValidate(propertyName);
    }

    public void NotifyPropertyChangedAndValidate(
      [CallerMemberName]string propertyName = "")
    {
      NotifyPropertyChanged(propertyName);
      Validate(propertyName, this[propertyName]);
    }

    public void Validate(string propertyName, IEnumerable<string> error)
    {
      if (errors.Any())
        errors.ForEach(e => AddValidationError(propertyName, e));
      else if (AllPropertyErrors.ContainsKey(propertyName))
        RemoveValidationError(propertyName);
    }

    private void AddValidationError(string propertyName, string error)
    {
      if (AllPropertyErrors.ContainsKey(propertyName))
      {
        if (!AllPropertyErrors[propertyName].Contains(error))
        {
          AllPropertyErrors[propertyName].Add(error);
          OnErrorsChanged(propertyName);
        }
      }
      else
      {
        AllPropertyErrors.Add(propertyName, new List<string>() { error });
```

```
      OnErrorsChanged(propertyName);
   }
}

private void RemoveValidationError(string propertyName)
{
  AllPropertyErrors.Remove(propertyName);
  OnErrorsChanged(propertyName);
}

#region INotifyDataErrorInfo Members

public event EventHandler<DataErrorsChangedEventArgs> ErrorsChanged;

public void OnErrorsChanged(string propertyName) =>
  ErrorsChanged?.Invoke(this,
  new DataErrorsChangedEventArgs(propertyName));

public IEnumerable GetErrors(string propertyName)
{
  List<string> propertyErrors = new List<string>();
  if (string.IsNullOrEmpty(propertyName)) return propertyErrors;
  allPropertyErrors.TryGetValue(propertyName, out propertyErrors);
  return propertyErrors;
}

public bool HasErrors =>
  allPropertyErrors.Any(p => p.Value != null && p.Value.Any());

#endregion

#region INotifyPropertyChanged Members

public virtual event PropertyChangedEventHandler PropertyChanged;
protected virtual void NotifyPropertyChanged(
  params string[] propertyNames)
{
  if (PropertyChanged != null) propertyNames.ForEach(
    p => PropertyChanged(this, new PropertyChangedEventArgs(p)));
}

protected virtual void NotifyPropertyChanged(
  [CallerMemberName]string propertyName = "")
{
  PropertyChanged?.Invoke(this,
    new PropertyChangedEventArgs(propertyName));
}
```

```
    #endregion
  }
}
```

In our first implementation, we see the declaration of the `allPropertyErrors` backing field and the `AllPropertyErrors` expression bodied property that returns it. For this collection, we use the type `Dictionary<string, List<string>>`, where the name of each property in error is used as the dictionary key, and multiple errors for that property can be stored in the related string list.

We then see an abstract string indexer that returns an `IEnumerable` of type string, which is responsible for returning multiple validation errors from derived classes, that relate to the property specified by the `propertyName` input parameter. We'll see how we can implement this in the derived classes in the *Varying Levels of Validation* section shortly.

We add two convenient `NotifyPropertyChangedAndValidate` methods, that we can use to both notify of changes to our property and to validate it in a single operation. In these methods, we call our implementation of the `NotifyPropertyChanged` method and then our private `Validate` method, passing the relevant property name to both and the indexer error output to the `Validate` method.

If the `errors` collection input parameter in the `Validate` method contains any errors, we iterate through them, calling the `AddValidationError` method to add each of them, otherwise we call the `RemoveValidationError` method to remove any other errors, if they exist.

Next, we see the definition of the `AddValidationError` method, where we first check for the existence of an entry for the property name in the keys of the `AllPropertyErrors` dictionary object. If one exists, we then check whether the error already exists within the related list and if it doesn't, we add it and raise the `ErrorsChanged` event.

If there is no existing entry, we add a new one, along with a new string list containing the error, and raise the `ErrorsChanged` event. In the `RemoveValidationError` method, we remove the entry for the `propertyName` input parameter from the `AllPropertyErrors` dictionary and raise the `ErrorsChanged` event.

Next, we see the required `INotifyDataErrorInfo` interface members. We declare the `ErrorsChanged` event and the related `OnErrorsChanged` expression bodied method that raises it using the null conditional operator, although this method is not technically part of the interface and we are free to raise the event as we see fit.

In the `GetErrors` method, we are required to return the errors for the `propertyName` input parameter and so, we utilize the `TryGetValue` method of the `Dictionary` class to attempt to retrieve the relevant errors, if any exist. Note that attempting to retrieve values from a `Dictionary` object using a non-existent key directly will raise a `KeyNotFoundException` error, so we return the empty collection if the property name value is `null` or equals `string.Empty`.

The simplified `HasErrors` expression bodied property follows and simply returns `true` if the `allPropertyErrors` field contains any errors, or `false` otherwise. Finally, we complete the class with our default implementation of the `INotifyPropertyChanged` interface. Note that we can simply omit this if we intend this base class to extend another with its own implementation of this interface.

If we remove the call to the `Validate` method from the constructor of the `ProductViewModel` class, this implementation would no longer work in a pre-emptive manner. It would instead initially hide any pre-existing validation errors, such as empty required values, until the user makes changes and there is a problem. Therefore, empty required values would never cause an error to be raised, unless a value was entered and then deleted, to once again be empty.

We could instead declare a `ValidateAllProperties` method that our View Models can call to force a new validation pass, either pre-emptively, before the user has a chance to enter any data, or on the click of a save button once all fields have been filled. We'll see an example of this later in this chapter, but for now, let's see the updated XAML of our `ProductView` class:

```xml
<UserControl x:Class="CompanyName.ApplicationName.Views.ProductView"
    xmlns="http://schemas.microsoft.com/winfx/2006/xaml/presentation"
    xmlns:x="http://schemas.microsoft.com/winfx/2006/xaml"
    xmlns:mc="http://schemas.openxmlformats.org/markup-compatibility/2006"
    xmlns:d="http://schemas.microsoft.com/expression/blend/2008"
    xmlns:Converters="clr-namespace:CompanyName.ApplicationName.Converters;
      assembly=CompanyName.ApplicationName.Converters"
    mc:Ignorable="d" d:DesignHeight="300" Width="600" FontSize="14">
  <Grid Margin="20">
    <Grid.Resources>
      ...
    </Grid.Resources>
    <Grid.ColumnDefinitions>
      <ColumnDefinition />
      <ColumnDefinition />
    </Grid.ColumnDefinitions>
    <ListBox ItemsSource="{Binding Products}" SelectedItem="{Binding
      Products.CurrentItem}" DisplayMemberPath="Name" Margin="0,0,20,0" />
```

```
<Grid Grid.Column="1">
  <Grid.RowDefinitions>
    <RowDefinition Height="Auto" />
    <RowDefinition Height="Auto" />
    <RowDefinition Height="Auto" />
  </Grid.RowDefinitions>
  <Grid.ColumnDefinitions>
    <ColumnDefinition Width="Auto" />
    <ColumnDefinition />
  </Grid.ColumnDefinitions>
  <Border Grid.ColumnSpan="2" BorderBrush="Red"
    BorderThickness="2" Background="#1FFF0000" CornerRadius="5"
    Visibility="{Binding Products.CurrentItem.HasErrors,
    Converter={StaticResource BoolToVisibilityConverter}}"
    Margin="0,0,0,10" Padding="10">
    <ItemsControl ItemsSource="{Binding Products.CurrentItem.Errors}"
      ItemTemplate="{StaticResource WrapTemplate}" />
  </Border>
  <TextBlock Grid.Row="1" Text="Name"
    Style="{StaticResource LabelStyle}" />
  <TextBox Grid.Row="1" Grid.Column="1"
    Text="{Binding Products.CurrentItem.Name,
    UpdateSourceTrigger=PropertyChanged,
    ValidatesOnNotifyDataErrors=True}"
    Style="{StaticResource TextBoxStyle}" />
  <TextBlock Grid.Row="2" Text="Price"
    Style="{StaticResource LabelStyle}" />
  <TextBox Grid.Row="2" Grid.Column="1"
    Text="{Binding Products.CurrentItem.Price,
    UpdateSourceTrigger=PropertyChanged,
    ValidatesOnNotifyDataErrors=True, Delay=250}"
    Style="{StaticResource TextBoxStyle}" />
</Grid>
  </Grid>
</UserControl>
```

Once again, note that the styles that were declared in the resources from the previous `ProductView` example have been omitted here for brevity, although they are still used in this example. Another point to note is that the `Visibility` property of the global error display's border has now been updated to work with the new `HasErrors` from the `INotifyDataErrorInfo` interface, rather than our previous base class `HasError` property.

The only other change was made to the text binding of the two textboxes; when using the `INotifyDataErrorInfo` interface, instead of setting the `ValidatesOnDataErrors` property to `true` as before, we now need to set the `ValidatesOnNotifyDataErrors` property to `true`. We'll update this example again shortly, but before that, let's explore another method of providing validation logic.

Annotating data

The .NET Framework also provides us with an alternative, attribute-based validation system in the `System.ComponentModel.DataAnnotations` namespace. It is mostly comprised of a wide range of attribute classes that we can decorate our data model properties with, to specify our validation rules. In addition to these attributes, it also includes a few validation classes, which will investigate later.

As an example, let's look at replicating the current validation rules from our `Product` class with these data annotation attributes. We need to validate that the `Name` property is entered and has a length of twenty-five characters or less, and that the `Price` property is more than zero. For the `Name` property, we can use the `RequiredAttribute` and the `MaxLengthAttribute`.

```
[Required(ErrorMessage = "Please enter the product name.")]
[MaxLength(25, ErrorMessage = "The product name cannot be longer than
  twenty-five characters.")]
public string Name
{
  get { return name; }
  set { if (name != value) { name = value;
    NotifyPropertyChangedAndValidate(); } }
}
```

As with all attributes, we can omit the word `Attribute` when using them to decorate properties with. Most of these data annotation attributes declare one or more constructors with a number of optional parameters. The `ErrorMessage` input parameter is used in each to set the message to output when the specified condition is not met.

The `RequiredAttribute` constructor has no input parameters and simply checks that the data bound value is not null or empty. The constructor of the `MaxLengthAttribute` class takes an integer, that specifies the maximum allowable length of the data bound value and it will raise a `ValidationError` instance if the input value is longer.

For the `Price` property, we can make use of the `RangeAttribute` with a really high maximum value, as there is no `MinimumAttribute` class available.

```
[Range(0.01, (double)decimal.MaxValue,
  ErrorMessage = "Please enter a valid price for the product.")]
public decimal Price
{
  get { return price; }
  set { if (price != value) { price = value;
    NotifyPropertyChangedAndValidate(); } }
}
```

The constructor of the `RangeAttribute` class takes two double values, that specify the minimum and maximum valid values and in this example, we set the minimum to one penny and the maximum to the maximum decimal value, as our `Price` property is of type decimal. Note that we could not use the `RequiredAttribute` class here, as numeric data bound values will never be null or empty.

There are a large number of these data annotation attribute classes, covering the most common validation situations, but when we have a requirement that does not have a pre-existing attribute to help us, we can create our own custom attribute class by extending the `ValidationAttribute` class. Let's create an attribute that only validates a minimum value:

```
using System.ComponentModel.DataAnnotations;

namespace CompanyName.ApplicationName.DataModels.Attributes
{
  public class MinimumAttribute : ValidationAttribute
  {
    private double minimumValue = 0.0;

    public MinimumAttribute(double minimumValue)
    {
      this.minimumValue = minimumValue;
    }

    protected override ValidationResult IsValid(object value,
      ValidationContext validationContext)
    {
      if (value.GetType() != typeof(decimal) ||
        (decimal)value < (decimal)minimumValue)
      {
        string[] memberNames =
          new string[] { validationContext.MemberName };
        return new ValidationResult(ErrorMessage, memberNames);
```

```
        }
      return ValidationResult.Success;
    }
  }
}
```

When we extend the `ValidationAttribute` class, we only need to override the `IsValid` method to return `true` or `false`, depending on our input value, which is specified by the `value` input parameter. In our simple example, we first declare the `minimumValue` field to store the target minimum allowable value to use during validation.

We populate this field in the class constructor, with the value that users of our class provide. Next, we override the `IsValid` method that returns a `ValidationResult` instance. In this method, we first check the type of the `value` input parameter and then cast it to decimal, in order to compare it with the value of our `minimumValue` field.

Note that we have hardcoded this double type as the type of our minimum value, because although our `Price` property is decimal, the decimal type is not considered primitive and therefore cannot be used in an attribute. A better, more reusable solution, would be to declare a number of constructors that accept different numerical types that could be used in a wider range of situations and to update our `IsValid` method to be able to compare the different types with the input value.

In our example, if the input value is either the incorrect type, or the cast value is less than the value of the `minimumValue` field, we first create the `memberNames` variable and insert the value of the `MemberName` property from the `validationContext` input parameter. We then return a new instance of the `ValidationResult` class, inputting the used error message and our `memberNames` collection.

If the input value is valid according to our particular validation logic, then we simply return the `ValidationResult.Success` field to signify successful validation. Let's see our new attribute being used on the `Price` property of the `Product` class now:

```
[Minimum(0.01,
  ErrorMessage = "Please enter a valid price for the product.")]
public decimal Price
{
  get { return price; }
  set { if (price != value) { price = value;
    NotifyPropertyChangedAndValidate(); } }
}
```

In effect, our new attribute will work exactly as the previously used `RangeAttribute` instance, but it clearly demonstrates how we can create our own custom validation attributes. Before we move on to see how we can read these errors with our code, let's first see how we can access the value of a second property from the data model in our attribute, as this is a common requirement when validating:

```
PropertyInfo propertyInfo =
   validationContext.ObjectType.GetProperty(otherPropertyName);
if (propertyInfo == null) throw new ArgumentNullException(
   $"Unknown property: {otherPropertyName}");
object otherPropertyValue =
   propertyInfo.GetValue(validationContext.ObjectInstance);
```

This example assumes that we have added a reference to the `System` and `System.Reflection` namespaces and declared a string field named `otherPropertyName`, that is populated with the name of the other property name in the constructor. Using reflection, we attempt to access the `PropertyInfo` object that relates to the specified property name.

If the `PropertyInfo` object is null, we throw an `ArgumentNullException` object, alerting the developer that they have used in non-existent property name. Otherwise, we use the `GetValue` method of the `PropertyInfo` object to retrieve the value from the other property.

Now that we've seen how to use and create our own custom validation attributes, let's see how we can use them to validate our data model instances from one of their base classes:

```
ValidationContext validationContext = new ValidationContext(this);
validationContext.MemberName = propertyName;
List<ValidationResult> validationResults = new List<ValidationResult>();
Validator.TryValidateObject(this, validationContext, validationResults,
   true);
```

We start by initializing a `ValidationContext` object, passing in the data model instance from the base class. We can optionally set the `MemberName` property to set the name of the property to validate. The context object is then passed to the `TryValidateObject` method of the `Validator` class, in order to retrieve any validation errors from any of the data annotation attributes.

We also initialize and pass a list of type `ValidationResult` into the `TryValidateObject` method, which will get filled with errors for the current data object. Note that the fourth, bool input parameter of this method specifies whether it will return errors for all properties, or just for those that have been decorated with `RequiredAttribute` from the data annotations namespace.

Later, we'll see how we can incorporate this into our application framework's base validation class, but now let's investigate how we can perform different levels of validation in different scenarios.

Varying levels of validation

One thing that is not addressed by either of the .NET validation interfaces is the ability to either turn validation on or off, or to set varying levels of validation. This can be useful in several different scenarios, such as having different Views to edit different properties of a data model object.

An example of this might be having a View that enables users to update the security settings of a `User` object, where we want to validate that each property has a value, but only for the properties that are currently displayed in the View. After all, there is no point in informing the user that a certain field must be entered if they can't do that in their current View.

The solution is to define a number of levels of validation, in addition to the levels that represent full and no validation. Let's take a look at a simple `ValidationLevel` enumeration that could fulfil this requirement.

```
namespace CompanyName.ApplicationName.DataModels.Enums
{
  public enum ValidationLevel
  {
    None, Partial, Full
  }
}
```

As we can see, in this simple example, we just have the three levels of validation, although we could have added many more. However, in practice, we could still manage with this enumeration. Let's see how we could use it to implement multi-level validation in our validation base class:

```
private ValidationLevel validationLevel = ValidationLevel.Full;

public ValidationLevel ValidationLevel
{
  get { return validationLevel; }
  set { if (validationLevel != value) { validationLevel = value; } }
}

private void Validate(string propertyName, IEnumerable<string> error)
{
```

```
  if (ValidationLevel == ValidationLevel.None) return;
  if (errors.Any())
    errors.ForEach(e => AddValidationError(propertyName, e));
  else if (AllPropertyErrors.ContainsKey(propertyName))
    RemoveValidationError(propertyName);
}
```

We add a `ValidationLevel` property, with its `validationLevel` backing field that defaults to the `Full` enumeration member, as that is the normal action. Then, in the `Validate` method, we add a new line that simply exits the method if the `ValidationLevel` property is set to the `None` enumeration member.

Finally, the developers of our application need to use the `ValidationLevel` property when validating their properties in the data model classes. Imagine a scenario where users could edit the names of our products directly in a collection control, or edit all of the product's properties in a separate View. Let's update our basic `Product` class indexer to demonstrate this:

```
public override IEnumerable<string> this[string propertyName]
{
  get
  {
    List<string> errors = new List<string>();
    if (propertyName == nameof(Name))
    {
      if (string.IsNullOrEmpty(Name))
        errors.Add("Please enter the product name.");
      else if (Name.Length > 25) errors.Add("The product name cannot be
        longer than twenty-five characters.");
      if (Name.Length > 0 && char.IsLower(Name[0])) errors.Add("The first
        letter of the product name must be a capital letter.");
    }
    else if (propertyName == nameof(Price) &&
      ValidationLevel == ValidationLevel.Full && Price == 0)
      errors.Add("Please enter a valid price for the product.");
    return errors;
  }
}
```

Using our implementation of the `INotifyDataErrorInfo` interface, we first initialize a string list named `errors` and then we check the value of the `propertyName` input parameter. As this implementation enables us to return multiple validation errors per property, we need to take care with our `if` and `else` statements.

For example, when the `propertyName` input parameter equals `Name`, we have two `if` statements and one `else` statement. The first `if` statement verifies that the `Name` property has a value, while the `else` statement checks that its value is no longer than twenty-five characters. As these two conditions cannot possibly both be true at the same time, we tie them together with the `if...else` statement.

On the other hand, the product name could be longer than twenty-five characters and start with a lowercase letter and so, the next condition has its own `if` statement. The remaining condition for the `Price` property is only to be validated when the `ValidationLevel` property is set to the `Full` member and so, that is simply added as a further condition.

To trigger partial validation on a data model variable, we can simply set its `ValidationLevel` property as follows:

```
product.ValidationLevel = ValidationLevel.Partial;
```

Incorporating multiple validation techniques

Now that we've had a good look at the two validation interfaces, the data annotation attributes and the ability to validate with different levels, let's take a look at how we can amalgamate these different techniques together.

Let's create a `BaseNotifyValidationModel` class by copying what we have in our previous implementation, to incorporate these new additions. First, we need to add some extra using directives to the ones used in the previous implementation:

```
using System.Collections.ObjectModel;
using System.Collections.Specialized;
using System.ComponentModel.DataAnnotations;
using CompanyName.ApplicationName.DataModels.Enums;
```

Next, we need to add our `validationLevel` and `errors` fields:

```
private ValidationLevel validationLevel = ValidationLevel.Full;
protected ObservableCollection<string> errors =
  new ObservableCollection<string>();
```

We need to add a constructor, in which we attach the
`ExternalErrors_CollectionChanged` event handler to the `CollectionChanged` event
of the `ExternalErrors` collection property, as we did earlier:

```
protected BaseNotifyValidationModel()
{
  ExternalErrors.CollectionChanged += ExternalErrors_CollectionChanged;
}
```

Now, let's add the familiar `ValidationLevel`, `Errors` and the `ExternalErrors`
properties, along with the abstract `ValidateAllProperties` method.

```
public ValidationLevel ValidationLevel
{
  get { return validationLevel; }
  set { if (validationLevel != value) { validationLevel = value; } }
}

public virtual ObservableCollection<string> Errors
{
  get
  {
    errors = new ObservableCollection<string>();
    IEnumerable<string> allErrors =
      AllPropertyErrors.Values.SelectMany(e => e);
    errors.Add(allErrors.Distinct());
    ExternalErrors.Where(
      e => !errors.Contains(e)).ForEach(e => errors.Add(e));
    return errors;
  }
}

public ObservableCollection<string> ExternalErrors { get; } =
  new ObservableCollection<string>();

public abstract void ValidateAllProperties();
```

Note that in this implementation, users of our framework will no longer need to override the `Errors` property in order to ensure that their validatable properties are validated. While we still declare this property as virtual, so that it can be overridden if necessary, this base class implementation already compiles all validation errors into the internal collection, ready for display.

This time, we first clear the `errors` collection, before adding all of the unique errors from each property error collection from the `AllPropertyErrors` property `Dictionary` object. We then add any errors from the `ExternalErrors` collection, if they do not already exist in the `errors` collection. This string `Errors` collection is primarily used because it is far easier to data bind to in the UI.

After the new `Errors` property, we see the `ExternalErrors` auto property with its initializer and the abstract `ValidateAllProperties` method that needs to be implemented in the derived classes and can be called to force a new validation pass, either pre-emptively, or on the click of a save button, once all fields have been filled.

Let's see an example for our `Product` class, which we should call after initializing the data collection in its constructor to instigate pre-emptive validation:

```
public override void ValidateAllProperties()
{
  Validate(nameof(Name), nameof(Price));
}
```

After the `ValidateAllProperties` method, we need to declare a couple of `Validate` methods, the first of which is a convenience method and simply calls the second, `private` method that should replace our previous method with the identical signature:

```
public void Validate(params string[] propertyNames)
{
  foreach (string propertyName in propertyNames)
    Validate(propertyName, this[propertyName]);
}

private void Validate(string propertyName, IEnumerable<string> errors)
{
  if (ValidationLevel == ValidationLevel.None) return;
  ValidationContext validationContext = new ValidationContext(this);
  List<ValidationResult> validationResults = new List<ValidationResult>();
  Validator.TryValidateObject(this, validationContext, validationResults,
    true);
  IEnumerable<ValidationResult> propertyValidationResults =
    validationResults.Where(v => v.MemberNames.Contains(propertyName));
  propertyValidationResults.ForEach(
```

```
      v => AddValidationError(propertyName, v.ErrorMessage));
  if (errors.Any())
    errors.ForEach(e => AddValidationError(propertyName, e));
  else if (propertyValidationResults.Count() == 0 &&
    AllPropertyErrors.ContainsKey(propertyName))
    RemoveValidationError(propertyName);
  NotifyPropertyChanged(nameof(Errors), nameof(HasErrors));
}
```

In this new `Validate` method, we incorporate the code that retrieves the validation errors from any used data annotation attributes, that was introduced in the earlier *Annotating data* section. We start by returning immediately if the `ValidationLevel` property is set to the `None` member, otherwise, we retrieve the data annotation related validation errors.

We then filter just the errors that relate to the current property that is specified by the `propertyName` input parameter and assign them to the `propertyValidationResults` collection variable. Next, we iterate through this collection, calling the `AddValidationError` method on each item.

If the `errors` collection input parameter contains any errors, we iterate through it, calling the `AddValidationError` method to add each item. If the `errors` collection is empty, we check that the `propertyValidationResults` collection is also empty and that the `AllPropertyErrors` dictionary actually contains one or more errors. If it does, we call the `RemoveValidationError` method to clear the dictionary entry.

Note that we have moved our call to notify of changes to our `Errors` and `HasErrors` properties from our `NotifyPropertyChanged` method to this method, which is only called for validatable properties and so, simplifies matters.

Finally, we just need to add the `ExternalErrors_CollectionChanged` method that is referenced in the constructor. It simply notifies of changes to the `Errors` collection and the `HasError` property, so that they will be updated each time an external error is added or removed.

```
private void ExternalErrors_CollectionChanged(object sender,
  NotifyCollectionChangedEventArgs e)
{
  NotifyPropertyChanged(nameof(Errors), nameof(HasErrors));
}
```

Now, our base validation class will manage errors that are defined in the indexer of each derived class, along with those defined in any data annotation attributes that may decorate the class properties. This implementation enables us to display multiple validation errors per property in our separate global error output collection control.

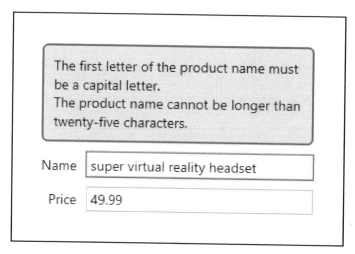

The `HasErrors` property can be used to set the visibility of such a collection control in the UI, so that it can display the complete collection of errors, whenever any exist and hide it when there are none. The last change that we need to make is to add an additional condition into the `HasErrors` property that listens out for external errors as well the internally generated ones.

```
public bool HasErrors => ExternalErrors.Any() ||
    allPropertyErrors.Any(p => p.Value != null && p.Value.Any());
```

Let's see how we can customize the way that we highlight these validation errors to the users now.

Customizing the error template

In addition to the essential `Errors` and `HasError` properties, the `Validation` class also declares an `ErrorTemplate` Attached Property of type `ControlTemplate`. The default template assigned to this property is responsible for defining the red rectangle that surrounds UI fields that have validation errors associated with them.

However, this property enables us to change this template and so, we are able to define how validation errors are highlighted to the application users. As this property is an Attached Property, this effectively means that we could apply a different template to be displayed for each control in the UI. However, this cannot be recommended, because it could make the application look less consistent.

This template actually uses an `Adorner` element to render its graphics in the adorner layer on top of the related control in error. Therefore, in order to specify where our error visual(s) should be rendered in relation to the related control, we need to declare an `AdornedElementPlaceholder` element in the error template.

Let's take a look at a simple example, where we define a slightly thicker, non-blurry border, unlike the default one, and paint over the background of the related control with feint red for added emphasis. We first need to define a `ControlTemplate` object in a suitable resource section:

```
<ControlTemplate x:Key="ErrorTemplate">
  <Border BorderBrush="Red" BorderThickness="2" Background="#1FFF0000"
    SnapsToDevicePixels="True">
    <AdornedElementPlaceholder />
  </Border>
</ControlTemplate>
```

In this example, we declare the `AdornedElementPlaceholder` element inside a `Border` element, so that the border will be rendered around the outside of the related control. Note that without declaring this `AdornedElementPlaceholder` element, our border would resemble a tiny red dot in the top left of the related control when an error occurred.

Let's see how we apply this template, using our earlier example of the control that was data bound to the `Product.Price` property and what it looks like now:

```
<TextBox Grid.Row="2" Grid.Column="1"
  Text="{Binding Products.CurrentItem.Price,
  UpdateSourceTrigger=PropertyChanged,
  ValidatesOnNotifyDataErrors=True, Delay=250}"
  Style="{StaticResource TextBoxStyle}"
  Validation.ErrorTemplate="{StaticResource ErrorTemplate}" />
```

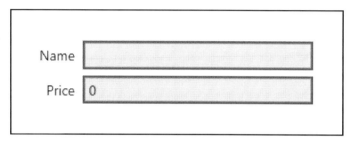

If we wanted to position our error highlighting elements in a different position with relation to the related control in error, we could use one of the panels to position them. Let's take a look at a slightly more advanced error template that we could use. Let's start with declaring some resources in a suitable resource section:

```
<ToolTip x:Key="ValidationErrorsToolTip">
  <ItemsControl ItemsSource="{Binding}">
    <ItemsControl.ItemTemplate>
      <DataTemplate>
        <TextBlock Text="{Binding ErrorContent}" />
      </DataTemplate>
    </ItemsControl.ItemTemplate>
  </ItemsControl>
</ToolTip>
<ControlTemplate x:Key="WarningErrorTemplate">
  <StackPanel Orientation="Horizontal"
    ToolTip="{StaticResource ValidationErrorsToolTip}">
    <AdornedElementPlaceholder Margin="0,0,2,0" />
    <Image Source="pack://application:,,,/CompanyName.ApplicationName;
      component/Images/Warning_16.png" Stretch="None" />
  </StackPanel>
</ControlTemplate>
```

In this example, we declare a `ToolTip` resource named `ValidationErrorsToolTip`. In it, we declare an `ItemsControl` element to display all of the validation errors together. We define a `DataTemplate` element in the `ItemTemplate` property, that will output the value of the `ErrorContent` property of each `ValidationError` object in the `Validation.Errors` collection. This collection will be implicitly set as the data context of the control template.

Next, we declare a `ControlTemplate` element to set to the `ErrorTemplate` property with the key `WarningErrorTemplate`. In it, we define a horizontal `StackPanel` control and apply the `ValidationErrorsToolTip` resource to its `ToolTip` property. Within the panel, we declare the required `AdornedElementPlaceholder` element, followed by the warning icon taken from the Visual Studio icon set that was discussed in the previous chapter.

We can apply this template using the `ErrorTemplate` property as follows:

```
<TextBox Grid.Row="2" Grid.Column="1"
  Text="{Binding Products.CurrentItem.Price,
  UpdateSourceTrigger=PropertyChanged,
  ValidatesOnNotifyDataErrors=True, Delay=250}"
  Style="{StaticResource TextBoxStyle}"
  Validation.ErrorTemplate="{StaticResource WarningErrorTemplate}" />
```

When a validation error now occurs on this textbox, it will look like this:

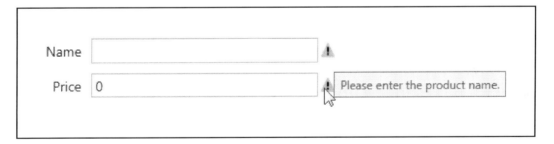

Avoiding UI-based validation errors

In the last example from the previous section, we data bound the whole `Validation.Errors` collection to a tooltip in the error template for our textbox. We also data bound our own `Errors` collection from our base class to the items control above the form fields.

Our `Errors` collection can display all of the errors for all of the properties in each data model. However, the `Validation.Errors` collection has access to UI-based validation errors that never make it back to the View Models. Take a look at the following example:

The UI-based validation error says **Value '0t' could not be converted** and that explains why the View Models never see this error. The type of value expected in the data bound property is decimal, but an unconvertible value has been entered. Therefore, the input value cannot be converted to a decimal and so, the data bound value is never updated.

However, the `Validation.Errors` collection is a UI element and each data bound control has its own collection and so, we have no simple way to access them all from our View Model classes. Furthermore, the `ValidationError` class is in the `System.Windows.Controls` UI assembly, so we don't want to add a reference of that to our `ViewModels` project.

Instead of trying to control the UI-based validation errors from the View Models, we can alternatively extend controls, or define Attached Properties that restrict the ability of the users to enter invalid data in the first place, thereby avoiding the need for UI-based validation. Let's take a look at one way that we can create a textbox that will only accept numerical input, using our `TextBoxProperties` class:

```
using System.Text.RegularExpressions;
using System.Windows;
using System.Windows.Controls;
using System.Windows.Input;

namespace CompanyName.ApplicationName.Views.Attached
```

```
{
  public class TextBoxProperties : DependencyObject
  {
    #region IsNumericOnly

    public static readonly DependencyProperty IsNumericOnlyProperty =
      DependencyProperty.RegisterAttached("IsNumericOnly",
      typeof(bool), typeof(TextBoxProperties),
      new UIPropertyMetadata(default(bool), OnIsNumericOnlyChanged));

    public static bool GetIsNumericOnly(DependencyObject dependencyObject)
    {
      return (bool)dependencyObject.GetValue(IsNumericOnlyProperty);
    }

    public static void SetIsNumericOnly(DependencyObject dependencyObject,
      bool value)
    {
      dependencyObject.SetValue(IsNumericOnlyProperty, value);
    }

    public static void OnIsNumericOnlyChanged(DependencyObject
      dependencyObject, DependencyPropertyChangedEventArgs e)
    {
      TextBox textBox = (TextBox)dependencyObject;
      bool newIsNumericOnlyValue = (bool)e.NewValue;
      if (newIsNumericOnlyValue)
      {
        textBox.PreviewTextInput += TextBox_PreviewTextInput;
        textBox.PreviewKeyDown += TextBox_PreviewKeyDown;
        DataObject.AddPastingHandler(textBox, TextBox_Pasting);
      }
      else
      {
        textBox.PreviewTextInput -= TextBox_PreviewTextInput;
        textBox.PreviewKeyDown -= TextBox_PreviewKeyDown;
        DataObject.RemovePastingHandler(textBox, TextBox_Pasting);
      }
    }

    private static void TextBox_PreviewTextInput(object sender,
      TextCompositionEventArgs e)
    {
      string text = GetFullText((TextBox)sender, e.Text);
      e.Handled = !IsTextValid(text);
    }

    private static void TextBox_PreviewKeyDown(object sender,
```

```
      KeyEventArgs e)
    {
      TextBox textBox = (TextBox)sender;
      e.Handled = e.Key == Key.Space || (textBox.Text.Length == 1 &&
        (e.Key == Key.Delete || e.Key == Key.Back));
    }

    private static void TextBox_Pasting(object sender,
      DataObjectPastingEventArgs e)
    {
      if (e.DataObject.GetDataPresent(typeof(string)))
      {
        string text = GetFullText((TextBox)sender,
          (string)e.DataObject.GetData(typeof(string)));
        if (!IsTextValid(text)) e.CancelCommand();
      }
      else e.CancelCommand();
    }

    private static string GetFullText(TextBox textBox, string input)
    {
      return textBox.SelectedText.Length > 0 ?
        string.Concat(textBox.Text.Substring(0, textBox.SelectionStart),
        input, textBox.Text.Substring(textBox.SelectionStart +
        textBox.SelectedText.Length)) :
        textBox.Text.Insert(textBox. SelectionStart, input);
    }

    private static bool IsTextValid(string text)
    {
      return Regex.Match(text, @"^-?\d*\.?\d*$").Success;
    }

    #endregion

    ...
  }
}
```

Excluding the other, existing members from our `TextBoxProperties` class, we first declare the `IsNumericOnly` Attached Property and its getter and setter methods and attach the `OnIsNumericOnlyChanged` handler.

In the `OnIsNumericOnlyChanged` method, we first cast the `dependencyObject` input parameter to a `TextBox` and then cast the `NewValue` property of the `DependencyPropertyChangedEventArgs` class to the bool `newIsNumericOnlyValue` variable.

If the `newIsNumericOnlyValue` variable is `true`, we attach our event handlers for the `PreviewTextInput`, `PreviewKeyDown` and `DataObject.Pasting` events. If the `newIsNumericOnlyValue` variable is `false`, we detach the handlers.

We need to handle all of these events in order to create a textbox that can only enter numerical values. The `UIElement.PreviewTextInput` event is raised when the textbox receives a text input from any device, the `Keyboard.PreviewKeyDown` event occurs specifically when a keyboard key is pressed and the `DataObject.Pasting` event is raised when we paste from the clipboard.

The `TextCompositionEventArgs` object in the `TextBox_PreviewTextInput` handler method only provides us with the last typed character through its `Text` property, along with `TextComposition` details. At the stage that this tunneling event is called, the `Text` property of the relevant textbox is not yet aware of this latest character.

Therefore, in order to correctly validate the whole entered text value, we need to combine the existing value with this new character. We do that in the `GetFullText` method and pass the returned value to the `IsTextValid` method.

We then set the inverted return value of the `IsTextValid` method to the `Handled` property of the `TextCompositionEventArgs` input parameter. Note that we invert this bool value, because setting the `Handled` property to `true` will stop the event from being routed any further and result in the latest character not being accepted. Therefore, we do this when the input value is invalid.

Next, we see the `TextBox_PreviewKeyDown` event handler method and in it, we again start by casting the `sender` input parameter to a `TextBox` instance. We specifically need to handle this event, because the `PreviewTextInput` event does not get raised when the *Space bar*, *Delete*, or *Backspace* keys on the keyboard are pressed.

Therefore, we stop the event being routed any further by setting the `Handled` property of the `KeyEventArgs` input parameter to `true` if the key pressed is the *Space bar* key, or if the length of the entered text is a single character and the *Delete* or *Backspace* key is pressed; this stops the user from deleting the last character from the textbox, which would result in a UI-based validation error.

In the `TextBox_Pasting` handler method, we check whether the `DataObject` property that is accessed from the `DataObjectPastingEventArgs` input parameter has any string data available and call its `CancelCommand` method to cancel the paste operation if not.

If string data is present, we cast the `sender` input parameter to a `TextBox` instance and then pass the data from the `DataObject` property to the `GetFullText` method to reconstruct the whole entered string. We pass the reconstructed text to the `IsTextValid` method and if it is invalid, then we call the `CancelCommand` method to cancel the paste operation.

Next is the `GetFullText` method, where the entered text from the textbox is reconstructed. In this method, if any text is selected in the textbox, we rebuild the string by concatenating the portion of text before the selection with the newly entered or pasted text and the portion of text after the selection. Otherwise, we use the `Insert` method of the `String` class, along with the textbox's `SelectionStart` property to insert the new character into the appropriate place in the string.

At the end of the class, we see the `IsTextValid` method, which simply returns the `Success` property value of the `Regex.Match` method. The regular expression that we validate with is as follows:

```
@"^-?\d*\.?\d*$".
```

The ampersand marks the string as a verbatim string literal, which is useful when using characters that normally need to be escaped, the caret signifies the start of the input line, the `-?` states that we can accept zero or one minus signs at the start, the `\d*` indicates that we can then have zero or more numerical digits, the `\.?` specifies that zero or one periods are then valid, the `\d*` again indicates that we can then have zero or more numerical digits and finally, the `$` signifies the end of the input line.

When attached to an ordinary `TextBox` control, we can now only enter numeric values, but both integer and decimal values are allowed. Continuing to use our earlier `ProductView` example, we can attach our new property like this:

```
xmlns:Attached="clr-namespace:CompanyName.ApplicationName.Views.Attached"
...
<TextBox Grid.Row="2" Grid.Column="1"
  Text="{Binding Products.CurrentItem.Price,
  UpdateSourceTrigger=PropertyChanged,
  ValidatesOnNotifyDataErrors=True, Delay=250}"
  Style="{StaticResource TextBoxStyle}"
  Validation.ErrorTemplate="{StaticResource WarningErrorTemplate}"
  Attached:TextBoxProperties.IsNumericOnly="True" />
```

However, those that have been experimenting with this ProductView example may have noticed something peculiar occurring when attempting to enter a price. In .NET 4.5, Microsoft decided to introduce a breaking change to the way that data is entered into the TextBox control when the binding UpdateSourceTrigger is set to PropertyChanged.

From .NET 4.5, we can no longer enter a numerical separator, neither a period nor a comma, when we have data bound to a float, double, or decimal data type. There are a number of ways around this, with the first being introduced with the change in .NET 4.5. A new related property has been added to WPF, which we can set to address this issue.

The KeepTextBoxDisplaySynchronizedWithTextProperty property was added to the FrameworkCompatibilityPreferences class, which indicates whether a textbox should display the same as its data bound property or not. If we set this to false, it should return the previous behavior, although in practice, there are still some side effects:

```
FrameworkCompatibilityPreferences.
    KeepTextBoxDisplaySynchronizedWithTextProperty = false;
```

Note that we need to set this property very early in the application lifetime, such as in the constructor of the App.xaml.cs file. Once set, it cannot be changed. Another way is to avoid this problem is to set the UpdateSourceTrigger property to a value other than PropertyChanged, however, this is no use if we want to validate or want our data source to update with each key press.

```
<TextBox Text="{Binding Products.CurrentItem.Price,
    Style="{StaticResource TextBoxStyle}"
    UpdateSourceTrigger=LostFocus ... />
```

Alternatively, we could simply data bind a string property to our textbox and perform our own number parsing in our View Model. Another option would be to utilize the Delay property of the Binding class that we discussed in Chapter 4, *Becoming Proficient with Data Binding*. If we set this to a figure of just a few hundred milliseconds, it can give the user enough time to enter their number including the decimal point:

```
<TextBox Text="{Binding Products.CurrentItem.Price,
    UpdateSourceTrigger=PropertyChanged, Delay=250}" ... />
```

This is the option that we used in our examples, primarily because it is a simple and quick fix for this problem. However, care should be taken when using this method with actual monetary properties, as mistakes can easily be made if the user types slowly and does not pay attention to the entered value.

A more robust solution would be to declare an `IValueConverter` implementation to use in these situations, that will correctly convert our string text input into valid numbers. We could either add a property, or use the converter parameter to specify which type of number we want to convert to and provide a few alternative conversion methods.

As always with WPF, there are a number of different ways to implement any solution. There are also several other ways to stop users from entering invalid data; we could build, or make use of a third-party numeric up/down control, enable users to enter time values using a custom clock control, or even use combo boxes to restrict the value that users can select to a set of allowable values.

Amalgamating validation and visuals

Let's now utilize some of the techniques that we discussed in the previous chapter to design a visually appealing user interface that highlights validation errors in a novel way, using our glowing example. We'll first need to add some more resources to use in this example. Let's start by adding two further glow brush resources to the `GreenGlow` brush resource from the previous chapter:

```
<RadialGradientBrush x:Key="BlueGlow" Center="0.5,0.848"
  GradientOrigin="0.5,0.818" RadiusX="-1.424" RadiusY="-0.622"
  RelativeTransform="{StaticResource GlowTransformGroup}">
  <GradientStop Color="#CF01C7FF" Offset="0.168" />
  <GradientStop Color="#4B01C7FF" Offset="0.478" />
  <GradientStop Color="#1101C7FF" Offset="1" />
</RadialGradientBrush>
<RadialGradientBrush x:Key="RedGlow" Center="0.5,0.848"
  GradientOrigin="0.5,0.818" RadiusX="-1.424" RadiusY="-0.622"
  RelativeTransform="{StaticResource GlowTransformGroup}">
  <GradientStop Color="#CFFF0000" Offset="0.168" />
  <GradientStop Color="#4BFF0000" Offset="0.478" />
  <GradientStop Color="#00FF0000" Offset="1" />
</RadialGradientBrush>
```

Let's now see the styles that use these brush resources:

```
<Style x:Key="GlowStyle" TargetType="{x:Type Rectangle}">
  <Setter Property="SnapsToDevicePixels" Value="True" />
  <Setter Property="Opacity" Value="1.0" />
  <Setter Property="StrokeThickness" Value="0" />
  <Setter Property="RadiusX" Value="2.5" />
  <Setter Property="RadiusX" Value="2.5" />
  <Setter Property="IsHitTestVisible" Value="False" />
  <Setter Property="VerticalAlignment" Value="Stretch" />
```

```
        <Setter Property="HorizontalAlignment" Value="Stretch" />
        <Setter Property="Fill" Value="{StaticResource BlueGlow}" />
    </Style>
```

This first style is reusable and can be declared in the global application resources, while the following styles extend it, are data model specific and could be declared locally in our `ProductView` class:

```
    <Style x:Key="ProductGlowStyle" TargetType="{x:Type Rectangle}"
        BasedOn="{StaticResource GlowStyle}">
        <Style.Triggers>
            <DataTrigger Binding="{Binding Products.CurrentItem.HasChanges,
                FallbackValue=False, Mode=OneWay}" Value="True">
                <Setter Property="Fill" Value="{StaticResource GreenGlow}" />
            </DataTrigger>
            <DataTrigger Binding="{Binding Products.CurrentItem.HasErrors,
                FallbackValue=False, Mode=OneWay}" Value="True">
                <Setter Property="Fill" Value="{StaticResource RedGlow}" />
            </DataTrigger>
        </Style.Triggers>
    </Style>
    <Style x:Key="ProductItemGlowStyle" TargetType="{x:Type Rectangle}"
        BasedOn="{StaticResource GlowStyle}">
        <Style.Triggers>
            <DataTrigger Binding="{Binding HasChanges, FallbackValue=False,
                Mode=OneWay}" Value="True">
                <Setter Property="Fill" Value="{StaticResource GreenGlow}" />
            </DataTrigger>
            <DataTrigger Binding="{Binding HasErrors, FallbackValue=False,
                Mode=OneWay}" Value="True">
                <Setter Property="Fill" Value="{StaticResource RedGlow}" />
            </DataTrigger>
        </Style.Triggers>
    </Style>
```

We declare the `ProductGlowStyle` style for our form rectangle, and the `ProductItemGlowStyle` style for our data items in the `Products` collection. The only differences can be found in the binding paths of the two data triggers.

In these styles, we add a `DataTrigger` element that sets the rectangle `Fill` property to the `GreenGlow` resource when the `HasChanges` property of the current item in the `Products` collection is `true` and another that sets it to the `RedGlow` resource when the `HasErrors` property of the current item is `true`.

As the trigger that highlights errors is declared after the other one, it will override it if both conditions are `true`, which is essential for this example. Let's now see the `Product` class data template resource that makes use of this rectangle style:

```
xmlns:DataModels="clr-namespace:CompanyName.ApplicationName.DataModels;
   assembly=CompanyName.ApplicationName.DataModels"
xmlns:Views="clr-namespace:CompanyName.ApplicationName.Views"
...
<DataTemplate DataType="{x:Type DataModels:Product}">
  <Border CornerRadius="3" BorderBrush="{StaticResource TransparentBlack}"
    BorderThickness="1" Background="{StaticResource TransparentWhite}">
    <Border Name="InnerBorder" CornerRadius="2" Margin="1"
      Background="{StaticResource LayeredButtonBackground}">
      <Grid>
        <Rectangle IsHitTestVisible="False" RadiusX="2" RadiusY="2"
          Style="{StaticResource ProductItemGlowStyle}" />
        <Grid>
          <Grid.ColumnDefinitions>
            <ColumnDefinition Width="Auto" />
            <ColumnDefinition />
            <ColumnDefinition Width="Auto" />
          </Grid.ColumnDefinitions>
          <Image Width="24" Height="24"
            Source="pack://application:,,,/CompanyName.ApplicationName;
            component/Images/Product.ico" VerticalAlignment="Center"
            Margin="3,2,5,2" />
          <TextBlock Grid.Column="1" HorizontalAlignment="Left"
            VerticalAlignment="Center" Text="{Binding Name}"
            TextWrapping="Wrap" Margin="0,1,5,3" Foreground="White"
            FontSize="14" />
          <Button Grid.Column="2"
            Command="{Binding DataContext.DeleteCommand,
            RelativeSource={RelativeSource FindAncestor,
            AncestorType={x:Type Views:ProductView}}}"
            CommandParameter="{Binding}" Margin="0,2,4,2"
            Width="20" Height="20">
            <Image Width="16" Height="16"
              Source="pack://application:,,,/CompanyName.ApplicationName;
              component/Images/Delete_16.png"
              HorizontalAlignment="Center" VerticalAlignment="Center" />
          </Button>
        </Grid>
      </Grid>
    </Border>
  </Border>
</DataTemplate>
```

In this example, we reuse our double border technique from the previous chapter, so there's no need to examine that code again. Inside the borders, we declare a `Grid` panel that contains a rectangle that has our new `ProductItemGlowStyle` style applied to it and another `Grid` panel to display each user's name and a couple of images.

These images are from the Visual Studio 2015 icon set and the first signifies that these objects are products. The `VerticalAlignment` property of each of the three elements is set to `Center` to ensure that they are all aligned vertically and the `TextWrapping` property of the `TextBlock` element is set to `Wrap` in case any products have a long name.

The second image specifies that each of these items can be deleted. Note that it is declared within a `Button` control and while we have not attempted to style that button, it could also be given the double border treatment, or any other custom style. This button is optional, but has been included merely as an example of linking a command from the View Model to each data object.

Note that the binding path in the button's `Command` property uses a `RelativeSource` binding to reference the ancestor of type `ProductView`. In particular, it references the `DeleteCommand` property of the `DataContext` of the View, which in our case, is an instance of our `ProductViewModel` class.

The `CommandParameter` property is then data bound to the whole data context of each data template, which means that the whole data model object will be passed through as the command parameter. Using our `ActionCommand` class, this is specified by the `action` and `canExecute` fields in the following example, which should be added to the `ProductViewModel`, along with the related methods:

```
using System.Windows.Input;
using CompanyName.ApplicationName.ViewModels.Commands;

...

public ICommand DeleteCommand
{
  get { return new ActionCommand(action => Delete(action),
    canExecute => CanDelete(canExecute)); }
}

private bool CanDelete(object parameter)
{
  return Products.Contains((Product)parameter);
}

private void Delete(object parameter)
```

```
{
  Products.Remove((Product)parameter);
}
```

In this example, our `CanDelete` method simply returns `true` if the command parameter product is contained in the `Products` collection, but this can be replaced with your own condition. For example, you could check whether the item has any changes, or whether the current user has the correct security permission to delete objects. Our `Delete` method simply removes the cast `Product` input parameter from the `Products` collection.

Now that we have styled our `Product` items in the `ListBox` with this data template, there is something else that we can do to improve the look further; we can remove the default selection rectangle of the `ListBoxItem` elements that wrap our data models. In .NET 3.5 and before, we could simply add some resources into a style for the `ListBoxItem` class that would do the job for us:

```xml
<Style TargetType="{x:Type ListBoxItem}">
  <Style.Resources>
    <SolidColorBrush x:Key="{x:Static SystemColors.HighlightBrushKey}"
      Color="Transparent" />
    <SolidColorBrush x:Key="{x:Static SystemColors.ControlBrushKey}"
      Color="Transparent" />
    <SolidColorBrush x:Key="{x:Static SystemColors.HighlightTextBrushKey}"
      Color="Black" />
    <SolidColorBrush x:Key="{x:Static SystemColors.ControlTextBrushKey}"
      Color="Black" />
  </Style.Resources>
</Style>
```

However, from .NET 4.0 onwards, this will no longer work. Instead, we now need to define a new `ControlTemplate` object for the `ListBoxItem` class that does not highlight its background when selected, or when the user's mouse cursor is over it.

```xml
<Style TargetType="{x:Type ListBoxItem}">
  <Setter Property="Padding" Value="0" />
  <Setter Property="Margin" Value="2,2,2,0" />
  <Setter Property="BorderThickness" Value="1" />
  <Setter Property="Template">
    <Setter.Value>
      <ControlTemplate TargetType="{x:Type ListBoxItem}">
        <Border x:Name="Bd" BorderBrush="{TemplateBinding BorderBrush}"
          BorderThickness="{TemplateBinding BorderThickness}"
          Background="{TemplateBinding Background}"
          Padding="{TemplateBinding Padding}" SnapsToDevicePixels="True">
          <ContentPresenter
            ContentTemplate="{TemplateBinding ContentTemplate}"
```

```
                Content="{TemplateBinding Content}"
                ContentStringFormat="{TemplateBinding ContentStringFormat}"
                HorizontalAlignment="{TemplateBinding
                HorizontalContentAlignment}"
                SnapsToDevicePixels="{TemplateBinding SnapsToDevicePixels}"
                VerticalAlignment="{TemplateBinding VerticalContentAlignment}"
                />
        </Border>
        <ControlTemplate.Triggers>
            <Trigger Property="IsEnabled" Value="False">
                <Setter Property="TextElement.Foreground"
                    TargetName="Bd" Value="{DynamicResource
                    {x:Static SystemColors.GrayTextBrushKey}}" />
            </Trigger>
        </ControlTemplate.Triggers>
    </ControlTemplate>
  </Setter.Value>
 </Setter>
</Style>
```

To create the `ControlTemplate` element in this style, we first accessed the default template of the `ListBoxItem` class, as described in the *Modifying Existing Controls* section of Chapter 5, *Using the Right Controls for the Job*, and then simply removed the triggers that colored the background. We then added it to a style with no `x:Key` directive, so that it will be implicitly applied to all `ListBoxItem` elements within scope.

Next, we have the `ErrorBorderStyle` style that styles the border of our global validation error display and uses our `BoolToVisibilityConverter` class to set the `Visibility` property to show the control when the `HasErrors` property of the current item in the `Products` collection is `true`:

```
<Style x:Key="ErrorBorderStyle" TargetType="{x:Type Border}">
  <Setter Property="BorderBrush" Value="#7BFF0000" />
  <Setter Property="Background" Value="#FFFFDFE1" />
  <Setter Property="BorderThickness" Value="1" />
  <Setter Property="CornerRadius" Value="2.75" />
  <Setter Property="Padding" Value="5,3" />
  <Setter Property="Margin" Value="0,0,0,5" />
  <Setter Property="SnapsToDevicePixels" Value="True" />
  <Setter Property="Visibility"
    Value="{Binding Products.CurrentItem.HasErrors,
    Converter={StaticResource BoolToVisibilityConverter},
    FallbackValue=Collapsed, Mode=OneWay}" />
</Style>
```

For this example, we want the ability to know when the data has changed, so we'll also need to update our `BaseNotifyValidationModel` class to extend our earlier `BaseSynchronizableDataModel` class. In order to do that, we'll need to make it generic and add the same generic constraints for the `T` generic type parameter to its declaration:

```
public abstract class BaseNotifyValidationModel<T> :
  BaseSynchronizableDataModel<T>,
  INotifyPropertyChanged, INotifyDataErrorInfo
  where T : BaseDataModel, ISynchronizableDataModel<T>, new()
```

We'll need to remove its default implementation of the `INotifyPropertyChanged` interface and make use of the existing implementation from the `BaseSynchronizableDataModel` class. We'll also need to implement the base class' required members in our `Product` class:

```
public class Product : BaseNotifyValidationModel<Product>
{
  ...

  public override void CopyValuesFrom(Product product)
  {
    Id = product.Id;
    Name = product.Name;
    Price = product.Price;
  }

  public override bool PropertiesEqual(Product otherProduct)
  {
    if (otherProduct == null) return false;
    return Id == otherProduct.Id && Name == otherProduct.Name &&
      Price == otherProduct.Price;
  }
}
```

The `CopyValuesFrom` method is used by the base class to make cloned copies of the data object and the `PropertiesEqual` method is used to compare its property values with other `Product` instances.

Now that we have updated our `BaseNotifyValidationModel` class to extend our earlier `BaseSynchronizableDataModel` class and extended this in our `Product` class, we can now update the `Products` class to extend our earlier `BaseSynchronizableCollection` class:

```
public class Products : BaseSynchronizableCollection<Product> { }
```

With our new `Products` collection, we can now call the `Synchronize` method in the constructor of the `ProductViewModel` class, after adding the two products to it:

```
Products.Synchronize();
```

Now that we've updated the `ProductViewModel` class, let's see move onto the `ProductView` class:

```xml
<Grid>
  <Grid.ColumnDefinitions>
    <ColumnDefinition />
    <ColumnDefinition />
  </Grid.ColumnDefinitions>
  <ListBox ItemsSource="{Binding Products}"
    SelectedItem="{Binding Products.CurrentItem}" Margin="0,0,20,0"
    HorizontalContentAlignment="Stretch" />
  <Border Grid.Column="1" CornerRadius="3"
    BorderBrush="{StaticResource TransparentBlack}" BorderThickness="1"
    Background="{StaticResource TransparentWhite}">
    <Border Name="InnerBorder" CornerRadius="2" Margin="1"
      Background="{StaticResource LayeredButtonBackground}">
      <Grid>
        <Rectangle IsHitTestVisible="False" RadiusX="2" RadiusY="2"
          Style="{StaticResource ProductGlowStyle}" />
        <Grid Margin="10">
          <Grid.RowDefinitions>
            <RowDefinition Height="Auto" />
            <RowDefinition Height="Auto" />
            <RowDefinition Height="Auto" />
          </Grid.RowDefinitions>
          <Grid.ColumnDefinitions>
            <ColumnDefinition Width="Auto" />
            <ColumnDefinition />
          </Grid.ColumnDefinitions>
          <Border Grid.ColumnSpan="2" Style="{StaticResource
            ErrorBorderStyle}" Margin="0,0,0,10" Padding="10">
            <ItemsControl
              ItemsSource="{Binding Products.CurrentItem.Errors}"
              ItemTemplate="{StaticResource WrapTemplate}" />
          </Border>
```

```
            <TextBlock Grid.Row="1" Text="Name"
              Style="{StaticResource LabelStyle}" />
            <TextBox Grid.Row="1" Grid.Column="1"
              Text="{Binding Products.CurrentItem.Name,
              UpdateSourceTrigger=PropertyChanged}"
              Style="{StaticResource TextBoxStyle}" />
            <TextBlock Grid.Row="2" Text="Price"
              Style="{StaticResource LabelStyle}" />
            <TextBox Grid.Row="2" Grid.Column="1"
              Text="{Binding Products.CurrentItem.Price
              UpdateSourceTrigger=PropertyChanged}"
              Style="{StaticResource TextBoxStyle}"
              Attached:TextBoxProperties.IsNumericOnly ="True" />
          </Grid>
        </Grid>
      </Border>
    </Border>
  </Grid>
```

We have the same `Grid` panel, with a `ListBox` control on the left and some form controls on the right. Note that we set the `HorizontalContentAlignment` property to `Stretch` on the `ListBox` control to ensure that its `ListBoxItem` elements stretch to fit its whole width.

On the right, we then see the double borders and the rectangle that is painted with the glow color resource that we created in the previous chapter. Rather than hardcoding one particular color resource as we did earlier, we instead apply our new `ProductGlowStyle` style to it, that will change the color with its data triggers.

Note that we have added an outer `Grid` panel that only contains the glow rectangle and the original `Grid` panel, which now adds an outer margin to our form. The original panel remains much unchanged, although the error display border now uses our new `ErrorBorderStyle` style.

The form fields also remain unchanged, although when using our extended implementation, we no longer need to set the `ValidatesOnNotifyDataErrors` property to `true` on each binding. We also updated the `LabelStyle` style to add a setter to color the label foreground white and edited the `TextBoxStyle` style to add a setter to set the `Validation.ErrorTemplate` Attached Property to `x:Null` to hide the default red error border when there are validation errors.

When running this View now, it would render the following visual output, with a red glow on the form and the item in error:

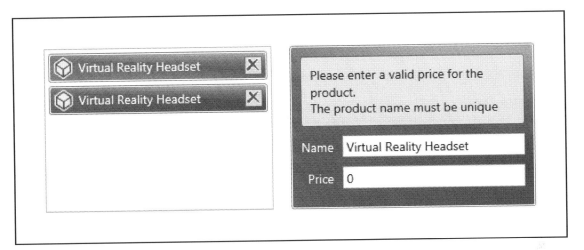

After correcting the errors, we'll see a green glow on the form and the edited item:

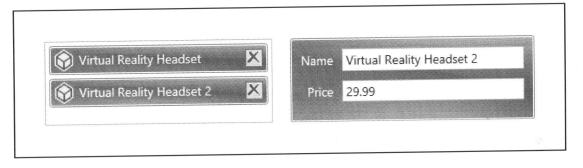

After saving the changes, we'd need to call the `Synchronize` method on the `Products` collection again and then we'd see this, where all objects are now painted with the blue glow:

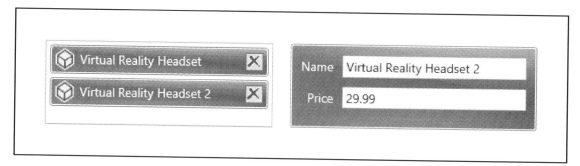

Summary

In this chapter, we had a thorough look at the data validation options that the .NET Framework offers us, primarily concentrating on a variety of ways to implement the two available validation interfaces. We investigated the use of the data annotation validation attributes, explored providing custom error templates and aggregated our new found knowledge with that from the previous chapter to build up a visually pleasing validation example.

In the next chapter, we'll look a number of ways that we can provide users of our applications with a great user experience, from asynchronous programming to feedback mechanisms. We will also examine how to make use of application settings to provide user preferences and examine a variety of ways of supplying in-application help to the application users. We will end with a further look into additional ways of improving the user experience for the end users.

9
Completing That Great User Experience

As we have seen, it is easy to add form fields to a View and produce visually appealing and functionally adequate applications. However, it can take a lot more work to provide the end user with an interface that truly ticks all of the boxes. For example, how many times have you clicked on a button in an application and had the whole application freeze while it does some work?

In this chapter, we'll look into solving this problem by using asynchronous programming, along with a number of other ways of improving the user experience of the end user. For example, we'll investigate enabling the users to customize their versions of the application using their own user preference settings.

We'll discuss keeping the users informed, by providing user feedback and update our application framework by adding a feedback system. We'll explore a few alternative methods of providing in-application help files and/or documentation and a number of other ways of making the application more user friendly and the life of the users that much easier.

Providing user feedback

One essential facet of a great application is keeping the end users up to date with what's going on in the application. If they click on a function button, they should be informed as to the progress and/or the status of the operation. Without adequate feedback, the user can be left wondering whether a particular operation worked and may attempt to run it several times, possibly causing errors.

It is therefore essential to implement a feedback system into our application framework. So far in this book, we've seen the name of the `FeedbackManager` class in a few places, although we've seen very little implementation. Let's now see how we can implement a working feedback system in our application framework, starting with the `Feedback` class that holds the individual feedback messages:

```
using System;
using System.ComponentModel;
using CompanyName.ApplicationName.DataModels.Enums;
using CompanyName.ApplicationName.DataModels.Interfaces;
using CompanyName.ApplicationName.Extensions;

namespace CompanyName.ApplicationName.DataModels
{
  public class Feedback : IAnimatable, INotifyPropertyChanged
  {
    private string message = string.Empty;
    private FeedbackType type = FeedbackType.None;
    private TimeSpan duration = new TimeSpan(0, 0, 4);
    private bool isPermanent = false;
    private Animatable animatable;

    public Feedback(string message, FeedbackType type, TimeSpan duration)
    {
      Message = message;
      Type = type;
      Duration = duration == TimeSpan.Zero ? this.duration : duration;
      IsPermanent = false;
      Animatable = new Animatable(this);
    }

    public Feedback(string message, bool isSuccess, bool isPermanent) :
      this(message, isSuccess ? FeedbackType.Success :
      FeedbackType.Error, TimeSpan.Zero)
    {
      IsPermanent = isPermanent;
    }

    public Feedback(string message, FeedbackType type) : this(message,
      type, TimeSpan.Zero) { }

    public Feedback(string message, bool isSuccess) : this(message,
      isSuccess ? FeedbackType.Success : FeedbackType.Error,
      TimeSpan.Zero) { }

    public Feedback() : this(string.Empty, FeedbackType.None) { }
```

```
public string Message
{
  get { return message; }
  set { message = value; NotifyPropertyChanged(); }
}

public TimeSpan Duration
{
  get { return duration; }
  set { duration = value; NotifyPropertyChanged(); }
}

public FeedbackType Type
{
  get { return type; }
  set { type = value; NotifyPropertyChanged(); }
}

public bool IsPermanent
{
  get { return isPermanent; }
  set { isPermanent = value; NotifyPropertyChanged(); }
}

#region IAnimatable Members

public Animatable Animatable
{
  get { return animatable; }
  set { animatable = value; }
}

#endregion

#region INotifyPropertyChanged Members

...

#endregion
  }
}
```

Note that our Feedback class implements the IAnimatable interface that we saw earlier, along with the INotifyPropertyChanged interface. After declaring the private fields, we declare a number of useful constructor overloads.

In this example, we have hardcoded a default feedback display duration of four seconds for the `duration` field. In the main constructor, we set the `Duration` property, dependent upon the value of the `duration` input parameter; if the input parameter is the `TimeSpan.Zero` field, then the default value is used, but if the input parameter is a non-zero value, it will be used.

The `Message` property will hold the feedback message, the `Duration` property specifies the length of time that the message will be displayed, the `Type` property uses the `FeedbackType` enumeration that we saw earlier to specify the type of the message and the `IsPermanent` property dictates whether the message should be permanently displayed until the user manually closes it or not.

The implementation of our `IAnimatable` class is shown beneath the other properties and simply consists of the `Animatable` property, but our implementation of the `INotifyPropertyChanged` interface has been omitted for brevity, as we are using the default implementation that we saw earlier.

Let's now see the `FeedbackCollection` class that will contain the individual `Feedback` instances:

```
using System.Collections.Generic;
using System.Linq;

namespace CompanyName.ApplicationName.DataModels.Collections
{
  public class FeedbackCollection : BaseAnimatableCollection<Feedback>
  {
    public FeedbackCollection(IEnumerable<Feedback> feedbackCollection) :
      base(feedbackCollection) { }

    public FeedbackCollection() : base() { }

    public new void Add(Feedback feedback)
    {
      if (!string.IsNullOrEmpty(feedback.Message) && (Count == 0 ||
        !this.Any(f => f.Message == feedback.Message))) base.Add(feedback);
    }

    public void Add(string message, bool isSuccess)
    {
      Add(new Feedback(message, isSuccess));
    }
  }
}
```

The `FeedbackCollection` class extends our `BaseAnimatableCollection` class that we saw earlier and sets its generic type parameter to the `Feedback` class. This is a very simple class and declares a couple of constructors, passing any input parameters straight through to the base class constructors.

In addition to this, it declares two `Add` methods, with the second simply creating a `Feedback` object from its input parameters and passing it to the first method. The first method first checks that the feedback message is not null or empty and that an identical message is not already contained in the feedback collection, before adding the new message to the collection.

Let's now look at the `FeedbackManager` class that uses these two classes internally:

```
using System.ComponentModel;
using System.Runtime.CompilerServices;
using CompanyName.ApplicationName.DataModels;
using CompanyName.ApplicationName.DataModels.Collections;

namespace CompanyName.ApplicationName.Managers
{
  public class FeedbackManager : INotifyPropertyChanged
  {
    private static FeedbackCollection feedback = new FeedbackCollection();
    private static FeedbackManager instance = null;

    private FeedbackManager() { }

    public static FeedbackManager Instance =>
      instance ?? (instance = new FeedbackManager());

    public FeedbackCollection Feedback
    {
      get { return feedback; }
      set { feedback = value; NotifyPropertyChanged(); }
    }

    public void Add(Feedback feedback)
    {
      Feedback.Add(feedback);
    }

    public void Add(string message, bool isSuccess)
    {
      Add(new Feedback(message, isSuccess));
    }

    #region INotifyPropertyChanged Members
```

```
      . . .

    #endregion
  }
}
```

The `FeedbackManager` class also implements the `INotifyPropertyChanged` interface and in it, we see the static `FeedbackCollection` field. Next, we see the static `instance` field, the private constructor and the static `Instance` property of type `FeedbackManager`, that instantiates the `instance` field on the first use and tells us that this class follows the Singleton pattern.

The `Feedback` property follows and is the class' access to the `FeedbackCollection` field. After that, we see a number of convenient overloads of the `Add` method that enable developers to add feedback using different parameters. Our implementation of the `INotifyPropertyChanged` interface here has again been omitted for brevity, but it uses our default implementation that we saw earlier.

Let's now focus on the XAML of the `FeedbackControl` object:

```
<UserControl
  x:Class="CompanyName.ApplicationName.Views.Controls.FeedbackControl"
  xmlns="http://schemas.microsoft.com/winfx/2006/xaml/presentation"
  xmlns:x="http://schemas.microsoft.com/winfx/2006/xaml"
  xmlns:mc="http://schemas.openxmlformats.org/markup-compatibility/2006"
  xmlns:d="http://schemas.microsoft.com/expression/blend/2008"
  xmlns:Controls="clr-namespace:CompanyName.ApplicationName.Views.Controls"
  xmlns:Converters="clr-namespace:CompanyName.ApplicationName.Converters;
    assembly=CompanyName.ApplicationName.Converters"
  xmlns:DataModels="clr-namespace:CompanyName.ApplicationName.DataModels;
    assembly=CompanyName.ApplicationName.DataModels"
  xmlns:Panels="clr-namespace:CompanyName.ApplicationName.Views.Panels"
  mc:Ignorable="d" d:DesignHeight="22" d:DesignWidth="300">
  <UserControl.Resources>
    <Converters:FeedbackTypeToImageSourceConverter
      x:Key="FeedbackTypeToImageSourceConverter" />
    <Converters:BoolToVisibilityConverter
      x:Key="BoolToVisibilityConverter" />
    <ItemsPanelTemplate x:Key="AnimatedPanel">
      <Panels:AnimatedStackPanel />
    </ItemsPanelTemplate>
    <Style x:Key="SmallImageInButtonStyle" TargetType="{x:Type Image}"
      BasedOn="{StaticResource ImageInButtonStyle}">
      <Setter Property="Width" Value="16" />
      <Setter Property="Height" Value="16" />
    </Style>
```

```xml
    <DataTemplate x:Key="FeedbackTemplate" DataType="{x:Type
      DataModels:Feedback}">
      <Grid Margin="2,1,2,0" MouseEnter="Border_MouseEnter"
        MouseLeave="Border_MouseLeave">
        <Grid.ColumnDefinitions>
          <ColumnDefinition Width="16" />
          <ColumnDefinition />
          <ColumnDefinition Width="24" />
        </Grid.ColumnDefinitions>
        <Image Stretch="None" Source="{Binding Type,
          Converter={StaticResource FeedbackTypeToImageSourceConverter}}"
          VerticalAlignment="Top" Margin="0,4,0,0" />
        <TextBlock Grid.Column="1" Text="{Binding Message}"
          MinHeight="22" TextWrapping="Wrap" Margin="5,2,5,0"
          VerticalAlignment="Top" FontSize="14" />
        <Button Grid.Column="2" ToolTip="Removes this message from the
          list" VerticalAlignment="Top" PreviewMouseLeftButtonDown=
          "DeleteButton_PreviewMouseLeftButtonDown">
          <Image Source="pack://application:,,,/
            CompanyName.ApplicationName;component/Images/Delete_16.png"
            Style="{StaticResource SmallImageInButtonStyle}" />
        </Button>
      </Grid>
    </DataTemplate>
    <DropShadowEffect x:Key="Shadow" Color="Black" ShadowDepth="6"
      Direction="270" Opacity="0.4" />
  </UserControl.Resources>
  <Border BorderBrush="{StaticResource TransparentBlack}"
    Background="White" Padding="3" BorderThickness="1,0,1,1"
    CornerRadius="0,0,5,5" Visibility="{Binding HasFeedback,
    Converter={StaticResource BoolToVisibilityConverter},
    RelativeSource={RelativeSource Mode=FindAncestor,
    AncestorType={x:Type Controls:FeedbackControl}}}"
    Effect="{StaticResource Shadow}">
    <ListBox MaxHeight="89" ItemsSource="{Binding Feedback,
      RelativeSource={RelativeSource Mode=FindAncestor,
      AncestorType={x:Type Controls:FeedbackControl}}}"
      ItemTemplate="{StaticResource FeedbackTemplate}"
      ItemsPanel="{StaticResource AnimatedPanel}"
      ScrollViewer.HorizontalScrollBarVisibility="Disabled"
      ScrollViewer.VerticalScrollBarVisibility="Auto" BorderThickness="0"
      HorizontalContentAlignment="Stretch" />
  </Border>
</UserControl>
```

We start by adding a number of XML namespace prefixes for some of our application projects. Using the `Converters` prefix, we add instances of the `FeedbackTypeToImageSourceConverter` and `BoolToVisibilityConverter` classes that we saw earlier into the `UserControl.Resources` section. We also reuse our `AnimatedStackPanel` class from Chapter 6, *Mastering Practical Animations*.

Next, we see the `SmallImageInButtonStyle` style, that is based on the `ImageInButtonStyle` style that we also saw earlier, and adds some sizing properties. After that, we see the `FeedbackStyle` style that defines what each feedback message will look like in our feedback control.

Each `Feedback` object will be rendered in three columns; the first contains an image that specifies the type of feedback, using the `FeedbackTypeToImageSourceConverter` class that we saw earlier, the second displays the message, with a `TextWrapping` value of `Wrap`, and the third holds a button with an image, using our `SmallImageInButtonStyle` style, that users can use to remove the message.

Note that, as this is purely a UI control with no business logic in, we are able to use the code behind file, even when using MVVM. As such, we attach event handlers for the `MouseEnter` and `MouseLeave` events to the `Grid` panel containing each `Feedback` object and another for the `PreviewMouseLeftButtonDown` event to the delete button. The final resource that we have here is a `DropShadowEffect` instance that defines a small shadow effect.

For the feedback control, we define a `Border` element that uses a semi-transparent border brush and has a `BorderThickness` value of `1,0,1,1` and a `CornerRadius` value of `0,0,5,5`. These four values work like the `Margin` property and enable us to set different values for each of the four sides, or corners in the case of the `CornerRadius` property. In this way, we can display a rectangle that is only bordered on three sides, with rounded corners on two.

Note that the `Visibility` property on this border is determined by the `HasFeedback` property of the `FeedbackControl` class via an instance of our `BoolToVisibilityConverter` class. Therefore, when there are no feedback objects to display, the border will be hidden. Also note that our `Shadow` resource is applied to the border's `Effect` property.

Inside the border, we declare a `ListBox` control, with its `ItemsSource` property set to the `Feedback` property of the `FeedbackControl` class and its height restricted to a maximum of three feedback items, after which, vertical scrollbars will be shown. Its `ItemTemplate` property is set to the `FeedbackTemplate` that we defined in the resources section.

Its `ItemsPanel` property is set to the `AnimatedPanel` resource that we declared to animate the entrance and exit of the feedback items. Next, we remove the default border of the `ListBox` by setting the `BorderThickness` property to 0 and stretch the autogenerated `ListBoxItem` objects to fit the width of the `ListBox` control by setting the `HorizontalContentAlignment` property to `Stretch`.

Let's now see the code behind of our feedback control:

```
using System;
using System.Collections.Generic;
using System.Collections.Specialized;
using System.Linq;
using System.Windows;
using System.Windows.Controls;
using System.Windows.Input;
using System.Windows.Threading;
using CompanyName.ApplicationName.DataModels;
using CompanyName.ApplicationName.DataModels.Collections;
using CompanyName.ApplicationName.Extensions;

namespace CompanyName.ApplicationName.Views.Controls
{
  public partial class FeedbackControl : UserControl
  {
    private static List<DispatcherTimer> timers =
      new List<DispatcherTimer>();

    public FeedbackControl()
    {
      InitializeComponent();
    }

    public static readonly DependencyProperty FeedbackProperty =
      DependencyProperty.Register(nameof(Feedback),
      typeof(FeedbackCollection), typeof(FeedbackControl),
      new UIPropertyMetadata(new FeedbackCollection(),
      (d, e) => ((FeedbackCollection)e.NewValue).CollectionChanged +=
      ((FeedbackControl)d).Feedback_CollectionChanged));

    public FeedbackCollection Feedback
    {
      get { return (FeedbackCollection)GetValue(FeedbackProperty); }
      set { SetValue(FeedbackProperty, value); }
    }

    public static readonly DependencyProperty HasFeedbackProperty =
      DependencyProperty.Register(nameof(HasFeedback), typeof(bool),
```

```
      typeof(FeedbackControl), new PropertyMetadata(true));

  public bool HasFeedback
  {
    get { return (bool)GetValue(HasFeedbackProperty); }
    set { SetValue(HasFeedbackProperty, value); }
  }

  private void Feedback_CollectionChanged(object sender,
    NotifyCollectionChangedEventArgs e)
  {
    if ((e.OldItems == null || e.OldItems.Count == 0) &&
      e.NewItems != null && e.NewItems.Count > 0)
    {
      e.NewItems.OfType<Feedback>().Where(f => !f.IsPermanent).
        ForEach(f => InitializeTimer(f));
    }
    HasFeedback = Feedback.Any();
  }

  private void InitializeTimer(Feedback feedback)
  {
    DispatcherTimer timer = new DispatcherTimer();
    timer.Interval = feedback.Duration;
    timer.Tick += Timer_Tick;
    timer.Tag = new Tuple<Feedback, DateTime>(feedback, DateTime.Now);
    timer.Start();
    timers.Add(timer);
  }

  private void Timer_Tick(object sender, EventArgs e)
  {
    DispatcherTimer timer = (DispatcherTimer)sender;
    timer.Stop();
    timer.Tick -= Timer_Tick;
    timers.Remove(timer);
    Feedback feedback = ((Tuple<Feedback, DateTime>)timer.Tag).Item1;
    Feedback.Remove(feedback);
  }

  private void DeleteButton_PreviewMouseLeftButtonDown(object sender,
    MouseButtonEventArgs e)
  {
    Button deleteButton = (Button)sender;
    Feedback feedback = (Feedback)deleteButton.DataContext;
    Feedback.Remove(feedback);
  }
```

[434]

```
      private void Border_MouseEnter(object sender, MouseEventArgs e)
      {
        foreach (DispatcherTimer timer in timers)
        {
          timer.Stop();
          Tuple<Feedback, DateTime> tag =
            (Tuple<Feedback, DateTime>)timer.Tag;
          tag.Item1.Duration = timer.Interval = tag.Item1.Duration.
            Subtract(DateTime.Now.Subtract(tag.Item2));
        }
      }

      private void Border_MouseLeave(object sender, MouseEventArgs e)
      {
        foreach (DispatcherTimer timer in timers)
        {
          Feedback feedback = ((Tuple<Feedback, DateTime>)timer.Tag).Item1;
          timer.Tag = new Tuple<Feedback, DateTime>(feedback, DateTime.Now);
          timer.Start();
        }
      }
    }
  }
```

We start by declaring the collection of `DispatcherTimer` instances that will be responsible for timing when each feedback object should be removed from the collection, according to its `Duration` property. We then see the declaration of the `Feedback` and `HasFeedback` Dependency Properties, along with their CLR wrappers and the `Feedback` property's `CollectionChanged` handler.

In the attached `Feedback_CollectionChanged` handler method, we call the `InitializeTimer` method, passing in each new, non-permanent feedback item. Note that we need to use the `OfType` LINQ Extension method to cast each item in the `NewItems` property of the `NotifyCollectionChangedEventArgs` class from the `object` type to `Feedback`. Before returning control to the caller, we set the `HasFeedback` property accordingly.

In the `InitializeTimer` method, we initialize a `DispatcherTimer` instance and set its interval to the value from the `Duration` property of the `feedback` input parameter. We then attach the `Timer_Tick` event handler, add the current time and the feedback object into the `Tag` property of the timer for later use, start the timer and add it into the `timers` collection.

In the `Timer_Tick` method, we access the timer from the `sender` input parameter and the `Feedback` instance from its `Tag` property. The feedback item is then removed from the `Feedback` collection, the timer is stopped and removed from the `timers` collection and the `Tick` event handler is detached.

In the `DeleteButton_PreviewMouseLeftButtonDown` method, we first cast the delete button from the `sender` input parameter. We then cast the `Feedback` object from the button's `DataContext` property and remove it from the `Feedback` collection.

In the `Border_MouseEnter` method, we iterate through the `timers` collection and stop each timer. The interval of each timer and duration of each associated `Feedback` object is then set to the remaining time that they should be displayed for, in effect, pausing their durations.

Finally, we see the `Border_MouseLeave` method, which re-initializes the `Tag` property of each timer in the timers collection, with the same feedback item and the current date and time, and restarts it when the user's mouse pointer leaves the feedback control.

This means that the length of time that temporary feedback messages are displayed for can be extended if the user moves their mouse pointer over the feedback control. This feature will hold the feedback messages in the control for as long as the user keeps their mouse pointer over the control, giving them ample time to read the messages. Let's now see what this control looks like:

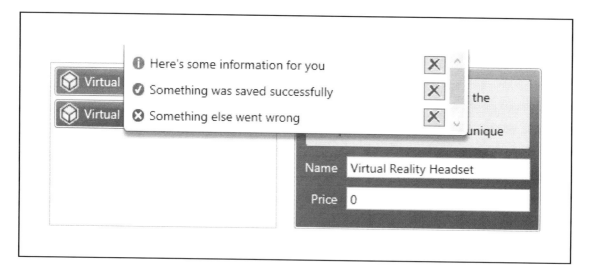

If you have menu buttons at the top of your Views, then you could alternatively have the feedback appear at the bottom of the application, or even sliding in from one of the sides. Also note that the delete buttons have not been styled, so as to shorten this example, but they should be styled in line with the other controls in a real application.

If you remember from `Chapter 3`, *Writing Custom Application Frameworks*, all of our View Models will have access to our new `FeedbackManager` class through the `FeedbackManager` property in our `BaseViewModel` class, and so we can replicate the feedback in the preceding image from any View Model like this:

```
FeedbackManager.Add(new Feedback("Here's some information for you",
    FeedbackType.Information));
FeedbackManager.Add("Something was saved successfully", true);
FeedbackManager.Add("Something else went wrong", false);
FeedbackManager.Add("Something else went wrong too", false);
```

Utilizing multiple threads

Traditionally, all applications were developed as single threaded applications. However, when long running background processes were running, the application UI would freeze and become unresponsive, because the single thread was busy elsewhere. This problem and other performance bottlenecks led to the current era of asynchronous programming and multi-threaded applications.

In days gone by, creating multi-threaded applications was a complicated matter. With each successive version of the .NET Framework, Microsoft have striven to make this task easier. Originally, we only had the Thread class and then the `BackgroundWorker` class in .NET 2.0, but in .NET 4.0, they introduced the `Task` class and in .NET 4.5, they introduced the `async` and `await` keywords.

In this section, we will explore the latter methods of multithreading and add functionality to our application framework that will enable us to perform our data retrieval and update actions asynchronously. Let's start by looking at the `async` and `await` keywords first.

Discovering the Async and Await keywords

Along with these new keywords, Microsoft have also added a plethora of new methods across the .NET Framework that end with the suffix `Async`. As the suffix hints, these new methods are all asynchronous and can be used in conjunction with the new keywords. Let's start with the basic rules.

First of all, in order to use the `await` keyword in a method, the method signature must be declared with the `async` keyword. The `async` keyword enables us to use the `await` keyword in the method and returns just the `T` generic type parameter from a method that actually returns the `Task<T>` type. A method that is modified with the `async` keyword is known as an async method.

Async methods actually execute in a synchronous manner, until they reach an `await` expression. If there is no `await` keyword in the method, then the whole method will run synchronously and the compiler will output a warning.

While a portion of async methods run asynchronously, they don't in fact run on their own threads. No additional threads are created using the `async` and `await` keywords. Instead, they give the appearance of multithreading by using the current synchronization context, but only when the method is active and not when it is paused while running an `await` expression.

When execution reaches an `await` keyword, the method is suspended until the awaited task has completed asynchronously. During this time, execution returns to the method caller. When the asynchronous action is complete, program execution returns to the method and the remainder of the code in it is run synchronously.

Async methods are required to have a particular signature. They all need to use the `async` modifier keyword and in addition to this, the names of async methods should end with the `Async` suffix to clearly signify that they are asynchronous methods. Another requirement of declaring async methods is that they cannot contain any `ref` or `out` input parameters.

The final requirement is that async methods can only use one of three return types; `Task`, the generic `Task<TResult>`, or `void`. Note that the generic `TResult` type parameter is the same as and can be replaced with `T`, but Microsoft refer to it as `TResult` simply because it specifies a return type.

All async methods that return some meaningful result will use the `Task<TResult>` type, where the actual type of the return value will be specified by the `TResult` generic type parameter. Therefore, if we want to return a `string` from our async method, we would declare that our async method returns a parameter of type `Task<string>`. Let's see an example of this in action:

```
using System;
using System.IO;
using System.Threading.Tasks;

...
```

```
public async Task<string> GetTextFileContentsAsync(string filePath)
{
  string fileContents = string.Empty;
  try
  {
    using (StreamReader streamReader = File.OpenText(filePath))
    {
      fileContents = await streamReader.ReadToEndAsync();
    }
  }
  catch { /*Log error*/ }
  return fileContents;
}
```

Here we have a simple async method that returns a string that represents the contents of the text file specified by the `filePath` input parameter. Note that the actual return type of the method is in fact `Task<string>`. In it, we first initialize the `fileContents` variable and then attempt to create a `StreamReader` instance from the `File.OpenText` method within the `using` statement.

Inside the `using` statement, we attempt to populate the `fileContents` variable by awaiting the result of the `ReadToEndAsync` method of the `StreamReader` class. Up until this point, the method will run synchronously. The `ReadToEndAsync` method will be called and then control will immediately return to the caller of our async method.

When the return value of the `ReadToEndAsync` method is ready, control returns to our async method and continues where it left off. In our example, there is nothing else to do but return the result string, although async methods can contain any number of lines after the `await` keyword, or even multiple `await` keywords. Note that in a real-world application, we would log any exceptions that might be thrown from this method.

If our async method just performs some function asynchronously, but does not return anything, then we use a return type of `Task`. That is, the task-based async method will return a `Task` object that enables it to be used with the `await` keyword, but the actual method will not return anything to the caller of that method. Let's see an example of this:

```
using System.Text;

. . .

public async Task SetTextFileContentsAsync(string filePath,
  string contents)
{
  try
  {
```

```
      byte[] encodedFileContents = Encoding.Unicode.GetBytes(contents);
      using (FileStream fileStream = new FileStream(filePath,
        FileMode.OpenOrCreate, FileAccess.Write, FileShare.None, 4096, true))
      {
        await fileStream.WriteAsync(encodedFileContents, 0,
          encodedFileContents.Length);
      }
    }
    catch { /*Log error*/ }
  }
```

In the `SetTextFileContentsAsync` method, we first need to convert our input string to a byte array. For this reason, we now need to add a `using` directive for the `System.Text` namespace in addition to the three originally specified. Note that in this particular example, we are using `Unicode` encoding, but you are free to use any other encoding value here.

After using the `GetBytes` method to obtain a byte array from the `contents` input parameter, we initialize a new `FileStream` object within another `using` statement. Apart from the `booluseAsync` input parameter, the remaining parameters used in the `FileStream` constructor in this example are unimportant and you are free to replace them with values that suit your requirements better.

Inside the `using` statement, we see the `await` keyword used with the `WriteAsync` method. Up until this point, this method will run synchronously and on this line, it will start execution of the `WriteAsync` method and then return control to the method caller.

As execution leaves the `using` statement, the `FileStream` instance will be closed and disposed of. As this method has nothing to return, the return type of the async method is `Task`, which enables it to be awaited by the calling code. Again, we would typically log any exceptions that might be thrown from this method, but this is omitted here for brevity.

Most of us will never use the third return type option of `void` when using MVVM, because it is primarily used in event handling methods. Note that async methods that return `void` cannot be awaited and that calling code cannot catch exceptions thrown from such async methods.

One of the most commonly asked questions regarding async methods is "How can I create an async method from a synchronous method?" Luckily, there is a very simple solution to this using the `Task.Run` method, so let's take a quick look at it now.

```
await Task.Run(() => SynchronousMethod(parameter1, parameter2, etc));
```

Here we use a Lambda expression to specify the synchronous method to run in an asynchronous context. That's all that we have to do to run a synchronous method asynchronously. However, what about the opposite requirement? Let's now see how we can run an asynchronous method synchronously. Again, the `Task` class provides us with a solution:

```
Task task = SetFileContentsAsync(filePath, contents);
task.RunSynchronously();
```

As we saw at the end of Chapter 1, *A Smarter Way of Working with WPF*, in order to run an asynchronous method synchronously, we first need to instantiate a `Task` instance from our asynchronous method. Then, all we have to do is call the `RunSynchronously` method on that instance and it will run synchronously.

Building asynchrony into our framework

Using the `Task` class, we can add functionality into our application framework that will enable us to call any data access method asynchronously. Furthermore, it will also enable us to run our data operations asynchronously when the application is running and synchronously while testing. In order to achieve this, we will need to implement several parts, that go together to provide this functionality.

Let's look at the first part, that will wrap each data operation and hold the result value, if applicable, along with any feedback messages and/or error details.

```
using System;
using System.Data.SqlClient;
using CompanyName.ApplicationName.DataModels.Enums;
using CompanyName.ApplicationName.Extensions;

namespace CompanyName.ApplicationName.DataModels
{
  public abstract class DataOperationResult<T>
  {
    public DataOperationResult(string successText)
    {
      Description = string.IsNullOrEmpty(successText) ?
        "The data operation was successful" : successText;
    }

    public DataOperationResult(Exception exception, string errorText)
    {
      Exception = exception;
      if (Exception is SqlException)
```

```
    {
      if (exception.Message.Contains("The server was not found"))
        Error = DataOperationError.DatabaseConnectionError;
      else if (exception.Message.Contains("constraint"))
        Error = DataOperationError.DatabaseConstraintError;
      // else Description = Exception.Message;
    }
    if (Error != DataOperationError.None)
      Description = Error.GetDescription();
    else
    {
      Error = DataOperationError.UndeterminedDataOperationError;
      Description = string.IsNullOrEmpty(errorText) ?
        Error.GetDescription() : errorText;
    }
  }

  public DataOperationResult(Exception exception) :
    this(exception, string.Empty) { }

  public string Description { get; set; }

  public DataOperationError Error { get; set; } =
    DataOperationError.None;

  public Exception Exception { get; set; } = null;

  public bool IsSuccess =>
    Error == DataOperationError.None && Exception == null;
  }
}
```

In our abstract `DataOperationResult` class, we have a number of properties and constructor overloads. The first constructor is used for a successful set data operation and merely takes the `successText` input parameter, which is used to populate the `Description` property, unless it is null or empty, in which case a default successful operation message is used instead.

The second constructor is to be used when an exception has been thrown during the data operation and takes the exception and an error message as input parameters. In it, we first set the `Exception` property to the exception specified by the `exception` input parameter and then, we have a chance to catch common exceptions and replace their error messages with custom messages in plain English.

Although we are only checking for exceptions of type `SqlException` in this example, we could easily extend this to capture other well-known and/or expected exceptions and replace their messages with custom messages using laymen terms, by adding further `else...if` conditions.

Note that the `Error` property of enumeration type `DataOperationError` is used here to set and output the predefined error messages and we'll see that in a moment. If the exception is not one that we were expecting, then we could chose to output the actual exception message, although that would mean little to the users and could be deemed confusing, or even worrying.

Instead, we could log the exception in the database and output the message from the `errorText` input parameter. We check whether the `Error` property has been set and if it has, we call our `GetDescription` Extension method to retrieve the message that relates to the set enumeration member and set it to the `Description` property.

Otherwise, we set the `Error` property to the `UndeterminedDataOperationError` member and the `Description` property to the value of the `errorText` input parameter if is not null or empty, or the text associated with the selected enumeration member if it is. The third constructor is also used when an exception has been thrown, but when there is no predefined feedback message.

After the constructors, we see the properties of the `DataOperationResult` class, most of which are self-explanatory. Of particular note is the `IsSuccess` property, which can be used by the calling code to determine what to do with the result. Let's now take a look at the `DataOperationError` enumeration class that is used to hold the error descriptions:

```
using System.ComponentModel;

namespace CompanyName.ApplicationName.DataModels.Enums
{
  public enum DataOperationError
  {
    [Description("")]
    None = 0,
    [Description("A database constraint has not been adhered to, so this
      operation cannot be completed")]
    DatabaseConstraintError = 9995,
    [Description("There was an undetermined data operation error")]
    UndeterminedDataOperationError = 9997,
    [Description("There was a problem connecting to the database")]
    DatabaseConnectionError = 9998,
  }
}
```

As you can see, we utilize the `DescriptionAttribute` class to relate a humanized error message with each enumeration member. We can use the `GetDescription` Extension method that we saw earlier to access the text values from the attributes.

Each enumeration member is assigned a number and this could work well with the SQL Server error numbers, if you were using SQL stored procedures or queries directly. For example, we could cast the SQL error code to the particular enumeration member to get the custom message for each error. Let's now take a look at the two classes that extend the `DataOperationResult` class:

```
using System;

namespace CompanyName.ApplicationName.DataModels
{
  public class GetDataOperationResult<T> : DataOperationResult<T>
  {
    public GetDataOperationResult(Exception exception, string errorText) :
      base(exception, errorText)
    {
      ReturnValue = default(T);
    }

    public GetDataOperationResult(Exception exception) :
      this(exception, string.Empty) { }

    public GetDataOperationResult(T returnValue, string successText) :
      base(successText)
    {
      ReturnValue = returnValue;
    }

    public GetDataOperationResult(T returnValue) :
      this(returnValue, string.Empty) { }

    public T ReturnValue { get; private set; }
  }
}
```

We start with the `GetDataOperationResult` class, which is used to return the result of get data operations, or the exception details, if an error occurred. It adds a `ReturnValue` property of generic type `T` to hold the return value of the data operation. Apart from this single member, it simply adds a number of constructors that each call the base class constructors.

The first is used when an exception has been thrown and sets the `ReturnValue` property to its default value, rather than leaving it as null. The second constructor is also used when an exception has been thrown, but when there is no predefined error message.

The third constructor is used for a successful data operation and sets the `ReturnValue` property to the returned value. The fourth is also used for a successful data operation, but when there is no predefined success message. It calls the third constructor, passing the returned value and an empty string for the success message. Let's now see the other class that extends the `DataOperationResult` class:

```
using System;

namespace CompanyName.ApplicationName.DataModels
{
  public class SetDataOperationResult : DataOperationResult<bool>
  {
    public SetDataOperationResult(Exception exception, string errorText) :
       base(exception, errorText) { }

    public SetDataOperationResult(string successText) :
       base(successText) { }
  }
}
```

The `SetDataOperationResult` class is used for set operations and so has no return value. Like the `GetDataOperationResult` class, its two constructors call the relevant base class constructors. The first is used when an exception has been thrown and the second is used for a successful data operation and accepts an input parameter for the operation's success message.

We'll need to add a new method into our `FeedbackManager` class to enable us to add the feedback messages from our `GetDataOperationResult` and `SetDataOperationResult` classes directly. We'll also include a parameter that allows us to override whether each message will be displayed for its set duration, or until the user closes it manually. Let's take a look at that now:

```
public void Add<T>(DataOperationResult<T> result, bool isPermanent)
{
  Add(new Feedback(result.Description, result.IsSuccess, isPermanent));
}
```

Note that we use the `DataOperationResult` base class as the input parameter here, so that either of our derived classes can be used with it. This method simply initializes a `Feedback` object from the `Description` and `IsSuccess` properties of the `DataOperationResult` class and passes it to the `Add` method that actually adds it to the `Feedback` collection.

If we're going to be making asynchronous calls to the UI feedback control, then we'll also need to ensure that they are made on the UI thread, so as to avoid the common `calling thread cannot access this object because a different thread owns it` exception.

To enable this, we need to add a reference to the `UiThreadManager` class that we discussed earlier into our `FeedbackManager` class, although here, we add a reference to the `IUiThreadManager` interface instead, to enable us to use a different implementation while testing:

```
using System;
using CompanyName.ApplicationName.Managers.Interfaces;

...

private IUiThreadManager uiThreadManager = null;

...

public IUiThreadManager UiThreadManager
{
  get { return uiThreadManager; }
  set { uiThreadManager = value; }
}

...

public void Add(Feedback feedback)
{
  UiThreadManager.RunOnUiThread((Action)delegate
  {
    Feedback.Add(feedback);
  });
}
```

Using the `IUiThreadManager` interface, we simply need to wrap our single call to add feedback to the `FeedbackManager.Feedback` collection property with the `RunOnUiThread` method to run it on the UI thread. However, our `uiThreadManager` field needs to be initialized before any feedback is displayed and we can do that from the first use of the `BaseViewModel` class:

```
public BaseViewModel()
{
  if (FeedbackManager.UiThreadManager == null)
    FeedbackManager.UiThreadManager = UiThreadManager;
}

...

public IUiThreadManager UiThreadManager
{
  get { return DependencyManager.Instance.Resolve<IUiThreadManager>(); }
}
```

The first time that any View Model is instantiated, this base class constructor will be called and the instance of the `IUiThreadManager` interface in the `FeedbackManager` class will be initialized. Of course, in order to correctly resolve our instance of the `IUiThreadManager` interface at runtime, we'll first need to register it in the `App.xaml.cs` file, along with the other registrations.

```
DependencyManager.Instance.Register<IUiThreadManager, UiThreadManager>();
```

Let's take a look at this interface and the classes that implement it now:

```
using System;
using System.Threading.Tasks;
using System.Windows.Threading;

namespace CompanyName.ApplicationName.Managers.Interfaces
{
  public interface IUiThreadManager
  {
    object RunOnUiThread(Delegate method);

    Task RunAsynchronously(Action method);

    Task<TResult> RunAsynchronously<TResult>(Func<TResult> method);
  }
}
```

The IUiThreadManager interface is a very simple affair and declares just three methods. The RunOnUiThread method is used to run code on the UI thread, the first RunAsynchronously method is used to run code asynchronously and the second RunAsynchronously method is used to run methods that return something asynchronously. Let's now see the classes that implement it:

```
using System;
using System.Threading.Tasks;
using System.Windows;
using System.Windows.Threading;
using CompanyName.ApplicationName.Managers.Interfaces;

namespace CompanyName.ApplicationName.Managers
{
  public class UiThreadManager : IUiThreadManager
  {
    public object RunOnUiThread(Delegate method)
    {
      return Application.Current.Dispatcher.Invoke(
        DispatcherPriority.Normal, method);
    }

    public Task RunAsynchronously(Action method)
    {
      return Task.Run(method);
    }

    public Task<TResult> RunAsynchronously<TResult>(Func<TResult> method)
    {
      return Task.Run(method);
    }
  }
}
```

In the UiThreadManager class, the RunOnUiThread method calls the Invoke method on the Application.Current.Dispatcher object, to ensure that the method that is passed to it is queued to run on the UI thread.

Basically, a dispatcher is responsible for maintaining the queue of work items for a particular thread and each thread will have its own dispatcher. The Application.Current property returns the Application object for the current AppDomain object and its Dispatcher property returns the dispatcher of the thread that was running when the application started – the UI thread.

As was seen earlier, the `RunAsynchronously` methods simply pass the methods specified by the `method` input parameters to the `Task.Run` method. We also saw an example of mocking the `RunAsynchronously` method in Chapter 1, *A Smarter Way Of Working With WPF*, but now let's see the whole `MockUiThreadManager` class, that we could use while testing our application:

```
using System;
using System.Threading.Tasks;
using System.Windows.Threading;
using CompanyName.ApplicationName.Managers.Interfaces;

namespace Test.CompanyName.ApplicationName.Mocks.Managers
{
  public class MockUiThreadManager : IUiThreadManager
  {
    public object RunOnUiThread(Delegate method)
    {
      return method.DynamicInvoke();
    }

    public Task RunAsynchronously(Action method)
    {
      Task task = new Task(method);
      task.RunSynchronously();
      return task;
    }

    public Task<TResult> RunAsynchronously<TResult>(Func<TResult> method)
    {
      Task<TResult> task = new Task<TResult>(method);
      task.RunSynchronously();
      return task;
    }
  }
}
```

In the `RunOnUiThread` method, we simply call the `DynamicInvoke` method of the `Delegate` class to run the method specified by the `method` input parameter. As we saw earlier, the `RunAsynchronously` methods use the `RunSynchronously` method of the `Task` class to run the methods specified by the `method` input parameters synchronously, to avoid timing problems during testing.

In them, we first create a new `Task` object with the method specified by the `method` input parameter, then call the `RunSynchronously` method on it and finally return the task. When called using the `await` keyword, this will actually return the result of the method instead.

Let's now see perhaps, the most important part of this functionality, where the `IUiThreadManager` interface is used, the `DataOperationManager` class.

```
using System;
using System.Diagnostics;
using System.Threading.Tasks;
using System.Windows.Threading;
using CompanyName.ApplicationName.DataModels;
using CompanyName.ApplicationName.Managers.Interfaces;

namespace CompanyName.ApplicationName.Managers
{
  public class DataOperationManager
  {
    private const int maximumRetryCount = 2;
    private IUiThreadManager uiThreadManager;

    public DataOperationManager(IUiThreadManager uiThreadManager)
    {
      UiThreadManager = uiThreadManager;
    }

    private IUiThreadManager UiThreadManager
    {
      get { return uiThreadManager.Instance; }
      set { uiThreadManager = value; }
    }

    private FeedbackManager FeedbackManager
    {
      get { return FeedbackManager.Instance; }
    }

    public GetDataOperationResult<TResult> TryGet<TResult>(
      Func<TResult> method, string successText, string errorText,
      bool isMessageSupressed)
    {
      Debug.Assert(method != null, "The method input parameter of the
        DataOperationManager.TryGet<TResult>() method must not be null.");
      for (int index = 0; index < maximumRetryCount; index++)
      {
        try
        {
          TResult result = method();
          return WithFeedback(
            new GetDataOperationResult<TResult>(result, successText),
            isMessageSupressed);
        }
```

```
  catch (Exception exception)
  {
    if (index == maximumRetryCount - 1)
    {
      return WithFeedback(
        new GetDataOperationResult<TResult>(exception, errorText),
        isMessageSupressed);
    }
    Task.Delay(TimeSpan.FromMilliseconds(300));
  }
}
return WithFeedback(
  new GetDataOperationResult<TResult>(default(TResult), successText),
  isMessageSupressed);
}

private GetDataOperationResult<TResult>WithFeedback<TResult>(
  GetDataOperationResult<TResult> dataOperationResult, bool
  isMessageSupressed)
{
  if (isMessageSupressed && dataOperationResult.IsSuccess)
    return dataOperationResult;
  FeedbackManager.Add(dataOperationResult, false);
  return dataOperationResult;
}

public Task<GetDataOperationResult<TResult>> TryGetAsync<TResult>(
  Func<TResult> method, string successText, string errorText,
  bool isMessageSupressed)
{
  return UiThreadManager.RunAsynchronously(() =>
    TryGet(method, successText, errorText, isMessageSupressed));
}

public SetDataOperationResult TrySet(Action method,
  string successText, string errorText, bool isMessagePermanent,
  bool isMessageSupressed)
{
  Debug.Assert(method != null, "The method input parameter of the
    DataOperationManager.TrySet<TResult>() method must not be null.");
  for (int index = 0; index < maximumRetryCount; index++)
  {
    try
    {
      method();
      return WithFeedback(new SetDataOperationResult(successText),
        isMessagePermanent, isMessageSupressed);
    }
```

```
        catch (Exception exception)
        {
          if (index == maximumRetryCount - 1)
          {
            return WithFeedback(new SetDataOperationResult(exception,
              errorText), isMessagePermanent, isMessageSupressed);
          }
          Task.Delay(TimeSpan.FromMilliseconds(300));
        }
      }
      return WithFeedback(new SetDataOperationResult(successText),
        isMessagePermanent, isMessageSupressed);
    }

    private SetDataOperationResult WithFeedback(
      SetDataOperationResult dataOperationResult,
      bool isMessagePermanent, bool isMessageSupressed)
    {
      if (isMessageSupressed && dataOperationResult.IsSuccess)
        return dataOperationResult;
      FeedbackManager.Add(dataOperationResult, isMessagePermanent);
      return dataOperationResult;
    }

    public Task<SetDataOperationResult> TrySetAsync(Action method)
    {
      return TrySetAsync(method, string.Empty, string.Empty);
    }

    public Task<SetDataOperationResult> TrySetAsync(Action method,
      string successText, string errorText)
    {
      return TrySetAsync(method, successText, errorText, false, false);
    }

    public Task<SetDataOperationResult> TrySetAsync(Action method,
      string successText, string errorText, bool isMessagePermanent,
      bool isMessageSupressed)
    {
      return UiThreadManager.RunAsynchronously(() => TrySet(method,
        successText, errorText, isMessagePermanent, isMessageSupressed));
    }
  }
}
```

The `DataOperationManager` class starts with a couple of private fields, that represent the maximum number of attempts to retry each data operation in case there is a problem and the instance of the `IUiThreadManager` interface to use to run our functions asynchronously when running the application.

The constructor enables us to inject the `IUiThreadManager` dependency that will be used into the class and sets it to the private `UiThreadManager` property, which can only be accessed from within the class. Likewise, the `FeedbackManager` property is also private and enables us to pass feedback messages to the manager class to display them in the UI.

Next, we see the generic `TryGet<TResult>` method that returns an object of type `GetDataOperationResult<TResult>`. More specifically, it returns a generic object of type `TResult`, that is wrapped in one of our `GetDataOperationResult` objects. It first asserts that the `method` input parameter is not null, as this class is based around this required parameter.

In this method, we create a loop, with the number of its iterations determined by the value of the `maximumRetryCount` field and inside the loop, we try to run the function specified by the `method` input parameter. If the data operation is successful, we initialize a `GetDataOperationResult` object, passing the return value and success feedback message and return it via the `WithFeedback` method.

If an error occurs and the maximum number of attempts have not yet been reached, then we use the asynchronous `Task.Delay` method to wait before attempting to run the method again. If the maximum number of errors have been reached, then the exception and error feedback message are wrapped in a `GetDataOperationResult` object and returned via the `WithFeedback` method.

One improvement that we could implement here would be to increase this delay time each time we retry the data operation. We could implement a function that returns an exponentially increasing number, based on the `maximumRetryCount` field, representing the millisecond value that will be passed to the `Task.Delay` method. This would be more likely to better handle short network drop outs.

The `WithFeedback` method enables developers to suppress successful feedback messages, as they might not always need the users to receive feedback. For example, we may not need to inform them that their data objects were fetched from the database successfully, if they have or will soon be displayed on the screen.

Therefore, if the data operation was successful and the `isMessageSupressed` input parameter is `true`, the data operation result is returned directly, without feedback. Otherwise, the `dataOperationResult` input parameter object is passed to the `FeedbackManager` class to display the associated message, using the new methods that we added earlier.

Next, we see the asynchronous `TryGetAsync` method, that simply calls the `TryGet` method via the `RunAsynchronously` method of the `UiThreadManager` class. After that, we have the `TrySet` method that is responsible for running all set data operations and returns an object of type `SetDataOperationResult`.

This method is very similar to the `TryGet` method, except that it works for set data operations. Similarly, it first asserts that the `method` input parameter is not null and then runs the remainder of the code within a for loop. This again enables our retry capability and is limited by the value of the `maximumRetryCount` field.

In the method, we try to run the function specified by the `method` input parameter and if the data operation is successful, we initialize a `SetDataOperationResult` object, passing just the success feedback message and return it via the `WithFeedback` method.

If an error occurs and the number of attempts specified by the `maximumRetryCount` field have not yet been reached, then we use the `Task.Delay` method to wait before attempting to run the method again. If the maximum number of errors have been reached, then the exception and error feedback message are wrapped in a `SetDataOperationResult` object and returned via the `WithFeedback` method.

The `WithFeedback` method used with the `SetDataOperationResult` objects works exactly the same as the earlier one that works with the generic `GetDataOperationResult` objects. Finally, we have some overloaded `TrySetAsync` methods, that end up calling the `TrySet` method asynchronously via the `RunAsynchronously` method of the `UiThreadManager` class.

One point to note here is that currently, this class is located in the `Managers` project. If we were at all likely to need to swap out our data access technology, then we might prefer to move this class to the data access project for ease of removal. As it stands, we don't have that requirement and so, it is fine where it is.

We can make use of this `DataOperationManager` class in the `DataController` class that we saw earlier, with just a few changes. We can also replace its previous `SetAuditCreateFields` and `SetAuditUpdateFields` methods with some new methods that also update our data models that implement the `ISynchronizableDataModel` interface. Let's take a look at the new code in there:

```
using System;
using System.Threading.Tasks;
using CompanyName.ApplicationName.DataModels;
using CompanyName.ApplicationName.DataModels.Collections;
using CompanyName.ApplicationName.DataModels.Enums;
using CompanyName.ApplicationName.DataModels.Interfaces;
using CompanyName.ApplicationName.Managers;
using CompanyName.ApplicationName.Models.Interfaces;

namespace CompanyName.ApplicationName.Models.DataControllers
{
  public class DataController
  {
    ...

    private DataOperationManager dataOperationManager;

    public DataController(IDataProvider dataProvider,
      DataOperationManager dataOperationManager, User currentUser)
    {
      ...
      DataOperationManager = dataOperationManager;
      CurrentUser = currentUser.Clone();
    }

    protected DataOperationManager DataOperationManager
    {
      get { return dataOperationManager; }
      private set { dataOperationManager = value; }
    }

    ...

    public Task<SetDataOperationResult> AddProductAsync(Product product)
    {
      return DataOperationManager.TrySetAsync(() =>
        DataProvider.AddProduct(InitialiseDataModel(product)),
        $"{product.Name} was added to the data source successfully", $"A
        problem occurred and {product.Name} was not added to the data
        source.");
    }
```

```
public Task<SetDataOperationResult> DeleteProductAsync(
  Product product)
{
  return DataOperationManager.TrySetAsync(() =>
    DataProvider.DeleteProduct(DeleteDataModel(product)),
    $"{product.Name} has been deleted from the data source
    successfully.", $"A problem occurred and {product.Name} was not
    deleted from the data source.", true, false);
}

public Task<GetDataOperationResult<Products>> GetProductsAsync()
{
  return DataOperationManager.TryGetAsync(() =>
    DataProvider.GetProducts(), string.Empty, "A problem occurred when
    trying to retrieve the products.", true);
}

public SetDataOperationResult UpdateProduct(Product product)
{
  return DataOperationManager.TrySet(() =>
    DataProvider.UpdateProduct(UpdateDataModel(product)),
    $"{product.Name} was saved in the data source successfully.", $"A
    problem occurred and {product.Name} was not updated in the data
    source.", false, false);
}

private T InitialiseDataModel<T>(T dataModel)
  where T : class, IAuditable, new()
{
  dataModel.Auditable = new Auditable(dataModel, CurrentUser);
  if (dataModel is ISynchronizableDataModel<T>)
  {
    ISynchronizableDataModel<T> synchronisableDataModel =
      (ISynchronizableDataModel<T>)dataModel;
    synchronisableDataModel.ObjectState = ObjectState.Active;
  }
  return dataModel;
}

private T DeleteDataModel<T>(T dataModel)
  where T : class, IAuditable, new()
{
  dataModel.Auditable.UpdatedOn = DateTime.Now;
  dataModel.Auditable.UpdatedBy = CurrentUser;
  if (dataModel is ISynchronizableDataModel<T>)
  {
    ISynchronizableDataModel<T> synchronisableDataModel =
      (ISynchronizableDataModel<T>)dataModel;
```

```
        synchronisableDataModel.ObjectState = ObjectState.Deleted;
      }
      return dataModel;
    }

    private T UpdateDataModel<T>(T dataModel)
      where T : class, IAuditable, new()
    {
      dataModel.Auditable.UpdatedOn = DateTime.Now;
      dataModel.Auditable.UpdatedBy = CurrentUser;
      return dataModel;
    }
  }
}
```

We start this class with the `dataOperationManager` field of type `DataOperationManager`. We don't need to use an interface here, as this class is safe to be used during testing. However, it contains a member of type `IUiThreadManager`, and we need to be able to use different implementations of this, dependent upon whether we're running or testing the application.

Therefore, we still need to inject the instance of the `dataOperationManager` field to use through the constructor, so that it's instance of the `IUiThreadManager` interface can be resolved in the calling code. After the constructor, we see the private `DataOperationManager` property, that can only be set from within the class.

The first of the new methods is the `AddProductAsync` method and as a set operation, it returns a `Task` of type `SetDataOperationResult`. Internally and like all async set operations here, it calls the `TrySetAsync` method of the `DataOperationManager` class. It passes the method to run asynchronously and the success and unspecified error text to be displayed as user feedback.

Note that we pass the `product` input parameter to the `InitialiseDataModel` method, before passing it to the `AddProduct` method of the `IDataProvider` instance, to initialize the base class `Auditable` property before it is stored in the database.

If the current instance also extends the `ISynchronizableDataModel` interface, then its `ObjectState` property will be set to the `Active` member of the `ObjectState` enumeration. This idea could easily be extended; if we had an `IIdentifiable` interface with a single identification property, we could initialize that here also.

The DeleteProductAsync method also returns a Task of type SetDataOperationResult and calls the TrySetAsync method of the DataOperationManager class, but it uses a different overload, which enables the feedback message to be displayed permanently, or until the user manually closes it. In this example, it is used to ensure that the user is aware that the product was deleted.

In this method, we pass the product input parameter to the DeleteDataModel method, before passing it to the DeleteProduct method of the IDataProvider instance. This sets the UpdatedOn property of the Auditable class to the current date and time and the UpdatedBy property to the currently logged in user. If the current instance extends the ISynchronizableDataModel interface, then its ObjectState property will also be set to a state of Deleted.

The next new method is the GetProductsAsync method, which is a get operation and returns a Task of type GetDataOperationResult<Products>. Internally and like all async get operations, it calls the TryGetAsync method of the DataOperationManager class. It passes the method to run asynchronously and the unspecified error text to be displayed as user feedback.

Of particular note here is the bool parameter that it passes, which suppresses any successful feedback message from being displayed. If there is an error, either the provided error message or a more well defined custom error message will be displayed still, but as no successful message will be displayed, we simply pass an empty string through for that parameter.

The final new data operation method is the UpdateProduct method, which is not asynchronous, and returns a SetDataOperationResult directly. Instead of the TrySetAsync method, it calls the TrySet method of the DataOperationManager class and passes the method to run, the success and error messages and two bool parameters to signify that it should display the feedback normally.

Internally, it passes the product input parameter to the UpdateDataModel method, before passing it to the UpdateProduct method of the IDataProvider instance. This sets the UpdatedOn property of the Auditable class to the current date and time and the UpdatedBy property to the currently logged in user.

This gives an example of how we might build up our data operation methods, predominantly using asynchronous access methods, but not restricted to having to do so. Of course, there are many ways of accessing data in an application and you should experiment with the way that suits you best. This way would suit larger scale applications best, as there is a fair amount of overhead in creating this system.

However, there's still one piece of the puzzle missing. Now that we've changed the constructor of the `DataController` class, we'll also need to update our `BaseViewModel` class, which exposes it, again.

```
protected DataController Model
{
  get { return new DataController(
    DependencyManager.Instance.Resolve<IDataProvider>(),
    new DataOperationManager(UiThreadManager),
    StateManager.CurrentUser); }
}

...

public IUiThreadManager UiThreadManager
{
  get { return DependencyManager.Instance.Resolve<IUiThreadManager>(); }
}
```

Now, the `IDataProvider` implementation is resolved by the `DependencyManager` instance, along with the `IUiThreadManager` implementation that gets injected into the `DataOperationManager` object. In addition to this, we pass the value of the `StateManager.CurrentUser` property to the `DataController` class constructor to instantiate it each time it is requested.

Now, we have a system in place that can run our data operations either synchronously or asynchronously and retry our data operations a specified number of times if they fail, before finally reporting custom feedback messages to the user.

We can customize how long these messages remain visible, before automatically disappearing, or whether they will automatically disappear or not, or even whether they are displayed in the first place or not. Even with these options, the system remains lightweight and can be easily added to.

Going the extra mile

Most privately developed applications are primarily functional, with little time and effort spent on design concerns and even less on usability. How many times have we seen applications that throw out a stack trace to the end user when an error occurs, or validation messages that highlight errors with the camel case code names for fields, rather than the labels used in the UI?

In a good application, the end user should never be presented with any code-based terminology. If we were writing an English based application, we wouldn't output error messages in Spanish, so why output them in C#? This can confuse the user and even alarm them in some cases.

How many times have you used an application that has an awkward process flow to perform each task, that involves far more mouse clicks than is necessary? This section is dedicated to avoiding these kinds of situations and suggests a number of ways of improving the usability of our applications.

Producing in-application help

In an ideal world, we would all create applications that were so intuitive that we wouldn't need to provide in-application help. However, with the complexity of some of today's applications, this is not always possible. It is therefore often helpful to provide the end users of our applications with some form of help that they can refer to when necessary.

There are a number of ways of doing this, with the first simply being to provide a link to a separate help file from the application. If we have a PDF, or other type of file that contains help for the users, we can add it to our solution in Visual Studio as a resource.

To do this, we can add a `Resources` folder into our solution and then select the **Add New Item** option in the new folder's context menu. After navigating to the help file in the **Add New Item** dialog and successfully adding it, we can view its properties, by selecting it in the **Solution Explorer** and pressing F4, or right clicking it and selecting **Properties** from the context menu.

Once the properties are displayed, we can verify that the file has been added with a **Build Action** of **Content** and a **Copy to Output Directory** value of **Copy always** or **Copy if newer**, which ensures that our help file and its `Resources` folder will be copied to the folder that contains the application executable file and that the newest version will always be used.

We can then add a menu item or button to our application, that the users can select to open the document directly. In our View Model command that is data bound to this control, we can call the `Start` method of the `Process` class, passing the path of the help file, to open the file in the default application on the user's computer.

```
System.Diagnostics.Process.Start(filePath);
```

We can get the folder path of the application executable file using the following code:

```
string filePath = System.AppDomain.CurrentDomain.BaseDirectory;
```

Therefore, if our `Resources` folder is in the startup project, we could attain its folder path like this:

```
string filePath = Path.Combine(
    new DirectoryInfo(System.AppDomain.CurrentDomain.BaseDirectory).
    Parent.Parent.FullName, "Resources");
```

This utilizes the `DirectoryInfo` class to access the parent folder of the parent folder of the executable file, or the root directory of the project, and the `Combine` method of the `Path` class to create a file path that combines the new `Resources` folder with that path.

If we don't have a complete documentation file for our application, a quick and simple alternative would be to add an information icon to each View. This image control could display pertinent information to the users in a tooltip when they place their mouse pointer over it.

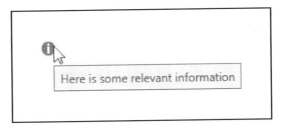

Using the information icon from the Visual Studio Image Library that was discussed in `Chapter 7`, *Creating Visually Appealing User Interfaces*, we can create these help points like this:

```
<Image Source="pack://application:,,,/CompanyName.ApplicationName;
    component/Images/Information_16.png" Stretch="None" ToolTip="Here is
    some relevant information" />
```

Either way, the idea is to provide the users of the application with any help that they may need right from the application itself. This not only improves the usability of our applications, but also reduces user errors and increases data quality.

Enabling user preferences

The users of our applications are likely to be very different to each other, or at least have their individual preferences. One user may prefer to work in one way, while another may have different preferences. Providing the ability for them to customize the application to suit the way that they work will increase the usability of the application for them.

This may relate to the View that they prefer to see when the application starts, or to which particular options in each View that they prefer to use, or even to the size and position of the application when it was last used. There are any number of preferences that we can offer each user.

Luckily, we can offer this customization functionality with minimal work, as the .NET Framework provides us with settings files for just this purpose. These settings can either have application or user scope and can be mixed and matched in each settings file.

Application settings are the same for each user and are suited to storing configuration settings, such as e-mail server details or credentials. User settings can be different for each user and are suited to the kind of personal customizations just discussed.

Typically, the startup project will already have a settings file named `Settings.settings`. It can be found by opening the `Properties` folder in the **Solution Explorer** in Visual Studio and opened by double-clicking on it. Alternatively, you can right-click on the project in the **Solution Explorer**, select the **Properties** option and then select the **Settings** tab.

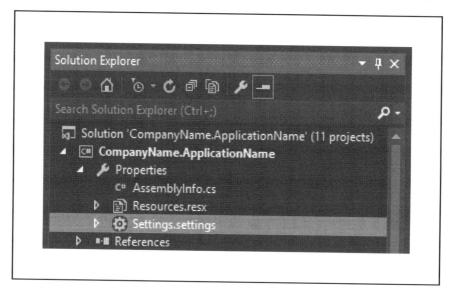

Settings files can also be added to other projects, although they are not typically available by default. In order to add a settings file to another project, we first need to open the project properties by right clicking on the project in the **Solution Explorer** and selecting the **Properties** option.

In the project properties window, select the **Settings** tab and click the link that says **This project does not contain a default settings file. Click here to create one**. A settings file will be created within the project `Properties` folder in the **Solution Explorer**. We are then free to start adding our user preferences.

	Name	Type		Scope		Value
	AreAuditFieldsVisible	bool	∨	User	∨	False
	AreSearchTermsSaved	bool	∨	User	∨	False
*	Setting	string	∨	User	∨	

To add our custom settings, click a blank row in the settings file and enter the name, data type, scope and default value of the setting. The name will be used in code and so, cannot contain spaces. We can select our own custom data types, although whichever type we select must be serializable. The default value is the initial value that the setting will have before the user changes it.

Settings will usually be loaded upon application startup and saved just before application shutdown. As such, it is customary to attach event handlers to the `Loaded` and `Closed` events in the `MainWindow.xaml.cs` file, although we can also do it in the `App.xaml.cs` file if we have configured the application to use it. We can see a typical example here:

```
using System;
using System.Windows;
using CompanyName.ApplicationName.ViewModels;

namespace CompanyName.ApplicationName
{
  public partial class MainWindow : Window
  {
    public MainWindow()
    {
      InitializeComponent();
```

```
        Loaded += MainWindow_Loaded;
        Closed += MainWindow_Closed;
    }

    private void MainWindow_Loaded(object sender, RoutedEventArgs e)
    {
      MainWindowViewModel viewModel = new MainWindowViewModel();
      viewModel.LoadSettings();
      DataContext = viewModel;
    }

    private void MainWindow_Closed(object sender, EventArgs e)
    {
      MainWindowViewModel viewModel = (MainWindowViewModel)DataContext;
      viewModel.SaveSettings();
    }
  }
}
```

We attach the two event handlers in the constructor, right after the components are initialized. In the `MainWindow_Loaded` method, we instantiate an instance of the `MainWindowViewModel` class, call its `LoadSettings` method and set it as the window's `DataContext` property value.

In the `MainWindow_Closed` method, we access the instance of the `MainWindowViewModel` class from the `DataContext` property, but this time, call its `SaveSettings` method. Now, let's see these methods in the `MainWindowViewModel.cs` file:

```
using CompanyName.ApplicationName.ViewModels.Properties;

...

public void LoadSettings()
{
  Settings.Default.Reload();
  StateManager.AreAuditFieldsVisible =
    Settings.Default.AreAuditFieldsVisible;
  StateManager.AreSearchTermsSaved = Settings.Default.AreSearchTermsSaved;
}

public void SaveSettings()
{
  Settings.Default.AreAuditFieldsVisible =
    StateManager.AreAuditFieldsVisible;
  Settings.Default.AreSearchTermsSaved = StateManager.AreSearchTermsSaved;
  Settings.Default.Save();
}
```

The first thing that we need to do in the `LoadSettings` method is to call the `Reload` method on the default instance of the settings file. This loads the settings from the settings file into the `Default` object. From there, we set each settings property to its corresponding property that we created in our `StateManager` class, for use in the application.

Note that the values of each user's personal settings are not stored in the `Settings.settings` file. Instead, they are stored in their `AppData` folder, which is hidden by default. The exact file path can be found using the `ConfigurationManager` class, but to find it, we'll need to add a reference to the `System.Configuration` DLL and use the following code:

```
using System.Configuration;

...

string filePath = ConfigurationManager.OpenExeConfiguration(
    ConfigurationUserLevel.PerUserRoamingAndLocal).FilePath;
```

In my case, that resolves to the following file path:

```
C:\Users\Sheridan\AppData\Local\CompanyName\
    CompanyName.ApplicationNa_Url_0nu0qp14li5newll2223u0ytheisf2gh\
    1.0.0.0\user.config
```

Note that the folder in the `CompanyName` folder is named using a particular identification number that relates to the current settings and application version. Over time and after making changes, new folders will appear here with new identification numbers, but this is all totally transparent to the users, as their previous settings will be safely transferred.

Extending common courtesies

One area of application development where we can easily make great improvements is usability. Many applications these days are created with little or no concern for the end users that will be using the application each day.

We've probably all seen applications that spew out exception stack traces when errors occur and while we, as developers, may find that useful, it can be confusing, or even alarming for the end users. Instead of worrying the end users unnecessarily, we can output stack traces and any other pertinent information about each error to an `Errors` table in our database.

Extending this idea further, it is good working practice to totally avoid using any development terms or phrases anywhere in the application that the users can see. That includes all UI labels, along with any additional external help files and/or documentation. Using terms of this kind will make the application more difficult to use, especially for new users. All but the best known abbreviations should also be avoided.

We can further humanize our application by paying attention to the small details. How often have you come across an application that displays a label that says something like "1 passengers", or "2 item". While this is a very simple problem to fix, it is commonly found in many applications. Let's create a new Extension method to encapsulate this useful functionality in an `IntegerExtensions` class:

```
public static string Pluralize(this int input, string wordToAdjust)
{
  return $"{wordToAdjust}{(input == 1 ? string.Empty : "s")}";
}
```

In this example, we simply use string interpolation to append an `s` to the end of the `wordToAdjust` input parameter when the value of the this `input` parameter is not 1. While this will work for most words that we are likely to use, it is worth noting that there are some groups of words that this will not work with.

For example, some words, such as "Activity", end with a "y" in their singular form and will end with "ies" when pluralized. However, this problem can be easily addressed by either adding a new overload of our `Pluralize` method, or an additional input parameter that enables the users of our code to specify the transformation that they require.

With this method, we now have a really simple way to always ensure that our spelling is correct when dealing with quantities. Let's see how we might use this method to pluralize the word `Ticket`, but only when the amount of tickets in the `Tickets` collection is not 1.

```
public string TicketCountText => Tickets.Count.Pluralize("Ticket");
```

An extension to this method could combine this functionality with the actual number to output 6 `Tickets` for example. Let's take a look at this new method.

```
public static string Combine(this int input, string wordToAdjust)
{
  return $"{input} {wordToAdjust}{(input == 1 ? string.Empty : "s")}";
}
```

The `Combine` method is very similar to the `Pluralize` method, except that also includes the value of the `input` input parameter in the text output. We could also extend this method in the same way that we could extend the `Pluralize` method, to handle the pluralization of words other than those that just require an s to be appended. We can also use it in the same way:

```
public string TicketCountText => Tickets.Count.Combine("Ticket");
```

Another way that we could humanize our textual output would be to provide a selection summary field that displays a comma-separated list of the selected items in a collection control. Clearly, this would be unrequired for controls that only allow single selections to be made however, it could be a useful confirmation for those using multiple selection collection controls. Let's see how we could declare a `ToCommaSeparatedString` method now:

```
using System.Text;

...

public static string ToCommaSeparatedString<T>(
  this IEnumerable<T> collection)
{
  StringBuilder stringBuilder = new StringBuilder();
  int index = 0;
  foreach (T item in collection)
  {
    if (index > 0)
    {
      if (index < collection.Count() - 1) stringBuilder.Append(", ");
      else if (index == collection.Count() - 1)
        stringBuilder.Append(" and ");
    }
    stringBuilder.Append(item.ToString());
    index++;
  }
  return stringBuilder.ToString();
}
```

Here, we have a method that we can call on any collection that is either of the type of, or extends the `IEnumerable<T>` interface and receive a string back that contains a comma-separated list of each contained element. We can either call it with a string collection, or implement the `object.ToString` method in our classes, as that will be called on each element.

This method uses the `StringBuilder` class to build the comma-separated list. As the `StringBuilder` class has a slight overhead when being initialized and when exporting the constructed string, tests have shown that it only really offers an improvement in time over basic string concatenation when appending ten or more strings.

You may therefore prefer to refactor this method to remove the `StringBuilder` object, although you may also find that the difference in milliseconds is negligible. Returning to the method, after declaring the `StringBuilder` object, we initialize the `index` variable, which is used to specify which separator to join each string with.

When the `index` variable equals zero and no strings have yet been added to the `StringBuilder` object, no separator will be appended. After that, we check whether the current string is the last in the collection and if it is, we prepend " and" to it, otherwise we prepend a comma and space to it.

After each iteration, we increment the `index` variable and when finished, we return the output from the `StringBuilder` object. It could be used to display a comma-separated list of the products that a user has selected like this:

```
SelectedProducts.Select(p => p.Name).ToCommaSeparatedString();
```

As you can see, there are many ways that we can humanize our output for the end users, in order to make them feel more at ease when using our applications. Let's now move on to see other ways that we can provide that great user experience for our users.

Un-burdening the end user

There are many things that we can do to make the life of the end users easier. One simple example would be to set the focus in a form to the first field, so that users can start typing as soon as they load a view, without first needing to focus it manually.

We saw one way to do this using an Attached Property in Chapter 4, *Becoming Proficient With Data Binding*, but we can also achieve this easily, by first adding a new `bool` property into our `BaseViewModel` class.

```
private bool isFocused = false;

...

public bool IsFocused
{
  get { return isFocused; }
  set { if (isFocused != value) { isFocused = value;
```

```
      NotifyPropertyChanged(); } }
  }
```

Next, we can add a style resource into the application resources in the `App.xaml` file:

```xml
<Style TargetType="{x:Type TextBox}">
  <!-- Define default TextBox style here -->
</Style>
<Style x:Key="FocusableTextBoxStyle" TargetType="{x:Type TextBox}"
  BasedOn="{StaticResource {x:Type TextBox}}">
  <Style.Triggers>
    <DataTrigger Binding="{Binding IsFocused}" Value="True">
      <Setter Property="FocusManager.FocusedElement"
        Value="{Binding RelativeSource={RelativeSource Self}}" />
    </DataTrigger>
  </Style.Triggers>
</Style>
```

This assumes that we already have a default style that we want to use for our textboxes and that our new style will be based on that, but add this additional focusable functionality. It simply consists of a single data trigger that uses the `FocusedElement` property of the `FocusManager` class to focus the textbox element that has this style applied to it when the `IsFocused` property is set to `true`.

Therefore, all we need to do to focus a particular textbox in a View is to apply this style to it and set the `IsFocused` property from the `BaseViewModel` class to `true` in the appropriate place in the related View Model.

```
IsFocused = true;
```

Note that the textbox will become focused as the property becomes `true` and so, if the property is already `true`, we may need to first set it to `false` before again setting it to `true` to get this to work. For example, if the property was true before the View was loaded, then the textbox would not become focused.

Another simple example of making our application users' lives easier would be to pre-populate any form fields that we may be able to. For example, if our application has a login screen that uses the users' Windows username, we could fill in the user name field in the form after accessing it from the `WindowsIdentity` class like this:

```
UserName = WindowsIdentity.GetCurrent().Name;
```

Another example of this might be to pre-populate form fields with the most commonly used values. We could perhaps fill in a date field to today's date, or an Amount Paid field to the total amount, if that is what the users typically do.

We do however need to be careful when doing this, because if we get the default value(s) wrong, it could backfire and actually take the users longer to delete the default value and replace it with the value that they want than to just input the value directly. Remember, the idea is to save the users time and make them more productive.

Quite often, we can save the users of our applications a great amount of time. If we have the chance to ask them exactly what they do and how they would use the application on a day to day basis, then we can usually program a lot of their operations into functions in the application.

For example, if any users have to repeatedly edit a number of files with the same data, perhaps to add, remove, or update a particular field, then we could build that functionality straight into the application.

Instead of making them edit a single record at a time, we could provide a View where they set the field or fields to change and the new value(s), along with the ability to select multiple records, and therefore save them a great deal of time and effort.

All menial, or repetitive tasks can be programmed into functions and so, writing a good application is not just restricted to making pretty and asynchronous UIs, but also to making it highly usable. Furthermore, the more useful the application is, the more productive the users will become, and the more lavish the praise that will be bestowed on us and our development teams, if applicable.

Summary

In this chapter, we discussed further ways to improve our applications, making them as useful to the end users as possible. We investigated how we could implement a custom user feedback system to keep the users informed with the status of the operations that they perform.

We also examined how to make our applications asynchronous, so that our UI won't freeze when the application is performing long running operations. We then looked at one way of building this asynchronous behavior right into our application framework, so that we can run any data access operation asynchronously, with minimal code.

We ended with a short section dedicated to improving the way that our applications are perceived by the end users. In it, we detailed a number of ways of accomplishing this, from providing in-application help and user preferences to paying attention to the smaller details and implementing work-heavy functions to save the users from having to manually do the same.

In the next chapter, we'll be looking at a number of ways that we can improve the performance of our applications, from utilizing the power of installed graphics cards, to writing more efficient code. We'll also look into how we can improve the efficiency of our data bindings and resources and investigate other techniques, such as data virtualization.

10
Improving Application Performance

The performance of WPF applications in general is one of their biggest problems. The more visual layers that our rendered data objects and UIs contain, the more time it takes to render them, so we often need to maintain a balance between making our applications visually appealing and making them perform better.

This situation can be improved by running our WPF applications on more powerful computers. This explains why these applications are most prevalent in the financial industry. However, not everyone can afford to update all of their users' computers for this purpose.

Luckily, there are a number of ways that we can improve the performance of our WPF applications and we'll investigate them here. The art of improving application performance really comes down to making a lot of small improvements that together, add up to a noticeable difference.

In this chapter, we'll explore how we can better utilize the graphics rendering power of our computer's graphics card and declare our resources more efficiently. We'll investigate how we can improve our application's performance by opting to use lighter weight UI controls, more efficient data binding modes and employing other techniques, such as virtualization.

Leveraging the power of hardware rendering

As we've learnt, the visuals that WPF can output, while beautiful, can be very CPU intensive and we often need to bear this in mind when designing our Views. However, rather than compromising our designs, we can offload the intensive rendering processes to the host computer's **Graphics Processing Unit (GPU)** instead.

While WPF will default to utilize its software rendering pipeline, it is also able to take advantage of a hardware rendering pipeline. This hardware pipeline leverages features of Microsoft DirectX, as long as the host PC has DirectX version 7 or higher installed. Furthermore, if the version of DirectX that is installed is version 9 or higher, increased performance improvements will be seen.

The WPF Framework looks at the graphics hardware that is installed on the computer that it is running on and puts it into one of three categories, depending on its features, such as video RAM, shaders, and support for multi-textures. If it does not support version 7 of DirectX or higher, then it is classed in **Rendering Tier 0** and will not be used for hardware rendering at all.

However, if it does support DirectX version 7 or higher, but less than version 9, then it is classed in **Rendering Tier 1** and will be used for partial hardware rendering. But as practically all new graphics cards support versions of DirectX higher than 9, they would all be classed in **Rendering Tier 2** and would be used for full hardware rendering.

As the UI will freeze during the rendering time, care should be taken to minimize the number of visual layers that are rendered. Therefore, for WPF applications that will run on computers that have graphics hardware classed in Rendering Tier 0 and use software rendering, we need to take extra care.

However, if our application is likely to be run on older computers, or computers with older graphics hardware, we can detect this using the rendering tier and run more efficient code in these instances. We can find out the rendering tier of the host computer's graphics hardware using the static `Tier` property of the `RenderCapability` class.

Unfortunately, instead of the type of this property being some kind of useful enumeration, it is in fact an integer, where just the high-order word represents the value of the tier and can be either 0, 1, or 2. We can attain it by shifting the bits in the integer to read the value from just the last two bytes:

```
using System.Windows.Media;

...

int renderingTier = RenderCapability.Tier >> 16;
```

Once we know the rendering tier of the host computer's graphics hardware, we can write code accordingly. For example, let's imagine that we had a processor-intensive View, with lots of visuals making up each item in a collection. We could set the tier value into a property and data bind it to the View, where we could select different data templates to use dependent upon the processing power of the host computer. Let's examine this example, by first creating that missing enumeration:

```
namespace CompanyName.ApplicationName.DataModels.Enums
{
  public enum RenderingTier
  {
    Zero = 0,
    One = 1,
    Two = 2
  }
}
```

Next, we need to add a property of type `RenderingTier` into our `StateManager` class from `Chapter 3`, *Writing Custom Application Frameworks*.

```
public RenderingTier RenderingTier { get; set; }
```

We don't need to inform the `INotifyPropertyChanged` interface of changes to this property because it will only be set once upon application startup. Let's adjust our previous example:

```
public App()
{
  StateManager.Instance.RenderingTier =
    (RenderingTier)(RenderCapability.Tier >> 16);
}
```

After casting the bit shifted integer value into our `RenderingTier` enumeration and setting it to the new `RenderingTier` property in the `StateManager` class, we can then start to use it in our Views to determine the level of visualizations that we can employ:

```
<ListBox ItemsSource="{Binding Products}">
  <ListBox.Style>
    <Style TargetType="{x:Type ListBox}">
      <Setter Property="ItemTemplate"
        Value="{StaticResource SimpleDataTemplate}" />
      <Style.Triggers>
        <DataTrigger Binding="{Binding
          StateManager.Instance.RenderingTier}" Value="One">
          <Setter Property="ItemTemplate"
            Value="{StaticResource MoreComplexDataTemplate}" />
        </DataTrigger>
```

```
        <DataTrigger Binding="{Binding
          StateManager.Instance.RenderingTier}" Value="Two">
          <Setter Property="ItemTemplate"
            Value="{StaticResource MostComplexDataTemplate}" />
        </DataTrigger>
      </Style.Triggers>
    </Style>
  </ListBox.Style>
</ListBox>
```

In this example, we have a `ListBox` control that is displaying a collection of products. The idea is that we can declare three different data templates to define what each product will look like. We have a `SimpleDataTemplate` template that might just provide a text-based output, a `MoreComplexDataTemplate` template, that could contain some basic visuals and a `MostComplexDataTemplate` template, that could contain several layers of visuals.

In the style that is applied to the list box, we set the default `SimpleDataTemplate` template as the value of its `ItemTemplate` property. Using the `RenderingTier` property of the `StateManager` class, we then declare a couple of data triggers to switch the value of the `ItemTemplate` property to one of the more complex templates, dependent upon the rendering tier of the host computer.

Making more efficient resources

When we reference our resources, we can either use a `StaticResource` or a `DynamicResource`. If you remember from Chapter 5, *Using The Right Controls for The Job*, a `StaticResource` will look up the value of the resource just once, which is comparative to a compile-time lookup. A `DynamicResource` will repeatedly look up the value of the resource each time it is requested, whether it has changed or not, like a runtime lookup.

For this reason, we should only ever use a `DynamicResource` if we really need to and can attain much better performance by using the `StaticResource` class instead. If we find that we need to use a lot of `DynamicResource` references to access our resources, then we can refactor our code to data bind to properties in our `StateManager` class instead of the resources, to increase performance.

Another simple way to improve the performance of our resources is to reuse them. Instead of declaring them inline in the place that they are used in the XAML, we should declare them in a suitable resource section and reference them.

In this way, each resource is created just once and shared. To extend this idea further, we could define all of our shared resources in the application resources in the `App.xaml` file and share them between all of the application Views.

Imagine a situation where some brush resources were declared inline with the XAML within a `DataTemplate` element. Now imagine that this template is set as the `ItemTemplate` of an `ItemsControl` object and that the collection that is data bound to its `ItemsSource` property contains a thousand elements.

The application will therefore create a thousand brush objects with identical properties for each brush that is declared locally within the data template. Now compare this to the situation where we declare each required brush just once in a resource section and reference it from the template. It's clear to see the benefit of this method and the huge savings that can be made of the computer's resources.

Furthermore, this idea also affects the `Resources` sections of our Views, if we will be displaying more than one of them at once. If we declare a View to define how each object in a collection should be rendered, then all of the resources that are declared in the View will be initialized once for each element in the collection. In this case, it is better to declare them at the application level.

Freezing objects

In WPF, certain resource objects, such as animations, geometries, brushes and pens, can be made `Freezable`. This provides special features that can help to improve the performance of our WPF applications. `Freezable` objects can either be frozen or unfrozen. In the unfrozen state, they behave like any other object, but when frozen, they become immutable and can no longer be modified.

The main benefit of freezing objects is that it can improve application performance, because frozen objects no longer require resources to be consumed on monitoring and issuing change notifications. Another benefit is that a frozen object is also safe to be shared across threads, unlike unfrozen objects.

Many UI-related objects extend the `Freezable` class to provide this functionality and most `Freezable` objects relate to the graphics sub-system, as rendering visuals is one of the areas where performance improvements are most needed.

Classes such as the `Brush`, `Geometry` and `Transform` classes contain unmanaged resources and the system must monitor them for changes. By freezing these objects and making them immutable, the system is able to free up its monitoring resources and better utilize them elsewhere. Furthermore, even the memory footprint of a frozen object is considerably less than its unfrozen counterpart.

Therefore, in order to make the greatest performance improvements, we should get used to freezing all of our resources in all `Resource` sections, as long as we have no plans to modify them. As most resources typically remain unmodified, we are usually able to freeze the vast majority of them and gain significant and noticeable improvements in performance by doing so.

In `Chapter 7`, *Creating Visually Appealing User Interfaces,* we saw how we can freeze a `Freezable` object in code by calling its `Freeze` method. Let's now see how we can freeze our resources in XAML. First, we need to add an XML namespace prefix to the presentation options namespace to access its `Freeze` attribute:

```
xmlns:PresentationOptions=
  "http://schemas.microsoft.com/winfx/2006/xaml/presentation/options
"xmlns:mc="http://schemas.openxmlformats.org/markup-compatibility/2006"
mc:Ignorable="PresentationOptions"
```

Note that we also include another XML namespace prefix to be able to access the `Ignorable` attribute and we set our `PresentationOptions` prefix as its value. This is because the `Freeze` attribute is primarily only recognized by the WPF XAML processor and in order to maintain compatibility with other XAML readers, we need to specify that the attribute can be ignored.

We'll see a full example in the *Drawing Conclusions* section coming up soon, but for now and using a resource from an earlier example, let's see how to freeze a `Freezable` object in XAML:

```
<DropShadowEffect x:Key="Shadow" BlurRadius="10" Direction="270"
  ShadowDepth="7" Opacity="0.5" PresentationOptions:Freeze="True" />
```

Some `Freezable` objects, such as the animation and geometry objects, can contain other `Freezable` objects. When a `Freezable` object is frozen, its child objects are also frozen. However, there are a few cases where a `Freezable` object cannot be frozen.

One case happens if it has any properties that might change value, due to either animations, data binding, or `DynamicResource` references. The other case occurs when the `Freezable` object has any child objects that cannot be frozen.

If we are freezing resource type objects in the code behind of a custom control, for example, then we can call the `CanFreeze` property of the `Freezable` class to check whether each `Freezable` object can be frozen before attempting to freeze them.

```
EllipseGeometry ellipseGeometry =
   new EllipseGeometry(new Rect(0, 0, 500, 250));
if (ellipseGeometry.CanFreeze) ellipseGeometry.Freeze();
Path.Data = ellipseGeometry;
```

Once a `Freezable` object is frozen, it cannot be modified and attempting to do so will cause an `InvalidOperationException` to be thrown. Note that a `Freezable` object cannot be unfrozen, so to avoid this situation, we can check the value of the `IsFrozen` property before attempting to modify the object. If it is frozen, we can make a copy of it using its `Clone` method and modify that instead:

```
if (ellipseGeometry.IsFrozen)
{
  EllipseGeometry ellipseGeometryClone = ellipseGeometry.Clone();
  ellipseGeometryClone.RadiusX = 400;
  Path.Data = ellipseGeometry;
}
else ellipseGeometry.RadiusX = 400;
```

If a `Freezable` object is cloned, any `Freezable` children that it may have will also be copied to enable modification. When a frozen object is animated, the animation system will make cloned copies of it in this way so that it can modify them, but as this adds an overhead to performance, it is advisable not to freeze a `Freezable` object if it is expected to be animated.

Using the right controls for performance

As was mentioned previously, there are usually several different ways of achieving the same functionality, or UI display when using WPF. Some ways will provide better performance than others. For example, we saw how some panels do more intensive layout work and therefore consume more CPU cycles and/or RAM than others.

Therefore, this is one area that we can investigate in order to make performance improvements. If we do not require the complex layout and resizing abilities of a `Grid` panel, then we can gain a performance improvement by utilizing a more efficient `StackPanel` or `Canvas` panel instead.

Another example could be that if we do not require the ability to select in a collection control, then we should use an `ItemsControl` element instead of a `ListBox`. While swapping one control will not make much of a performance improvement on its own, making this same swap in the `DataTemplate` of an item that will be displayed thousands of time will make a noticeable difference.

As we discovered in `Chapter 5`, *Using The Right Controls for The Job*, each time a UI element is rendered, the layout system must complete two passes, a measure pass and an arrange pass, collectively known as a layout pass. If the element has children and/or grandchildren, they will all need to complete the layout pass too. This process is intensive and the fewer passes that can be made, the quicker our Views will render.

As mentioned earlier, we need to be careful to ensure that we do not unnecessarily trigger additional passes of the layout system, as this can lead to poor performance. This can occur when adding or removing items to or from a panel, applying transforms on the elements, or by calling the `UIElement.UpdateLayout` method, which forces a new layout pass.

Because of the way that changes to a UI element will invalidate its children and force a new layout pass, we need to be especially careful when building hierarchical data in code. If we create the child elements first and then their parent objects and then the parents of those objects, and so on, then we will incur a huge performance hit, due to the existing child items being forced to perform multiple layout passes.

In order to address this issue, we need to always ensure that we build our tree from the top-down, rather than the top-up method just described. If we add the parent element(s) first and then add their children and their children if any, then we can avoid the additional layout passes. The performance improvement of using the top-down method is approximately five times quicker to render, and so is not insignificant. Let's look at some further control related performance benefits that we can employ.

Drawing conclusions

When we have a requirement to draw shapes in our UI, such as in our callout window example in `Chapter 7`, *Creating Visually Appealing User Interfaces*, we tend to use the abstract `Shape` class, or more accurately, one or more of its derived classes.

The `Shape` class extends the `FrameworkElement` class and so, it can make use of the layout system, be styled, have access to a range of stroke and fill properties and its properties can be data bound and animated. This makes it easy to use and generally the preferred method of drawing in WPF applications.

However, WPF also provides lower-level classes that can achieve the same end results, but more efficiently. The five classes that extend the abstract `Drawing` class have a much smaller inheritance hierarchy and as such, have a much smaller memory footprint than their `Shape` object-based counterparts.

The two most commonly used classes are the `GeometryDrawing` class, which is used to draw geometrical shapes, and the `DrawingGroup` class, which is used to combine multiple drawing objects into a single composite drawing.

Additionally, the `Drawing` class is also extended by the `GlyphRunDrawing` class, that renders text, the `ImageDrawing` class, that displays images and the `VideoDrawing` class, that enables us to play video files. As the `Drawing` class extends the `Freezable` class, further efficiency savings can be made by freezing its instances, if they do not need to be modified afterwards.

There is one other, potentially even more efficient method of drawing shapes in WPF. The `DrawingVisual` class does not provide event handling or layout functionality and so, its performance is improved compared with other drawing methods. However, this is a code only solution and there is no XAML based `DrawingVisual` option.

Furthermore, its lack of layout abilities means that in order to display it, we need to create a class that extends a class that provides layout support in the UI, such as the `FrameworkElement` class. To be even more efficient though, we could extend the `Visual` class, as that is the lightest weight class that can be rendered in the UI, with the fewest properties and no events to handle.

This class would be responsible for maintaining a collection of `Visual` elements to be rendered, creating one or more `DrawingVisual` objects to add to the collection and overriding a property and a method, in order to participate in the rendering process. It could also optionally provide event handling and hit testing capabilities, if user interaction was required.

It really depends on what we want to draw. Typically, the more efficient the drawing, the less flexible it is. For example, if we were just drawing some static clipart, background image, or perhaps logo, we could take advantage of the more efficient drawing methods, but if we need our drawing to grow and shrink as the application windows changes size, then we'll need to use the less efficient methods that provide more flexibility, or use another class in addition that provides that functionality.

Let's look at an example, that creates the same graphical image using each of the three different drawing methods. We'll define some smiley face emoticons, starting with the `Shape`-based method on the left-hand side, the `Drawing` object-based method in the center and the `DrawingVisual`-based method on the right. Let's first look at the visual output.

Now, let's inspect the XAML:

```
<UserControl x:Class="CompanyName.ApplicationName.Views.DrawingView"
   xmlns="http://schemas.microsoft.com/winfx/2006/xaml/presentation"
   xmlns:x="http://schemas.microsoft.com/winfx/2006/xaml"
   xmlns:Controls=
     "clr-namespace:CompanyName.ApplicationName.Views.Controls"
   xmlns:PresentationOptions=
     "http://schemas.microsoft.com/winfx/2006/xaml/presentation/options"
   Width="450" Height="150">
<Grid>
  <Grid.Resources>
    <RadialGradientBrush x:Key="RadialBrush" RadiusX="0.8" RadiusY="0.8"
      PresentationOptions:Freeze="True">
      <GradientStop Color="Orange" Offset="1.0" />
      <GradientStop Color="Yellow" />
    </RadialGradientBrush>
  </Grid.Resources>
  <Grid.ColumnDefinitions>
    <ColumnDefinition />
    <ColumnDefinition />
    <ColumnDefinition />
  </Grid.ColumnDefinitions>
  <Grid>
    <Grid.RowDefinitions>
      <RowDefinition Height="3*" />
```

```
      <RowDefinition Height="2*" />
      <RowDefinition Height="2*" />
      <RowDefinition Height="2*" />
      <RowDefinition Height="3*" />
    </Grid.RowDefinitions>
    <Grid.ColumnDefinitions>
      <ColumnDefinition />
      <ColumnDefinition />
      <ColumnDefinition />
      <ColumnDefinition />
      <ColumnDefinition />
    </Grid.ColumnDefinitions>
    <Ellipse Grid.RowSpan="5" Grid.ColumnSpan="5"
      Fill="{StaticResource RadialBrush}" Stroke="Black"
      StrokeThickness="5" />
    <Ellipse Grid.Row="1" Grid.Column="1" Fill="Black" Width="20"
      HorizontalAlignment="Center" />
    <Ellipse Grid.Row="1" Grid.Column="3" Fill="Black" Width="20"
      HorizontalAlignment="Center" />
    <Path Grid.Row="3" Grid.Column="1" Grid.ColumnSpan="3" Stroke="Black"
      StrokeThickness="10" StrokeStartLineCap="Round"
      StrokeEndLineCap="Round" Data="M0,10 A10,25 0 0 0 12.5,10"
      Stretch="Fill" HorizontalAlignment="Stretch" />
  </Grid>
  <Canvas Grid.Column="1">
    <Canvas.Background>
      <DrawingBrush PresentationOptions:Freeze="True">
        <DrawingBrush.Drawing>
          <DrawingGroup>
            <GeometryDrawing Brush="{StaticResource RadialBrush}">
              <GeometryDrawing.Geometry>
                <EllipseGeometry Center="50,50" RadiusX="50"
                  RadiusY="50" />
              </GeometryDrawing.Geometry>
              <GeometryDrawing.Pen>
                <Pen Thickness="3.5" Brush="Black" />
              </GeometryDrawing.Pen>
            </GeometryDrawing>
            <GeometryDrawing Brush="Black">
              <GeometryDrawing.Geometry>
                <EllipseGeometry Center="29.5,33" RadiusX="6.75"
                  RadiusY="8.5" />
              </GeometryDrawing.Geometry>
            </GeometryDrawing>
            <GeometryDrawing Brush="Black">
              <GeometryDrawing.Geometry>
                <EllipseGeometry Center="70.5,33" RadiusX="6.75"
                  RadiusY="8.5" />
```

```
                                  </GeometryDrawing.Geometry>
                                </GeometryDrawing>
                                <GeometryDrawing>
                                  <GeometryDrawing.Geometry>
                                    <PathGeometry>
                                      <PathGeometry.Figures>
                                        <PathFigure StartPoint="23,62.5">
                                          <ArcSegment Point="77,62.5" Size="41 41" />
                                        </PathFigure>
                                      </PathGeometry.Figures>
                                    </PathGeometry>
                                  </GeometryDrawing.Geometry>
                                  <GeometryDrawing.Pen>
                                    <Pen Thickness="7" Brush="Black" StartLineCap="Round"
                                      EndLineCap="Round" />
                                  </GeometryDrawing.Pen>
                                </GeometryDrawing>
                              </DrawingGroup>
                            </DrawingBrush.Drawing>
                          </DrawingBrush>
                        </Canvas.Background>
                      </Canvas>
                      <Canvas Grid.Column="2">
                        <Canvas.Background>
                          <VisualBrush>
                            <VisualBrush.Visual>
                              <Controls:SmileyFace />
                            </VisualBrush.Visual>
                          </VisualBrush>
                        </Canvas.Background>
                      </Canvas>
                    </Grid>
                  </UserControl>
```

The first thing that we can see straight away from this example is that the `Shape` object-based method of drawing is far simpler, achieving the same output as the far more verbose `Drawing` object-based method in far fewer lines of XAML. Let's now investigate the code.

After defining the `PresentationOptions` XML namespace, we declare a `RadialGradientBrush` resource and optimize its efficiency, by freezing it using the `Freeze` attribute that was discussed earlier in the chapter. Note that if we were planning on using this control multiple times simultaneously, then we could be even more efficient, by declaring all of our `Brush` and `Pen` objects in the application resources and reference them with `StaticResource` references.

We then declare an outer `Grid` panel, that has two columns. In the left column, we declare another `Grid` panel, with five rows and five columns. This inner panel is used to position the various `Shape` elements that make up the first smiley face. Note that we use star sizing on the row definitions of this panel in order to slightly increase the sizes of the top and bottom rows to better position the eyes and mouth of the face.

Inside the panel, we define an `Ellipse` object to create the overall shape of the face, fill it with our brush from the resources and add an outline with a black brush. We then use two further `Ellipse` elements filled with the black brush to draw the eyes and a `Path` element to draw the smile. Note that we do not fill the `Path` element, as that would look more like an open mouth than a smile.

Two other important points to note are that we must set the `Stretch` property to `Fill` to get the `Path` element to fill the available space that we provide it with and we must set the `StrokeStartLineCap` and `StrokeEndLineCap` properties to `Round` to produce the nice, rounded ends of the smile.

We specify the shape that the `Path` element should be using its `Data` property and the inline mini-language that we used previously. Let's break this value down into the various mini-language commands now:

```
M0,10 A10,25 0 0 0 12.5,10
```

As with the previous example before, we start with the Move command, which is specified by the `M` and the following co-ordinate pair and dictates the start point for the line. The remainder is taken up with the Elliptical Arc command, which is specified by the `A` and the following five figures.

In order, the five figures of the Elliptical Arc command relate to the size of the arc, or its *x* and *y* radii, its rotation angle, a bit field to specify whether the angle of the arc should be greater than 180° or not, another bit field to specify whether the arc should be drawn in a clockwise or anti-clockwise direction and finally, the end point of the arc.

Full details of this path syntax mini language can be found on the MSDN website. Note that we could change the bit field for the drawing direction to a `1` to draw a frown instead:

```
M0,10 A10,25 0 0 1 12.5,10
```

Now, let's move onto the second column of the outer `Grid` panel now. In this column, we recreate the same smiley face, but using the more efficient `Drawing` object-based objects. As they cannot render themselves like the `Shape` classes and we need to utilize other elements to do that job for us, we define them inside a `DrawingBrush` element and use that to paint the background of a `Canvas` object.

There are two important things to note here. The first is that we could have used the `DrawingBrush` element to paint any class that extends the `FrameworkElement` class, such as a `Rectangle`, or another type of panel.

The second is that as we have frozen the `DrawingBrush` element using the `Freeze` attribute, all of the inner elements that extend the `Freezable` type will also be frozen. In this case, that includes the `GeometryDrawing` objects, the `EllipseGeometry` and `PathGeometry` objects and even the `Brush` and `Pen` elements that were used to paint them.

When using a `DrawingBrush` object to render our drawings, we must define them using its `Drawing` property. As we want to build up our image from multiple `Drawing`-based objects, we need to wrap them all in a `DrawingGroup` object.

In order to recreate the overall shape of the face, we start with a `GeometryDrawing` element and specify an `EllipseGeometry` object as its `Geometry` property value. With this `GeometryDrawing` element, we paint the background by setting a reference of our `RadialGradientBrush` resource to its `Brush` property and define a new `Pen` instance in its `Pen` property to specify a stroke for it.

As with all `Geometry` objects, we specify its dimensions so that they are in scale with each other, rather than using exact pixel sizes. For example, our View is one hundred and fifty pixels high, but instead of setting the `Center` property of this `EllipseGeometry` object to seventy-five, which is half of the height, we have set it to fifty.

As the two radii properties are also set to fifty, they remain in scale with the position of the center and the resulting image is scaled to fit the container that it is rendered in. The scale that we use is up to our preference. For example, we could divide or multiply all of the co-ordinates, radii, brush and pen thicknesses in our drawing example by the same amount and we would end with the same face visual.

Next, we add another `GeometryDrawing` element with an `EllipseGeometry` object specified in its `Drawing` property for each of the two eyes on the face. These have no stroke and so have nothing assigned to the `Pen` property and are colored only using a black `Brush` set to their `Brush` properties. The final `GeometryDrawing` element hosts a `PathGeometry` object that draws the smile on the face.

Note that defining a `PathGeometry` in XAML is far more verbose than using the path syntax mini-language. In it, we need to specify each `PathFigure` element in the `PathFigures` collection property, although actually specifying this collection in XAML is optional. In the case of our smile, we just need to define a single `PathFigure` element containing an `ArcSegment` object.

The `StartPoint` property of the `PathFigure` element dictates where the arc should start, the `Size` property of the `ArcSegment` object relates to the size of the arc, or its *x* and *y* radii, while its `Point` property specifies the end point of the arc.

In order to define round ends for the smile, as we did with the previous smiley face, the `Pen` element that we specify for this `PathGeometry` object must have its `StartLineCap` and `EndLineCap` properties set to the `Round` member of the `PenLineCap` enumeration. This completes the second method of drawing a smiley face.

The third method uses `DrawingVisual` objects in code internally and results in a `Visual` object. As the items in the `Children` collection of the `Grid` panel are of type `UIElement`, we cannot add our `Visual` control to it directly. Instead, we can set it to the `Visual` property of a `VisualBrush` element and paint the background of an efficient container, such as a `Canvas` control, with it.

Let's take a look at the code in this `SmileyFace` class now:

```
using System;
using System.Collections.Generic;
using System.Windows;
using System.Windows.Media;

namespace CompanyName.ApplicationName.Views.Controls
{
  public class SmileyFace : Visual
  {
    private VisualCollection visuals;

    public SmileyFace()
    {
      visuals = new VisualCollection(this);
      visuals.Add(GetFaceDrawingVisual());
    }

    private DrawingVisual GetFaceDrawingVisual()
    {
      RadialGradientBrush radialGradientBrush =
        new RadialGradientBrush(Colors.Yellow, Colors.Orange);
      radialGradientBrush.RadiusX = 0.8;
      radialGradientBrush.RadiusY = 0.8;
      radialGradientBrush.Freeze();
      Pen outerPen = new Pen(Brushes.Black, 5.25);
      outerPen.Freeze();
      DrawingVisual drawingVisual = new DrawingVisual();
      DrawingContext drawingContext = drawingVisual.RenderOpen();
      drawingContext.DrawEllipse(radialGradientBrush, outerPen,
```

```
      new Point(75, 75), 72.375, 72.375);
    drawingContext.DrawEllipse(Brushes.Black, null,
      new Point(44.25, 49.5), 10.125, 12.75);
    drawingContext.DrawEllipse(Brushes.Black, null,
      new Point(105.75, 49.5), 10.125, 12.75);
    ArcSegment arcSegment =
      new ArcSegment(new Point(115.5, 93.75), new Size(61.5, 61.5), 0,
      false, SweepDirection.Counterclockwise, true);
    PathFigure pathFigure = new PathFigure(new Point(34.5, 93.75),
      new List<PathSegment>() { arcSegment }, false);
    PathGeometry pathGeometry =
      new PathGeometry(new List<PathFigure>() { pathFigure });
    pathGeometry.Freeze();
    Pen smilePen = new Pen(Brushes.Black, 10.5);
    smilePen.StartLineCap = PenLineCap.Round;
    smilePen.EndLineCap = PenLineCap.Round;
    smilePen.Freeze();
    drawingContext.DrawGeometry(null, smilePen, pathGeometry);
    drawingContext.Close();
    return drawingVisual;
  }

  protected override int VisualChildrenCount
  {
    get { return visuals.Count; }
  }

  protected override Visual GetVisualChild(int index)
  {
    if (index < 0 || index >= visuals.Count)
      throw new ArgumentOutOfRangeException();
    return visuals[index];
  }
}
}
```

There are several classes that we could have extended our `SmileyFace` class from, in order to display it in the UI. As we saw in `Chapter 5`, *Using The Right Controls for The Job*, most UI controls have a rich inheritance hierarchy, with each extended class offering some particular functionality.

In order to make the most efficient container for our `DrawingVisual`, we want to extend a class that enables it to take part in the layout process, but adds as little additional overhead via unused properties and unrequired event handling as possible. As such, we have chosen the `Visual` class, which cannot be used as a UI element directly in the XAML, but can be displayed as the visual of a `VisualBrush` element and used to paint a surface with.

To generate one or more `DrawingVisual` elements in our `SmileyFace` class, we need to declare and maintain a `VisualCollection` instance that will hold the `Visual` elements that we want to display. In the constructor, we initialize this collection and add the single `DrawingVisual` element that we want to render to it in this example, via the `GetFaceDrawingVisual` method.

In the `GetFaceDrawingVisual` method, we first declare a new version of our `RadialBrush` resource using the `RadialGradientBrush` class and a `Pen` element and freeze them using their `Freeze` methods. Next, we initialize a single `DrawingVisual` element and access a `DrawingContext` object from its `RenderOpen` method, with which to draw our shape.

We use the `DrawingContext` object to draw the ellipse that serves as the background for the face first. It is colored using the frozen `Brush` and `pen` elements. Note that as the `Visual` class has no `Stretch` property or concept of size, the dimensions that we use here are exact device-independent pixel dimensions, rather than relative values, as were used in the previous drawing methods.

In this example, our smiley faces are one hundred and fifty pixels wide by one hundred and fifty pixels tall and so the center position will be half of that. Therefore, these exact pixel values can be calculated by multiplying the relative values from the previous `Drawing`-based example by `1.5`.

However, we also need to consider the fact that the outline will be drawn half inside the drawing and half outside. As such, we need to adjust the two radii of this ellipse, reducing them by half of the outline size. As the pen used for this ellipse has a thickness of `5.25` device-independent pixels, we need to reduce each radii by `2.625`.

Next, we call the `DrawEllipse` method again to draw each of the eyes, passing in a black brush and no `Pen` element, along with their newly calculated positions and sizes. For the smile, we first need to create an `ArcSegment` element and add that to a collection of type `PathSegment`, while initializing a `PathFigure` object.

We then add the `PathFigure` object to a collection and pass that to the constructor of the `PathGeometry` object to initialize it. Next, we define the `Pen` that will be used to draw the smile, ensuring that we set its `StartLineCap` and `EndLineCap` properties to the `Round` member of the `PenLineCap` enumeration, as in the previous examples.

We then freeze this `Pen` object and pass it, along with the `PathGeometry` object, to the `DrawGeometry` method of the `DrawingContext` object to draw it. Finally, we close the drawing context using its `Close` method and return the single `DrawingVisual` element that we just created.

While we have now taken care of the code that draws our smiley face, we will not be able to see anything in the UI yet. In order to participate in the rendering process, we need to override a couple of members from the `Visual` class, the `VisualChildrenCount` property and the `GetVisualChild` method.

When overriding these members, we simply need to inform the `Visual` class of the visuals that we want it to render for us. As such, we simply return the number of items in our internal `VisualCollection` object from the `VisualChildrenCount` property and return the item in the collection that relates to the specified `index` input parameter from the `GetVisualChild` method.

In this example, we have added a check for invalid values from the `index` input parameter, although this shouldn't ever occur if we output the correct number of items from the `VisualChildrenCount` property in the first place.

So now, we have seen three different drawing methods for creating the same visual output, with each being more efficient than the previous. However, apart from the efficiency differences, we should also be aware of the differences in these drawing methods when it comes to manipulation and versatility of the elements.

As an example, let's adjust the `Width` of our `DrawingView` class, set its `ClipToBounds` property to `true` and see its new output.

```
Width="225" Height="150" ClipToBounds="True">
```

Let's now run the application again and see the output:

As we can see from the preceding image, these drawing methods behave differently when resized. The first method is redrawn at the current size and the thickness of each drawn line remains the same, even though the width of this face has been narrowed by the space provided to it from the parent `Grid` panel.

However, the second and third smiley faces actually look like a squashed image, where the thickness of each line is no longer static; the more vertical the line is, the thinner it now becomes. The overall width of these faces have also been adjusted by the parent `Grid` panel.

The third face however, has only been scaled by the `VisualBrush` object that is used to display it. If instead of extending the `Visual` class, we had wanted to derive from the `UIElement` class, to utilize some of its functionality, or perhaps to enable us to display our `SmileyFace` control directly in the XAML, then we would see a different output. Let's make a slight adjustment to our class declaration:

```
public class SmileyFace : UIElement
```

Let's also display it directly in the XAML now, replacing the `Canvas` and `VisualBrush` that previously displayed it:

```
<Controls:SmileyFace Grid.Column="2" />
```

Now, if we run the application again and see the output, it will look very different:

Because we specified exact values for our drawing, our `SmileyFace` control does not extend any class that would enable resizing or scaling and we no longer have the `VisualBrush` to resize it, the drawing remains exactly as it would be at full size, except that it now no longer fits into the space provided to it from the parent `Grid` panel.

In order to build the ability to draw the shape at different sizes into our class, we'll need to derive it from a class that provides us with additional properties and functionality. The `FrameworkElement` class supplies us with both dimension properties that we can use to draw our shape at the required size and a `Loaded` event that we can use to delay the construction of our shape until the relevant size has been calculated by the layout system. Let's see the changes that we'd need to make to achieve this:

```
public class SmileyFace : FrameworkElement
{
  ...

  public SmileyFace()
  {
    visuals = new VisualCollection(this);
    Loaded += SmileyFace_Loaded;
  }

  private void SmileyFace_Loaded(object sender, RoutedEventArgs e)
  {
    visuals.Add(GetFaceDrawingVisual());
  }

  private DrawingVisual GetFaceDrawingVisual()
  {
    ...
    DrawingVisual drawingVisual = new DrawingVisual();
    DrawingContext drawingContext = drawingVisual.RenderOpen();
    drawingContext.DrawEllipse(radialGradientBrush, outerPen,
      new Point(ActualWidth / 2, ActualHeight / 2), (ActualWidth -
      outerPen.Thickness) / 2, (ActualHeight - outerPen.Thickness) / 2);
    drawingContext.DrawEllipse(Brushes.Black, null, new Point(
      ActualWidth / 3.3898305084745761, ActualHeight / 3.0303030303030303),
      ActualWidth / 14.814814814814815, ActualHeight / 11.764705882352942);
    drawingContext.DrawEllipse(Brushes.Black, null, new Point(
      ActualWidth / 1.4184397163120568, ActualHeight / 3.0303030303030303),
      ActualWidth / 14.814814814814815, ActualHeight / 11.764705882352942);
    ArcSegment arcSegment = new ArcSegment(new Point(ActualWidth /
      1.2987012987012987, ActualHeight / 1.6), new Size(ActualWidth /
      2.4390243902439024, ActualHeight / 2.4390243902439024), 0, false,
      SweepDirection.Counterclockwise, true);
    PathFigure pathFigure = new PathFigure(new Point(ActualWidth /
```

```
      4.3478260869565215, ActualHeight / 1.6), new List<PathSegment>() {
      arcSegment }, false);
    PathGeometry pathGeometry =
      new PathGeometry(new List<PathFigure>() { pathFigure });

    ...
    return drawingVisual;
  }


  ...
}
```

The first change is that we need to move the call to generate the shape from the constructor to the `SmileyFace_Loaded` handling method. If we had not moved this, our shape would have no size, because the `ActualWidth` and `ActualHeight` properties that are used to define its size would not have been set by the layout system at that time.

Next, in the `GetFaceDrawingVisual` method, we need to replace the hardcoded values with divisions of the control's dimensions. The ellipse that draws the whole face is simple to calculate, with a position of half the width and height of the control and radii of half of the width and height of the control minus half of the thickness of the `Pen` element that draws its outline.

However, if you were wondering where all of the remaining long decimal divisor values came from, the answer is basic mathematics. The original drawing was one hundred and fifty pixels wide by one hundred and fifty pixels tall and so we can divide this by the various position and sizes of the drawn lines from the previous example.

For example, the ellipse that draws the first eye was previously centered with an X position of 44.25, so to calculate our required width divisor, we simply divide 150 by 44.25, which equals 3.3898305084745761. Therefore, when the control is provided with 150 pixels of space, it will draw the left eye at an X position of 44.25 and it will now scale correctly at all other sizes.

The divisors for each position and size of the drawn shapes were all calculated using this method, to ensure that they would be sized appropriately for the space provided to our control. Note that we could have altered the brush and pen thicknesses likewise, but have opted not to do so in this example for brevity.

When running this example now, we again have a slightly different output:

Now, the first and third faces look more similar, with the thicknesses of their drawn lines being static and unchanging along their length, unlike the second face. So, we see that we have many options when it comes to creating custom drawings and we need to balance the need for efficiency with the ease of use of the drawing method and also take the use of the resulting image into consideration.

Before moving onto the next topic in this chapter, there are a few further efficiency savings that we can make when drawing complex shapes. If our code uses a large number of PathGeometry objects, then we can replace them by using a StreamGeometry object instead.

The StreamGeometry class is specifically optimized to handle multiple path geometries and shows better performance than can be attained from using multiple PathGeometry instances. In fact, we have already been using the StreamGeometry class inadvertently, as that is what is used internally when the binding path syntax mini-language is parsed by the XAML reader.

It can be thought of in a similar way to the StringBuilder class, in that it is more efficient at drawing complex shapes than using multiple instances of the PathGeometry class, but that it has some overhead and so only benefits us when replacing a fair number of them.

Finally, rather than display our DrawingVisual using a VisualBrush, which is refreshed during each layout pass, if our drawings are never to be manipulated in the UI, it is even more efficient to create actual images from them and display those instead.

The `RenderTargetBitmap` class provides a simple way for us to create images from `Visual` instances, using its `Render` method. Let's see an example of this:

```
using System.IO;
using System.Windows.Media;
using System.Windows.Media.Imaging;

...

RenderTargetBitmap renderTargetBitmap = new RenderTargetBitmap(
   (int)ActualWidth, (int)ActualHeight, 96, 96, PixelFormats.Pbgra32);
renderTargetBitmap.Render(drawingVisual);
renderTargetBitmap.Freeze();
PngBitmapEncoder image = new PngBitmapEncoder();
image.Frames.Add(BitmapFrame.Create(renderTargetBitmap));
using (Stream stream = File.Create(filePath))
{
   image.Save(stream);
}
```

We start by initializing a `RenderTargetBitmap` object with the required dimensions, resolution and pixel format of the image to create. Note that the `Pbgra32` member of the static `PixelFormats` class specifies a pixel format that follows the sRGB format, using 32 bit per pixel, with each of the four alpha, red, green and blue channels receiving 8 bits each per pixel.

Next, we pass our `DrawingVisual` element, or any other element that extends the `Visual` class, to the `Render` method of the `RenderTargetBitmap` class to render it. To make the operation more efficient still, we then call its `Freeze` method to freeze the object.

In order to save a PNG image file, we first initialize a `PngBitmapEncoder` object and add the `renderTargetBitmap` variable to its `Frames` collection via the `Create` method of the `BitmapFrame` class. Finally, we initialize a `Stream` object using the `File.Create` method, passing in the desired file name and path, and call its `Save` method to save the file to the computer's hard drive. Alternatively, the `JpegBitmapEncoder` class can be used to create a JPG image file.

Let's now move on to find ways of using images more efficiently.

Imaging more efficiently

When an image is displayed in a WPF application, it is loaded and decoded at its full size by default. If your application displays a number of thumbnails from the original images, then you can gain enhanced performance by copying your full size images and resizing them to the correct size for the thumbnails, rather than letting WPF do it for you.

Alternatively, you can request that WPF decodes your images to the size required by the thumbnails, although if you want to display the full size images, you would really need to decode each full size image separately. Let's see how we can achieve this using a `BitmapImage` object as the source for an `Image` control:

```
<Image Width="64">
  <Image.Source>
    <BitmapImage DecodePixelWidth="64" UriSource="pack://application:,,,/
      CompanyName.ApplicationName;component/Images/Image1.png" />
  </Image.Source>
</Image>
```

The important part of this example is the `DecodePixelWidth` property of the `BitmapImage` class, which specifies the actual size of the image to decode to. In this example, this would result in a smaller memory footprint as well as faster rendering.

Note that if the `DecodePixelHeight` and `DecodePixelWidth` properties of the `BitmapImage` class are both set, a new aspect ratio will be calculated from their values, but if only one of these properties is set, then the image's original aspect ratio will be used. It is therefore customary to only set one of these properties in order to decode to a different size from the original, while maintaining its aspect ratio.

Normally, when images are used in a WPF application, they are all cached into memory at load time. Another benefit that can be gained if using code in the aforementioned scenario is to set the `CacheOption` property of the `BitmapImage` class to the `OnDemand` enumeration member, which postpones the caching of the relevant image until the image is actually requested to be displayed.

This can save a significant amount of resources at load time, although each image will take a tiny bit longer to display the first time they are displayed. Once the image is cached however, it will work in exactly the same way as images created in the default way.

There is one additional property in the BitmapImage class that can be used to improve the performance when loading multiple image files. The CreateOptions property is of enumeration type BitmapCreateOptions and enables us to specify initialization options that relate to the loading of images. This enumeration can be set using bitwise combinations as it specifies the FlagsAttribute attribute in its declaration.

The DelayCreation member can be used to delay the initialization of each image until it is actually required, thereby speeding up the process of loading the relevant View, while adding a tiny cost to the process of requesting each image when it is actually required.

This would benefit a photo gallery type application, for example, where the initialization of each full size image could be delayed until the user clicks on the appropriate thumbnail. It is only at that point that the image would be created, but as there would only be a single image to create at that point, the initialization time would be negligible.

While it is possible to set more than one of these members to the CreateOptions property using the bitwise OR operator (|), care should be taken not to also set the PreservePixelFormat member, unless specifically required, as that can result in lower performance. When it is not set, the system will chose the pixel format with the best performance by default. Let's see a short example:

```
private Image CreateImageEfficiently(string filePath)
{
    Image image = new Image();
    BitmapImage bitmapImage = new BitmapImage();
    bitmapImage.BeginInit();
    bitmapImage.CacheOption = BitmapCacheOption.OnDemand;
    bitmapImage.CreateOptions = BitmapCreateOptions.DelayCreation;
    bitmapImage.UriSource = new Uri(filePath, UriKind.Absolute);
    bitmapImage.EndInit();
    image.Source = bitmapImage;
    return image;
}
```

When creating images in code, we need to initialize an instance of the BitmapImage class to use as the source for the actual Image object that we will be displaying in the UI. When doing so, we need to call its BeginInit method before making changes to it and call its EndInit method afterwards. Note that all changes made after initialization will be ignored.

During initialization, we set the CacheOption property to the OnDemand member and the CreateOptions property to the DelayCreation member. Note that we do not set the DecodePixelWidth or DecodePixelHeight properties here, because this code example is setup for initializing the full size images in our gallery example.

Also note that in this particular example, we initialize the `Uri` object using an absolute file path, by passing the `Absolute` member of the `UriKind` enumeration into the constructor. If you prefer to work with relative file paths, you can change this line to specify a relative file path by passing the `Relative` member to the constructor instead:

```
bitmapImage.UriSource = new Uri(filePath, UriKind.Relative);
```

Now that we've seen some tips on how to display our images more efficiently, let's investigate how we might do the same for our application's textual output.

Enhancing the performance of textual output

WPF provides similar options for creating text as it does for drawing shapes; the more versatile the output method, the easier it is to use, but the less efficient it is and vice versa. The vast majority of us opt for the simplest, but least efficient method of using the high-level `TextBlock` or `Label` elements.

While this doesn't typically cause us any problems when used in typical forms, there is definitely room for improvement when displaying thousands of text blocks in a data grid, or other collection control. If we require formatted text, we can utilize the more efficient `FormattedText` object, otherwise we can use the lowest level method and the most efficient `Glyphs` elements.

Let's see an example:

```
<UserControl x:Class="CompanyName.ApplicationName.Views.TextView"
  xmlns="http://schemas.microsoft.com/winfx/2006/xaml/presentation"
  xmlns:x="http://schemas.microsoft.com/winfx/2006/xaml"
  xmlns:Controls=
    "clr-namespace:CompanyName.ApplicationName.Views.Controls"
  Height="250" Width="325">
  <Grid ShowGridLines="True">
    <Grid.RowDefinitions>
      <RowDefinition />
      <RowDefinition />
      <RowDefinition />
      <RowDefinition />
    </Grid.RowDefinitions>
    <Label Content="Quite Efficient" FontFamily="Times New Roman"
      FontSize="50" FontWeight="Bold" FontStyle="Italic"
      Foreground="Red" Margin="10,0,0,0" Padding="0" />
    <TextBlock Grid.Row="1" Text="More Efficient"
      FontFamily="Times New Roman" FontSize="50" FontWeight="Bold"
      FontStyle="Italic" Foreground="Black" Margin="10,0,0,0" />
```

```
      <Controls:FormattedTextOutput Grid.Row="2" Text="More Efficient" />
      <Glyphs Grid.Row="3" UnicodeString="Most Efficient"
        FontUri="C:\WINDOWS\Fonts\timesbi.TTF" FontRenderingEmSize="50"
        Fill="Black" OriginX="10" OriginY="45" />
    </Grid>
  </UserControl>
```

Here we have a View that has a `Grid` panel with four rows. The first row holds a `Label` control, which although fairly efficient, is the least efficient of the textual output methods shown here and as we'll see soon, should only be used in very specific circumstances. On it, we specify the `FontFamily`, `FontSize`, `FontWeight`, `FontStyle` and `Foreground` properties to define how its text should look.

The second row contains a `TextBlock` element, which is slightly more efficient and like the `Label` element, we specify the `FontFamily`, `FontSize`, `FontWeight` and `FontStyle` and `Foreground` properties on it directly. It's worth noting that to result in the same visual output, we don't need to set its `Padding` property to `0`, which was required with the `Label` control.

In the third row, we have a custom `FormattedTextOutput` control that uses a `FormattedText` object internally and is slightly more efficient still. As we'll see shortly, we need to specify the relevant properties of this text object in code.

Finally, we see a `Glyphs` element in the fourth row and this represents the most efficient method of outputting text in a WPF application. Note that when using this method of textual output, we don't specify a font family by name, but instead set an exact font file path to its `FontUri` property.

As we want to match the bold italic version of the Times New Roman font, we specifically need to set the file path to that exact file. Therefore, we need to specify the `timesbi.ttf` file, rather than the normal `times.ttf` version. Other than setting the font size to the `FontRenderingEmSize` property and the margin to the `OriginX` and `OriginY` properties, this class is fairly self-explanatory.

Before continuing, let's first see the visual output of this View:

Let's now take a look at the code inside the `FormattedTextOutput` class:

```
using System.Globalization;
using System.Windows;
using System.Windows.Media;

namespace CompanyName.ApplicationName.Views.Controls
{
  public class FormattedTextOutput : FrameworkElement
  {
    public static readonly DependencyProperty TextProperty =
      DependencyProperty.Register(nameof(Text), typeof(string),
      typeof(FormattedTextOutput), new FrameworkPropertyMetadata(
      string.Empty, FrameworkPropertyMetadataOptions.AffectsRender));

    public string Text
    {
      get { return (string)GetValue(TextProperty); }
      set { SetValue(TextProperty, value); }
    }

    protected override void OnRender(DrawingContext drawingContext)
    {
      FormattedText formattedText = new FormattedText(Text,
```

```
        CultureInfo.GetCultureInfo("en-us"), FlowDirection.LeftToRight,
        new Typeface("Times New Roman"), 50, Brushes.Red);
      formattedText.SetFontStyle(FontStyles.Italic);
      formattedText.SetFontWeight(FontWeights.Bold);
      drawingContext.DrawText(formattedText, new Point(10, 0));
    }
  }
}
```

The `FormattedTextOutput` class is a fairly simple affair, with a single Dependency
Property and its associated CLR wrapper and a single overridden base class method. One
very important point to note is our use of the `AffectsRender` member of the
`FrameworkPropertyMetadataOptions` enumeration to specify that changes to this
property needs to cause a new rendering pass.

Typically, the `Text` property will be updated from any data binding after the `OnRender`
method is called by the `UIElement` base class. Without specifying this option, our class will
never output any data bound values. By specifying this option, we are in fact, telling the
Framework to call the `OnRender` method again each time this property value changes.

In the overridden `OnRender` method, we first initialize a `FormattedText` object with basic
properties, such as the text to render, the current culture and the color, size and type of the
font to use. Additional style properties can be set using the various set methods that the
class exposes. Finally, we call the `DrawText` method of the `DrawingContext` object
specified by the `drawingContext` input parameter, passing in the `FormattedText` object
and the position to render it.

Note that we can use data binding with all of these text rendering methods, so let's update
our previous example now to demonstrate:

```
. . .
<Label Content="{Binding Text}" FontFamily="Times New Roman"
  FontSize="50" FontWeight="Bold" FontStyle="Italic" Foreground="Red"
  Margin="10,0,0,0" Padding="0" />
<TextBlock Grid.Row="1" Text="{Binding Text}"
  FontFamily="Times New Roman" FontSize="50" FontWeight="Bold"
  FontStyle="Italic" Foreground="Red" Margin="10,0,0,0" />
<Controls:FormattedTextOutput Grid.Row="2" Text="{Binding Text}" />
<Glyphs Grid.Row="3" UnicodeString="{Binding Text}" FontUri=
  "C:\WINDOWS\Fonts\timesbi.TTF" FontRenderingEmSize="50"
  Fill="Black" OriginX="10" OriginY="45" />
. . .
```

For this example, we can simply hardcode a value in our View Model.

```
namespace CompanyName.ApplicationName.ViewModels
{
  public class TextViewModel : BaseViewModel
  {
    public string Text { get; set; } = "Efficient";
  }
}
```

Although we can data bind when using all of these textual output methods, there are some caveats to be aware of. We've just learnt of one relating to the required metadata of the `Text` property in our custom `FormattedTextOutput` class and there is another relating to the `Glyphs` class.

It has a requirement that the `UnicodeString` property cannot be empty if the `Indicies` property, which represents an alternative method of providing the text to render, is also empty. Unfortunately, because of this requirement, attempting to data bind to the `UnicodeString` property as we did in our extended example will result in a compilation error:

Glyphs Indices and UnicodeString properties cannot both be empty.

To address this issue, we can simply provide a value for the `FallbackValue` property of the `Binding` class, so that the `Glyphs` class can rest assured that even if there is no data bound value, its `UnicodeString` property will have a non-empty value. Note that setting the `FallbackValue` property to an empty string will result in the same error being raised.

```
<Glyphs Grid.Row="3" UnicodeString="{Binding Text, FallbackValue='Data
    Binding Not Working'}" FontUri="C:\WINDOWS\Fonts\timesbi.TTF"
    FontRenderingEmSize="50" Fill="Black" OriginX="10" OriginY="45" />
```

There is one further issue regarding data binding, but this time, it involves the `Content` property of the `Label` class. Because strings are immutable, each time a data bound value updates the `Content` property, the previous string will be discarded and replaced with the new one.

Furthermore, if the default `ContentTemplate` element is used, it will generate a new `TextBlock` element and discard the previous element each time the property string is replaced. As a result, updating a data bound `TextBlock` is approximately four times quicker than updating a `Label`. Therefore, if we need to update our data bound text values, we should not use a `Label` control.

In fact, each method of rendering text has its own purpose. The `Label` control should specifically be used to label text fields in a form and in doing so, we can take advantage of its access key functionality and its ability to reference a target control. The `TextBlock` element is a general purpose text output method that should be used for the majority of the time.

The `FormattedText` object should really only be used when we specifically want to format some text in a particular way. It provides the ability to output text with a wide range of effects, such as being able to paint the stroke and fill of the text independently and to format particular ranges of characters within the rendered text string.

The `Glyphs` class extends the `FrameworkElement` class directly and is therefore extremely light-weight and should be utilized when we need to recreate our text output more efficiently than we can using the alternative methods. Although the `FormattedText` class can make use of lower, core level classes to render its output, the most efficient way to render text is to use `Glyphs` objects.

Liking the linking

As we have already seen, each UI element that we use in our Views takes time to render. Simply put, the fewer elements that we use, the quicker the View will be displayed. Those of us that have used `Hyperlink` elements in our Views will already be aware that we cannot display them on their own, but instead have to wrap them inside a `TextBlock` element.

However, as each `Hyperlink` element is self-contained, with its own navigation URI, content and property options, we can actually display more than one of them in a single `TextBlock` element. This will reduce the render time and so, the more `TextBlock` elements that we can remove, the quicker it will become. Let's see an example:

```
<ListBox ItemsSource="{Binding Products}" FontSize="14"
  HorizontalContentAlignment="Stretch">
  <ListBox.ItemTemplate>
    <DataTemplate DataType="{x:Type DataModels:Product}">
      <Grid>
        <Grid.ColumnDefinitions>
          <ColumnDefinition />
          <ColumnDefinition Width="Auto" />
          <ColumnDefinition Width="Auto" />
        </Grid.ColumnDefinitions>
        <TextBlock Text="{Binding Name}" />
        <TextBlock Grid.Column="1"
          Text="{Binding Price, StringFormat=C}" Margin="10,0" />
```

```
<StackPanel Grid.Column="2" TextElement.FontSize="14"
  Orientation="Horizontal">
  <TextBlock>
    <Hyperlink Command="{Binding ViewCommand,
      RelativeSource={RelativeSource
      AncestorType={x:Type Views:TextView}}}"
      CommandParameter="{Binding}">View</Hyperlink>
  </TextBlock>
  <TextBlock Text=" | " />
  <TextBlock>
    <Hyperlink Command="{Binding EditCommand,
      RelativeSource={RelativeSource
      AncestorType={x:Type Views:TextView}}}"
      CommandParameter="{Binding}">Edit</Hyperlink>
  </TextBlock>
  <TextBlock Text=" | " />
  <TextBlock>
    <Hyperlink Command="{Binding DeleteCommand,
      RelativeSource={RelativeSource
      AncestorType={x:Type Views:TextView}}}"
      CommandParameter="{Binding}">Delete</Hyperlink>
  </TextBlock>
</StackPanel>
      </Grid>
    </DataTemplate>
  </ListBox.ItemTemplate>
</ListBox>
```

Here, we have a collection of `Product` objects that are data bound to a `ListBox`, with each item displaying its name, price and three commands in the form of `Hyperlink` objects. Let's see what this looks like before continuing:

Virtual Reality Headset	£14.99 View | Edit | Delete
Mobile Phone Mount	£11.99 View | Edit | Delete

Focusing on the links now, our example uses nine UI elements per item to render these three links. The `StackPanel` element keeps them altogether, with each `Hyperlink` object having its own `TextBlock` element and a further two `TextBlock` elements to display the pipe separator characters.

The `Hyperlink` objects are data bound to commands in the View Model and the `CommandParameter` property is data bound to the whole `Product` object that is set as the data source for each item. In this way, we will have access to the relevant `Product` instance in the View Model when a link is clicked.

While there is nothing wrong with this XAML, if we need to be more efficient, then we can replace everything inside the `StackPanel` and the panel itself with the following `TextBlock` element:

```
<TextBlock Grid.Column="2" TextElement.FontSize="14" Foreground="White">
  <Hyperlink Command="{Binding ViewCommand, RelativeSource={
    RelativeSource AncestorType={x:Type Views:TextView}}}"
    CommandParameter="{Binding}">View</Hyperlink>
  <Run Text=" | " />
  <Hyperlink Command="{Binding EditCommand, RelativeSource={
    RelativeSource AncestorType={x:Type Views:TextView}}}"
    CommandParameter="{Binding}">Edit</Hyperlink>
  <Run Text=" | " />
  <Hyperlink Command="{Binding DeleteCommand, RelativeSource={
    RelativeSource AncestorType={x:Type Views:TextView}}}"
    CommandParameter="{Binding}">Delete</Hyperlink>
</TextBlock>
```

As you can see, we now host all three `Hyperlink` objects inside a single `TextBlock` element and have replaced the two `TextBlock` elements that displayed the pipe characters with `Run` objects. Using the `Run` class is moderately more efficient than using one `TextBlock` element inside another.

Now, we need only render six elements per item to produce the links, including using two more efficient elements, rendering three elements fewer per item. However, if we had a thousand products, we would end up rendering three thousand fewer UI elements, with two thousand more efficient replacements, so it is easy to see how this can soon add up to some real efficiency savings.

In this example, we could make further improvements, by simply removing the line under each link. Bizarrely, we can save up to twenty-five percent of the rendering time taken to render our `Hyperlink` elements if we remove their underlines. We can do this by setting their `TextDecorations` property to `None`:

```
<Hyperlink ... TextDecorations="None">View</Hyperlink>
```

Data binding

There are also a number of performance improvements that we can make when data binding in our applications. The simplest of which can be obtained by simply setting the `Binding.Mode` property correctly. In order to make data binding possible, the Framework attaches handlers to listen out for changes to our data bound properties.

For two-way bindings, event handlers will be attached to the `PropertyChanged` event of the `INotifyPropertyChanged` interface to listen to changes in our data model objects or View Models and to various other `XxxChanged` events in the relevant binding target controls to listen to UI-based property changes.

When we only require one way bindings, we can save some computing resources by setting the `Mode` property of the `Binding` class to the appropriate member of the `BindingMode` enumeration. If you remember, when a data bound property is for display purposes only, we should set its `Mode` property to `OneWay` and when we have no need to update an editable field from the View Model, we should set its `Mode` property to the `OneWayToSource` member.

In doing this, we cut down the number of event handlers listening for changes and therefore free up resources to be used where they are actually needed. Once again, the effect of doing this on one binding alone would be negligible, but if we practice this on every relevant binding, then the efficiency improvement will start to make a difference.

Another good practice to get into is to set the `FallbackValue` property of the `Binding` class on each binding that we declare. As mentioned in Chapter 4, *Becoming Proficient with Data Binding*, doing this will stop the WPF Framework from performing a lookup of the default value of the target Dependency Property when there are data binding errors and will prevent trace statements from being generated and output.

Likewise, setting the `TargetNullValue` property is similar to setting the `FallbackValue` property in that it is slightly more efficient than not setting it. Again, doing this on a single binding will have a negligible effect, yet if we do this on every binding, it will free up CPU cycles for rendering or other required processes.

In fact, the best binding related way to increase the performance of our applications is to simply fix any data binding errors that we may have. Each time a binding cannot be resolved, the Framework will perform a number of checks, using up valuable resources, as mentioned previously in this section. Therefore, keeping the **Output** window free of binding errors is a must when it comes to performance.

Registering Dependency Properties

As we saw in the *Using the right controls for performance* section earlier in this chapter, we need to be careful when setting the metadata for our Dependency Properties. Incorrectly specifying the framework metadata while registering our Dependency Properties can lower performance by forcing the layout system to unnecessarily perform additional layout passes.

In particular, we need to be careful when specifying any of the `AffectsMeasure`, `AffectsArrange`, `AffectsParentMeasure`, `AffectsParentArrange`, or the `AffectsRender` members of the `FrameworkPropertyMetadataOptions` enumeration and ensure that they are actually required.

Likewise, if we specify the `Inherits` member of the `FrameworkPropertyMetadataOptions` enumeration when registering our Dependency Property, we are effectively increasing the length of time that invalidation will take on the property. As such, we should ensure that this particular metadata member is only used when it is really necessary.

One last metadata option that can improve the performance of the application is the `SubPropertiesDoNotAffectRender` member. If the type of our Dependency Property is a reference type, we can specify this enumeration member to stop the layout system from checking for changes to all sub properties of the object, which it would otherwise do by default.

While we may need to call the `OverrideMetadata` method of the `DependencyProperty` class to override the metadata of the pre-existing properties in the .NET Framework, this comes with a small performance impact. When setting metadata for our own custom Dependency Properties, we should always use the appropriate `Register` or `RegisterAttached` method to specify our requirements, as this offers far better performance.

Likewise, when registering our custom Dependency Properties, we should also set their default values using the relevant `Register` or `RegisterAttached` method as they are created, rather than initializing each instance individually in a constructor, or by using some other method.

Binding to collections

As you are most probably aware, when dealing with collections that will be updated in a WPF application, we tend to prefer using the generic `ObservableCollection<T>` class. The reason for this is because this class implements the `INotifyCollectionChanged` interface, which notifies listeners of changes to the collection, such as adding, removing or clearing items.

What we may not realize is the incredible performance improvement that we get from using this class to hold our data collections. When comparing this with the generic `List<T>` class for example, we note that it does not automatically raise any collection changed event. In order to enable the View to display the updated collection, we need to reset it as the `ItemsSource` property value of the relevant collection control.

However, each time that the `ItemsSource` property is set, the data bound collection control will clear its current list of items and completely regenerate them again, which can be a time consuming process. So, to add a single item to an `ObservableCollection<T>` takes approximately 20 milliseconds to render, but to reset the `ItemsSource` property value could take over 1.5 seconds.

However, if our collection is immutable and we will not be altering it in any way, we do not need to use the generic `ObservableCollection<T>` class, as we have no need for its change handlers. Rather than wasting resources on unused change handlers, we can use a different type of collection class.

While there is not a preferred type of collection to use when data binding immutable collections to UI controls, we should try to avoid using the `IEnumerable` class as the collection container. This type cannot be used directly by the `ItemsControl` class and when it is used, the WPF Framework will generate a generic `IList<T>` collection to wrap the `IEnumerable` instance and this can also negatively affect performance.

In the next few sections, we'll see other ways that we can display large collections efficiently.

Shrinking data objects

Quite often, our applications will have fairly sizable data objects, with dozens, or even hundreds of properties. If we were to load all of the properties for each data object when we have thousands of them, our application would slow down and possibly even run out of memory.

We might think that we can save on RAM by simply not populating all of the property values, but if we use the same classes, we'll soon find that even the default or empty values for these properties may consume too much memory. In general and with a few exceptions, unset properties take the same amount of RAM as set properties.

If our data model object has a very large number of properties, one solution would be to break it down into much smaller pieces. For example, we could create a number of smaller, sub product classes, such as `ProductTechnicalSpecification`, `ProductDescription`, `ProductDimension`, `ProductPricing`, etc.

Rather than building one giant View to edit the whole product, we could then provide a number of smaller Views, perhaps even accessible from different tabs within the same View. In this way, we would be able to just load the `ProductDescription` objects for the user to select from and then load the individual sections of the product in each sub View.

There is a significant performance increase to be gained by this method, as binding to a single object with a great many properties can take up to four times longer than binding to a great many objects with fewer properties.

One alternative to breaking our data objects into smaller pieces would be to use the concept of thin data objects. For example, imagine that our `Product` class had dozens of properties and that we had thousands of products. We could create a `ThinProduct` class, that contains only the properties that would be used to identify the full data object to load when selected and those displayed in the product collection.

In this case, we might simply need two properties in our `ThinProduct` class, a unique identification property and a display name property. In this way, we can reduce the memory footprint of our products by a factor of ten or even more. This means that they can be loaded from the database and displayed in a fraction of the time of the full `Product` objects.

In order to facilitate easy transferal between the `Product` and `ThinProduct` classes, we can add constructors into each class that accepts the other type and updates the relevant properties.

```
using System;

namespace CompanyName.ApplicationName.DataModels
{
  public class ThinProduct : BaseDataModel
  {
    private Guid id = Guid.Empty;
    private string name = string.Empty;
```

```
    public ThinProduct(Product product)
    {
      Id = product.Id;
      Name = product.Name;
    }

    public Guid Id
    {
      get { return id; }
      set { if (id != value) { id = value;
        NotifyPropertyChanged(); } }
    }

    public string Name
    {
      get { return name; }
      set { if (name != value) { name = value;
        NotifyPropertyChanged(); } }
    }

    public override string ToString()
    {
      return Name;
    }
  }
}
```

The properties in this `ThinProduct` class basically mirror those from the `Product` class that we saw earlier, but only the ones that are used to identify each instance. A constructor is added that takes an input parameter of type `Product` to enable easy transferal between the two. A similar constructor is added to the `Product` class, but takes an input parameter of type `ThinProduct`.

```
public Product(ThinProduct thinProduct) : this()
{
  Id = thinProduct.Id;
  Name = thinProduct.Name;
}
```

The idea is that we have a View Model that displays a large number of products and in code, we actually load a large number of these much lighter `ThinProduct` instances. When the user selects one of the products to view or edit, we use the identification number of the selected item to then load the full `Product` object that relates to that identifier.

Given a base collection of these `ThinProduct` instances in a property named `Products`, we could achieve this as follows. First, let's bind our collection to a `ListBox` control:

```
<ListBox ItemsSource="{Binding Products}"
  SelectedItem="{Binding Products.CurrentItem}" ... />
```

When the user selects a product from the list, the collection's `CurrentItem` property will hold a reference to the selected item. If we attach a handler to the collection's `CurrentItemChanged` delegate when it is first loaded, we can be notified when the item is selected. At that point, we can load the full `Product` object using the identifier from the selected `ThinProduct` instance and output the associated feedback to the user.

```
private void Products_CurrentItemChanged(ThinProduct oldProduct,
  ThinProduct newProduct)
{
  GetDataOperationResult<Product> result =
    await Model.GetProductAsync(Products.CurrentItem.Id);
  if (result.IsSuccess) Product = result.ReturnValue;
  else FeedbackManager.Add(result, false);
}
```

In the next section, we'll find out how we can display our large collections more efficiently, using collection controls, rather than having to break up our large classes into smaller classes, or create associated thin data objects.

Virtualizing collections

When we display large numbers of items in our collection controls, it can negatively affect the application's performance. This is because the layout system will create a layout container, such as a `ComboBoxItem` in the case of a `ComboBox` for example, for every item in the data bound collection. As only a small subset of the complete number of items is displayed at any one time, we can take advantage of virtualization to improve the situation.

UI virtualization defers the generation and layout of these item containers until each item is actually visible in the relevant collection control, often saving on large amounts of resources. We can take advantage of virtualization without doing anything at all if we use `ListBox` or `ListView` controls to display our collections, as they use it by default.

Virtualization can also be enabled in `ComboBox`, `ContextMenu` and `TreeView` controls, although it will have to be done manually. When using a `TreeView` control, we can enable virtualization by simply setting the `VirtualizingStackPanel.IsVirtualizing` attached property to `True` on it.

```
<TreeView ItemsSource="{Binding Items}"
   VirtualizingStackPanel.IsVirtualizing="True" />
```

For other controls that use the `StackPanel` class internally, such as the `ComboBox` and `ContextMenu` controls, we can enable virtualization by setting an `ItemsPanelTemplate` element hosting an instance of the `VirtualizingStackPanel` class with its `IsVirtualizing` property set to `True` to its `ItemsPanel` property:

```
<ComboBox ItemsSource="{Binding Items}">
  <ComboBox.ItemsPanel>
    <ItemsPanelTemplate>
      <VirtualizingStackPanel IsVirtualizing="True" />
    </ItemsPanelTemplate>
  </ComboBox.ItemsPanel>
</ComboBox>
```

Apart from setting the `IsVirtualizing` property to `False`, there are a few other reasons why UI virtualization may not work. One case is when item containers have manually been added to an `ItemsControl` object or one of its derived controls. Another case is when the item containers are of different types.

The final reason why virtualization may not work is not so obvious and relates to the `CanContentScroll` property of the `ScrollViewer` class. This is an interesting property that specifies whether the `ScrollViewer` in a collection control will scroll its items in logical units, or physical units. The default value is `false`, which smoothly scrolls in terms of physical units.

Physical units relate to the device-independent pixels that WPF works with, while logical units relate to the widths or heights of the collection items, depending on the orientation of the control. As the default value of the `CanContentScroll` property is **false**, this will need to be set to `True` to enable virtualization, so that scrolling is performed item by item and not pixel by pixel.

When virtualization is employed in a collection control that extends the `ItemsControl` class and the user scrolls, new item containers are created for the newly visible items and the containers for the items that are no longer visible are disposed of.

In version 3.5 of the .NET Framework, an optimization of the virtualization system was introduced. Container recycling enables the collection control to reuse the item containers, instead of creating new ones and disposing of old ones as the user scrolls. This offers an additional performance benefit and can be enabled by setting the `VirtualizationMode` Attached Property to a value of `Recycling`.

```
<TreeView ItemsSource="{Binding Items}"
  VirtualizingStackPanel.IsVirtualizing="True" />
  VirtualizingStackPanel.VirtualizationMode="Recycling" />
```

One further optimization that WPF provides us with is deferred scrolling. Normally, scrolling in a collection control continuously updates the UI. However, if our data items or their item containers have several layers of visuals that define them and scrolling is slow, we can opt to defer the UI update until scrolling has finished.

In order to enable deferred scrolling on a collection control, we need to set the `ScrollViewer.IsDeferredScrollingEnabled` Attached Property to `True`. Although we don't generally use `ScrollViewer` elements in XAML directly, we can also attach this property to collection controls that host a `ScrollViewer` element in their control templates.

```
<ListBox ItemsSource="{Binding Items}"
  ScrollViewer.IsDeferredScrollingEnabled="True" />
```

Handling events

One of the most common causes of memory leaks appearing in an application is the failure to remove event handlers once objects are no longer needed. When we attach an event handler to an object's event in the usual way, we are effectively passing that object a reference to the handler and creating a hard reference to it.

When the object is no longer needed and could otherwise be disposed of, the reference in the object that raises the event will prevent that from occurring. This is because the garbage collector cannot collect an object that can be accessed from any part of the application code. In the worst case scenario, the object being kept alive may contain numerous other objects and so inadvertently keep them alive also.

The problem with this is that keeping objects alive after they are no longer needed will unnecessarily increase the memory footprint of the application, in some cases, with dramatic and irreversible consequences, leading to an `OutOfMemoryException` being thrown. It is therefore essential that we detach our event handlers from the events that they are subscribed to in objects that we have no further use for before trying to dispose of them.

There is however, an alternative method that we can use to avoid this situation. In the .NET Framework, there is a `WeakReference` class and it can be used to remove the hard references caused from attaching event handlers to events using the traditional method.

The basic idea is that the class that raises the event should maintain a collection of `WeakReference` instances and add to it each time another class attaches an event handler to the event. Let's update our `ActionCommand` class from earlier to use this `WeakReference` class now:

```
using System;
using System.Collections.Generic;
using System.Windows.Input;

namespace CompanyName.ApplicationName.ViewModels.Commands
{
  public class ActionCommand : ICommand
  {
    private readonly Action<object> action;
    private readonly Predicate<object> canExecute;
    private List<WeakReference> eventHandlers = new List<WeakReference>();

    public ActionCommand(Action<object> action) : this(action, null) { }

    public ActionCommand(Action<object> action,
      Predicate<object> canExecute)
    {
      if (action == null) throw new ArgumentNullException("The action
        input parameter of the ActionCommand constructor cannot be null.");
      this.action = action;
      this.canExecute = canExecute;
    }

    public event EventHandler CanExecuteChanged
    {
      add
      {
        eventHandlers.Add(new WeakReference(value));
        CommandManager.RequerySuggested += value;
      }
      remove
      {
        if (eventHandlers == null) return;
        for (int i = eventHandlers.Count - 1; i >= 0; i--)
        {
          WeakReference weakReference = eventHandlers[i];
          EventHandler handler = weakReference.Target as EventHandler;
          if (handler == null || handler == value)
```

```
        {
            eventHandlers.RemoveAt(i);
        }
      }
      CommandManager.RequerySuggested -= value;
    }
  }

  public void RaiseCanExecuteChanged()
  {
    eventHandlers.ForEach(
      r => (r.Target as EventHandler)?.Invoke(this, new EventArgs()));
  }

  public bool CanExecute(object parameter)
  {
    return canExecute == null ? true : canExecute(parameter);
  }

  public void Execute(object parameter)
  {
    action(parameter);
  }
 }
}
```

We start by adding a declaration of our new collection containing objects of type `WeakReference` to the pre-existing fields. The two constructors remain unchanged, but when attaching handlers in the `CanExecuteChanged` event, we now wrap the event handling delegate in a `WeakReference` object and add it to the collection. We still need to pass the references to the handlers that get attached through to the `RequerySuggested` event of the `CommandManager` class as before.

When an event handler is removed, we first double check that our `WeakReference` collection is not null and simply return control to the caller if it is. If not, we use a `for` loop to iterate through the collection in reverse, so that we can remove items with affecting the loop index.

We attempt to access the actual event handler from the `Target` property of each `WeakReference` object in turn, converting it to the base type `EventHandler` using the `as` keyword. We then remove the `WeakReference` instance if its event handler reference is either null, or matches the handler being removed.

Note that a null reference in the `Target` property would be the result of an event handler from a class that has been disposed of by the garbage collector. As before, we then also detach the event handler from the `CommandManager.RequerySuggested` event.

Finally, we need to update our `RaiseCanExecuteChanged` method to use our new collection of `WeakReference` objects. In it, we again iterate through each instance in the collection using our `ForEach` Extension method and after checking if its `Target` property is null using the null conditional operator, call it using the delegate's `Invoke` method.

So, the idea here is that we no longer directly hold on to any references to attached event handlers and are therefore free to dispose of those classes at any point without fear of them being kept alive unnecessarily.

Summary

In this chapter, we explored a number of options that we can use to increase the performance of our WPF applications. As we have now seen, this is more a case of making a large number of little changes to gain an overall noticeable performance benefit.

We saw that we can utilize the graphics rendering power of our computer's graphics card and declare our resources more efficiently. We investigated ways to improve our application's performance using lighter weight UI controls and more efficient methods of rendering drawings, images and text. We continued and also found how to data bind, display large objects and collections and handle events with improved performance.

In the next chapter, we will investigate the final requirement for all professional applications – deployment. In it, we will first cover the older method, using the Windows Installer software and then progress to investigate the more common and up-to-date method, using ClickOnce functionality.

11
Deploying Your Masterpiece Application

So, we've designed and constructed our application framework, resources and managers, added our Models, Views, and View Models and after completing the development of our application, now it's time for deployment. In this chapter, we'll be looking at an overview of the three main methods of deploying WPF applications.

We'll start by investigating the original **Windows Setup Project** method, move on to discover the newer **InstallShield Limited Edition Project** method and then progress to examine the preferred **ClickOnce** technology.

Installing Windows applications

In days gone by, creating a **Setup and Deployment** project in Visual Studio was a confusing and complicated process. However, as with just about everything in the .NET Framework, successive updates over the years have resulted in ever improved creation methods for these projects.

The latest deployment technologies are simpler to use and provide an easily understandable method of performing the same steps as the earlier technologies. However, in older versions of Visual Studio, we might only have access to the older **Visual Studio Installer** project types, so let's first investigate the standard **Setup Project**.

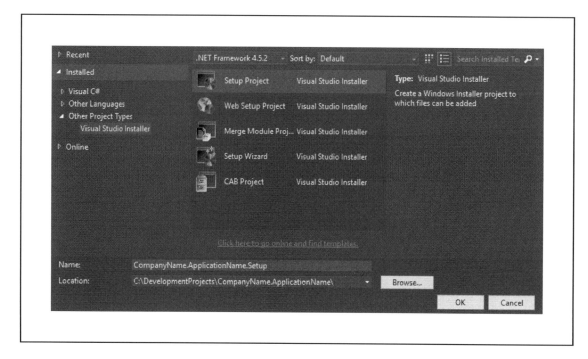

After adding a **Setup Project** to the solution, a page opens up showing the filesystem on the target computer. In this **File System Editor** page, we can specify what we would like to install and where. The page is divided into two, with a tree view of the folders to be installed on the users' computers on the left and their folder contents on the right. By default, the left pane contains the `Application`, `Desktop` and `Program Files` folders.

If we would prefer to use other pre-defined locations, such as the `Fonts`, `Favorites`, or the `Common Files` folders for example, then we can right-click on the background of these panes and select the **Add Special Folder** option. Typically, we would add a standard folder with our company's name into the `User's Programs Menu` folder and add a further folder named after our application into that.

However, if we want to install our application as a 64 bit application, then we'll need to use this option to add the 64 bit `Program Files` folder to install into. To do so, we need to right-click on the **File System on Target Machine** item at the top of the tree view, select the **Add Special Folder** option and then select the **Program Files (64-bit) Folder** item.

Note that we should only perform this step if we want to have a 64 bit installation. We then need to set the project output of our startup project to the folder in the left pane that represents our installation folder, whether 32 or 64 bit.

We'll need to right-click on that folder and select the **Add** option and then the **Project Outputs** option from the contextual menu and then select the **Primary Output** option that relates to our `CompanyName.ApplicationName` project. After doing so, we'll see a copy of the executable and other dependent files from its `bin` folder being included in our selected application folder.

Next, we can create a shortcut to our application on the machine that it was installed on, by right-clicking the icon for the project output in the right pane and selecting the **Create Shortcut to Primary output from CompanyName.ApplicationName (Active)** option from the menu.

We need to name it the same as our application name and set an icon for it, which we can do in its **Properties** window. We can then click and drag, or copy and paste it to the `User's Desktop` folder, or to whichever folder we want the shortcut to appear in.

In addition to the executable and shortcut files, we can right-click a folder in the left pane and select the **Add** option and then the **Folder** and/or **File** options from the contextual menu and choose any other files that we may need to install on the user's computer. Once we have finished configuring the **File System Editor**, we can right-click on the project node in the **Solution Explorer** and select another page to edit from the **View** menu.

The **Registry Editor** page is next and enables us to make entries in the Windows Registry of the host computer. The left window pane acts as the registry view of the target computer and we can use it in the same way as the **Registry Editor** to add new keys. This page also allows us to import registry keys from a `.reg` file if we right-click on an empty space and select **Import**.

The **File Types Editor** page follows in the **View** menu and enables us to associate any custom file types that we may have created with our application. In doing so, after installation Windows will then open our application whenever a file of one of the types specified in this page are clicked.

The **Setup Project** enables us to display a number of default dialogs during installation, such as welcome, confirmation and completion dialogs, and so on. It also provides the ability to reorder, or remove these default dialogs, or add new ones from a pre-defined list. Each dialog provides an image field and different options, such as whether a progress bar should be displayed, or what text to display at different stages of the installation. This is achieved in the **User Interface** page.

The **Custom Actions Editor** page enables us to specify assemblies that contain code in a particular form, that can be run after the application has been installed. These actions could be anything, such as popping up a small form and providing the user with some configuration options, or simply opening a particular web page after installation has completed.

The final option in the **View** menu of the **Setup Project** opens the **Launch Conditions Editor** page. Here, we can specify prerequisite conditions that must be satisfied in order for the application to be installed. For example, we might require a particular version of the .NET Framework to be installed, or the host computer to have a particular registry key setting.

Once the project pages have all been appropriately completed, we just need to build the **Setup and Deployment** project to generate the setup files. However, we need to ensure that we build it correctly, dependent upon the selections that we made in the **File System Editor** page.

For example, if we wanted to have a number of setup projects, let's say including 32 bit and 64 bit installations, then we need to only build the 32 bit version of the **Setup Project** in the 32 bit solution platform and only build the 64 bit version in the 64 bit solution platform.

We can do this in the **Configuration Manager** in Visual Studio, which we can open from the last option in either the solution configuration or solution platform drop-down controls. If the x86 and x64 solution platforms do not already exist, we can add them by selecting the **<New...>** option from the solution platform drop-down control in the **Configuration Manager** dialog window.

To add the new solution platforms in the **New Solution Platform** dialog that opens, type either x86 or x64 in the **Type or select the new platform** field, select the **<Empty>** option from the **Copy settings from** drop-down control and ensure that the **Create new project platforms** tick box is checked.

Once we have these two solution platforms, we can select them one at a time in the **Active solution platform** drop-down control in the **Configuration** Manager dialog window and tick and untick the relevant setup projects.

Here is a screenshot of the x86 solutions selected:

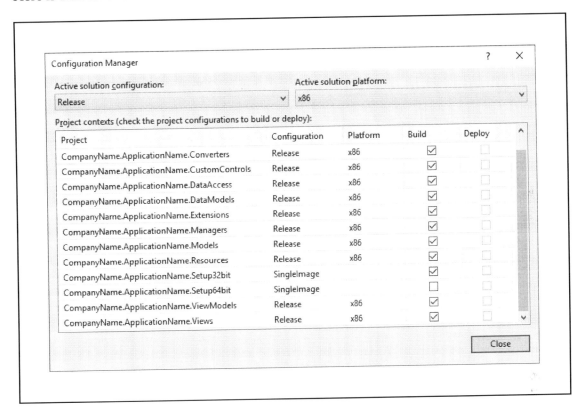

Here is a screenshot of the x64 solutions selected:

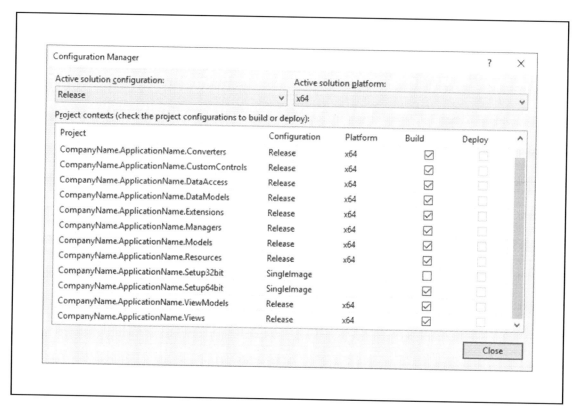

Note that we must select **Release** in the solution configuration drop-down and then build our project to generate the setup files. If we have setup our build configuration correctly, then building the x86 solution platform will generate the 32 bit setup files and building the x64 solution platform will generate the 64 bit setup files.

It can be useful to uncheck the **Build** tick boxes for our deployment projects on all solution platforms when the **Active solution configuration** is set to **Debug**. Doing this will stop the deployment files from being regenerated every time that the solution is built while debugging and will therefore save time during any future development.

To add a setup project in a modern version of Visual Studio, we need to select the **InstallShield Limited Edition Project** from the **Setup and Deployment** project type in the **Other Project Types** category in the left-hand pane of the **Add New Project** dialog window.

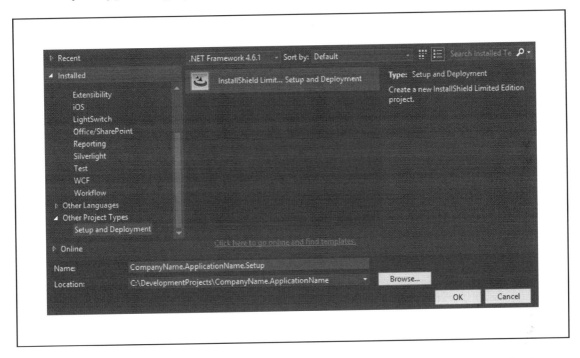

Note that this project type is already included with all paid versions of Visual Studio, but those who are using a free version may be directed to a website to download this functionality upon selection of the project type.

Once installed and the project has been successfully added, a help wizard, or **Project Assistant** window as InstallShield like to call it, will be opened in Visual Studio to aid the process of configuring the installation project. It walks us through the various tasks that we may need to perform when creating our installer, page by page.

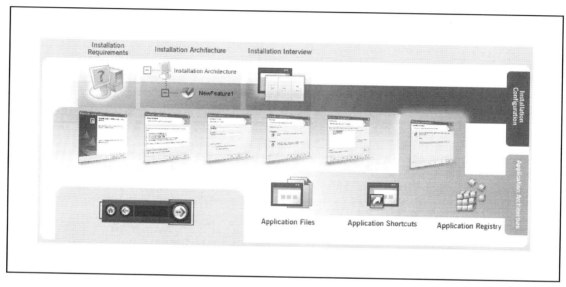

Each page is divided into two window panes; the right pane contains the various fields that we will edit to set our required specifications for the deployment and the left pane contains additional options and contextual help topics, relevant to each page.

The first page of the **Project Assistant** is the **Application Information** page, where we can provide general information about the application, such as the company name and website, the application name and version and the icon to display with the application.

The **Installation Requirements** page enables us to select one or more particular operating systems that our application is compatible with. In addition to this, we can also specify that our application has a dependency from a pre-existing list of third-party software, such as Adobe Reader, various versions of the .NET Framework and a number of Microsoft products.

While this list is short, it does contain the most likely pre-requisite software titles. However, there are a couple of additional options, one of which enables us to create custom installation requirements. Upon clicking on this option, the **System Search Wizard** opens and lets us search for additional installation requirements, either by folder path, registry key, or by `.ini` file value, and enables us to choose what happens if the new requirement is not met during the installation process.

The **Application Files** page is next and in it, we can add any required application files to the installation. The page is divided into two, with a tree view of the folders to be installed on the users' computers on the left and the folder contents on the right. The left pane contains a list of the most commonly used pre-defined folders, such as the App Data, Common and Program Files folders.

If we need to use other pre-defined locations, such as the Desktop, Favorites, or the My Pictures folders for example, then we can right-click on an item in this pane and select the **Show Predefined Folder** option. In fact, if we want to install our application as a 64 bit application, then we'll need to use this option to add the 64 bit Program Files folder, in a similar way to the Setup Project.

In order to do this, we can right-click on the **Destination Computer** item at the top of the tree view, select the **Show Predefined Folder** option and then select the ProgramFiles64Folder item. We would then need to set the project output of our startup project to the folder in the left pane that represents our installation folder. Note that it will be suffixed with [INSTALLDIR] and in our case, will be named ApplicationName.

We should click the **Add Project Outputs** button and select the **Primary Output** option that relates to our CompanyName.ApplicationName project to include a copy of the DLLs and other dependent files from its bin folder in the deployment. We can right-click the added output item to select further properties if required, or if we are using COM objects in our application.

Next up is the **Application Shortcuts** page, where we can control which custom shortcuts the installation will include on the users' computer. Note that default shortcuts will automatically be added for the executable files that we have specified, but this page enables us to delete these, as well as add new ones, or even specify uninstallation shortcuts, or alternative icons to use.

The **Application Registry** page follows and enables us to make entries in the Windows Registry of the computer that our application is being installed on. The left window pane mirrors the registry view of the destination computer and we can use it in the same way to add new keys. This page also allows us to import registry keys from a .reg file and open the registry editor on the source computer.

The last page is the **Installation Interview** page, where we can specify which dialog screens are displayed to the user during the installation. Here, we can optionally upload an End User License Agreement file in the **Rich Text Format (RTF)** file format to display to and require the user to agree to.

Additionally, we can prompt the user to enter their username and company name and provide them with options to select the installation location and whether the application should open after the installation is complete. We can also specify custom images to be displayed in these dialog windows from this page.

Once the project assistant pages have all been appropriately completed, we just need to build the setup and deployment project to generate the setup files. However, we need to ensure that we build it correctly, dependent upon the selections that we made in the project assistant.

When using and focusing the **InstallShield Limited Edition Project** in the **Solution Explorer** in Visual Studio, we get an extra **InstallShield LE** menu item and in it, we can find an **Open Release folder...** option. Clicking this option will open a folder window, showing the setup project folder, in which we can find the installation files to distribute to the users.

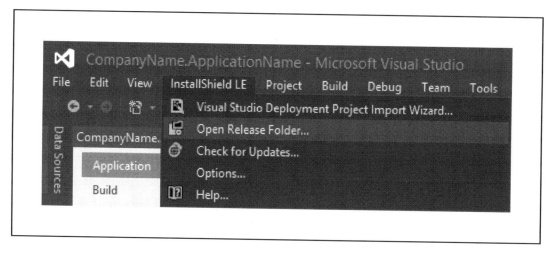

Utilizing ClickOnce functionality

ClickOnce is an application deployment technology that enables us to deploy applications that can be installed, run and updated with minimal interaction from the end user. In fact, the name ClickOnce comes from the ideal scenario, where each application could be installed with a single click.

Each ClickOnce application is deployed into its own self-contained area on the host computer, with no access to other applications, rather than in one of the standard program files folders that the other deployment technologies use. Furthermore, they only grant the exact security permissions required by the application and so, can generally also be installed by non-administrative users.

Another benefit of using ClickOnce is that it enables applications to be installed either from a web page, a network folder, or from physical media. We can also specify that applications installed using ClickOnce should check for updates at regular periods and can be easily updated by the end user, without requiring an administrator to be present.

ClickOnce deployments contain an application manifest and a deployment manifest. The application manifest contains details of the application, such as its dependencies, required security permissions, and the location where updates will be available. The deployment manifest contains details of the deployment, such as the location of the application manifest and the target version of the application.

ClickOnce is now the preferred method of deploying applications and is built right into the project properties of our startup project. We can open the properties window by either right-clicking on the `CompanyName.ApplicationName` project in the **Solution Explorer** and selecting the **Properties** option, by opening the project node and double clicking on the **Properties** item, or by selecting the project node and pressing the *Alt + Enter* keys on the keyboard together.

In the project properties window, we can find the ClickOnce configuration fields in the **Publish** tab. In this tab, we can set the location of the publishing folder to a network shared folder or FTP server. This represents the location that files will be published to. Optionally, we can also specify the location that users will install the application from, if that will be different.

We can dictate that the installation mode should make the application available online only, like a web application, or offline as well, like a typical desktop application. In this section, we also have the **Application Files** button that opens a dialog window where we can specify which additional files to include in the deployment.

All files from the solution that currently get built into the `bin` folder will be included by default, but we can exclude them if we prefer. Alternatively, we can add new files from the **Solution Explorer** by setting their **Build Action** to **Content** in the **Properties** window. We can also specify whether any executable files are prerequisites, or whether any other file types are data files. However this is set for us automatically and we do not need to make changes here, unless we have specific requirements.

Next, we see the **Prerequisites** button, which opens a dialog window that enables us to create a setup program to install any prerequisite components that we may have, such as the .NET Framework and the Windows Installer software. If the users' computers do not already have the required prerequisites installed, we can specify where the installer should access them from. This dialog is also automatically populated according to the requirements of the application.

In order to specify that the installed applications should check for updates, we can tick the **The application should check for updates** checkbox in the dialog that opens after clicking the **Updates** button in the **Publish** tab. We can also specify whether this occurs before or after the application starts, or after a certain period of time.

In the **Application Updates** dialog window, we can also stipulate that the application should be mandatorily updated to a particular version by ticking the **Specify a minimum required version for this application** checkbox and setting the version. Additionally, we can specify a further location that updates can be accessed from, if it would be different to the publish location.

Finally, in the **Install Mode and Settings** section, we come to the **Options** button, which opens the **Publish Options** dialog window, where we can specify details such as the publisher and product names, deployment and manifest settings and associate our applications with our custom file types, so that it will open when those file types are clicked.

The **Deployment** options enable us to specify a web page that users can use to download and install our ClickOnce application from, although if we enter `default.html`, we can use the default page that is generated for us. We can also specify whether the web page should automatically open, or whether the uploaded files should be verified after publishing the application.

The final section in the **Publish** tab is the **Publish Version** section, where we can specify the current version of the application. Rather than update this manually each time we publish, we can optionally tick the **Automatically increment revision with each publish** checkbox to update the revision for us.

In this section, we have two publishing options. The **Publish Wizard** button opens a multi-page dialog window that walks us through many of the more essential options described previously and ends with publishing the application. While this is useful for the first time that we publish the application, we tend to use the other option, the **Publish Now** button after that, which simply publishes the application.

Securing deployments

On the **Security** tab of the project properties window, we can specify the security permissions that our application requires. To do so, we can tick the **Enable ClickOnce security settings** checkbox and select whether our application is a full or partial trust application.

For a typical desktop application, it is common to specify that it is a full trust application, but otherwise we can specify just the trust level that we require. Note that unless the application publisher is set as a trusted publisher on the end user's computer, they might be required to grant any required permissions during installation.

If we specify that our application is a partial trust application, then we can either select from pre-configured zones that contain specific groups of permissions, or select custom permissions, in which case, we can manually specify our required permissions directly in the application manifest file.

Note that even if we have specified our application as a partial trust application, we usually have full trust when developing. In order to develop using the same permissions that our application requires and therefore see the same errors as the users, we can click the **Advanced** button and tick the **Debug this application with the selected permission set** checkbox.

On the **Signing** tab of the project properties window, we can optionally digitally sign the ClickOnce manifests by ticking the **Sign the ClickOnce manifests** checkbox. If we have a valid certificate that has been persisted in the computer's certificate store, then we can select it to sign the ClickOnce manifests using the **Select from Store** button.

Alternatively, if we have a **Personal Information Exchange (PFX)** file, we can sign the manifests with it by clicking on the **Select from File** button and selecting it in the file explorer that opens. If we don't currently have a valid certificate, we can optionally create one for testing purposes by clicking on the **Create Test Certificate** button.

Note however, that a test certificate should not be deployed with a production application as they do not contain verifiable information about the publisher. When installing the ClickOnce application with a test certificate, users will be informed that the publisher cannot be verified and asked to confirm whether they really want to install the application. For the peace of mind of the end users, a real certificate should be used and a copy stored in their Trusted Publishers Certificate Store.

We can also optionally sign the assembly by ticking the **Sign the assembly** checkbox and selecting a **Strong Name Key (SNK)** file from the associated drop-down control. If we haven't previously selected one, we can add a new one from the same drop-down control.

This completes the summary of the configuration pages used for a ClickOnce deployment. They provide practically the same settings as the other deployment technologies, except those to do with the location of the installed files and the security permissions that may be required to install. Let's now look at how we can safely store files on the host computer in non-full trust applications.

Isolating storage

One of the reasons why ClickOnce can be installed directly by the end users, without the need for administrator assistance is because it is installed into a self-contained eco system, separate from all other programs and in general, isolated from the rest of the user's computer.

When we have a requirement to store data locally, we can run into security problems if we have not specified our application as a full trust application. In these situations, we can take advantage of isolated storage, which is a data storage mechanism that abstracts the actual location of the data on the hard drive, which remains unknown to both users and developers.

When we use isolated storage, the actual data compartment where the data is stored is generated from some aspects of each application, so that it is unique. The data compartment contains one or more isolated storage files called stores, which reference where the actual data is stored. The amount of data that can be stored in each store can be limited by code in the application.

The actual physical location of the files will differ, depending upon the operating system running on the user's computer and whether the store has roaming enabled or not. For all operating systems since Vista, the location is in the hidden `AppData` folder in the user's personal user folder. Within this folder, it will either be found in the `Local` or `Roaming` folders, depending on the store's settings.

```
<SYSTEMDRIVE>\Users\<username>\AppData\Local
<SYSTEMDRIVE>\Users\<username>\AppData\Roaming
```

We can store any type of file in isolated storage, but as an example, let's take a look at how we could utilize it to store text files:

```
using System.IO;
using System.IO.IsolatedStorage;

namespace CompanyName.ApplicationName.Managers
{
  public class HardDriveManager
```

```
{
  private IsolatedStorageFile GetIsolatedStorageFile()
  {
    return IsolatedStorageFile.GetStore(IsolatedStorageScope.User |
      IsolatedStorageScope.Assembly | IsolatedStorageScope.Domain,
      null, null);
  }

  public void SaveTextFile(string filePath, string fileContents)
  {
    try
    {
      IsolatedStorageFile isolatedStorageFile = GetIsolatedStorageFile();
      using (IsolatedStorageFileStream isolatedStorageFileStream =
        new IsolatedStorageFileStream(filePath, FileMode.OpenOrCreate,
        isolatedStorageFile))
      {
        using (StreamWriter streamWriter =
          new StreamWriter(isolatedStorageFileStream))
        {
          streamWriter.Write(fileContents);
        }
      }
    }
    catch { /*Log error*/ }
  }

  public string ReadTextFile(string filePath)
  {
    string fileContents = string.Empty;
    try
    {
      IsolatedStorageFile isolatedStorageFile = GetIsolatedStorageFile();
      if (isolatedStorageFile.FileExists(filePath))
      {
        using (IsolatedStorageFileStream isolatedStorageFileStream =
          new IsolatedStorageFileStream(filePath, FileMode.Open,
          isolatedStorageFile))
        {
          using (StreamReader streamReader =
            new StreamReader(isolatedStorageFileStream))
          {
            fileContents = streamReader.ReadToEnd();
          }
        }
      }
    }
    catch { /*Log error*/ }
```

```
            return fileContents;
        }
    }
}
```

As with the other manager classes, we declare the `HardDriveManager` class in the `CompanyName.ApplicationName.Managers` namespace. In the private `GetIsolatedStorageFile` method, we obtain the `IsolatedStorageFile` object that relates to the isolated storage store that we will save the user's data in, by calling the `GetStore` method of the `IsolatedStorageFile` class.

This method has a number of overloads that enable us to specify the scope, application identity, evidence and evidence types, with which to generate the unique isolated storage file. In this example, we use the overload that takes the bitwise combination of the `IsolatedStorageScope` enumeration members and the domain and assembly evidence types, which we simply pass null for.

The scope input parameter here is interesting and requires some explanation. Isolated storage is always restricted to the user that was logged on and using the application when the store was created. However, it can also be restricted to the identity of the assembly, or to the assembly and application domain together.

When we call the `GetStore` method, it obtains a store that corresponds with the passed input parameters. When we pass the `User` and `AssemblyIsolatedStorageScope` enumeration members, this acquires a store that can be shared between applications that use the same assembly, when used by the same user. Typically, this is allowed under the Intranet security zone, but not the Internet zone.

When we pass the `User`, `Assembly` and `DomainIsolatedStorageScope` enumeration members, this acquires a store that can only be accessed by the user, when running the application that was used to create the store. This is the default and most common choice for most applications and so, these are the enumeration members that were used in our example.

Note that if we had wanted to enable the user to use roaming profiles, but still be able to access their data from their isolated storage file, then we could have additionally included the `Roaming` enumeration member with the other members.

Returning to the `HardDriveManager` class now, in the `SaveTextFile` method, we first call the `GetIsolatedStorageFile` method to obtain the `IsolatedStorageFile` object. We then initialize an `IsolatedStorageFileStream` object with the filename specified by the `filePath` input parameter, the `OpenOrCreate` member of the `FileMode` enumeration and the storage file object.

Next, we initialize a `StreamWriter` object with the `IsolatedStorageFileStream` variable and write the data from the `fileContents` input parameter to the file specified in the stream using the `Write` method of the `StreamWriter` class. Again, we enclose this in a `try...catch` block and would typically log any exceptions that might be thrown from this method, but omit this here for brevity.

In the `ReadTextFile` method, we initialize the `fileContents` variable to an empty string and then obtain the `IsolatedStorageFile` object from the `GetIsolatedStorageFile` method. We verify that the file specified by the `filePath` input parameter actually exists before attempting to access it.

We then initialize an `IsolatedStorageFileStream` object with the filename specified by the `filePath` input parameter, the `Open` member of the `FileMode` enumeration and the isolated storage file.

Next, we initialize a `StreamReader` object with the `IsolatedStorageFileStream` variable and read the data from the file specified in the stream into the `fileContents` input parameter using the `Read` method of the `StreamReader` object. Once again, this is all enclosed in a `try...catch` block and finally, we return the `fileContents` variable with the data from the file.

In order to use it, we can expose a reference to the new `HardDriveManager` class from our `BaseViewModel` class:

```
public HardDriveManager HardDriveManager
{
  get { return new HardDriveManager(); }
}
```

We can then use it to save files to, or read files from isolated storage from any View Model:

```
HardDriveManager.SaveTextFile("UserPreferences.txt", "AutoLogIn:True");

...

string preferences = HardDriveManager.ReadTextFile("UserPreferences.txt");
```

Realistically, if we were to save user preferences in this way, they would typically be in an XML file, or in another format that is more easily parsed. However, for the purposes of this example, a plain string will suffice.

As well as saving and loading files in an isolated storage store, we can also delete them and add or remove folders to better organize the data. We can add further methods to our `HardDriveManager` class, to enable us to manipulate the files and folders from within the user's isolated storage store. Let's take a look at how we can do this now:

```
public void DeleteFile(string filePath)
{
  try
  {
    IsolatedStorageFile isolatedStorageFile = GetIsolatedStorageFile();
    isolatedStorageFile.DeleteFile(filePath);
  }
  catch { /*Log error*/ }
}

public void CreateFolder(string folderName)
{
  try
  {
    IsolatedStorageFile isolatedStorageFile = GetIsolatedStorageFile();
    isolatedStorageFile.CreateDirectory(folderName);
  }
  catch { /*Log error*/ }
}

public void DeleteFolder(string folderName)
{
  try
  {
    IsolatedStorageFile isolatedStorageFile = GetIsolatedStorageFile();
    isolatedStorageFile.DeleteDirectory(folderName);
  }
  catch { /*Log error*/ }
}
```

Quite simply, the `DeleteFile` method accesses the `IsolatedStorageFile` object from the `GetIsolatedStorageFile` method and then calls its `DeleteFile` method, passing in the name of the file to delete, which is specified by the `filePath` input parameter, within another `try...catch` block.

Likewise, the `CreateFolder` method obtains the `IsolatedStorageFile` object from the `GetIsolatedStorageFile` method and then calls its `CreateDirectory` method, passing in the name of the folder to create, specified by the `folderName` input parameter, within a `try...catch` block.

Similarly, the `DeleteFolder` method acquires the `IsolatedStorageFile` object by calling the `GetIsolatedStorageFile` method and then calls its `DeleteDirectory` method, passing in the name of the folder to delete, that is specified by the `folderName` input parameter, within another `try...catch` block.

Now, let's adjust our previous example to demonstrate how we can use this new functionality:

```
HardDriveManager.CreateFolder("Preferences");
HardDriveManager.SaveTextFile("Preferences/UserPreferences.txt",
  "AutoLogIn:True");

...

string preferences =
  HardDriveManager.ReadTextFile("Preferences/UserPreferences.txt");

...

HardDriveManager.DeleteFile("Preferences/UserPreferences.txt");
HardDriveManager.DeleteFolder("Preferences");
```

In this extended example, we first create a folder named `Preferences` in the isolated storage store and then save the text file in that folder, by prefixing the filename with the name of the folder and separated from the name with a forward slash.

At a later stage, we can then read back the contents of the file by passing in the same file path to the `ReadTextFile` method. If we need to clear up the store afterwards, or if the file was temporary, we can delete it by passing the same file path to the `DeleteFile` method. Note that we must first delete the contents of a folder in the store before we can delete the folder itself.

Also note that we can create subdirectories in the isolated storage store, by chaining their names in the file path. For example, we can create a `Login` folder in the folder named `Preferences` by simply appending the subdirectory name to the end of the parent folder name and separating them with a forward slash again.

```
HardDriveManager.CreateFolder("Preferences");
HardDriveManager.CreateFolder("Preferences/Login");
HardDriveManager.SaveTextFile("Preferences/Login/UserPreferences.txt",
  "AutoLogIn:True");
```

Accessing application versions

In .NET, an application has a number of different versions and so, we have a number of alternative ways to access them. The version number that we discussed earlier and is displayed in the **Publish Version** section of the **Publish** tab of the project properties can be found using the `ApplicationDeployment` class from the `System.Deployment` DLL.

```
using System.Deployment.Application;

...

private string GetPublishedVersion()
{
  if (ApplicationDeployment.IsNetworkDeployed)
  {
    return ApplicationDeployment.CurrentDeployment.CurrentVersion.
      ToString();
  }
  return "Not network deployed";
}
```

Note that we need to verify that the application has actually been deployed before we can access the `CurrentVersion` property of the `ApplicationDeployment` class, otherwise an `InvalidDeploymentException` will be thrown. This means that we cannot attain the published version while debugging our WPF applications and so, should return some other value instead in these instances.

In order to view the remaining application versions, we first need to access the assembly that we want to know the version of. The code that we use to access the assembly will depend on where in the code we currently are. For example, we typically want to display the version of the startup assembly, but we may want to access it from a View Model in the `ViewModels` project instead.

We have a number of ways of accessing assemblies, depending on where they are in relation to the calling code. If we want to access the startup assembly from the startup project, the we can use the `Assembly.GetExecutingAssembly` method, after adding `using` statements for the following namespaces:

```
using System.Diagnostics;
using System.Reflection;
```

To access the same assembly from a different project, we can use the
`Assembly.GetEntryAssembly` method. Alternatively, we can access the startup project's
assembly from a different project if that project was called from the startup assembly, using
the `Assembly.GetCallingAssembly` method. For the remaining examples here, we'll use
the `GetEntryAssembly` method.

In addition to the published version, we may also need to access the application's assembly
or file versions. The assembly version that we can set in the **Assembly Information** dialog
window, which is accessible from the **Application** tab of the project properties window can
be accessed from the assembly, using the following code:

```
string assemblyVersion =
   Assembly.GetEntryAssembly().GetName().Version.ToString();
```

The assembly version is used by the .NET Framework to load and link references to other
assemblies at build and runtime. This is the version that is embedded when adding
references to our projects in Visual Studio and if an incorrect version is found during a
build, then an error will be raised.

Note that we can also set this value using the assembly level `AssemblyVersionAttribute`
class in the `AssemblyInfo.cs` file of the project, which can be found in the **Properties** node
of the project in the **Solution Explorer**.

Instead of converting the returned `Version` object to a string directly, we may prefer to
access the individual components that make up the version number. They are comprised of
the Major, Minor, Build and Revision component values. We could then chose to just output
the Major and Minor components, along with the product name for example:

```
Version assemblyVersion = Assembly.GetEntryAssembly().GetName().Version;
string productName = FileVersionInfo.GetVersionInfo(
   Assembly.GetEntryAssembly().Location).ProductName;
string output = $"{productName}: Version {version.Major}.{version.Minor}";
```

If we need the file version, which is used for non ClickOnce deployments, we can pass the
location of the assembly to the `GetVersionInfo` method of the `FileVersionInfo` class, as
shown in the preceding code, in the product name example, but access the `FileVersion`
property instead.

```
string fileVersion = FileVersionInfo.GetVersionInfo(
   Assembly.GetEntryAssembly().Location).FileVersion;
```

Note that we can also set this value in the **Assembly Information** dialog window, or by using the assembly level `AssemblyFileVersionAttribute` class in the `AssemblyInfo.cs` file of the project. This version can be seen in the **Details** tab of the file properties dialog window in Windows Explorer.

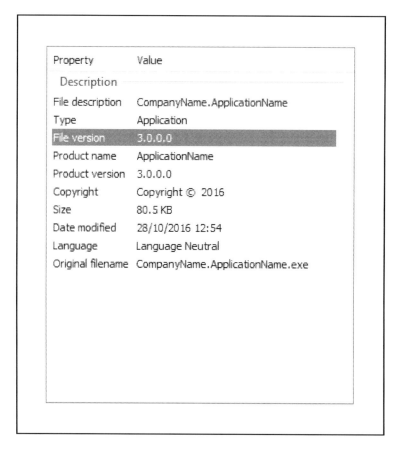

Property	Value
Description	
File description	CompanyName.ApplicationName
Type	Application
File version	3.0.0.0
Product name	ApplicationName
Product version	3.0.0.0
Copyright	Copyright © 2016
Size	80.5 KB
Date modified	28/10/2016 12:54
Language	Language Neutral
Original filename	CompanyName.ApplicationName.exe

The product version that the assembly is distributed with can be accessed in a similar way:

```
string productVersion = FileVersionInfo.GetVersionInfo(
    Assembly.GetEntryAssembly().Location).ProductVersion;
```

Note that this version can also be seen in the **Details** tab of the file properties dialog window in Windows Explorer, along with the product name that we accessed earlier. Also note that in a WPF application, this value typically comes from the assembly file version.

Summary

In this chapter, we explored a number of different ways to deploy our WPF applications. We looked over the older **Setup Project** type and the **InstallShield Limited Edition Project** type, but focused primarily on the newer ClickOnce technology. We investigated how ClickOnce deployments are made and how we can safely store and access data in isolated storage. We ended by looking at a number of ways to access the various application versions available to us in .NET.

In the final chapter, we'll take a look at a summary of what has been covered throughout this book and investigate what you can do next to continue this journey. We'll suggest a few possible ways that you could extend our application framework further and what you can do to advance your application development further in general.

12
What Next?

In this book, we discovered the MVVM architectural pattern and explored the process of developing a WPF application, while taking advantage of this pattern's Separation of Concerns and adhering to its principals. We investigated a number of different ways of communicating between the various application layers and structuring our code base.

Importantly, we considered a variety of ways of debugging our WPF applications and tracking down our coding problems. In particular, we revealed some tips and tricks to help us to identify the causes of our data binding errors. In addition, we also learnt how viewing trace information can help us to detect problems, even after our applications have been deployed.

We moved on to investigate the benefit of utilizing an application framework and began designing and developing our own. We structured it in a way that did not tie our framework to any particular feature or technology and experimented with a variety of ways to encapsulate our required functionality.

We devoted a whole chapter to the essential art of data binding and took a detailed look at the creation of Dependency Properties and Attached Properties. We looked at setting Dependency Property metadata and were introduced to the crucial Dependency Property Setting Precedence List. We then covered both standard and hierarchical data templates and studied some interesting data binding examples.

Investigating the rich inheritance hierarchy of the built-in WPF controls enabled us to see how their functionality is built up from each successive base class in the hierarchy. This in turn enabled us to see that some controls are better to use in some situations than others. We also found out how to customize the built-in controls and considered how best to make our own controls.

While the animation possibilities in a WPF application are practically endless, we investigated the more usable options, primarily focusing on the syntax used in XAML. We then added animation functionality directly into our application framework, where it could be used with little effort, on the part of the developers.

After turning our attention to the look of our applications, we investigated a number of techniques, such as borderless windows and adding shadows and glowing effects to more advanced methods for making our application stand out from the crowd. We also incorporated animations into our everyday controls, in order to bring about a sense of exclusivity to our applications.

We thoroughly investigated the data validation options that the .NET Framework offers us, primarily concentrating on the two available validation interfaces, and exploring a number of different ways of implementing them. We probed advanced techniques, such as multilevel validation and using data annotation attributes, and then added a complete validation system into our application framework.

We further extended our application framework with an asynchronous data operation system that was combined with a complete user feedback component, including an animated feedback display mechanism. We continued with investigating how we can provide in-application help and user preferences and implement work-heavy functions to save the users time and effort.

We also explored a number of options that we can use to increase the performance of our WPF applications, from declaring our resources more efficiently to using lighter weight controls and more efficient methods of rendering drawings, images and text. We saw more performant methods of data binding and discovered the importance of detaching event handlers.

Finally, we investigated the last task in any professional application's development, its deployment. We looked at a number of alternative methods, but primarily focused on the most popular ClickOnce technology. We investigated how ClickOnce deployments are made and how we can safely store and access data in isolated storage. We ended with a number of ways to access the various application versions available to us in .NET.

Overall, we've covered a plethora of information that together, will enable us to create efficient, visually appealing, highly usable and highly productive applications in WPF. What's more, we've now got our own application framework that we can reuse for each new application that we create. So, what is next?

Turning attention to future projects

You could apply the concepts and ideas from this book to other areas and continue to experiment and explore their effect in these new areas. For example, we've learnt about `Adorner` objects, so you could use that new found knowledge to implement some visual feedback for the common drag and drop functionality in the main window's adorner layer.

You could then further extend this idea, using what you've discovered about Attached Properties, and completely encapsulate this drag and drop functionality, enabling the developers that utilize your application framework to make use of this feature in a property-based manner.

For example, you could create a `DragDropProperties` class that declared Attached Properties, such as `IsDragSource`, `IsDragTarget`, `DragEffects`, `DragDropType` and `DropCommand`, and could be extended by your relevant Attached Property classes, such as a `ListBoxProperties` class.

You could then declare a `BaseDragDropManager` class to be used in the `DragDropProperties` class, that stitches everything together, by attaching and removing the appropriate event handlers, starting the drag and drop procedure, updating the cursor via the drag and drop effects as it moves across the screen and executing the `ICommand` object assigned to the `DropCommand` Property.

This leads to a further area that could be extended. Not only can we handle UI events in Attached Properties, but we can also combine them to perform more complex functionality. For example, let's say that we have an Attached Property of type `string`, named `Label`.

When this property is set, it could apply a particular `ControlTemplate` element from resources to the current `TextBox` object's `Template` property. This template could display the text from this property in a secondary text element and therefore act as an internal label. When the `TextBox` object has a value, the label text element could be hidden via an `IValueConverter` implementation that extends our `BaseVisibilityConverter` class:

```
<TextBlock Text="{Binding (Attached:TextBoxProperties.Label),
    RelativeSource={RelativeSource AncestorType=TextBox}, FallbackValue=''}"
    Foreground="{Binding (Attached:TextBoxProperties.LabelColor),
    RelativeSource={RelativeSource AncestorType=TextBox},
    FallbackValue=#FF000000}" Visibility="{Binding Text,
    RelativeSource={RelativeSource AncestorType=TextBox},
    Converter={StaticResource StringToVisibilityConverter},
    FallbackValue=Collapsed}" ... />
```

As shown in the preceding example, we could then declare another Attached Property, named LabelColor, of type Brush, that specifies the color to be used by the Label Attached Property when it is set. Note that if the LabelColor property is not set, then it will either use its default value if set, or the value specified in the FallbackValue property.

Improving our application framework

Another area that you can continue to work on is customizing our application framework further and adapting it to your individual requirements. With this in mind, you could continue to build up a complete collection of customized controls with a particular look and feel in an external resource file to use in all of your applications.

There are also many other examples provided throughout this book that could be easily extended. For example, you could update our DependencyManager class to enable multiple concrete classes to be registered for each interface.

Instead of using a Dictionary<Type, Type> object to store our registrations, you could define new custom objects. You could declare a ConcreteImplementation struct that has a Type property and an object array to hold any constructor input parameters that may be required for its initialization:

```
public ConcreteImplementation(Type type,
  params object[] constructorParameters)
{
  Type = type;
  ConstructorParameters = constructorParameters;
}
```

You could then declare a DependencyRegistration class that you could use to pair the interface type with the collection of concrete implementations:

```
public DependencyRegistration(Type interfaceType,
  IEnumerable<ConcreteImplementation> concreteImplementations)
{
  if (!concreteImplementations.All(c =>
    interfaceType.IsAssignableFrom(c.Type)))
    throw new ArgumentException("The System.Type object specified by the
    ConcreteImplementation.Type property must implement the interface type
    specified by the interfaceType input parameter.",
    nameof(interfaceType));
  ConcreteImplementations = concreteImplementations;
  InterfaceType = interfaceType;
}
```

In our `DependencyManager` class, you could change the type of the `registeredDependencies` field to a collection of this new `DependencyRegistration` type. The current `Register` and `Resolve` methods could then also be updated to use this new collection type.

Alternatively, you could include other common functionality that is contained within popular Dependency Injection and Inversion of Control containers, such as automatic registering of concrete classes to interfaces at assembly level. For this, you could use some basic reflection:

```
using System.Reflection;

...

public void RegisterAllInterfacesInAssemblyOf<T>() where T : class
{
  Assembly assembly = typeof(T).Assembly;
  IEnumerable<Type> interfaces =
    assembly.GetTypes().Where(p => p.IsInterface);
  foreach (Type interfaceType in interfaces)
  {
    IEnumerable<Type> implementingTypes = assembly.GetTypes().
      Where(p => interfaceType.IsAssignableFrom(p) && !p.IsInterface);
    ConcreteImplementation[] concreteImplementations = implementingTypes.
      Select(t => new ConcreteImplementation(t, null)).ToArray();
    if (concreteImplementations != null && concreteImplementations.Any())
      registeredDependencies.Add(interfaceType, concreteImplementations);
  }
}
```

This method first accesses the assembly that contains the generic type parameter and then gets a collection of the interfaces in that assembly. It then iterates through the interface collection and finds a collection of classes that implements each interface, instantiating a `ConcreteImplementation` element with each. Each match is added into the `registeredDependencies` collection with its relating interface type.

In this way, you could pass any interface type from our `Models`, `Managers` and `ViewModels` projects to automatically register all of the interfaces and concrete classes found inside their assemblies. There is a clear benefit to doing this in larger applications, as it will mean that you don't have to manually register each type.

```
private void RegisterDependencies()
{
  DependencyManager.Instance.ClearRegistrations();
  DependencyManagerAdvanced.Instance.
    RegisterAllInterfacesInAssemblyOf<IDataProvider>();
```

```
    DependencyManagerAdvanced.Instance.
      RegisterAllInterfacesInAssemblyOf<IUiThreadManager>();
    DependencyManagerAdvanced.Instance.
      RegisterAllInterfacesInAssemblyOf<IUserViewModel>();
  }
```

Additionally, you could declare another method that registers all types found in the assembly of the type specified by the generic type parameter T, where matches of implemented interfaces are found. This could be used during testing, so that you could just pass any type from the mock projects during testing, again saving time and effort.

```
  DependencyManager.Instance.
    RegisterAllConcreteImplementationsInAssemblyOf<MockUiThreadManager>();
```

As with all serious development projects, there is a need to test the code that makes up the code base. Doing so obviously helps to reduce the number of bugs in the application, but also alerts us when existing functionality has been broken, while adding new code. They also provide a safety net for refactoring, allowing us to continually improve our designs, while ensuring that existing functionality is not broken.

Therefore, one area that you could improve in the application would be to implement a full test suite. This book has explained a number of ways for us to swap out code during testing and this pattern can be easily extended. If a manager class uses some sort of resource that cannot be used during testing, then you can create an interface for it, add a mock class and use the DependencyManager class to instantiate the relevant concrete implementation during runtime and testing.

Another area from the book that could be extended relates to our AnimatedStackPanel class. You could extract the reusable properties and animation code from this class to an AnimatedPanel base class, so that it could service several different types of animated panel.

As suggested in Chapter 6, *Mastering Practical Animations*, you could then further extend the base class by exposing additional animation properties, so that users of your panel could have more control over the animations that it provides. For example, you could add alignment, direction, duration, and/or animation type properties to enable users of your framework to use a wide variety of animation options.

These properties could be divided between the entry and exit animations, to enable independent control over them. By providing a wide variety of these additional properties in a base class, you can vastly simplify the process of adding new animated panels.

For example, you could add a new `AnimatedWrapPanel`, or perhaps an `AnimatedColumnPanel`, by simply extending the base class and only have to implement the two `MeasureOverride` and `ArrangeOverride` methods in the new panel.

Logging errors

In a number of places in the code examples in this book, you may have seen `Log error` comments. In general, it is not only good practice to log errors, but it can also help you to track down bugs and improve the overall user experience of the users of your applications.

The easiest place to log errors to would be an `Errors` database and the minimum useful information fields that you'd want to store would include details of the current user, the time it occurred, the exception message, the stack trace and the assembly or area that it occurred in. This latter field can be found in the `Module` property of the exception's `TargetSite` property.

```
public Error(Exception exception, User createdBy)
{
  Id = Guid.NewGuid();
  Message = FlattenInnerExceptions(exception);
  StackTrace = exception.StackTrace;
  Area = exception.TargetSite.Module.ToString();
  CreatedOn = DateTime.Now;
  CreatedBy = createdBy;
}
```

Note the use of the custom `FlattenInnerExceptions` method that also outputs the messages from any inner exceptions that the thrown exception may contain. One alternative to building your own `FlattenInnerExceptions` method would be to simply save the `ToString` output of the exception, which will also contain details of any inner exceptions that it may contain, although it will also contain stack trace and other information as well.

Using online resources

As a final note, if you are not already familiar with the **Microsoft Developer Network (MSDN)** website, you really should acquaint yourself with it. It is maintained for the Microsoft developer community and includes everything from detailed APIs for their various languages, and tutorial walkthroughs and code examples through to downloads of their software.

It can be found at `https://msdn.microsoft.com` and should be the first place to look when questions arise over the various classes in the .NET framework. Should you not find your required information in their APIs, then you can ask questions in their forums and quickly receive answers from both the community and from Microsoft employees.

Another great developer resource is the Stack Overflow question and answer site for development professionals, where I still answer questions when I can find the time. It can be found online at `http://stackoverflow.com/` and with answers often provided by the community within seconds, it really is hard to beat and one of the best development forums around.

All that remains now is for me to wish you well with your future application development and your blossoming development careers.

Index

Made in the USA
San Bernardino, CA
13 July 2018